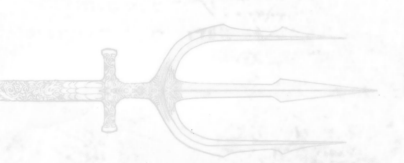

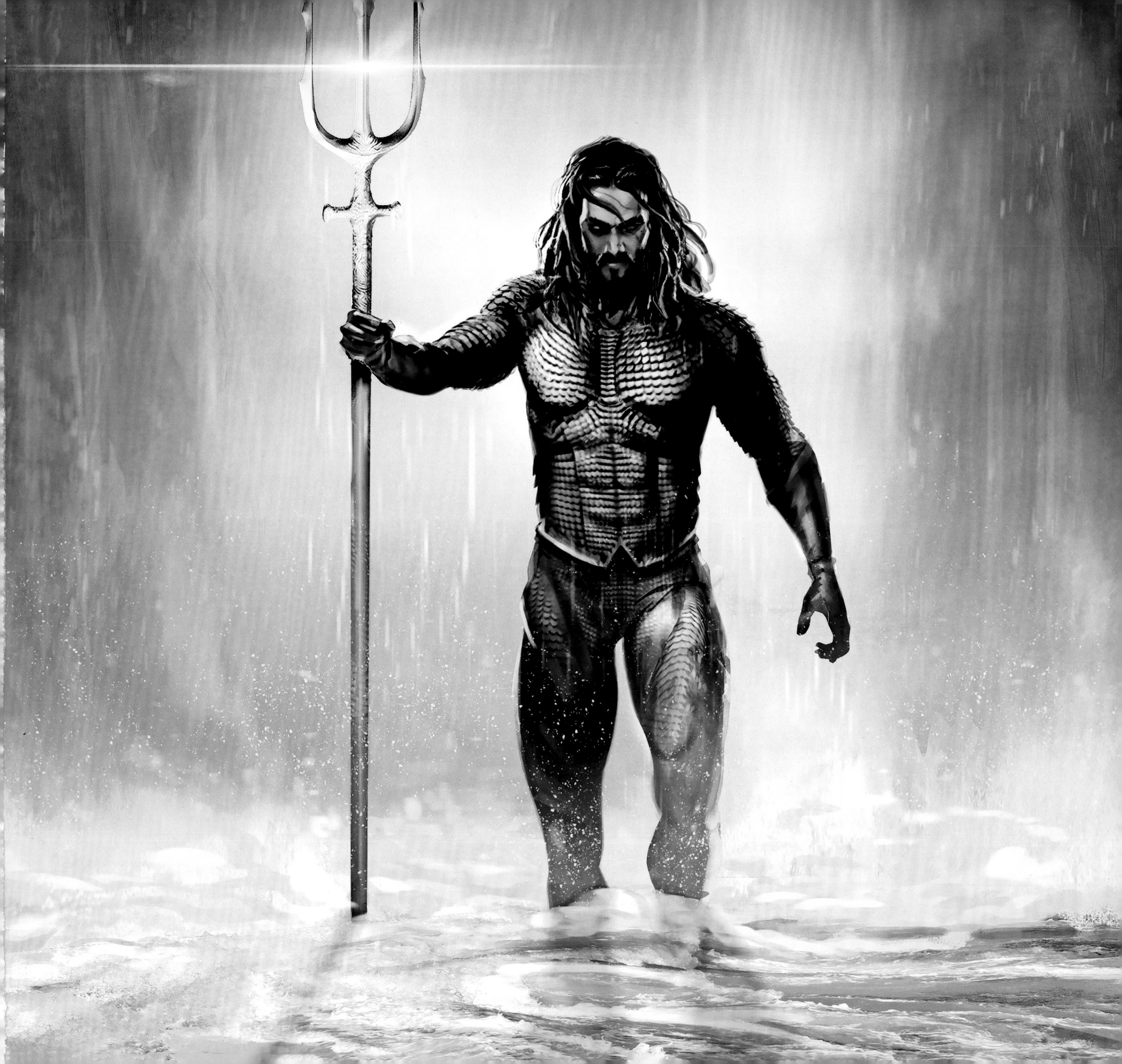

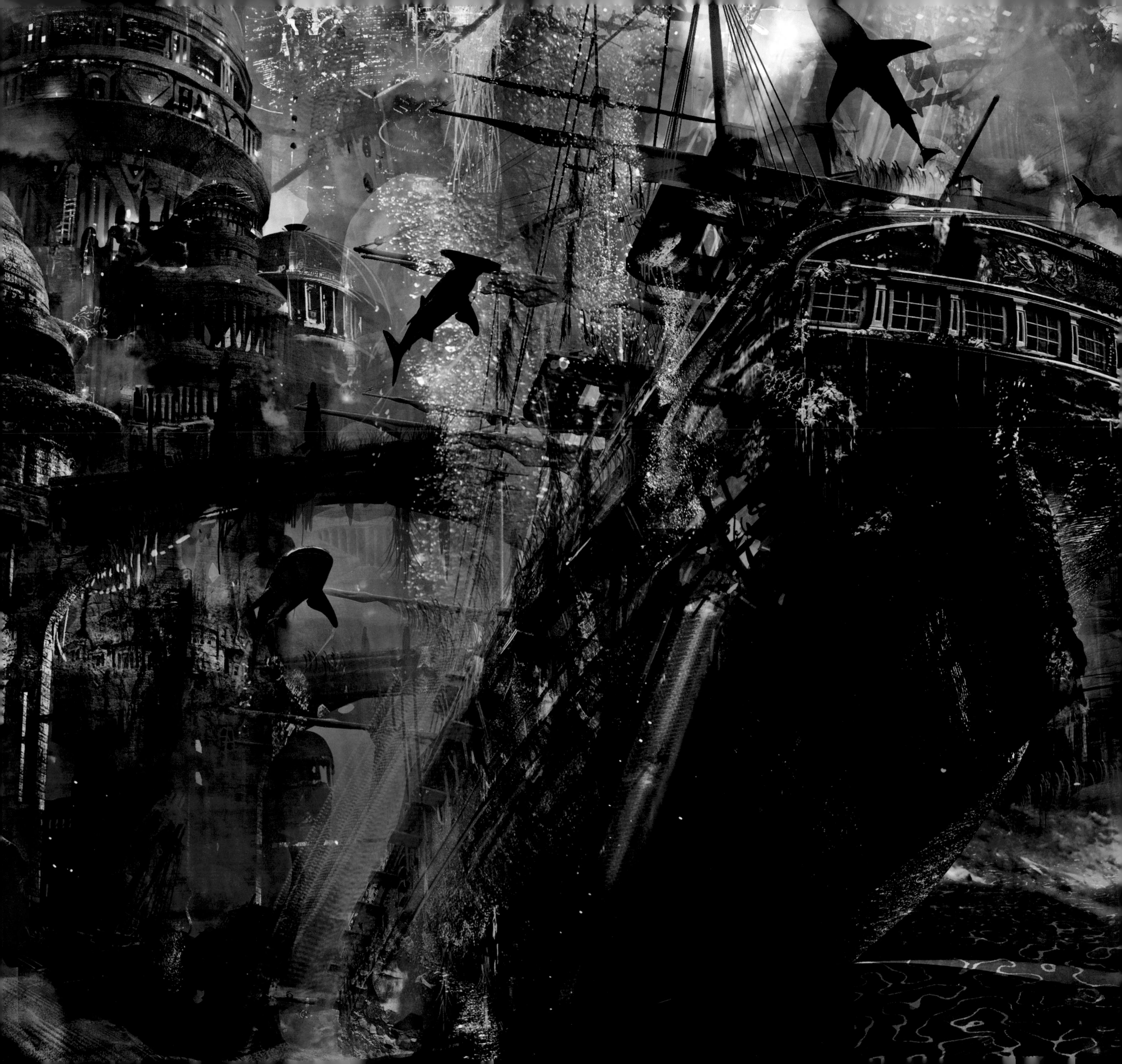

THE ART AND MAKING OF

AQUAMAN

MIKE AVILA

FOREWORD BY JASON MOMOA

INTRODUCTION BY JAMES WAN

AQUAMAN CREATED BY PAUL NORRIS AND MORT WEISINGER

INSIGHT EDITIONS

San Rafael, California

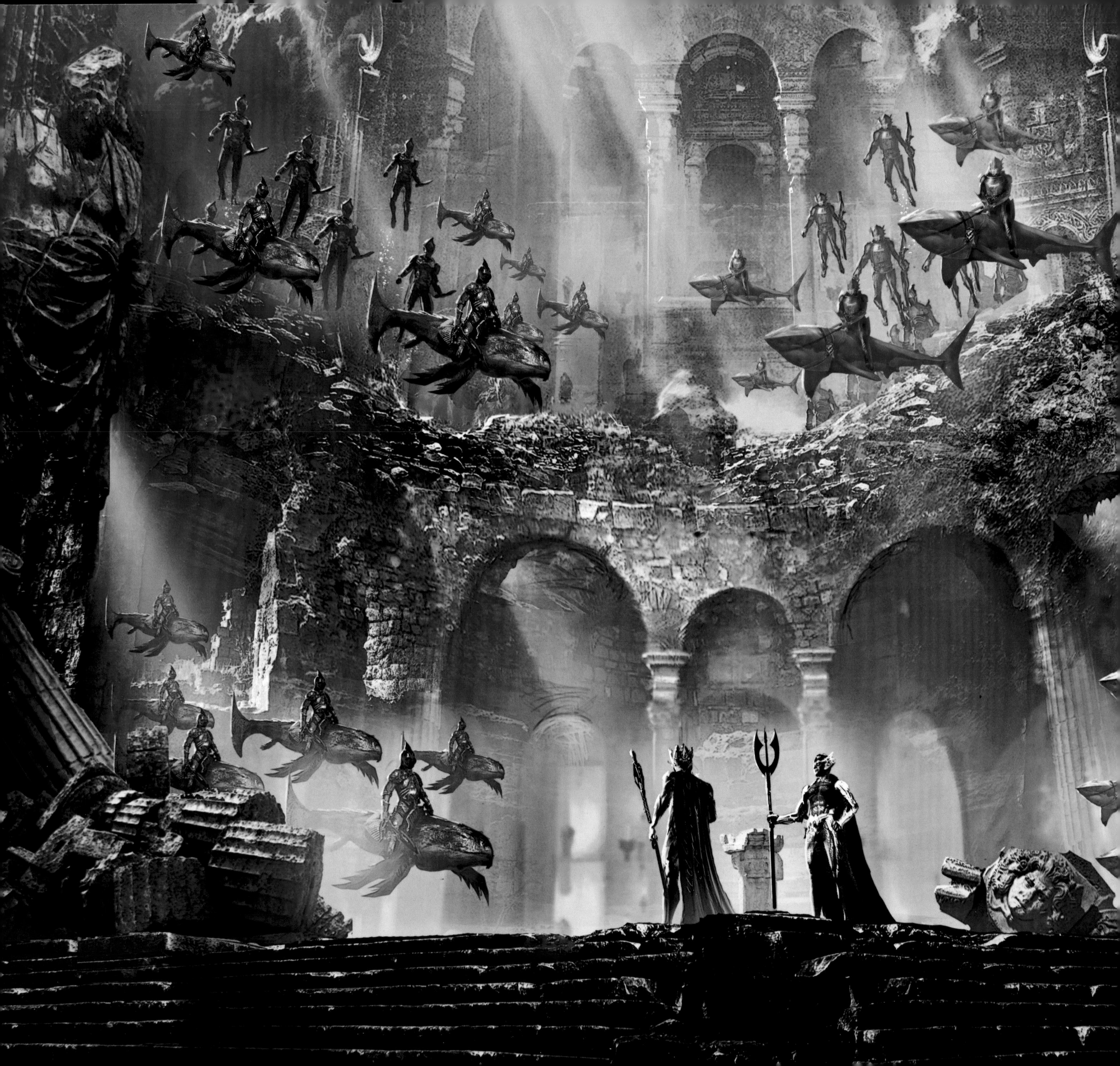

CONTENTS

FOREWORD BY
JASON MOMOA

Aquaman is the biggest secret I've ever kept in my life.

When I first got the role, I couldn't tell my friends or even family members. Had to straight up lie to everyone who asked me about it directly. I was hired years before the movie started production, even before James Wan came on as director. Hell, I was in the role before there was even a script. I was the first person officially involved with the film. Some people saw that as a leap of faith; others thought it insanity. To me, it was an opportunity—a chance to play a true hero and one of the most unique characters in the DC Comics lineup.

I was stoked when I saw a presentation James put together showcasing his vision for what an Aquaman movie should be. We hit it off immediately. We're both passionate and crazy. We both recognized what makes Arthur Curry such a special character. He's a man from two worlds who feels like an outcast in both. I felt a special connection with Aquaman because of my experience growing up; I get what it's like to feel like you don't fit in.

We wanted to blow apart people's expectations for a superhero movie. We wanted epic action, but also a true sense of adventure. And we wanted it to be *fun*. We took that entertaining adventure to the next level when Amber Heard joined the team as Mera, the undersea badass who gives Arthur all he can handle. Our scenes together were a blast, and they made the movie into a true classic adventure romance. But it's so much more.

I'm no stranger to physical roles. I've played some big, powerful characters in my career, but Aquaman was, without question, the most physically demanding role of my career. It's not even close. The way we shot this film, using all these different rigs and wires to replicate the movements underwater, was incredibly challenging. But if we did it right—and I've got no doubt that we did—you're never going to see half of that on-screen. What the audience will see is all of us floating weightlessly through the water as if the cast was born in the seas.

Maybe the most nerve-racking part of making this movie was the costume. Aquaman's been around since 1941. Everyone knows the gold and green outfit. I was scared as hell to try it on the first time, but our costume designer, Kym Barrett, did an amazing job creating the costume. She nailed the design. I really wanted the suit to look cool. And it does. Just like everything else in this film.

Making movies is all about trust. I've been entrusted with portraying this legendary DC Comics hero, and I take that responsibility very seriously. That's true of everyone else up and down the line in our production. This book is a culmination of that trust and that opportunity. Every page reveals the artistry that went into creating this awesome underwater world. I'm so thrilled that I got to be here in the beginning and now I get to be a part of this ending. Well, maybe not so much an ending. Aquaman's still got some stories to share. And I'm here for the ride.

PAGE 1: Aquaman concept art by Brad Nielsen.
PAGE 2: Sunken Galleon concept art by Christian Scheurer.
PAGES 4–5: Ancient ruins of Atlantis concept art by Sebastian Meyer.
OPPOSITE: Jason Momoa in the Aquaman hero costume.
PAGE 8: James Wan on the set of the sunken galleon.

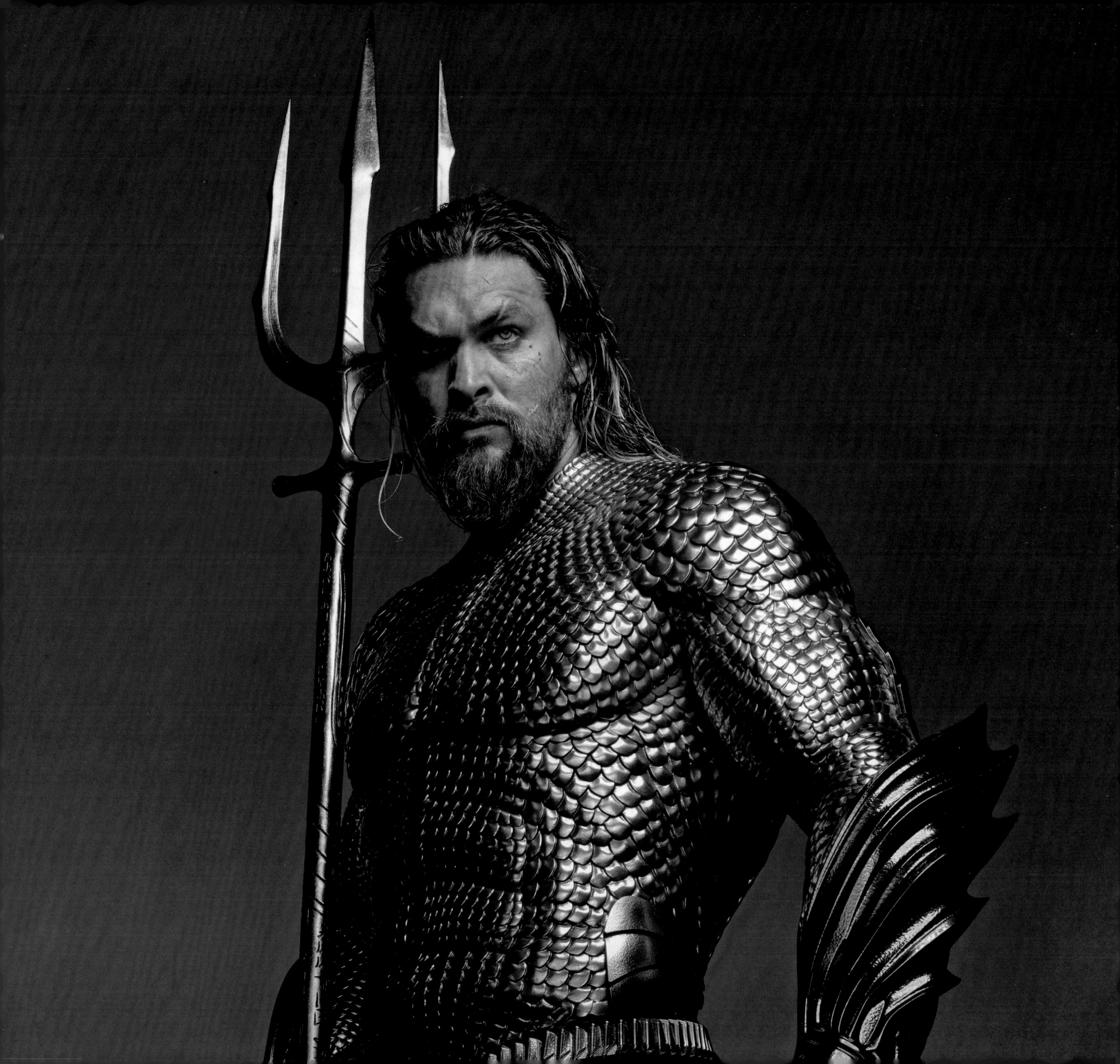

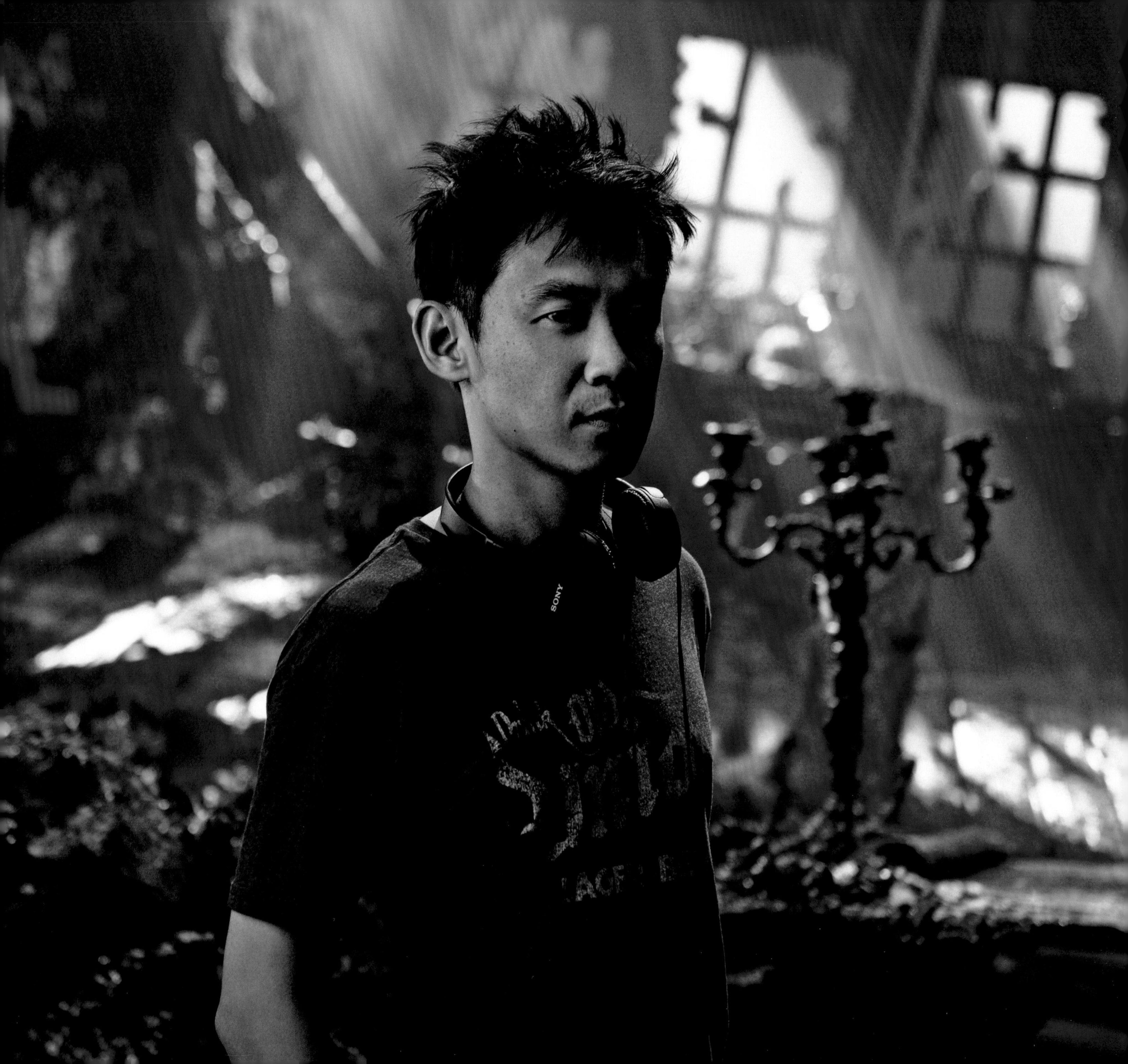
SONY

INTRODUCTION BY
JAMES WAN

I've spent years dreaming about which comic book property I would adapt for the big screen if given the chance, and for the life of me, I never would've guessed that Aquaman would be the one. However, when the opportunity arose, the more I thought about it, the more I realized that this legendary DC Comics Super Hero couldn't have been a better fit for my creative sensibility—playing with dramatic mythos, iconic heroes and heroines, scary sea creatures, and colorful villains. Ultimately, this film gave me the chance to do something I've always wanted to do—create and design an entire cinematic world unlike anything we've seen before. It was important for me to be as respectful and true to the source material as possible, while bringing my own voice to the film and introducing the character to a new generation that is not as familiar with him. Plus, the idea of taking a character that has been mercilessly mocked in pop culture and turning that on its head was a challenge too fun to resist.

Aquaman has always fascinated me as a character. He is more than just a guy with the ability to "talk to fish" and command the sea. It is the internal struggle of the character that inspires me. Arthur Curry is a man with ties to both Atlantis and the surface world, yet neither accepts him, causing him to feel like he doesn't belong in either world. It's Aquaman's human qualities that make him relatable, especially with modern audiences today, and make him all the more compelling to build a film around.

In making the movie, I eschewed the traditional superhero approach and developed it more in the grand spirit of classic sci-fi adventures and epic period pieces. I wanted to create a quest story that combines striking visuals of otherworldly beauty with wish fulfillment destinations, all taking place on our very own planet.

In this movie, Atlantis is a bioluminescent, zero-gravity metropolis assembled from organic elements of the sea. Here was an opportunity to let our imaginations run wild and bring the impossible to life—an advanced world and civilization adapted to underwater living. The oceanic world is wondrous, magical, and even scary at times, leaving us no shortage of material to draw inspiration from and a number of cinematic set pieces and genres to play with (horror, anyone?). Our brilliant production team gave purpose to everything we put in the film—from vehicles to marine life to the cities themselves. The best way we found to envision how a world like Atlantis could exist was by imagining ourselves as Atlanteans. From this we derived a number of questions, including: What materials would they use to build their structures? What light source would illuminate the darkness of the ocean floor? How would weapons and armor function both in and out of water? What sort of creatures and vehicles would be used for transportation? Anchoring the fantastic in practicality allowed us to create something truly special. From incredibly designed costumes to props to stunning locations both above and below the waterline, the concepts drawn up by our master craftspeople were more than simple blueprints. From the earliest concept designs all the way through to the final VFX imagery, they are works of art. The entire production team put every ounce of their creativity into what appears on-screen.

Aquaman is an action-packed, fun ride, but at the center of it all is Arthur Curry's personal journey from living as a lone-wolf outsider to ultimately becoming the King of Atlantis. Jason Momoa's charisma and personality breathe life into Aquaman in an exciting and refreshing way that we haven't seen in this character before. The love story between Arthur's mom and dad, Atlanna and Tom Curry, is the emotional backbone of the film, while the antics and chemistry between Jason and Amber Heard are the engine that drives the story. Arthur and Mera operate as a team of equals, both having formidable powers in their own right, so developing the dynamic of this relationship was as important as any fight sequence.

Shooting this film presented challenges that I've never quite experienced on any of my projects before—namely, trying to create the illusion of living, breathing, and talking underwater. This task required extensive stunt rigging and personnel and a great deal of patience and training on the part of the cast. When you're shooting a movie set beneath the sea, even your basic conversation between characters can be a major undertaking. Despite how much blue-screen work there was, we shot as much as possible with practical sets; there's just something tangible about having real props and sets that the actors can interact with. Our entire cast did an amazing job enduring long hours in uncomfortable rigs while still managing to bring forward compelling, strong performances. From Nicole Kidman to Patrick Wilson to Willem Dafoe and Dolph Lundgren, everyone gave 100 percent.

Aquaman is a unique, magical adventure that combines swashbuckling action with an emotional journey of romance and self-discovery. It has been an honor to bring this richly complex and iconic character to the big screen in his first-ever solo outing.

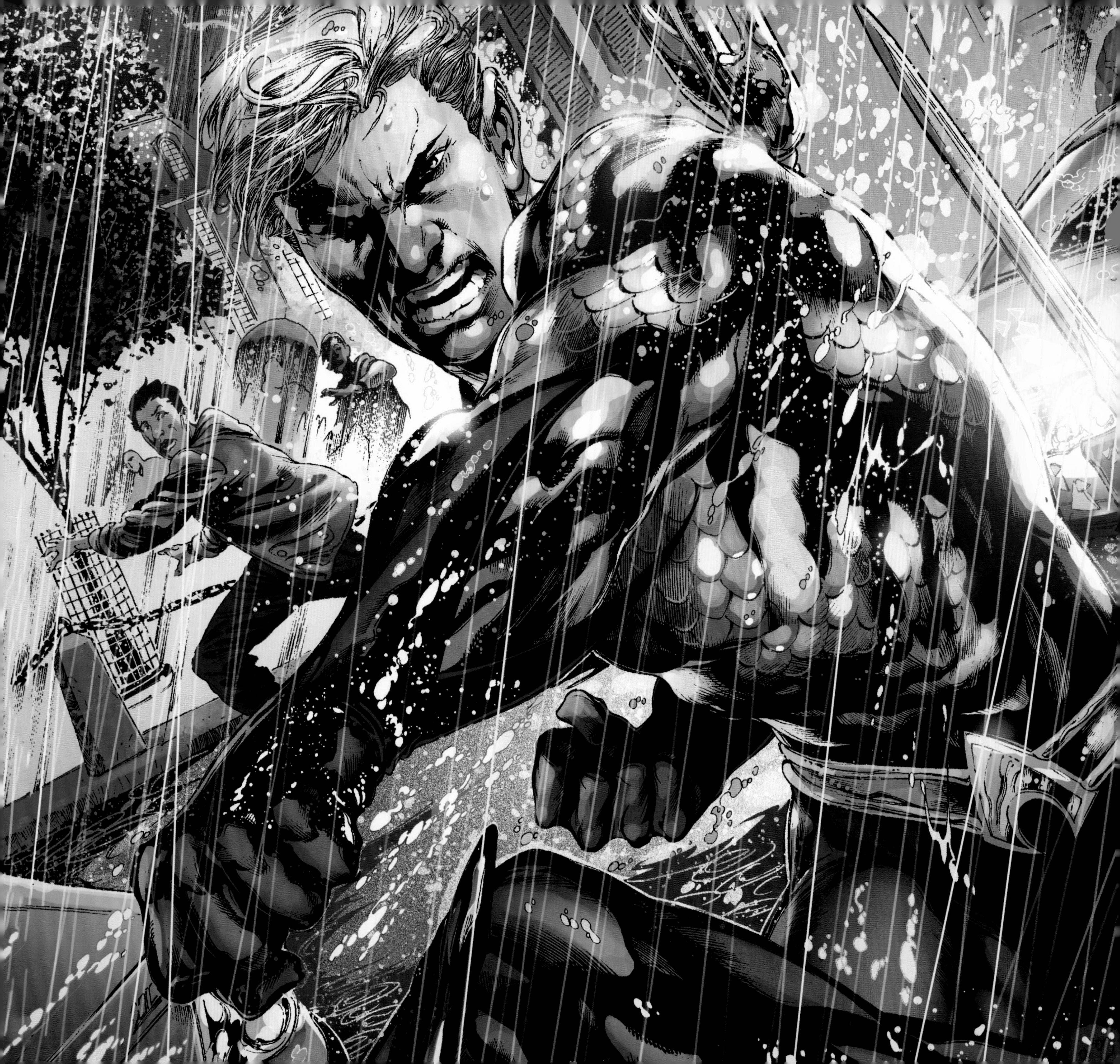

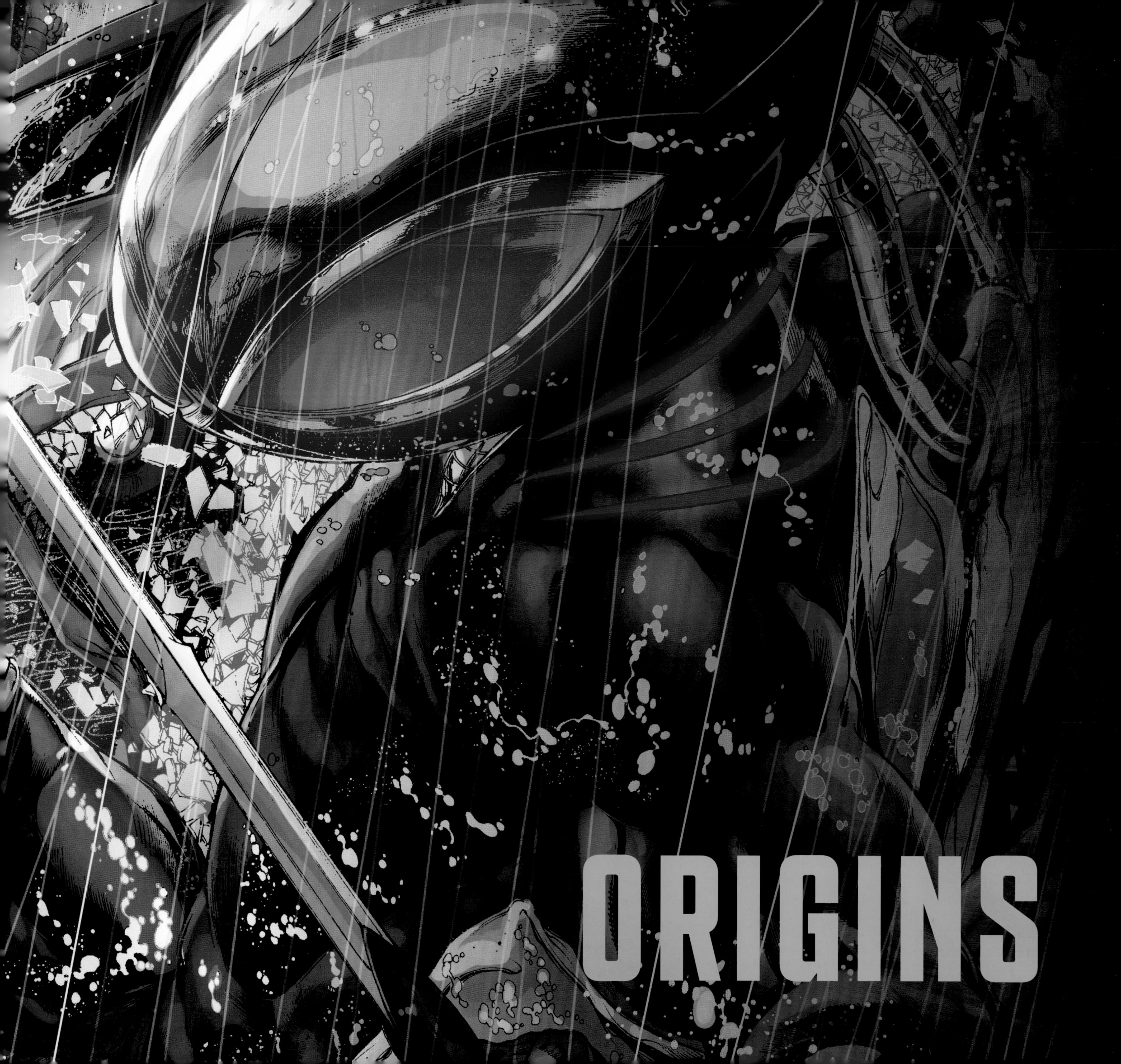

ORIGINS

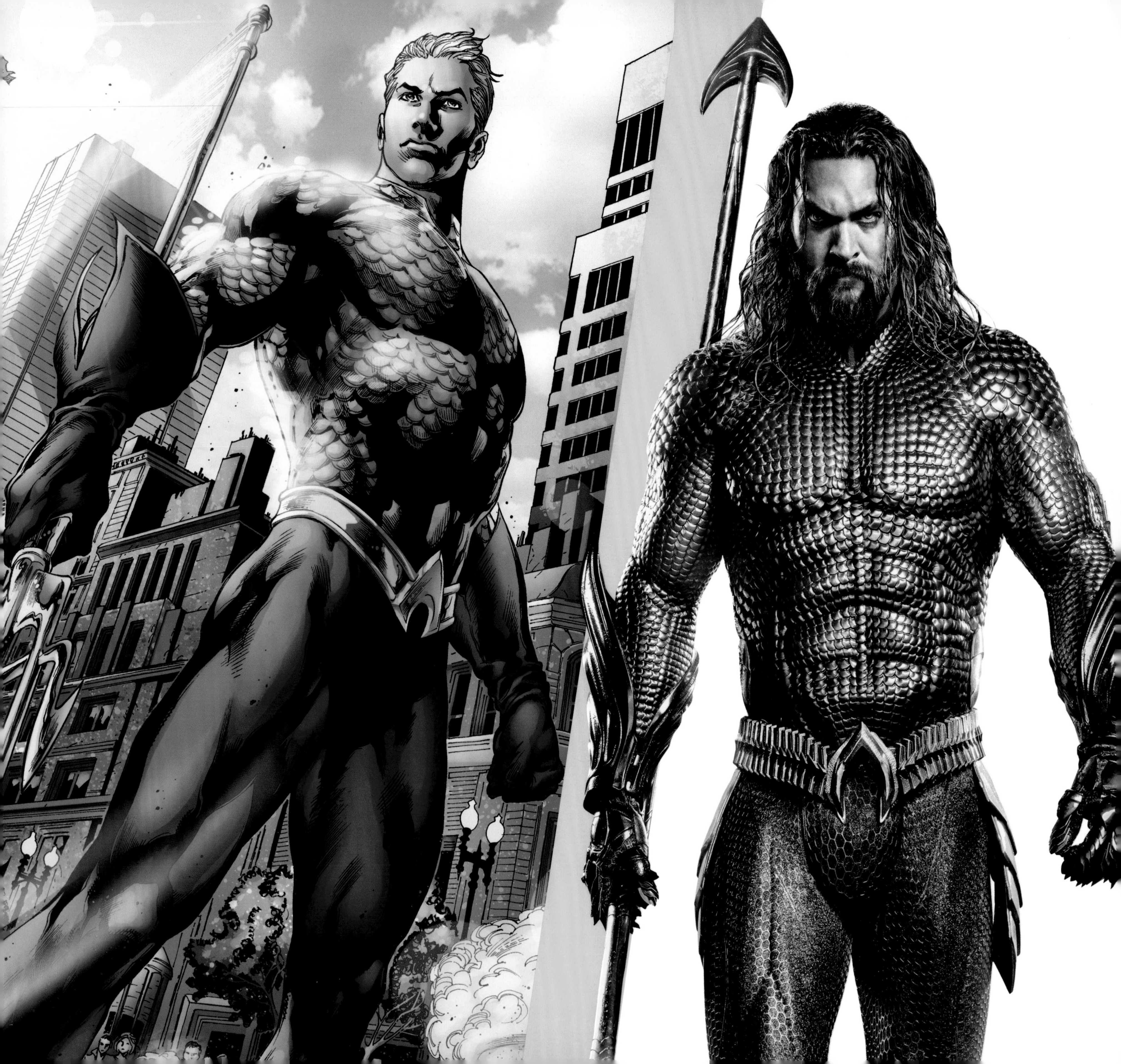

FROM PAGE TO SCREEN

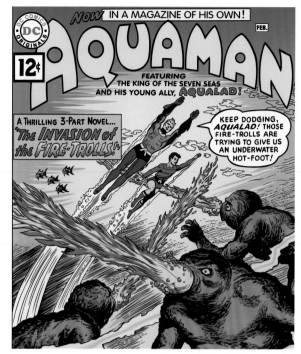

Aquaman is the culmination of more than three years of dedication and diligence to bring the epic tale of the legendary DC Comics Super Hero to life on-screen. Countless hours were spent in preproduction, getting the script right and assembling the talent to make the film; then more time was invested in capturing the intense action and dramatic moments in front of the cameras, leading to late nights with visual effects wizards hunched over computers in postproduction, finally crafting a universe unlike anything seen before in film. But that wasn't the beginning of the hero's path to the movie screen.

Created by Mort Weisinger and Paul Norris, Aquaman's storied history has evolved significantly over the decades. When the character made his debut in *More Fun Comics* #73 in 1941, Aquaman was born to a human undersea explorer and his wife who lived in a waterproof dome under the sea. Back then, the water-based hero fought Nazi villains in U-boats and other human enemies as part of his wartime adventures. After World War II, Aquaman's crusade against evil expanded and continued, uninterrupted. Aquaman is one of a very few comic book heroes to be continuously published—in one title or another—for nearly eighty years.

As the 1950s came to a close, Aquaman's origin changed to reflect the storytelling style of the approaching Silver Age of comics. He was now Arthur Curry, born to a lighthouse keeper named Tom Curry and Atlanna, a princess from the undersea realm of Atlantis, who died shortly after childbirth. This tale was told in *Adventure Comics* #260 in 1959. This era's Aquaman was blessed with superhuman strength and great underwater speed. He had a telepathic link with his fellow aquatic beings and often relied on them for the occasional rescue. Like any good hero of the day, he also had an Achilles' heel: If he were out of contact with water for more than an hour, he would perish.

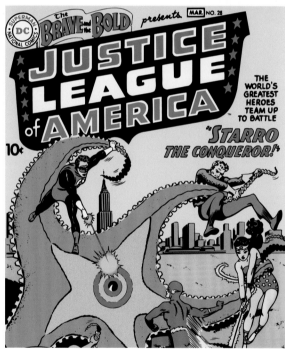

Mera was the most significant addition to Aquaman's universe during that time. The character—who would go on to become his wife in the comics—first appeared in 1963's *Aquaman* #11. At the time, she hailed from the kingdom of Xebel in the otherworldly Dimension Aqua. Like her beloved's, Mera's origin would also change with her both her and Xebel being moved to Earth in subsequent stories. Mera and Arthur's relationship has proven to be one of the most enduring and complex in the entire DC mythos, so much so that filmmakers knew that it had to be a key component of their film.

The title star of his own series, Aquaman was firmly ensconced as one of the cornerstones of the DC Universe during the Silver Age. He became a founding member of the Justice League of America (as it was originally called) in the landmark issue *The Brave and the Bold* #28. Aquaman not only received top billing in the page one roll call, but was also the first of the heroes seen in the story, when he encountered the villain Starro. This underscored the character's importance in the DC hierarchy.

NOW IN A MAGAZINE OF HIS OWN!
DC COMICS ORIGINALS
FEB.
12¢
AQUAMAN
FEATURING THE KING OF THE SEVEN SEAS AND HIS YOUNG ALLY, AQUALAD!
A THRILLING 3-PART NOVEL... "The INVASION of the FIRE-TROLLS!"
KEEP DODGING, AQUALAD! THOSE FIRE-TROLLS ARE TRYING TO GIVE US AN UNDERWATER HOT-FOOT!

SUPERMAN DC NATIONAL COMICS
The BRAVE and the BOLD presents
MAR. NO. 28
JUSTICE LEAGUE of AMERICA
THE WORLD'S GREATEST HEROES TEAM UP TO BATTLE
"STARRO THE CONQUEROR!"
10¢

PAGES 10–11: *Aquaman*, Vol. 7 #10 (August 2012) interior art by Ivan Reis, Joe Prado, Andy Lanning, and Rod Reis.

OPPOSITE LEFT: *Aquaman*, Vol. 7 #1 (November 2011) interior art by Ivan Reis, Joe Prado, and Rod Reis.

OPPOSITE RIGHT: Jason Momoa as Aquaman.

ABOVE: *Aquaman*, Vol. 1 #1 (February 1962) cover art by Nick Cardy and *The Brave and the Bold*, Vol. 1 #28 (March 1960) cover art by Mike Sekowsky, Murphy Anderson, and Jack Adler.

In 1967 Aquaman made the jump to television with Filmation's animated *The Superman/Aquaman Adventure Hour*. Six years later another key program was launched on the ABC television network: *Super Friends*. The series was an instant hit and reaffirmed the mainstream appeal of DC's biggest heroes: Superman, Batman, and Wonder Woman. It also became a gateway to the world of comic books for many young fans. But that wasn't Aquaman's last time appearing on the small screen. Arthur Curry showed up in several episodes of the long-running series *Smallville* as well as making several other TV appearances in the new millennium.

All this time, Aquaman was still going strong in comic books. Another key turning point for the character came during DC's company-wide relaunch, the New 52, in 2011. Writer Geoff Johns and artist Ivan Reis reintroduced an Aquaman more closely aligned to his Silver Age origins. Under Johns's direction, Arthur Curry was a warrior caught between both land and sea when tensions between both worlds rose to the point of war. Johns also introduced the seven undersea kingdoms and new denizens of the deep that would inhabit Aquaman's universe for years to come. The recent DC Rebirth initiative has framed Aquaman once again as the aquatic prince struggling to reconcile his responsibility to his people beneath the waves with his obligations to the surface world.

With so much history to pull from, the creative team behind *Aquaman* settled on the character's most recent incarnation established in the New 52 as their guidepost, but they never forgot his decades-old origin stories. The big screen version of Aquaman may look different from his blonde, blue-eyed comic book counterpart, but many of the facets of his personality remain the same. This strong, imposing hero with a bit of a twinkle in his eye now embodied by Jason Momoa comes straight from the comic page, with more than a little bit of the actor mixed in. It is a marriage of past nobility with a contemporary edge that breaths life into the film version of Aquaman. But the movie doesn't complete the hero's epic journey—not even remotely—it merely serves as another new beginning.

RIGHT: *Aquaman*, Vol. 7 #44 (November 2015) cover art by Trevor McCarthy and Guy Major.

OPPOSITE: *Aquaman*, Vol. 7 #6 (April 2012) cover art by Ivan Reis, Joe Prado, and Rod Reis.

PAGES 16–17: Submarine attack concept art by Rob McKinnon.

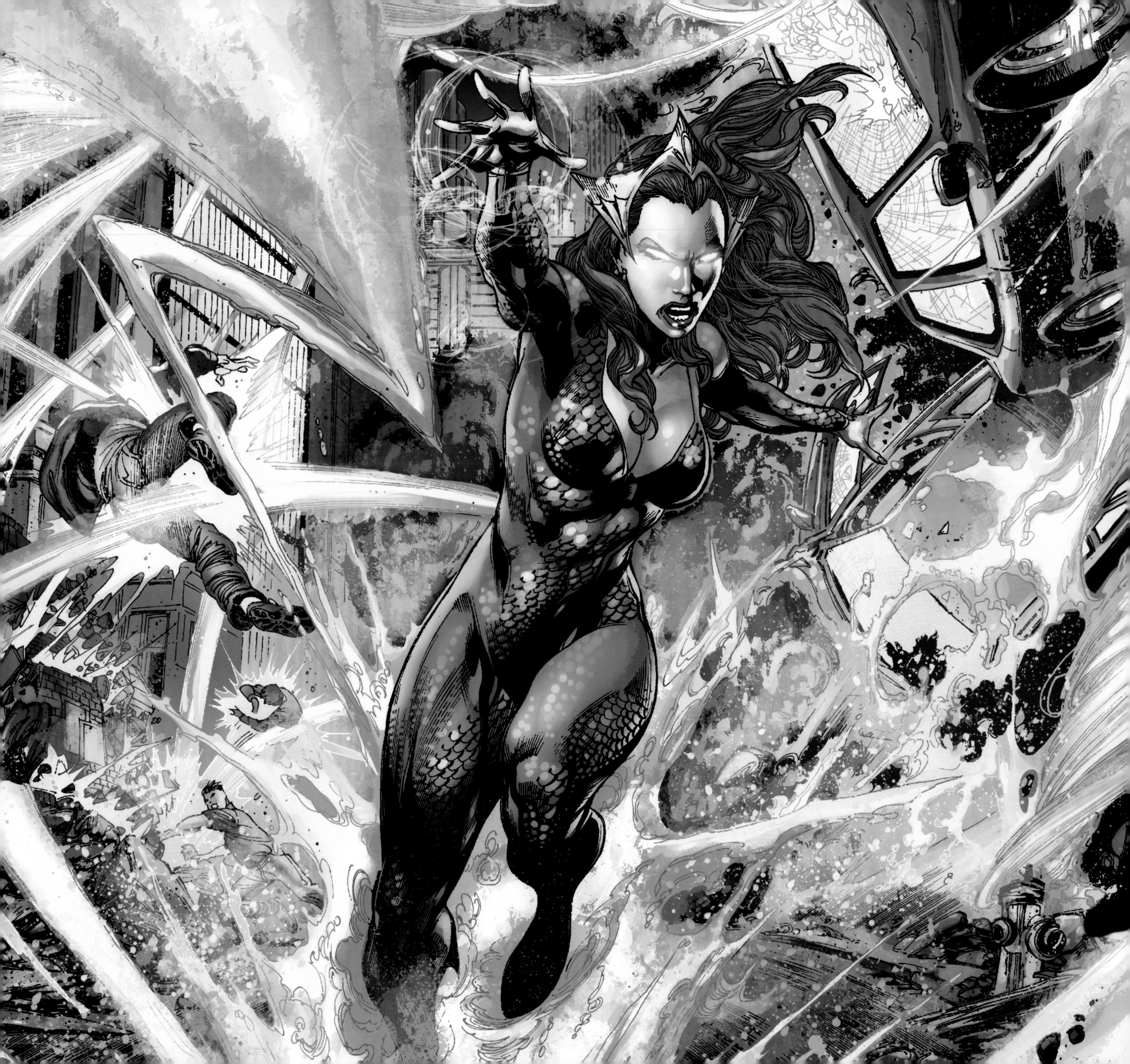

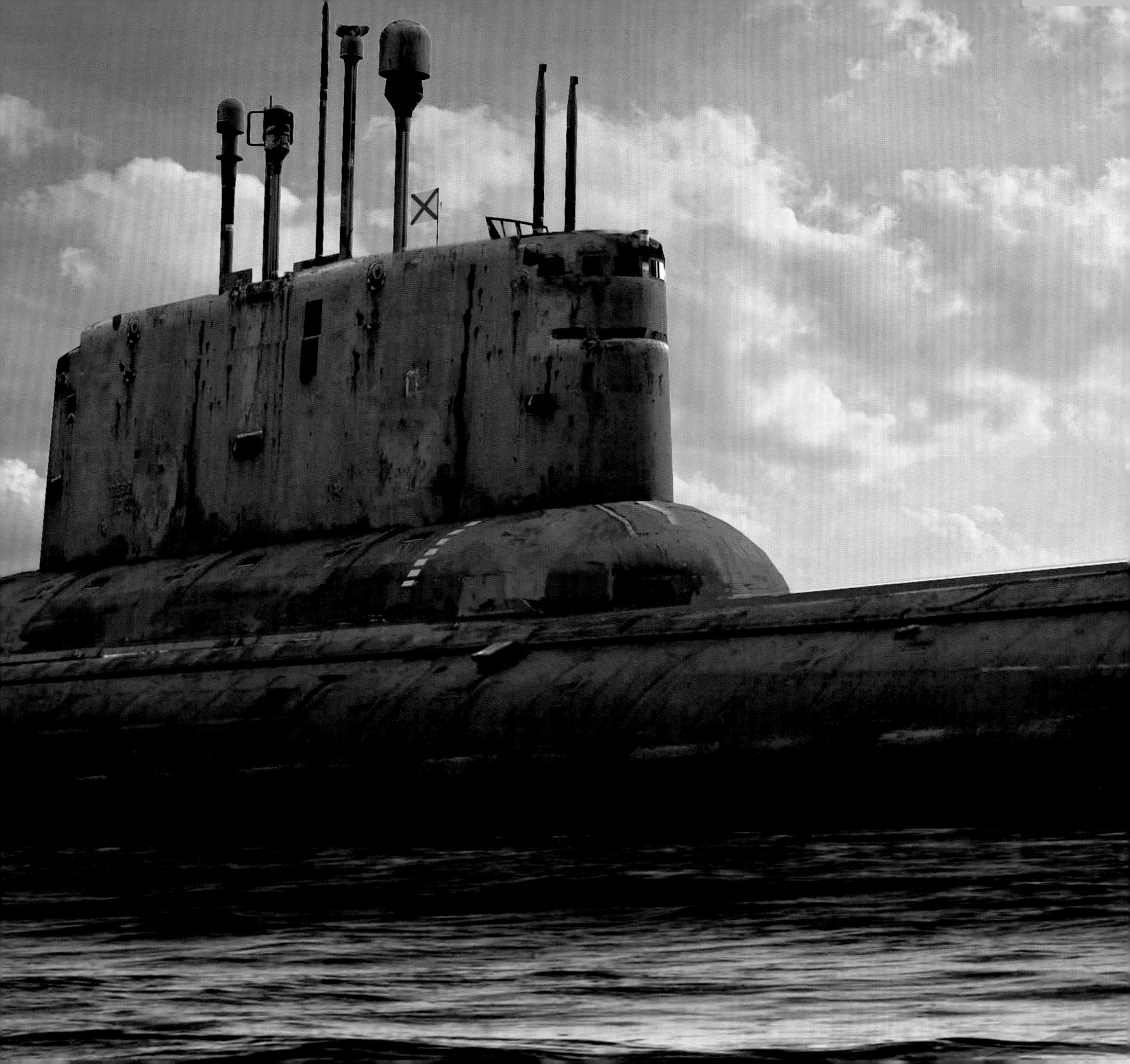

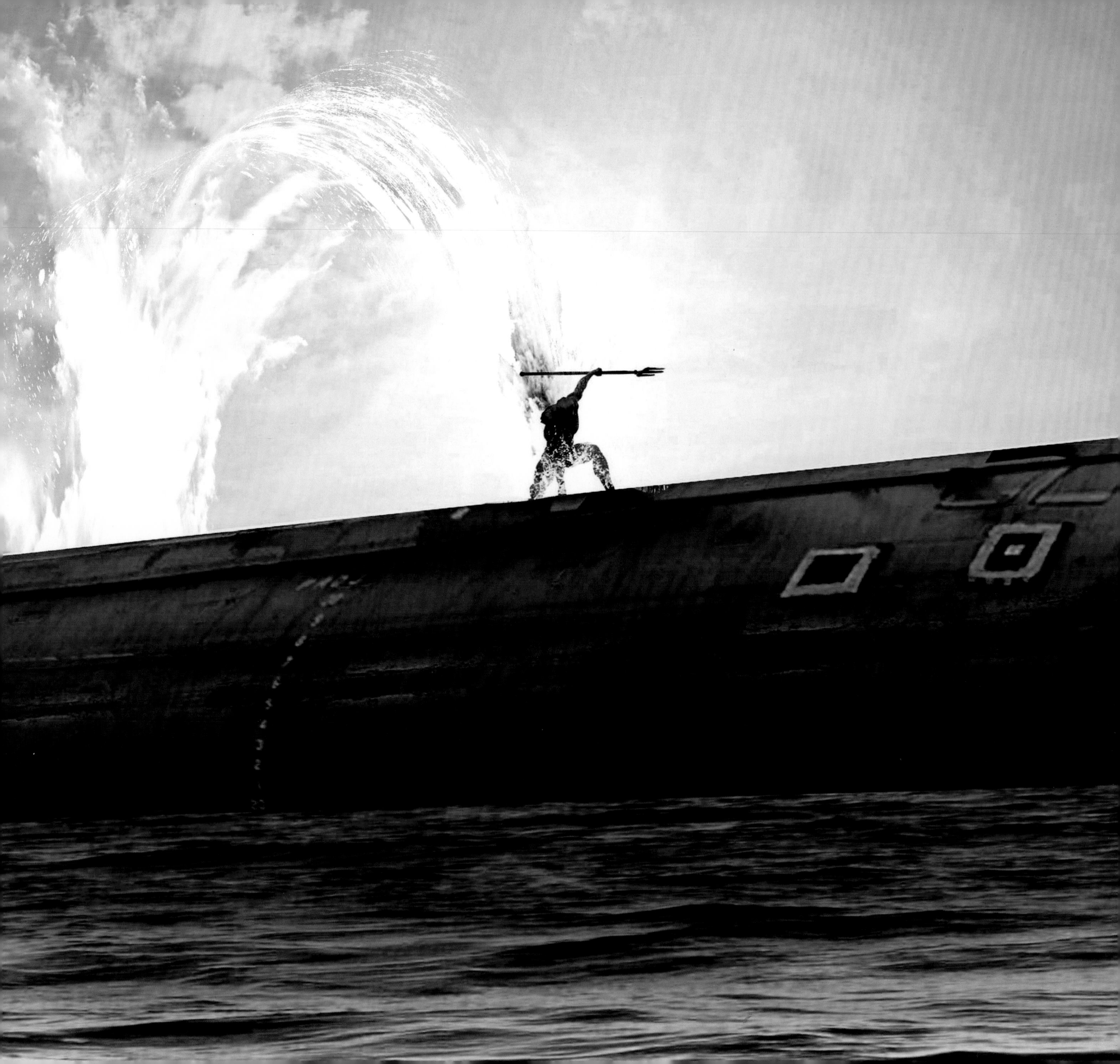

ARTHUR
SON OF TWO WORLDS

Jason Momoa has a history with the Arthur Curry that goes back before the filming of *Aquaman* began. It even predates the hiring of James Wan as director on the film. Wan was mindful of that when he joined the production and felt it was important to sit down with his star early and get on the same page regarding the kind of movie and the type of character they desired. "I wanted to be very respectful, because I know he's been living with this a long time," Wan says. "And here I am, the director coming in. I didn't want to freak him out too much."

Any concerns Wan may have had were erased once he and Momoa got together. The actor shared his ideas and thoughts on how he saw Arthur Curry-Aquaman, the character's relationship with his father, and his nomadic lifestyle. In the film, Arthur is a man who belongs to two different worlds—Atlantis and the surface world—and feels like an outsider in both. That was something the actor could relate to on a deeply personal level. "[He] doesn't know where to find his place, and that resonated with me instantly," Momoa says. The actor was born in Hawaii but raised in Iowa. He understands on an intimate level what it's like to feel like you don't belong. What Momoa took from his past and integrated into Aquaman was perfect for this particular role. Momoa just took a roundabout way of getting to him.

OPPOSITE: Arthur Curry costume concept art by Oksana Nedavniaya (*left*); Arthur steps through a waterfall into a new world.

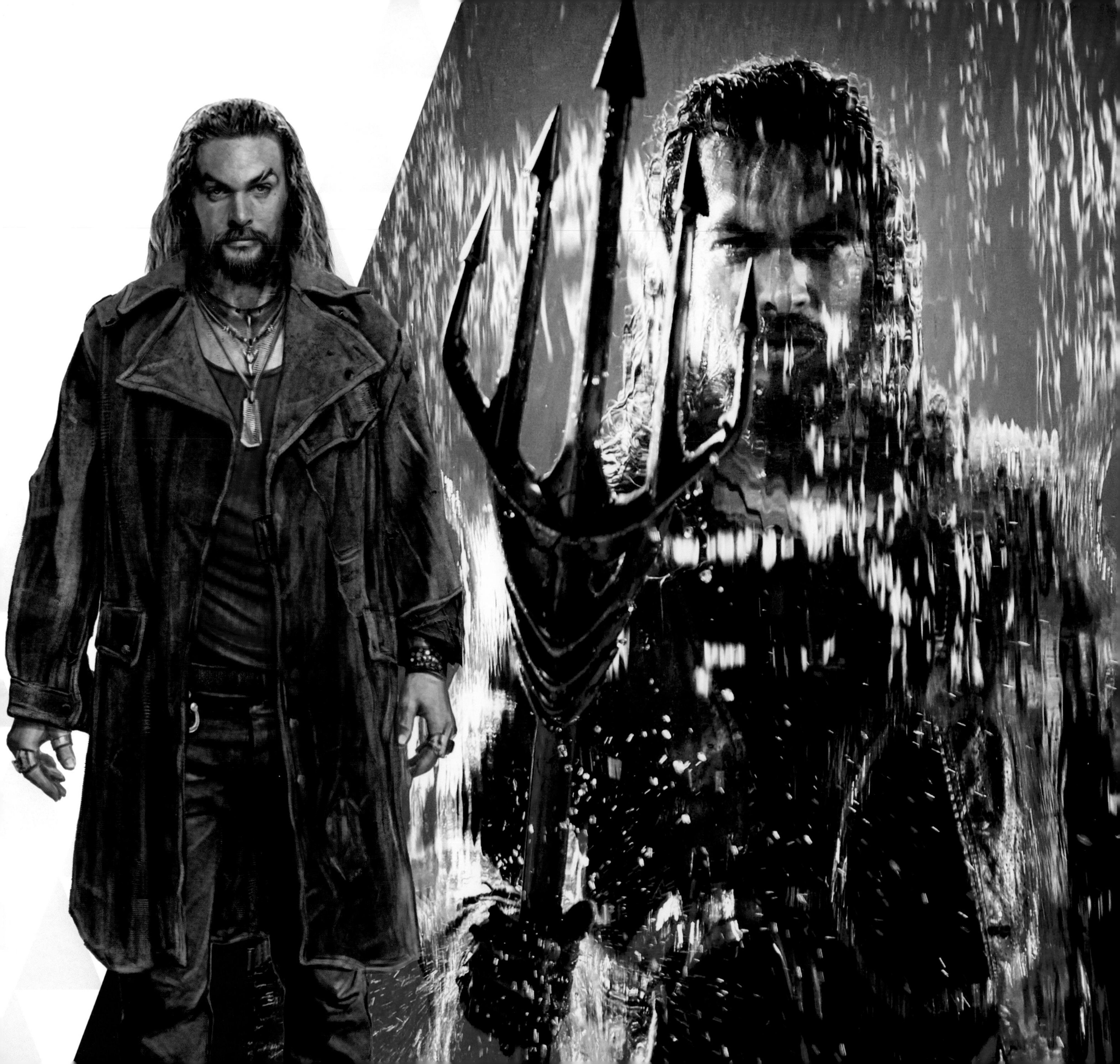

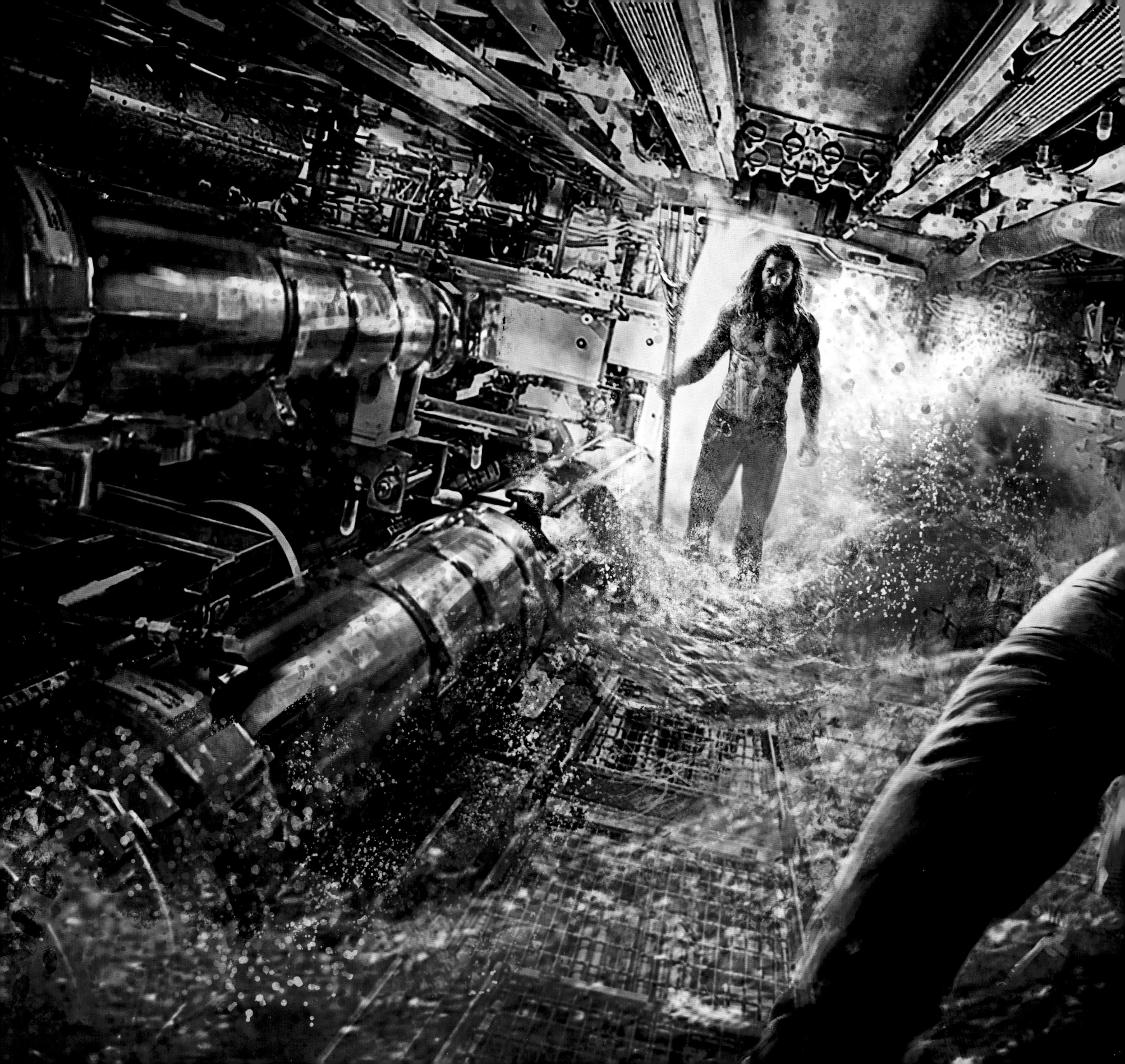

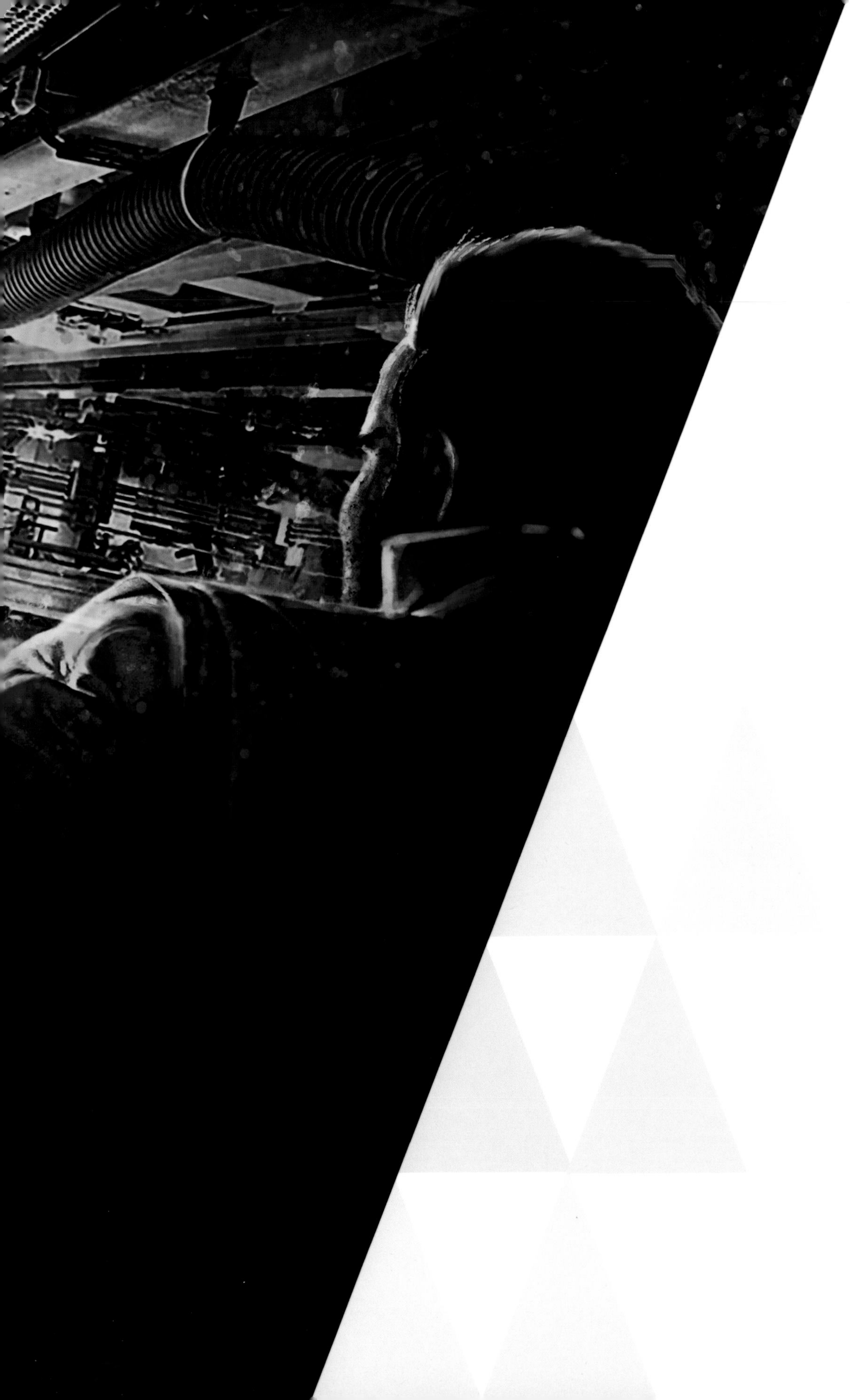

Following the release of *Man of Steel*, Zack Snyder had Momoa come in to test for the role of Gotham's Dark Knight. The actor, whose career was booming thanks to playing Khal Drogo on *Game of Thrones* and starring in a reboot of *Conan the Barbarian*, was stunned to be asked to read for the part. Still, he was game to try. "I think when I did the audition for *Batman*, I didn't play it like I was supposed to," he says. "I just played it completely different and I think that's what Zack liked."

The fearlessness Momoa portrayed in his audition was enough to impress Snyder, the director of *Batman v Superman: Dawn of Justice* and *Justice League*, who quickly offered the actor a different role. He was hired to play Aquaman, with one important caveat: He couldn't tell anyone about the part for quite a long time. That proved exceedingly difficult for the naturally gregarious Momoa. "I can't keep a secret to save my life. I can't keep a secret from my kids," he says, which is why keeping the secret for several years was its own special kind of torture for the actor. "I hated doing interviews," the actor says. "Everyone would be like, 'You're playing Aquaman!' And I would have to lie and say, 'Nope, not happening. I don't know what you're talking about.' I had to lie nonstop."

"There really is nobody who could play [Aquaman] in the way Jason does, from a physical and emotional perspective," says Peter Safran, the film's producer. "In many ways Jason mirrors Arthur Curry. Jason is a guy who comes from two different worlds. He never felt like he fit in when visiting Hawaii because he was growing up in Iowa, and he never felt like he fit in at home in Iowa because nobody there looked like him."

LEFT: Submarine attack concept art by Rob McKinnon.

"What I loved about him was that he was flawed," adds Momoa. "His dad was blue-collar, he worked on oil rigs. Arthur did underwater welding, and he saved people. He saved fishermen, and then he'd go drink." Much like his father, Arthur finds the camaraderie of a bar to be an escape mechanism. Talking about emotions does not come naturally to the Curry men, as that early scene at the Sunken Galleon shows. But there is one particular tragedy that haunts them both: the loss of Arthur's mother, Atlanna.

She named her son in honor of the Arthurian legend as well as a particularly memorable hurricane mentioned in the movie. Even when her child was an infant, Atlanna saw him as proof that the people above and below sea level could one day coexist. Even though she left Arthur when he was still a young child, the pain of her departure still looms over him and his father. According to Wan, that pain drives his desire to never go to Atlantis—"because he doesn't feel like those are his people," Wan says, "and

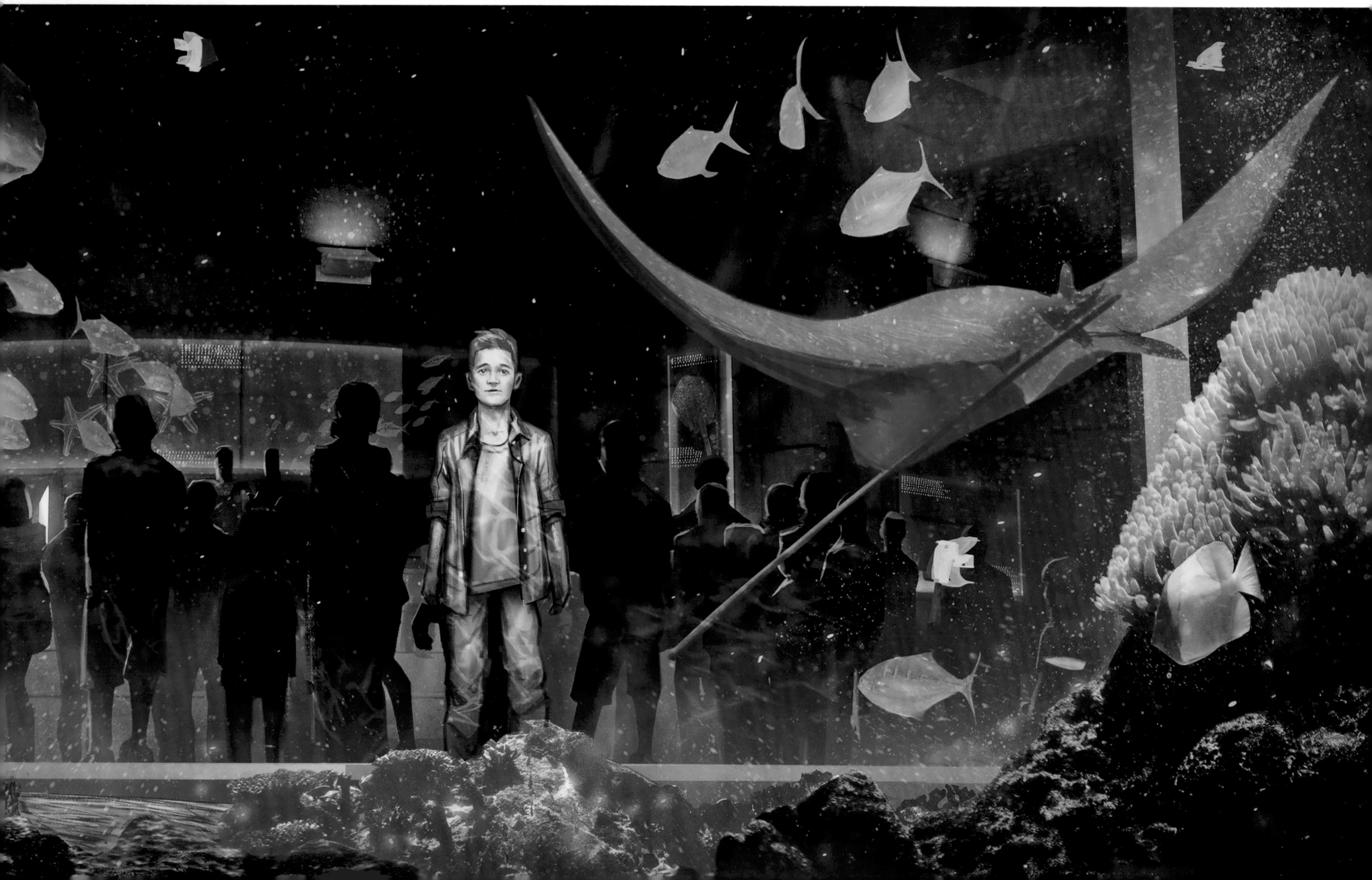

he doesn't really care about their culture." The impact of growing up without his mother resonates with Arthur throughout the movie.

Aquaman may not be the first time Jason Momoa has appeared on-screen as Arthur Curry, but this film is essentially Aquaman's origin story, which was consciously left out of his past screen outings. "If you had already seen it in *Justice League*, then it wouldn't be the same thing," notes Wan. "It was important to the growth of the character that we got to tell this story." The director worked with screenwriter Will Beall and executive producer Geoff Johns to reveal Aquaman's journey across the years, with various flashbacks used to show the manifestation of Arthur's powers. One flashback shows a young Arthur first noticing his unique abilities during a visit to the Boston Aquarium. It also reveals how other kids made fun of him for "talking with fish."

THESE PAGES: Boston Aquarium concept art by Brad Nielsen.

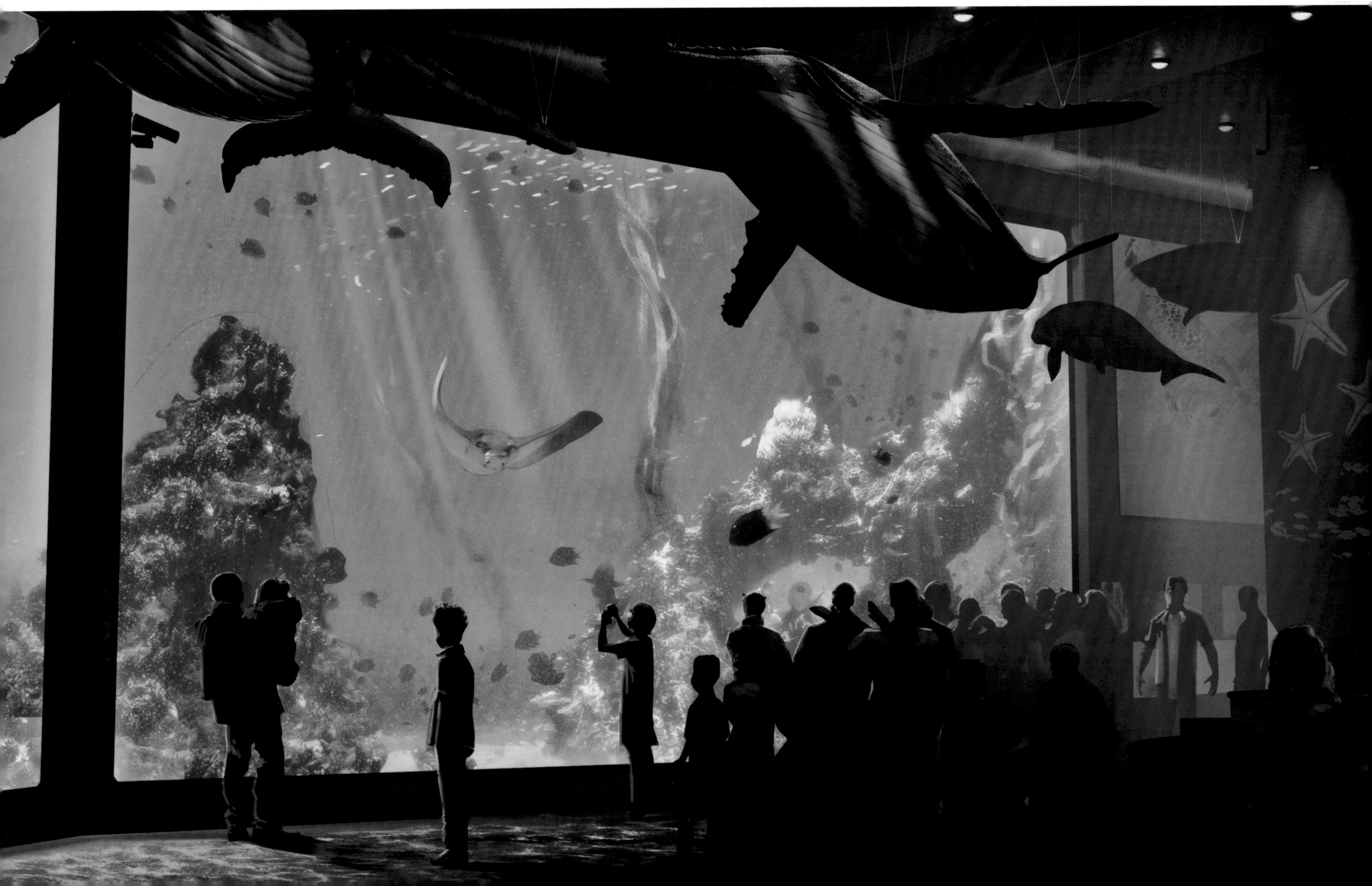

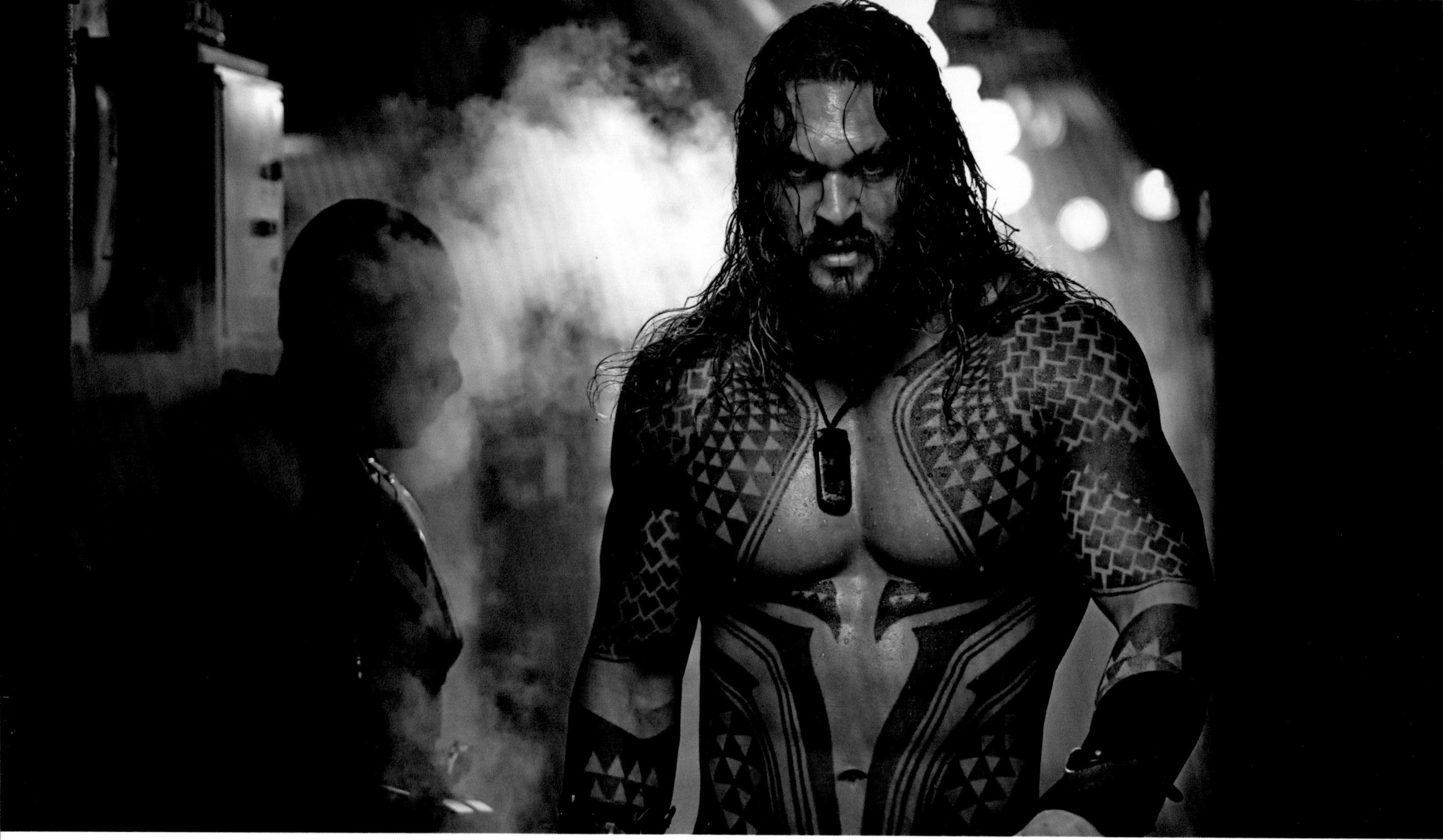

Screenwriter David Leslie Johnson-McGoldrick believes Arthur's duality is what makes him such a unique superhero. He's a very powerful being choosing to live a blue-collar life among humans even though he's royalty and, by all rights, should be the king of Atlantis. "This seemed like the right story to tell for Arthur. The story of how he became the leader of Atlantis," says Johnson. "He's a down-to-earth, dirt-under-his-fingernails guy. He's very relatable, like he's just there to do a job. He is not the guy you think is necessarily going to become a head of state."

Wan praises Momoa for helping to change Aquaman's public image. "That's something that is very important for me," Wan says. "Everyone knows that Aquaman [has been] the joke of the superhero world. He's the guy people love to make fun of. But the moment you cast Jason Momoa in this role, that all goes out the window."

THESE PAGES: Jason Momoa takes action in this physical role.

Johnson concurs, saying that the quaint Silver Age image some may have of the character will be irrevocably shattered by Momoa's rugged portrayal. "He is so clearly, from the moment you look at him, not the Aquaman you grew up with." The journey Arthur Curry takes in the movie changes the character in many surprising ways, and other ways that will be familiar. "At the start of the movie he has redefined who the character is," says Johnson. "But then you realize, as the story unfolds, that it's the origin story of how he became the iconic Aquaman we all know."

Momoa is an imposing, muscular figure who stands six foot four with long, flowing hair, who also worked exceptionally hard to look the part of a nearly invulnerable superhero. His training regimen included jujitsu, martial arts training, weight lifting, and rock climbing. The actor, who did a large number of his own stunts, said he did not overemphasize weight training because he was going for a more slimmed-down physique.

While his superpowers and fighting ability may make him nearly unstoppable, what makes Arthur Curry truly special is his humanity. And that human side is what could help him broker peace between the two worlds to which he belongs. "Yes, he's a super-being, and in my film he's very powerful," says Wan. "But at the end of the day what drives him comes from a very human place."

"There is nobody else who could play Aquaman other than Jason Momoa," adds Safran. "For generations to come, when they think of Aquaman, no one will think of a blonde-haired, blue-eyed guy. It will always be the wild man, Jason Momoa."

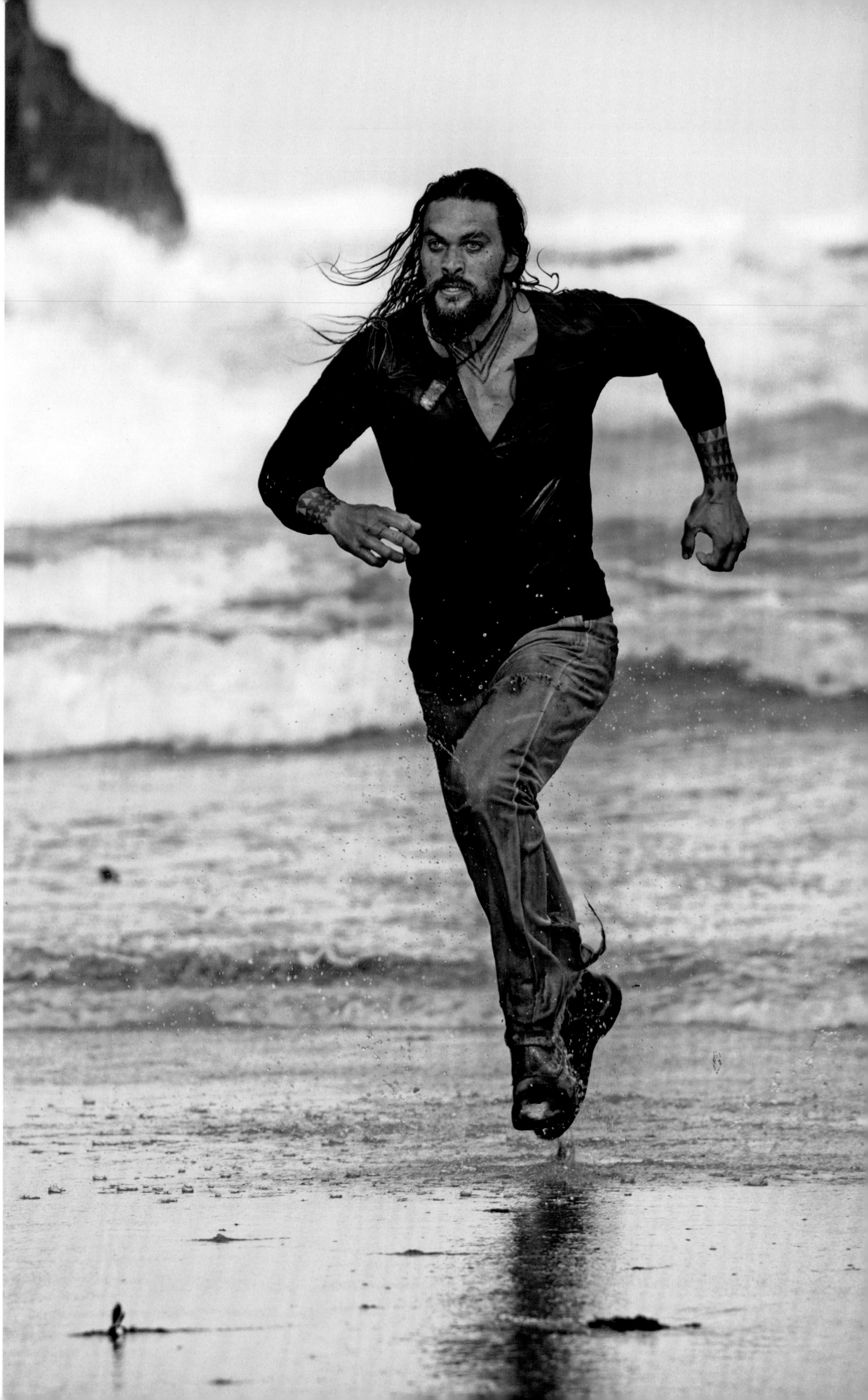

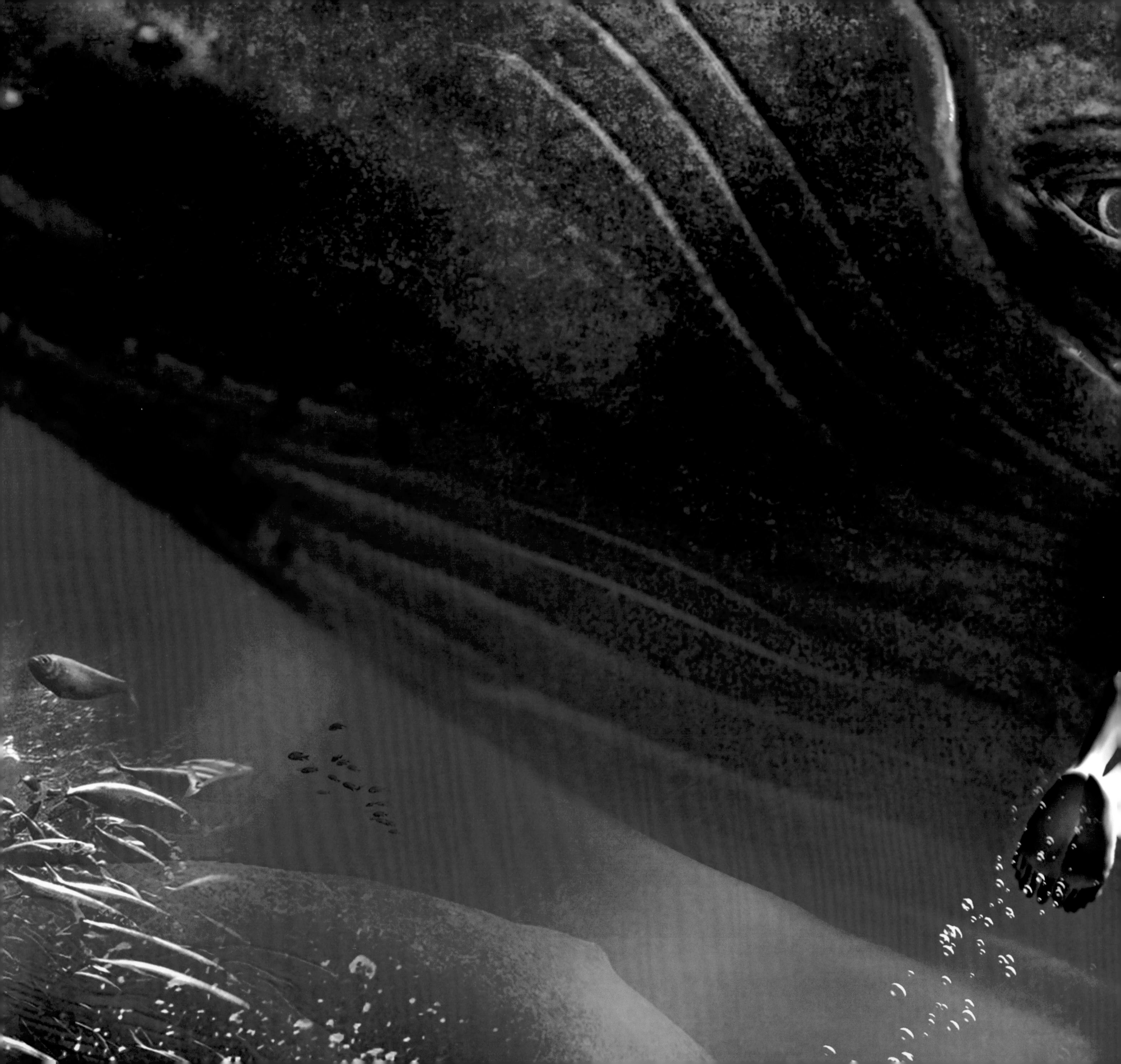

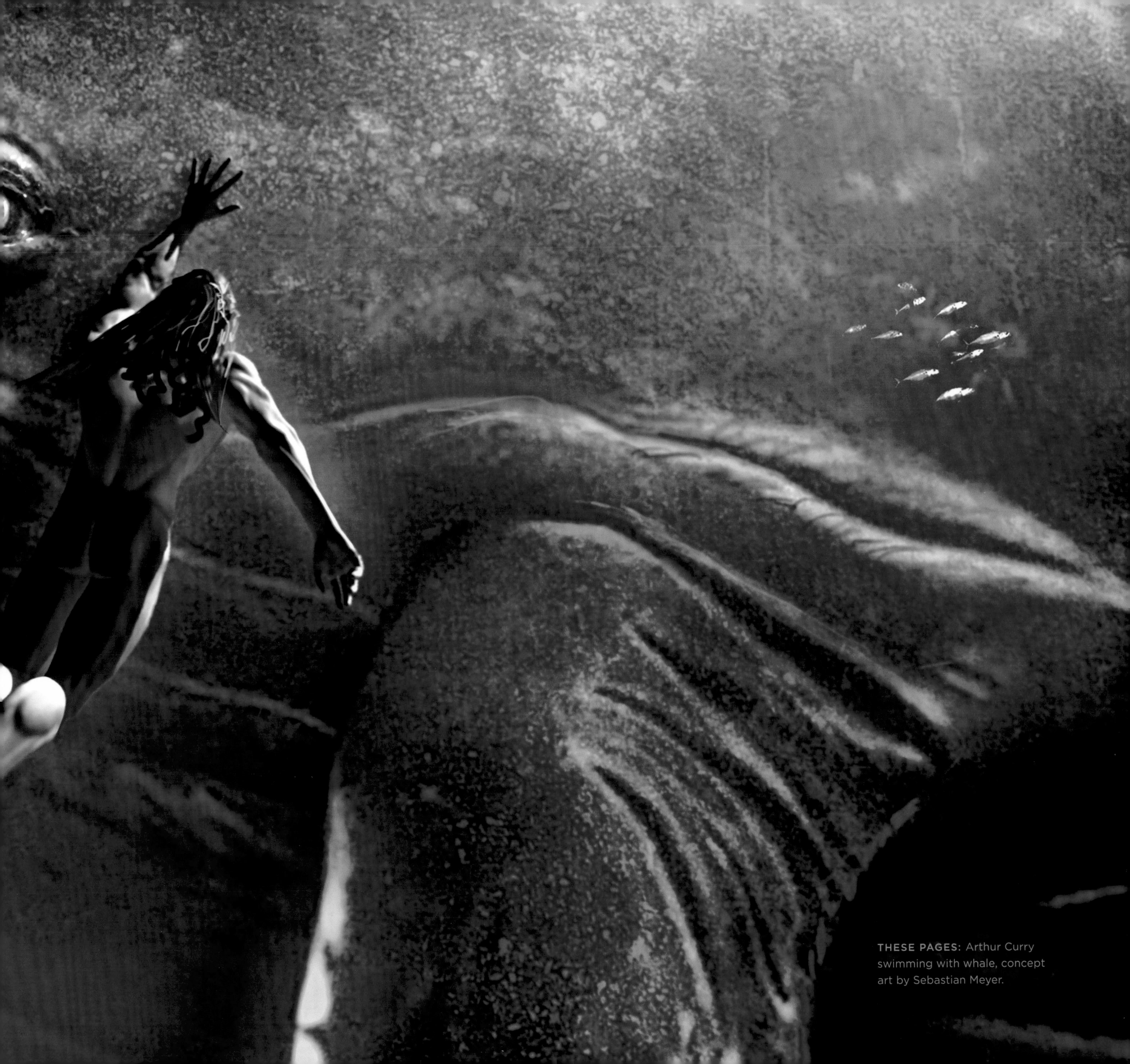

THESE PAGES: Arthur Curry swimming with whale, concept art by Sebastian Meyer.

TOM CURRY

MAN OF THE LAND

The impact of parents on superheroes' development is a foundational element of the DC mythos. Batman is driven by the enduring trauma of his parents' murder in Crime Alley. Superman is inspired by the example set and the beliefs taught by Jonathan and Martha Kent. Fast as the Flash may be, Barry Allen cannot outrun the trauma of losing his mother. Aquaman is no different.

Arthur Curry's shattered childhood looms large in the movie, affecting his relationship with his father, who is played by Temuera Morrison. Their relationship is built on the pain both men endured after Arthur's mother, Atlanna, was taken from them when Arthur was a little boy. Arthur may have understood that his mother had to leave him for noble reasons, but that did not diminish the loss. For his father, it also meant losing the love of his life. Tom Curry serves as the wayward hero's anchor to a life above the waves in Amnesty Bay. Tom also understands that his son's connections to Atlantis cannot be ignored. "The father and son relationship is a cool kind of thing where I've accepted way back that he's half Atlantean—because there were a few visits from Vulko and people like that to train up my son," Morrison says. "So I was aware that certain things are going to happen to my son and there was a certain amount of grooming my son for a bigger mission in life."

Momoa, a longtime fan of Morrison, greatly enjoyed the opportunity to work with the actor. "I based a lot of stuff of Drogo [on *Game of Thrones*] off of Jake 'the Muss,'" Momoa says, speaking of the memorable role Morrison played in *Once Were Warriors*. "There's a lot of history behind that, and so I really wanted him to play my father."

Morrison fondly recalls shooting the scene when Tom and Atlanna first meet. The scene that establishes the love at first sight that occurs between these two characters from vastly different worlds. According to Morrison, Kidman's collaborative nature and warmth helped make that instant connection feel natural. "She makes us all feel comfortable. No ego whatsoever, very open."

There's a moment when Tom Curry is at Terry's Sunken Galleon and sees clips of his son behaving as a hero on television. It's a key moment between father and son, but still Arthur Curry is not quite Aquaman at this juncture. "He's still dealing with the responsibility of it all," Morrison says. "I think that's where his dad comes in, too. Just to give him that reassuring pat on the shoulder."

TOP: Father and son embrace on the dock in Amnesty Bay.
BOTTOM: Tom rescues Atlanna in concept art by Scott Lukowski.
OPPOSITE RIGHT: Tom Curry costume concept art based on a design by costumer Kym Barrett.

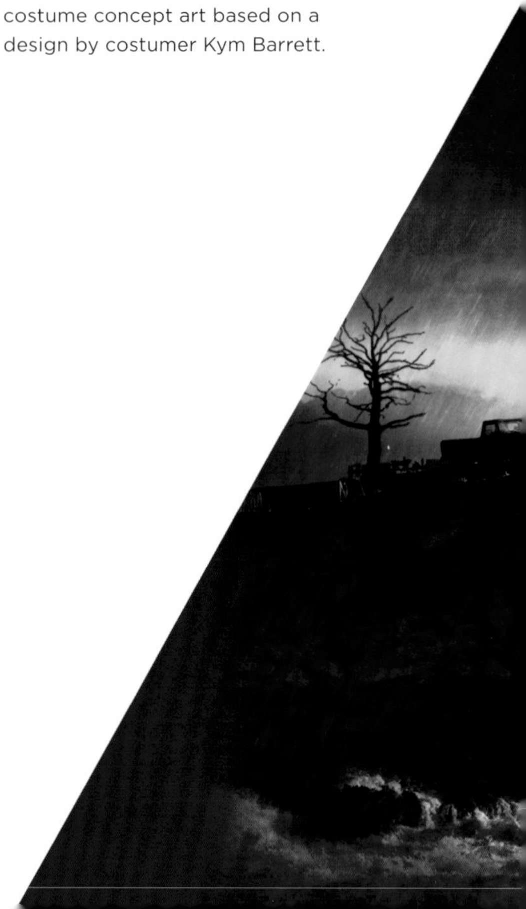

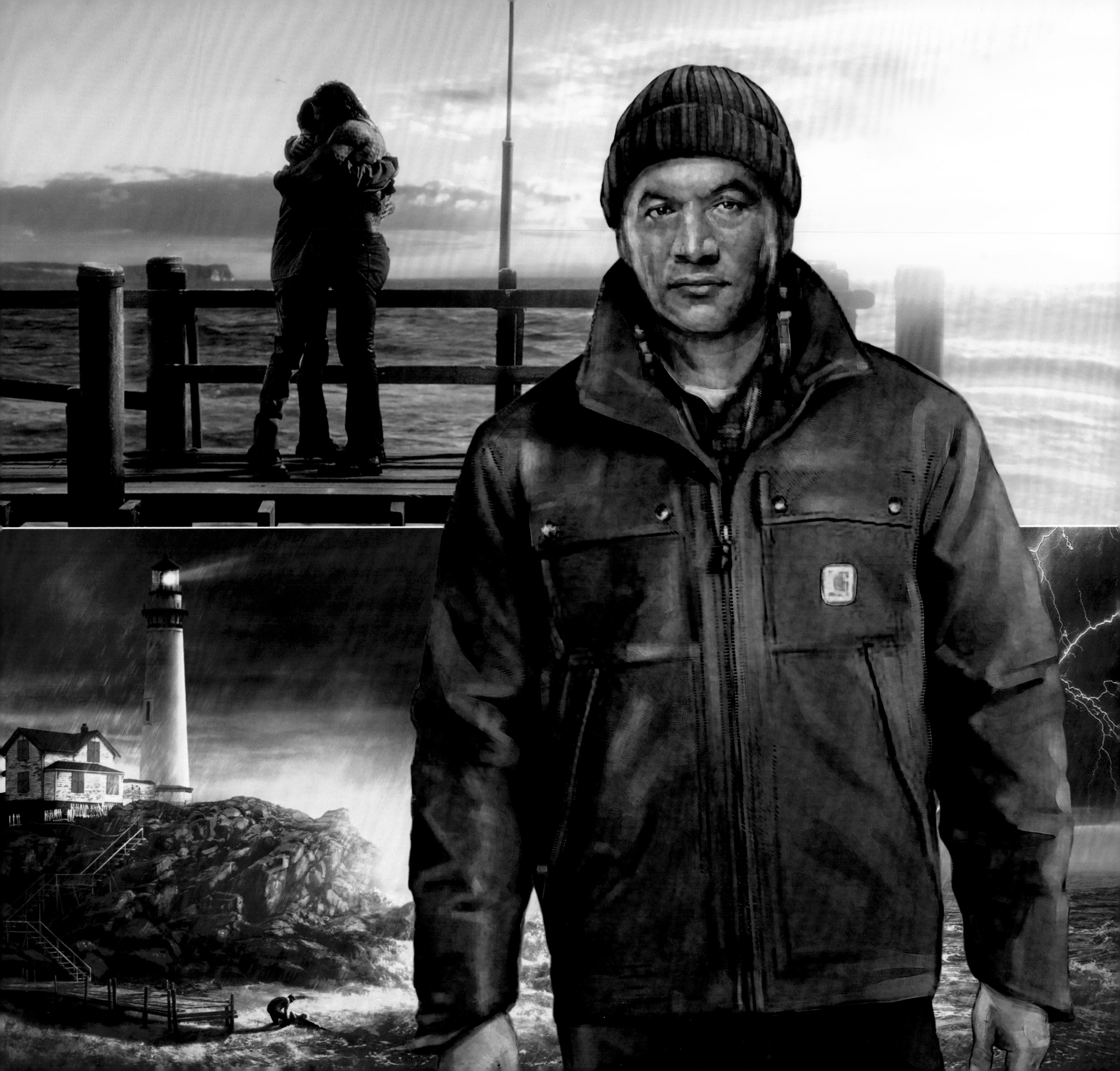

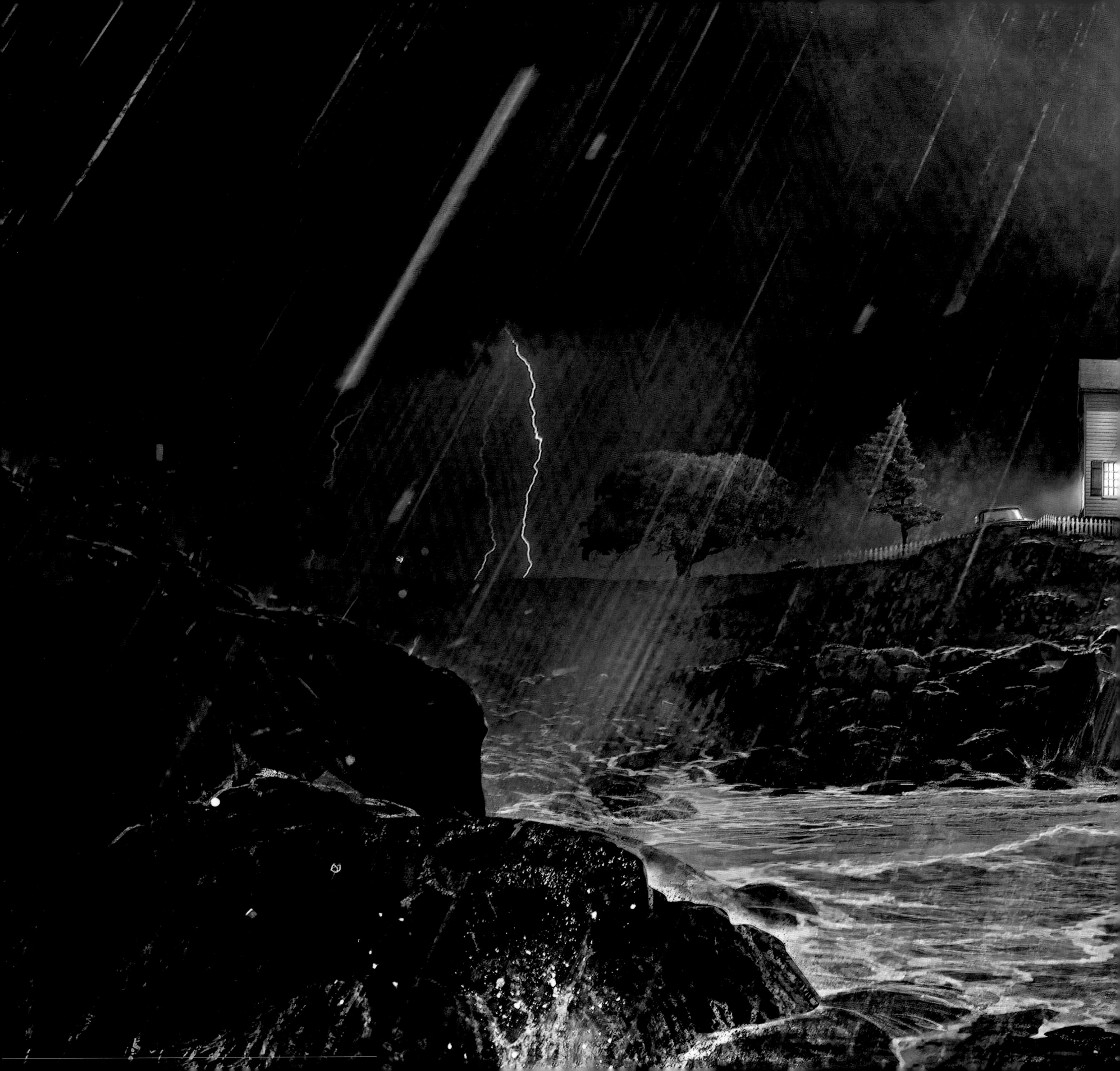

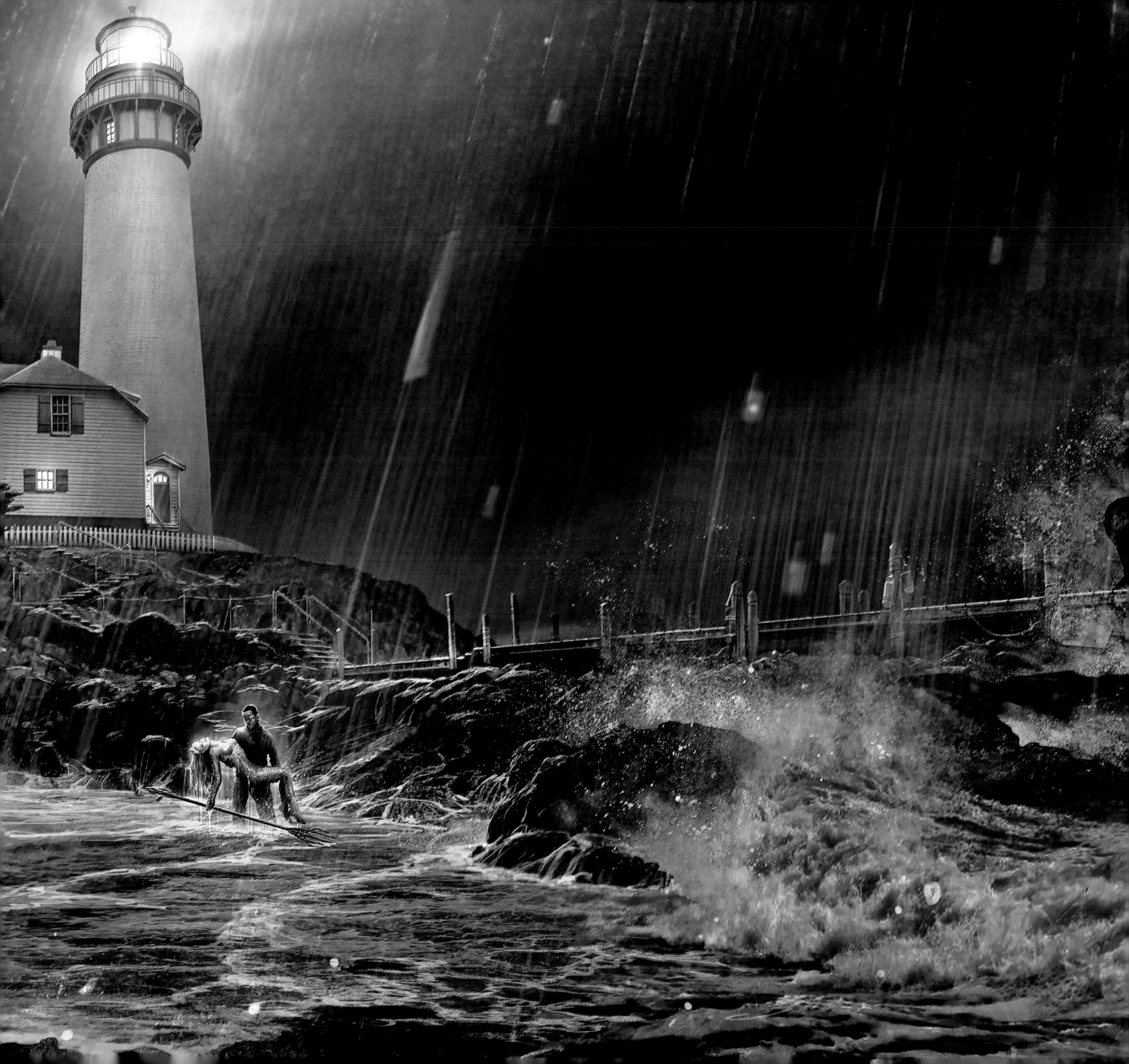

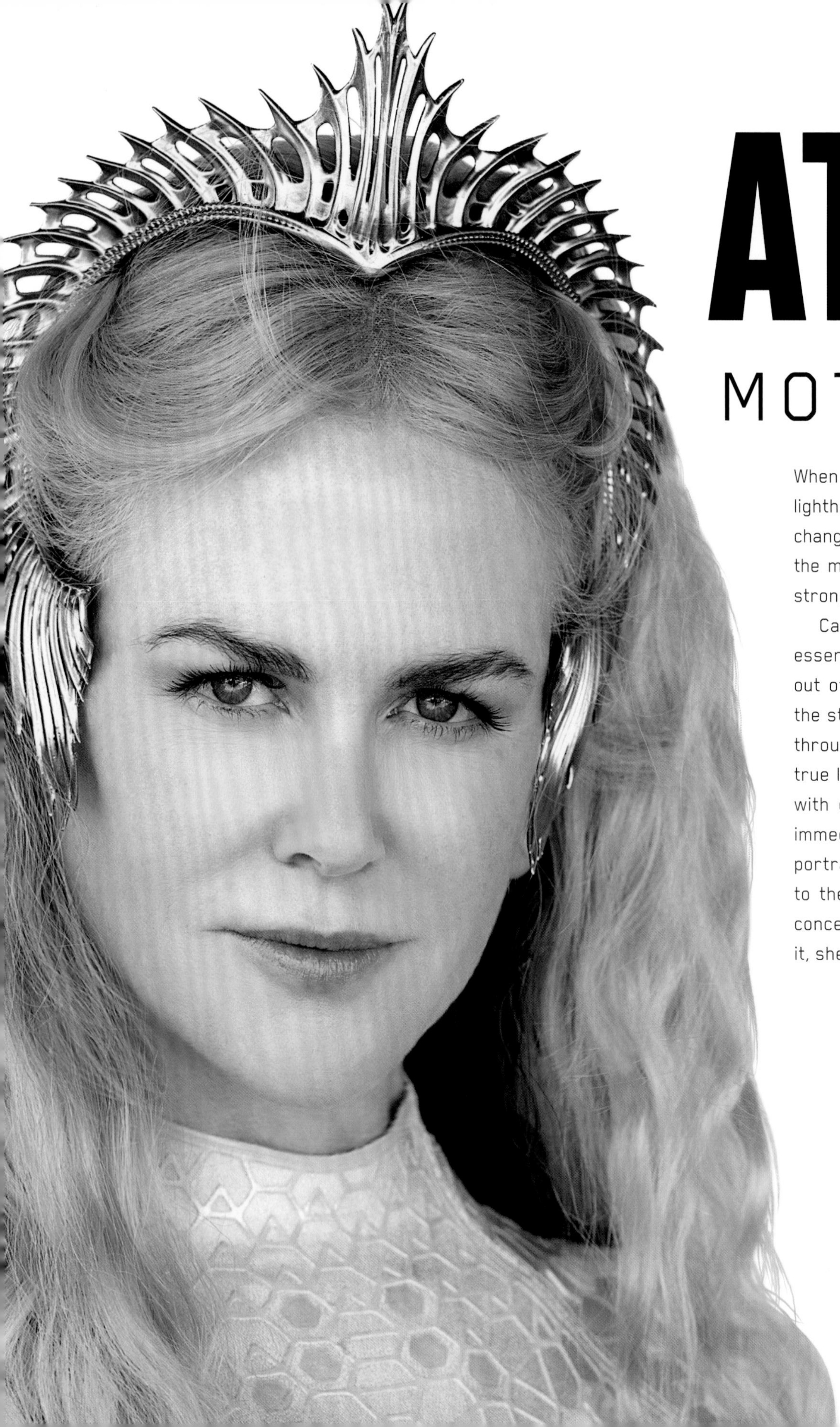

ATLANNA

MOTHER OF KINGS

When Tom Curry finds Atlanna badly hurt on the jagged shoreline by the lighthouse during a violent storm, he has no idea how much his life will change. In spite of the fact that the super-strong Atlantean almost kills Tom the moment she first lays eyes on him, their attraction soon proves too strong to resist.

Casting for the all-important role of the queen of Atlantis was essential. Her relationship with Tom Curry—as true an example of the "fish out of water" metaphor as has ever existed—is one of the linchpins of the story. Even when Atlanna is not on-screen, her impact reverberates through Arthur's pain and Tom Curry's tragic optimism that, one day, his true love will return. The production team knew they needed an actress with cinematic heft and undeniable charisma to portray Atlanna. They immediately aimed high, targeting Nicole Kidman as the ideal person to portray the regal and commanding queen. The filmmakers were so drawn to the possibility of casting Kidman that her likeness was used in the concept art and wardrobe drawings featuring Atlanna. As luck would have it, she was eager to sign on.

PAGES 30–31: Atlanna rescued by Tom concept art by Jeremy Love.
LEFT AND OPPOSITE RIGHT: Nicole Kidman as Atlanna.
OPPOSITE LEFT: Atlanna hero costume concept art by Oksana Nedavniaya.

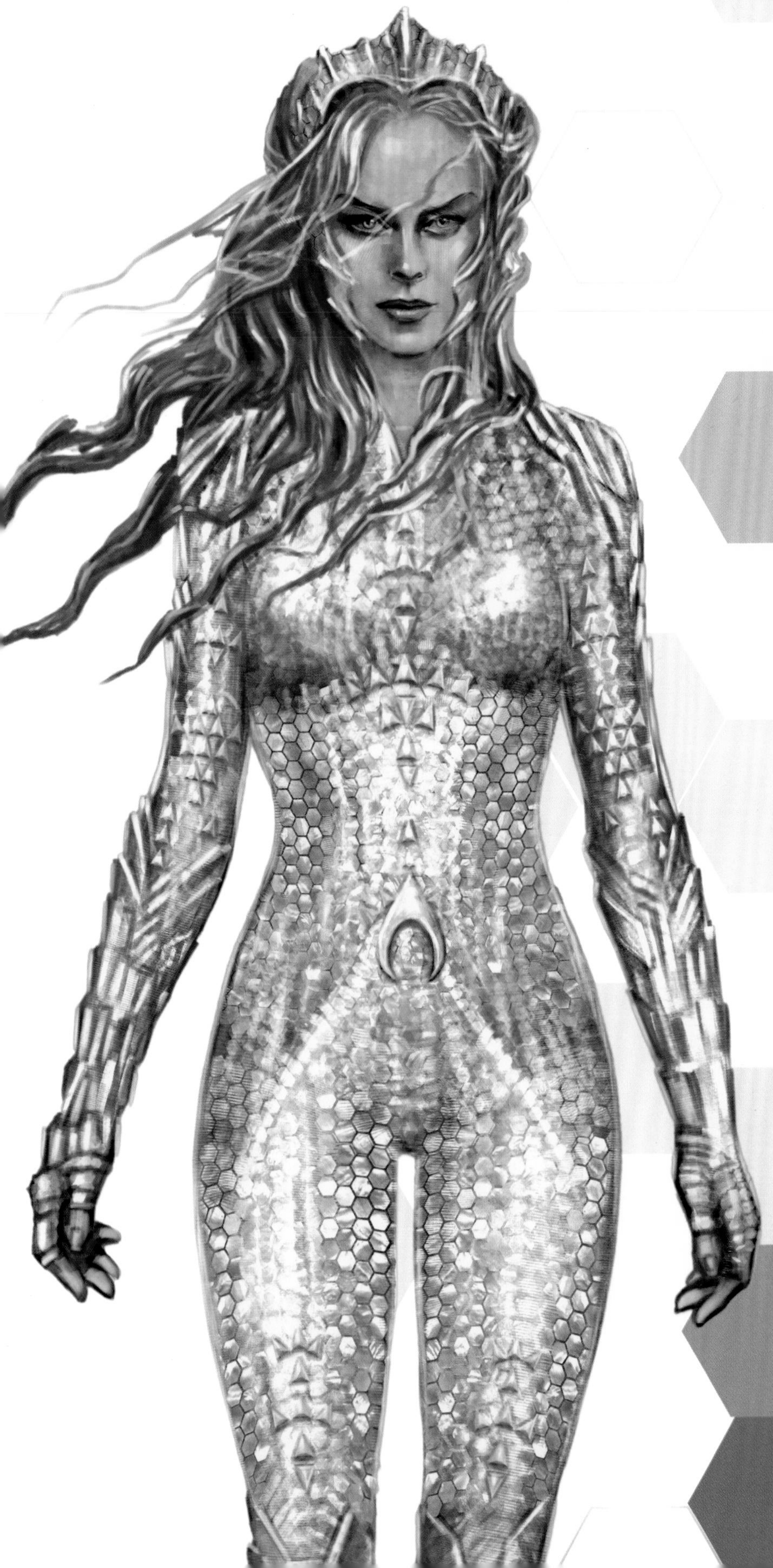
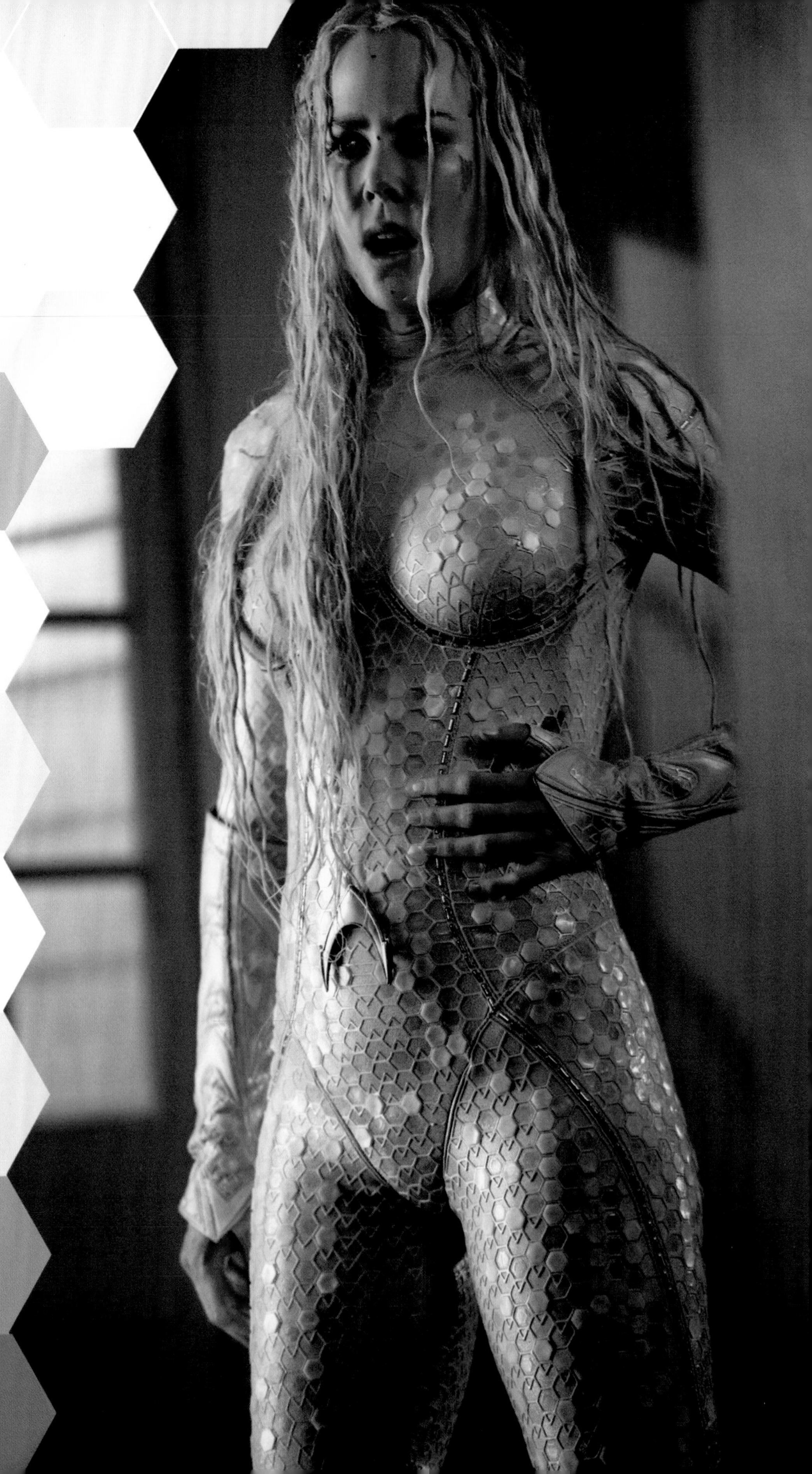

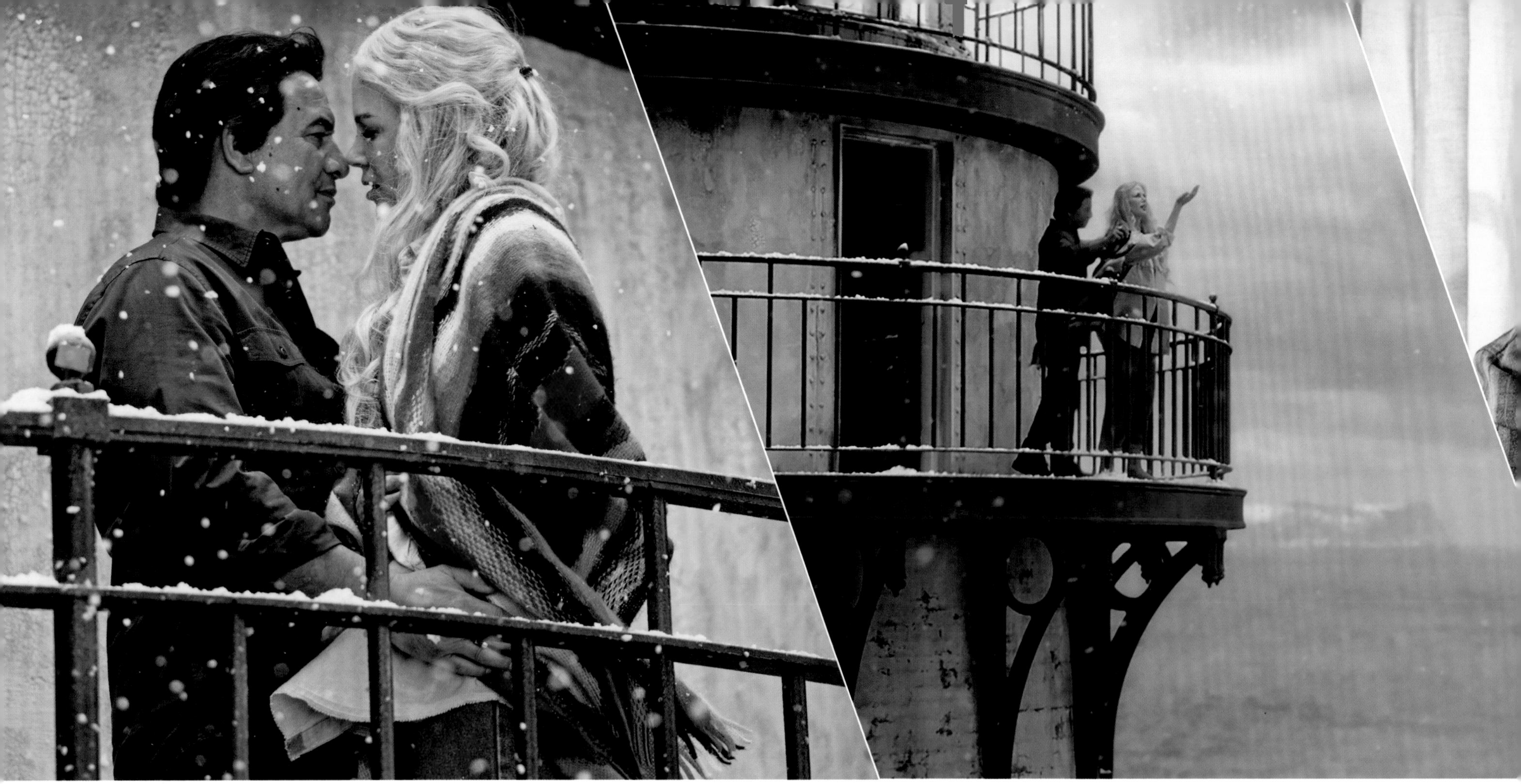

"When we started the process of casting the movie, we always knew that Atlanna had to be an iconic actress," producer Peter Safran says. "We knew it had to be somebody who would bring so much to the table just by looking at them and bring gravitas to the role." James Wan, an Australian like Kidman, mentioned to the producers that he had been told the star of *The Hours* and *Moulin Rouge* had always wanted to collaborate with him. "She had been looking for an interesting superhero film. When we reached out to Kidman we found out that she was very interested in working with James. "We walked her through the concept art, talked about the journey the movie took, and she said yes immediately." The producer praises Kidman for infusing Atlanna with great emotion and personality.

Atlanna's elegant costume is one of the production's standout designs. "It was an extension of what we were doing with Mera and the other characters," explains costume designer Kym Barrett." I wanted Atlanna's costume to have kind of mother-of-pearls-like-colors, very majestic. If you look closely, she also has a cellular-hex print on her outfit. She also has lots of gold, silver, and copper in her highlights. It's also important that when we meet Atlanna that we see how out of place the texture and color is in Tom Curry's lighthouse. It's a working-class fishing village. So Atlanna and what she is wearing gives the audience its first glimpse at how different Atlantis is." Atlanna's costume exemplified the way the production fused design and practical elements. The light source for scenes shot in the undersea realms was crucial. Given Wan's mandate that the world depicted in the film have functional logic, the filmmakers used the bioluminescence that many marine creatures produce naturally as the primary light source for Atlantis. That includes several design elements in Atlanna's shimmering costume. The lighting added to the character's ethereal quality, perfectly embodied by the statuesque actress.

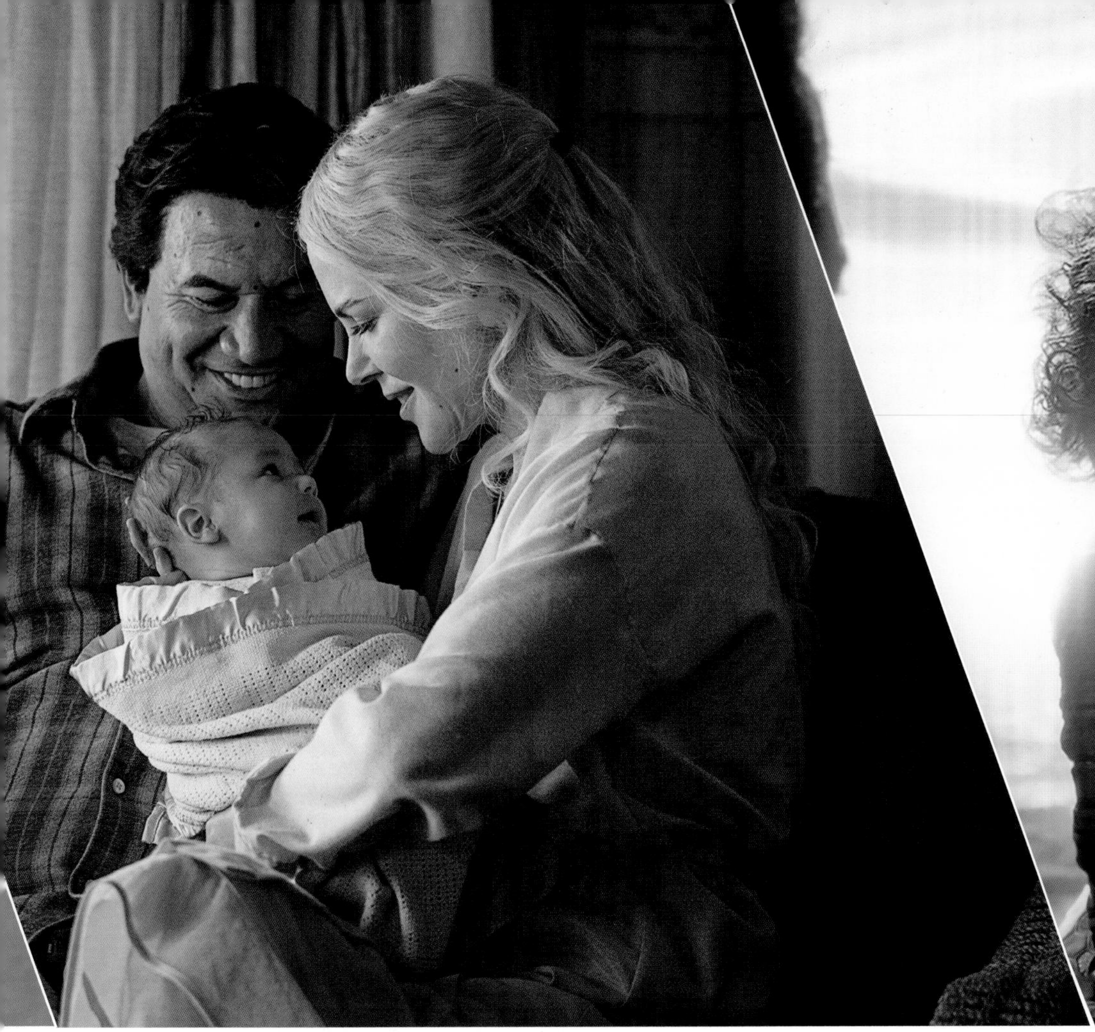

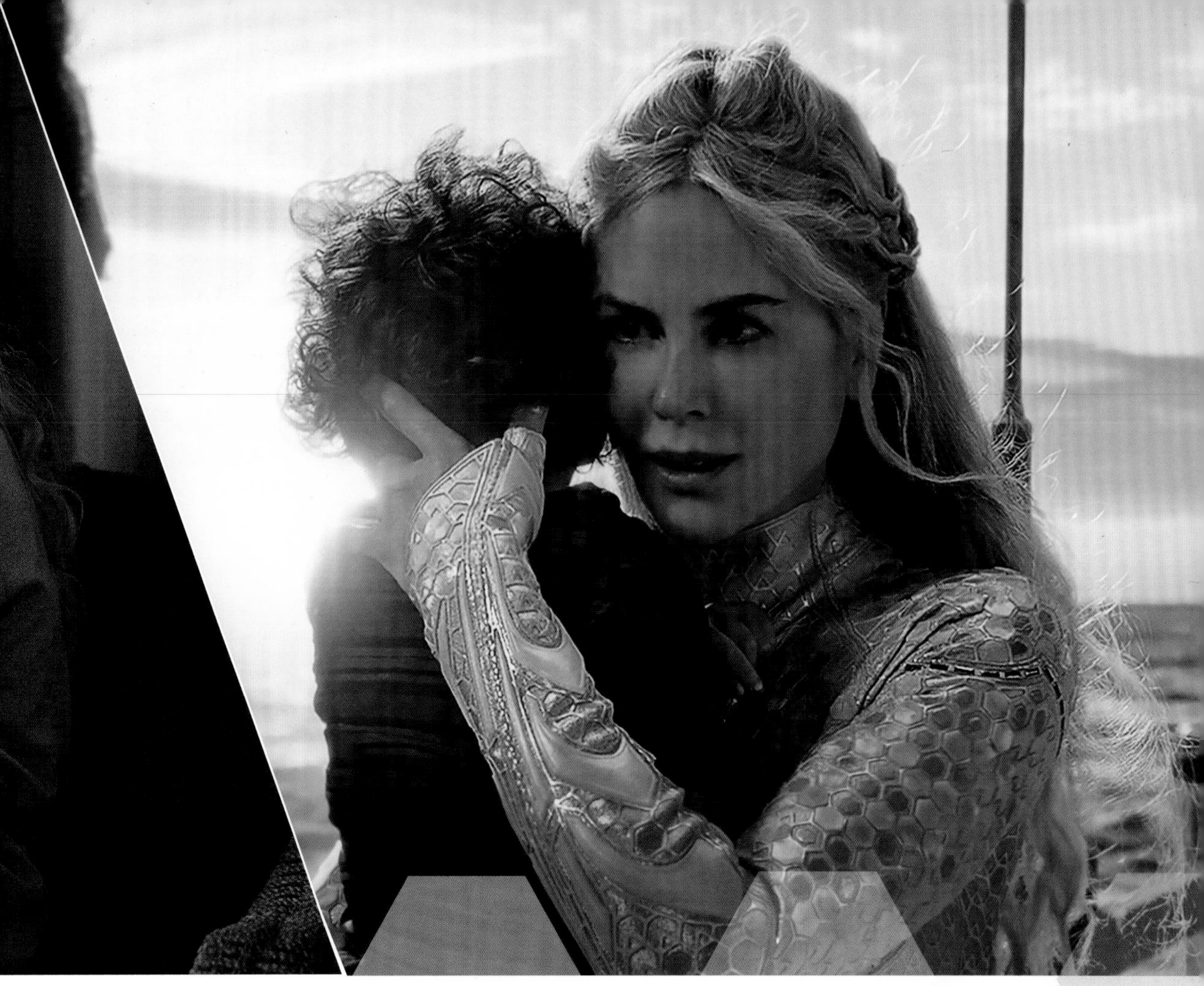

OPPOSITE LEFT AND RIGHT: Temuera Morrison and Nicole Kidman, as Tom Curry and Atlanna, share a tender moment alone. The black dots on their faces serve as marks for the visual effects work that makes their characters appear younger in the final VFX shot.
TOP LEFT: Tom and Altanna with baby Arthur. Again, the adult actors sport black dots on their faces as marks for the VFX work.
TOP RIGHT: Atlanna says goodbye to a young Arthur in a shot digitally altered to add the sunset background and make the actress appear years younger.

AMNESTY BAY

Director James Wan's goal was to create a different type of superhero movie. He wanted an action-packed global travelogue that harkened back to classic adventure stories like *Raiders of the Lost Ark* and *Romancing the Stone*. He wanted to create an entirely new universe, unlike anything seen before on Earth or in film. Step one in this plan was to establish a home base for the hero: a place that would provide a starting point on his journey and introduce the life of Arthur Curry before his world expands into Aquaman's.

The cove in Maine where Arthur Curry was raised by his lighthouse-keeper father is a working-class community of commercial fishermen. It's a place where the land meets the sea, but it rests firmly in the surface world. The locale will be familiar to audiences—unlike the realms in the imaginative new seascape the film will later explore—but Amnesty Bay still has its own unique charm that makes it special. To create this picturesque human enclave, the production needed to find the appropriate setting.

Amnesty Bay has been a beacon of comfort for Aquaman since Geoff Johns and Ivan Reis introduced it in the comic *Blackest Night* #2 in 2009, and that familiarity continues into Aquaman's first film. Arthur Curry is a loner by nature. He doesn't trust many people and feels like an outsider, which fits with a place like Amnesty Bay: Fishing outposts often are isolated and on the fringe of a community, the weather is often harsh, and people that work on boats spend months out at sea, returning for just brief moments before heading out again. "It's a different sort of life here," says production designer Bill Brzeski. "This is the kind of place Arthur feels comfortable in, where he will be mostly left alone."

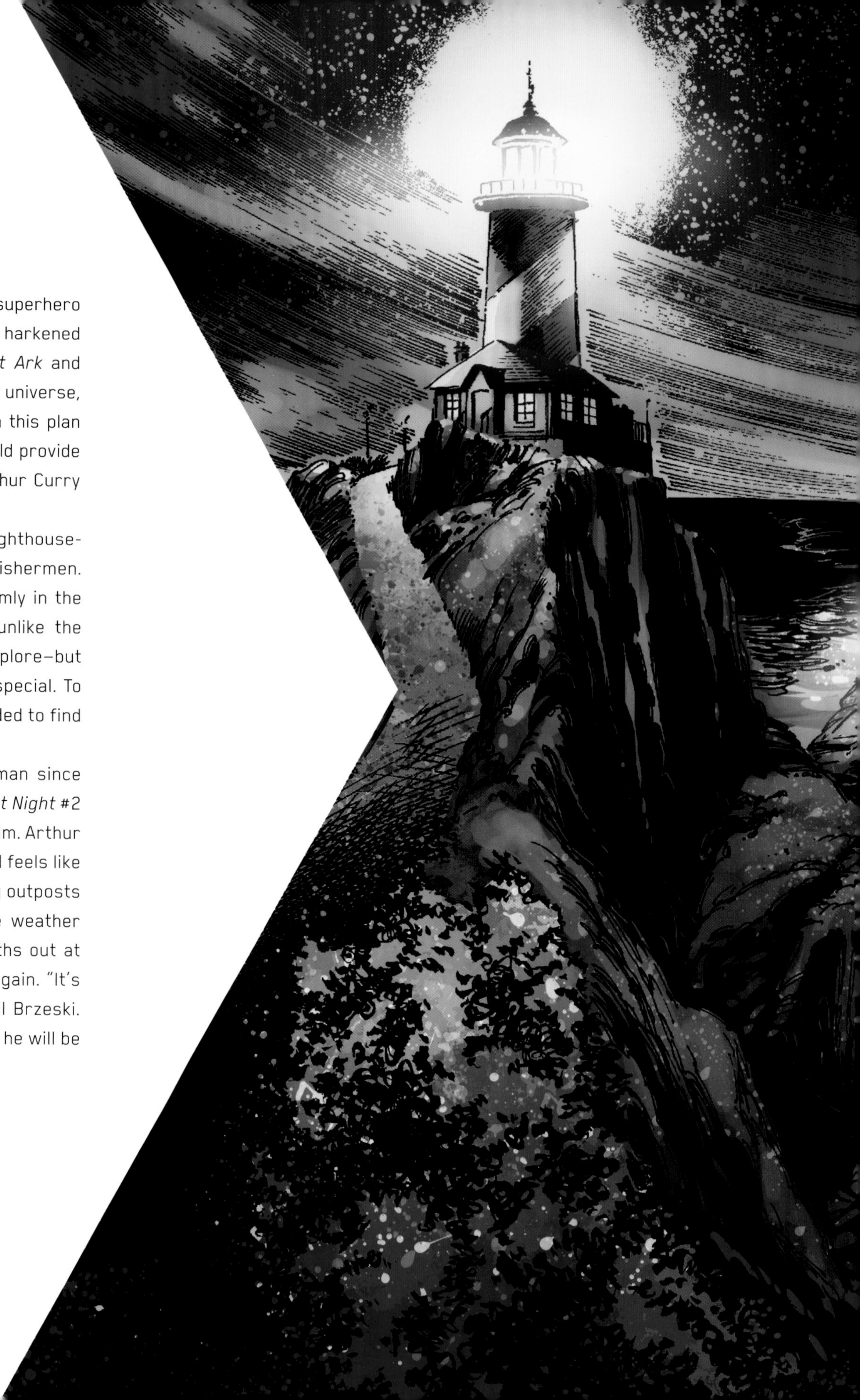

RIGHT: *Aquaman: The Trench* graphic novel interior art by Ivan Reis, Joe Prado, and Rod Reis.
OPPOSITE: Lighthouse concept art by Ray Don.

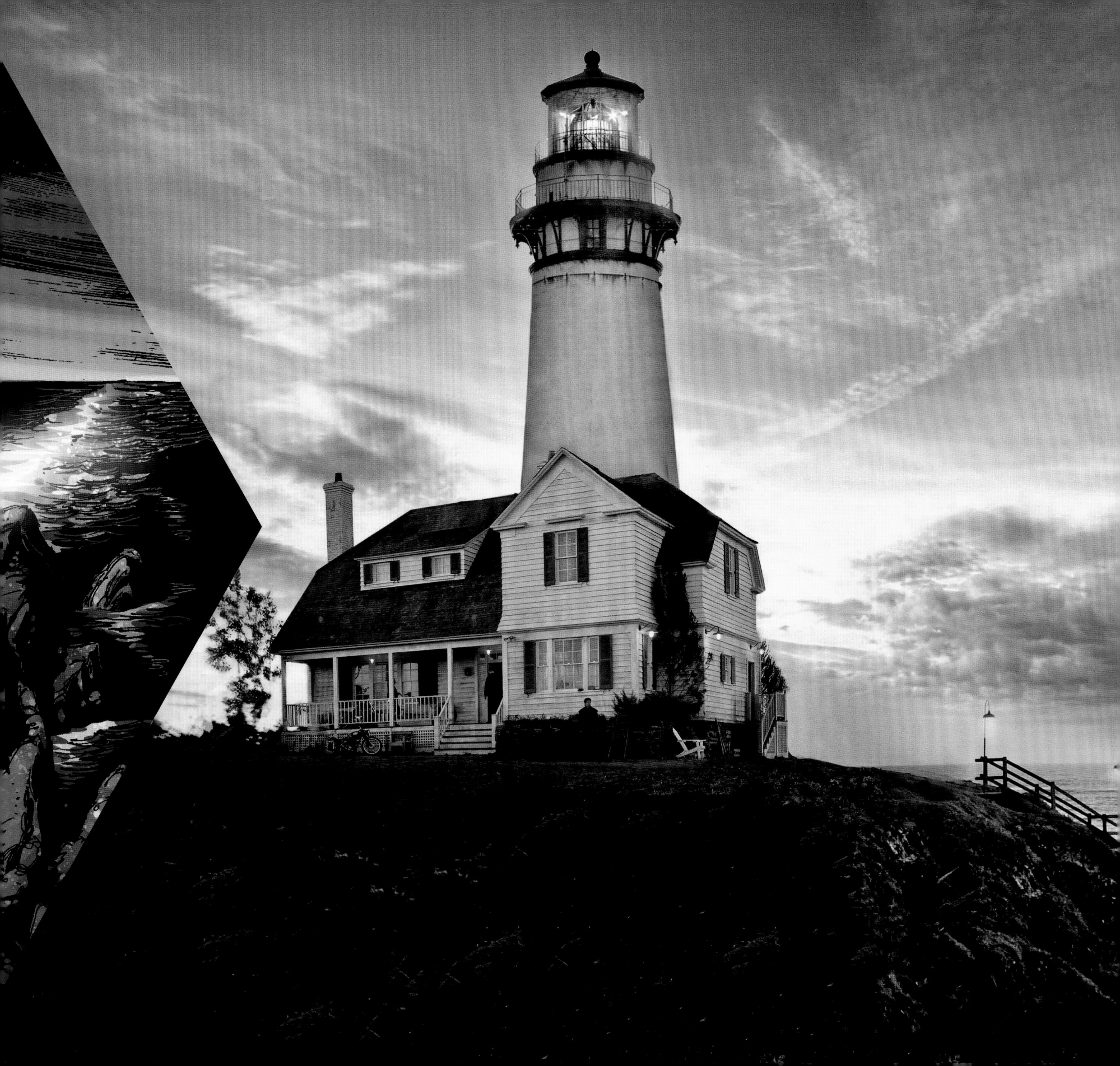

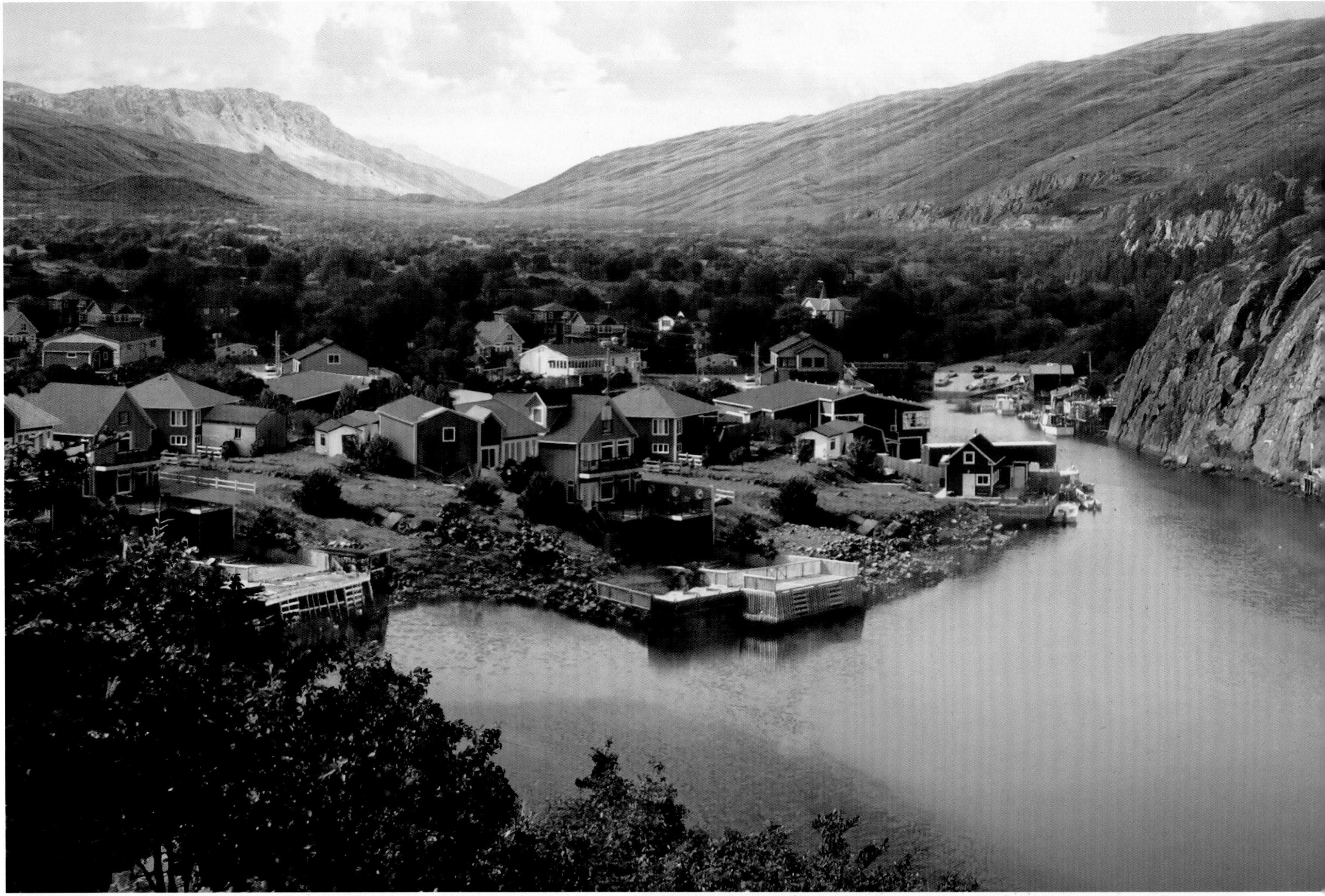

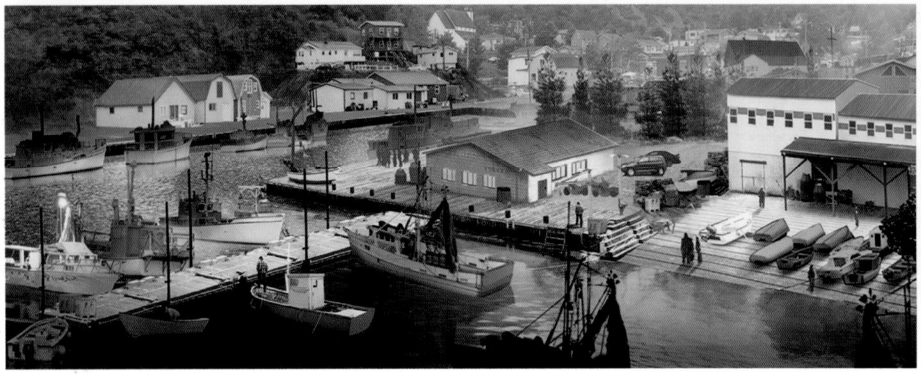

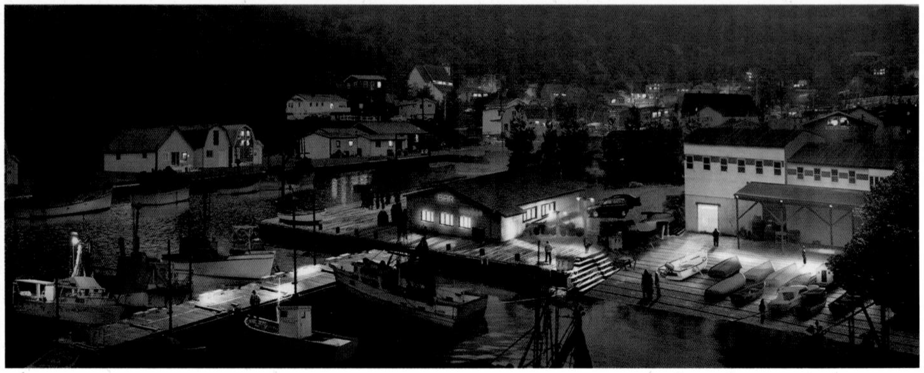

The logistics of shooting a megabudget motion picture that heavily relies on computer-generated effects meant the production team had to get creative with locations and set design. *Aquaman* was shot entirely in Australia, and the actual sets used to depict Amnesty Bay, Maine, were assembled on the Gold Coast. A stand-in fishing village was re-created near Main Beach, an ocean-side stretch popular with local Australian surfers. Brzeski, who worked with Wan on *Furious 7* and also oversaw design on blockbusters such as *The Fate of the Furious* and *Iron Man 3*, says this location represents home for Aquaman. Brzeski's inspiration came from a small, picturesque harbor called Petty Harbour–Maddox Cove, just south of St. John's in Newfoundland. He stumbled upon the Main Beach location almost by accident. "I came here to look at this [location] for something else," says Brzeski. "I can't even remember what it was."

That bit of chance was a real boon to the production, as the crew tasked with finding a suitable location for Amnesty Bay had run into a problem: Classic northeastern fishing villages don't really exist anymore, at least not in the US. "It's really sad. Up and down the East Coast, fishing villages are disappearing," notes Brzeski, who grew up in the New England area, surrounded by many such harbors. "Now everything is so gentrified, and the fishing industry has kind of turned away from this small-boat fishing towards industrial trawlers. We couldn't find this kind of location even in Maine, believe it or not. It sounds crazy. I mean, there's some but they're very touristy looking."

Once locations were secured, the next step in the production process was to shoot photographic plates in Newfoundland to provide clean background footage. The fishing enclave Brzeski's team assembled in Australia was then digitally inserted in Petty Harbour to create Amnesty Bay. A similar process was used for the lighthouse and the Curry home. The home was a set built in Hastings Point, Australia, along with the interior of the lighthouse. The exterior shots of the full lighthouse were digitally inserted in postproduction, but everything else—the stairs and the rest of the interior—was actually assembled on site. The location provided one particularly memorable moment that Temuera Morrison, who plays Tom Curry, won't soon forget.

"It was quite special the day I actually went out to the lighthouse. The whales were there so they came to say hi to the lighthouse keeper," says Morrison. "The crew kind of just stopped for a moment while we gazed at the whales. That's one of those moments where you sort it out on set. You're dealing with makeup and wardrobe and people and costumes. Then all of a sudden, the whales start jumping up and down. It's kind of a special feeling."

ABOVE: Amnesty Bay concept art by Scott Lukowski.
BOTTOM: Amnesty Bay bar location day and night concept art by Brad Nielsen.
PAGES 40–41: Close-up of the Terry's Sunken Galleon sign (*left*); bar interior concept art by Jeremy Love (*right*).

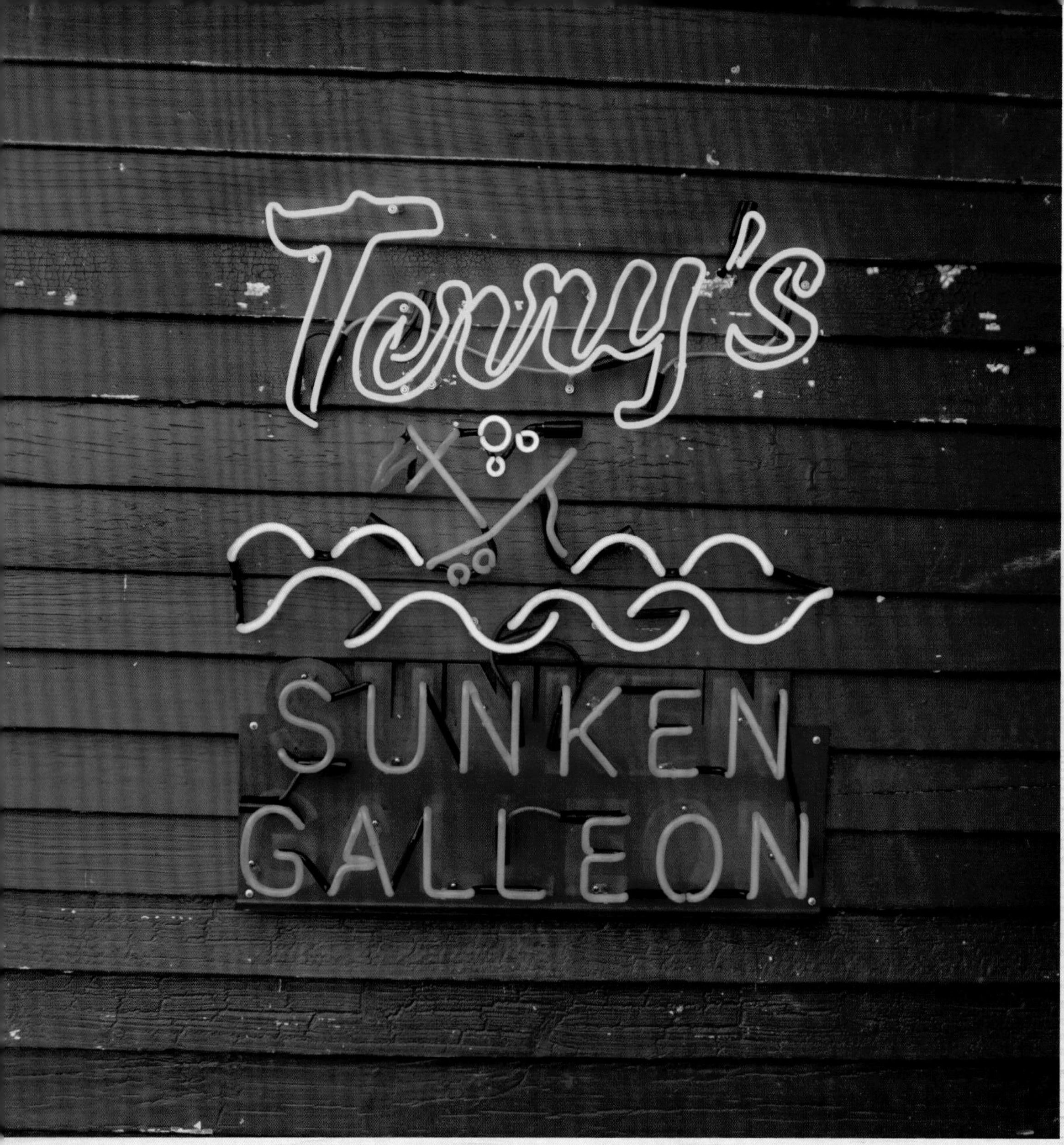
Terry's
SUNKEN
GALLEON

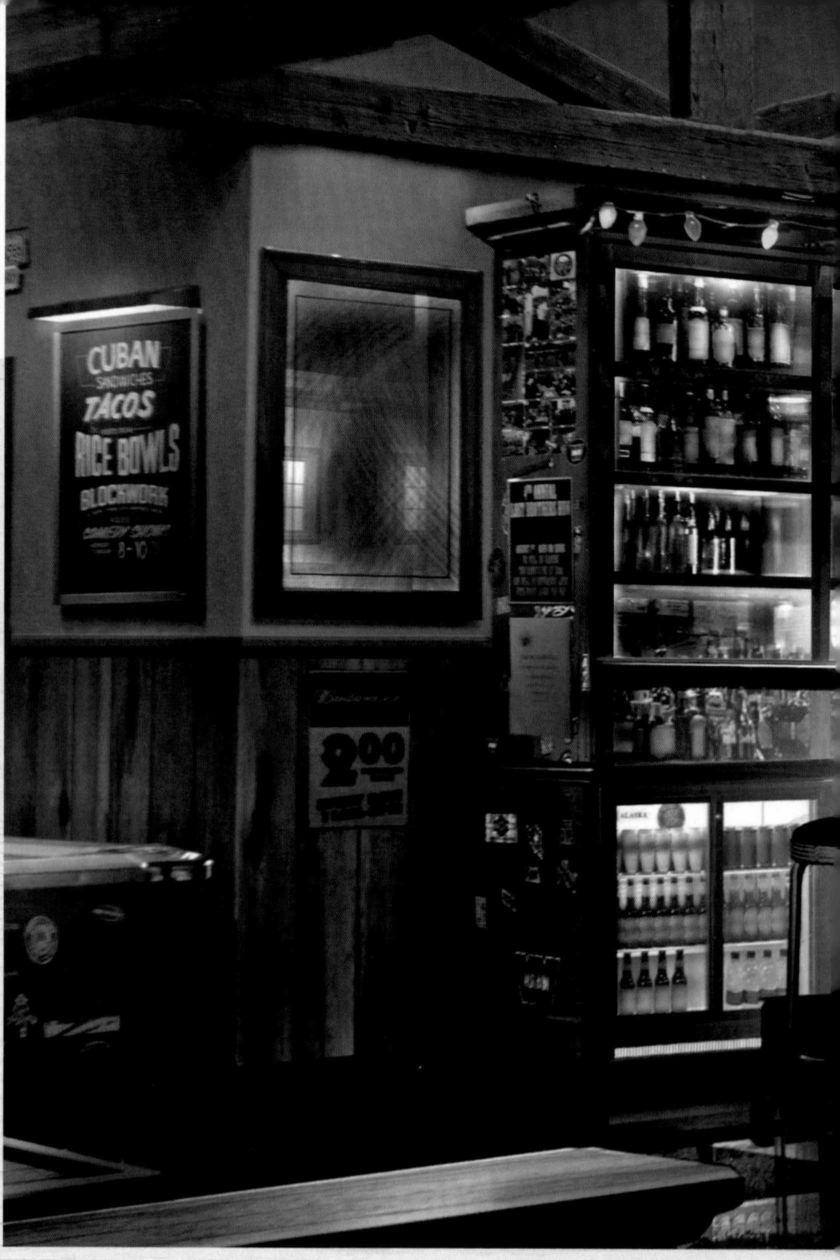
CUBAN
SANDWICHES
TACOS
RICE BOWLS
BLOCKWORK

Ask anyone who has spent a lot of time in a fishing community, and you'll understand that a fishermen's bar is a unique place. As Brzeski says, "It's where people who work really hard out on the ocean come in, after doing two- to three-week stints on a boat, and blow off steam. And that's what it is supposed to represent in our story." For *Aquaman*, this special location is Terry's Sunken Galleon, where Arthur Curry and his father go for some quality time together.

The set for Terry's was erected on land that was once an industrial boatyard. In the process of scouting for suitable locations, Brzeski's team went all over the place looking for bars and found themselves with an interesting problem. "We realized we couldn't get a parking lot that didn't show Australia out the window," Brzeski reveals. The solution? After building the set for Terry's, the production team filled the boat basin with old vessels that looked authentic to New England. With some digital filmmaking magic to piece it all together, the set had the look of a classic fishing village.

Terry's Sunken Galleon is one of Brzeski's favorite sets from the film. "I've done so many sets in my career, but it's fun when you make a set that evokes an emotion to the crew, that they feel really comfortable in it. This set just hit the mark." Set decorator Beverley Dunn gets much of the credit for capturing the aesthetic many neighborhood bars develop over time. In fact, it was so realistic that locals were pulling up to the location

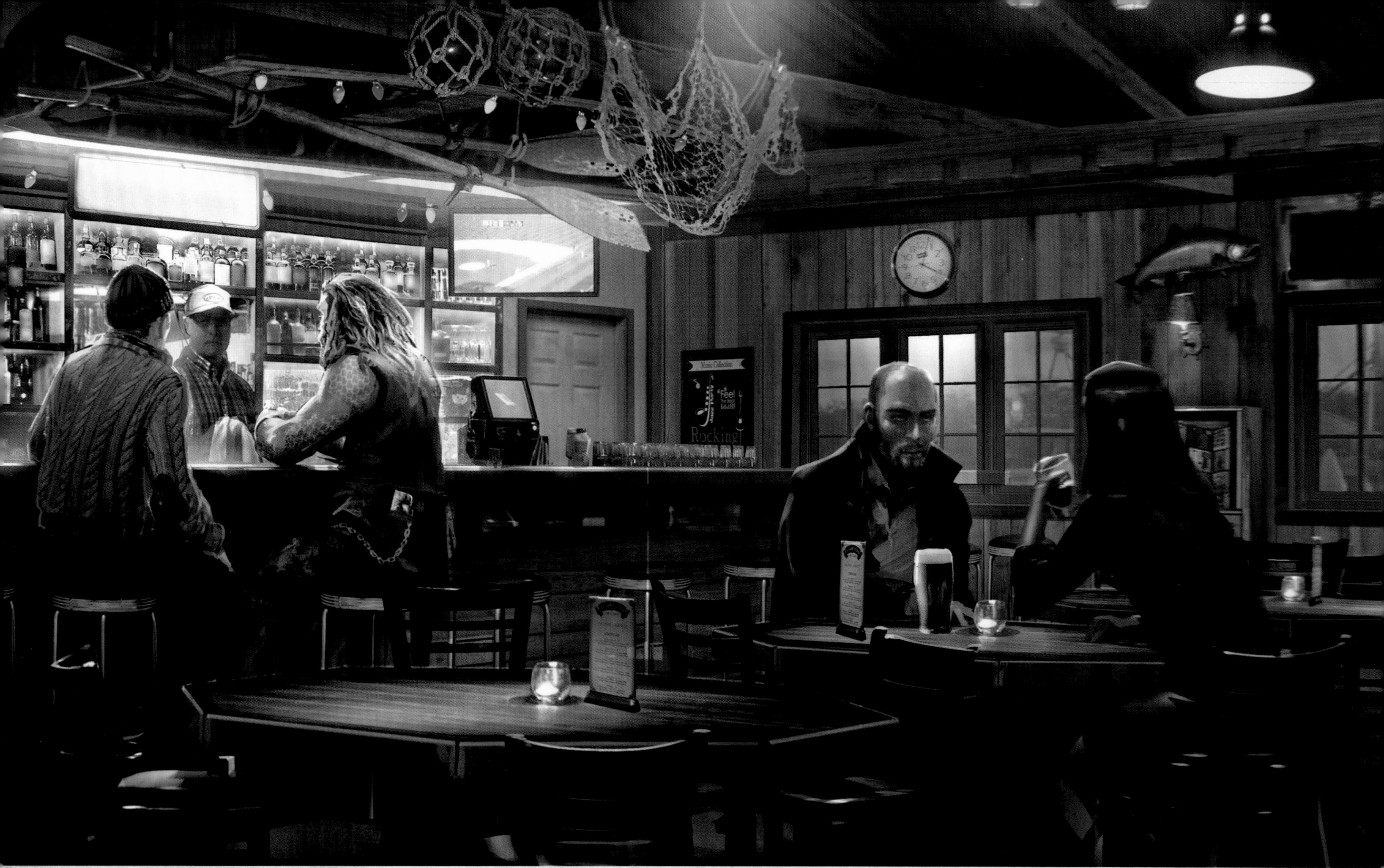
Music Collection
Rocking

thinking it was a real bar. "You know you've done your job well when you have people who live in the area saying, 'My gosh, when is this going to open to the public?'" Dunn says with pride.

The bar is the appropriate backdrop for a key early scene between Arthur and his father Tom that provides a glimpse into Aquaman's human side. It's a father-son moment meant to show how this incredibly powerful hero and his dad, both scarred by loss, reconnect over a few cold beers. It's a scene that illustrates how important Tom is to Arthur as the one constant, the one member of his family who remained with him. Terry's is also a place of comfort for Arthur. The locals know him there. He's one of their own, a local hero who likes a brew just like the average fishermen. For someone who is constantly struggling with his identity, the bar provides someplace familiar to return to.

Within Amnesty Bay, the Sunken Galleon is relatively close to the lighthouse, no more than a mile or so away. On the drive back home on the coastal road, Arthur and Tom are nearly killed by a surging tsunami that slams into Amnesty Bay and causes massive devastation. The battering waves hurl Arthur away from the pickup truck, where Tom is trapped inside. It is only Mera's dramatic arrival that saves his father's life. She uses her powers to part the waters, and then pulls the water from Tom's lungs to keep him from drowning. The destruction of Amnesty Bay—Arthur's home—starts him on his journey into a larger world beyond the cove.

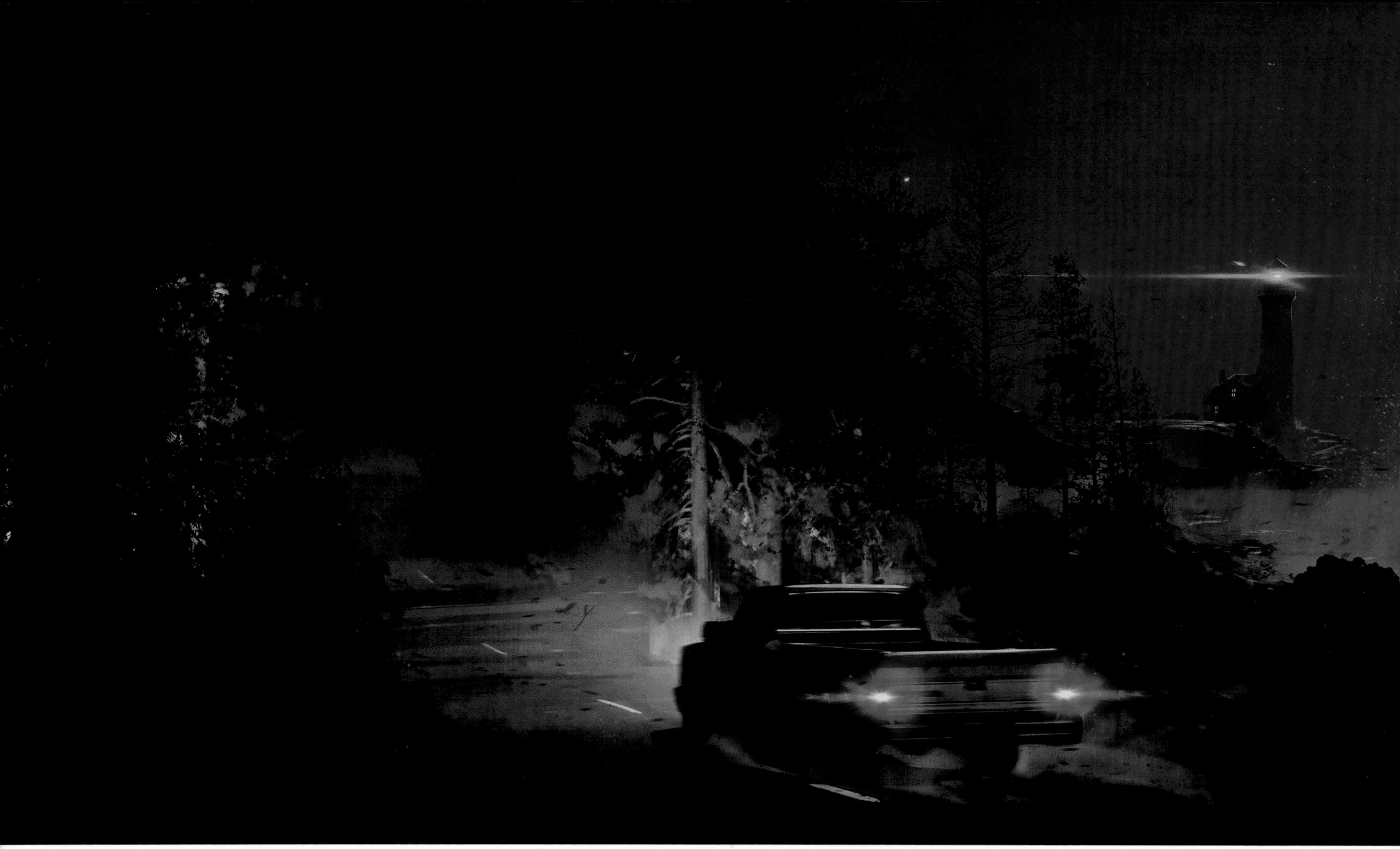

ORM'S FIRST ATTACK

"The tidal wave sequence is a beautifully executed piece finished by VFX supervisor Bryan Hirota at Scanline VFX and of course imagined/designed by James Wan. Scanline VFX is one of only a handful of companies that are capable of doing fluid dynamics CG effects on this scale and at the level of detail that James demanded. They really pulled out some next-level work for us on this project. . . . The wave and all of the interactions are CG. Keep in mind however, that I shot extensive plate photography in Newfoundland of the landscape and hero vehicle that the CG wave gets set into. My philosophy is that sequences such as this should always be based on actual plate photography and CG is only used when absolutely necessary. We exerted significant effort to acquire ground-based and aerial plates that the CG wave was then incorporated into. I think that is the secret to the success and reality of shots like this."

—Kelvin McIlwain, Visual Effects Supervisor

THESE PAGES: Concept artwork by Brad Nielsen detailing the pivotal tsunami sequence and its aftermath. **PAGES 44–45:** Mera saves Tom and Arthur in concept art by Brad Nielsen.

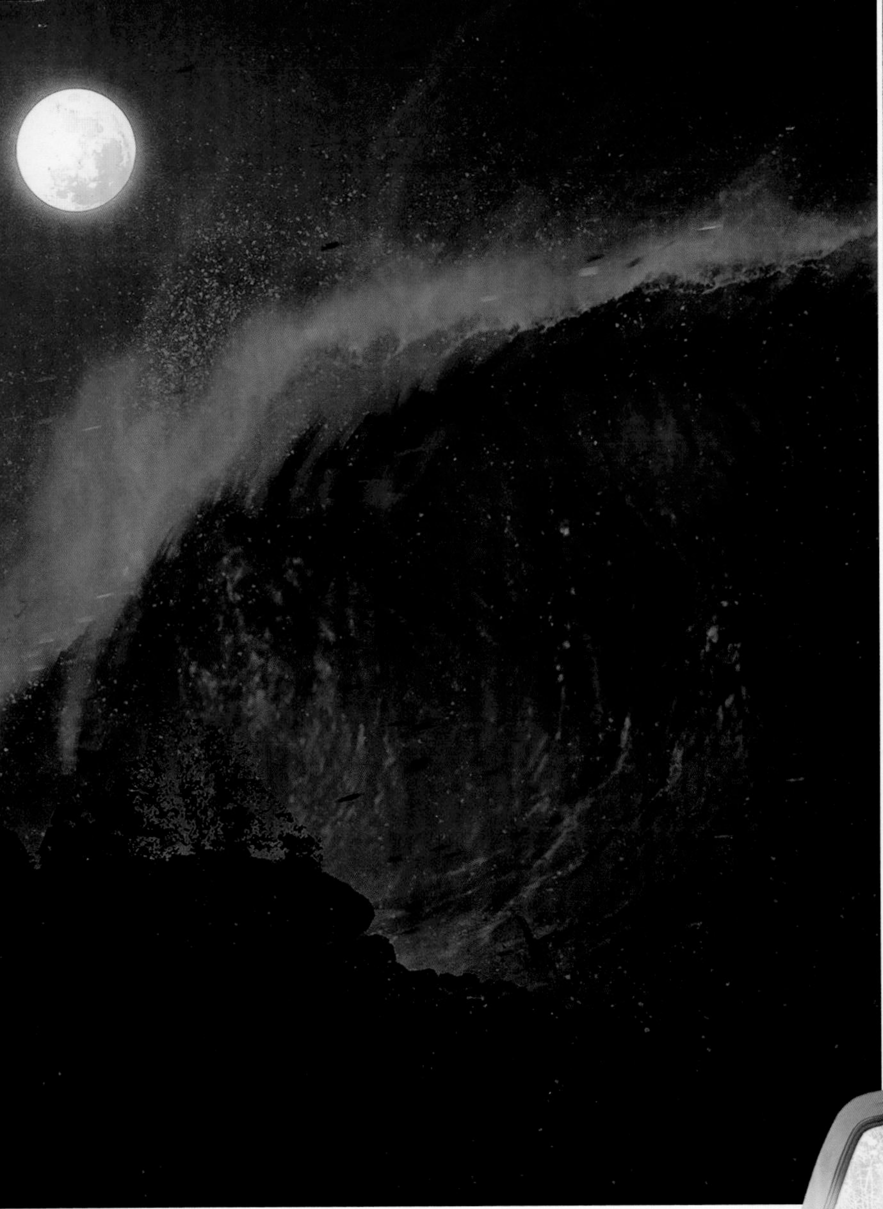
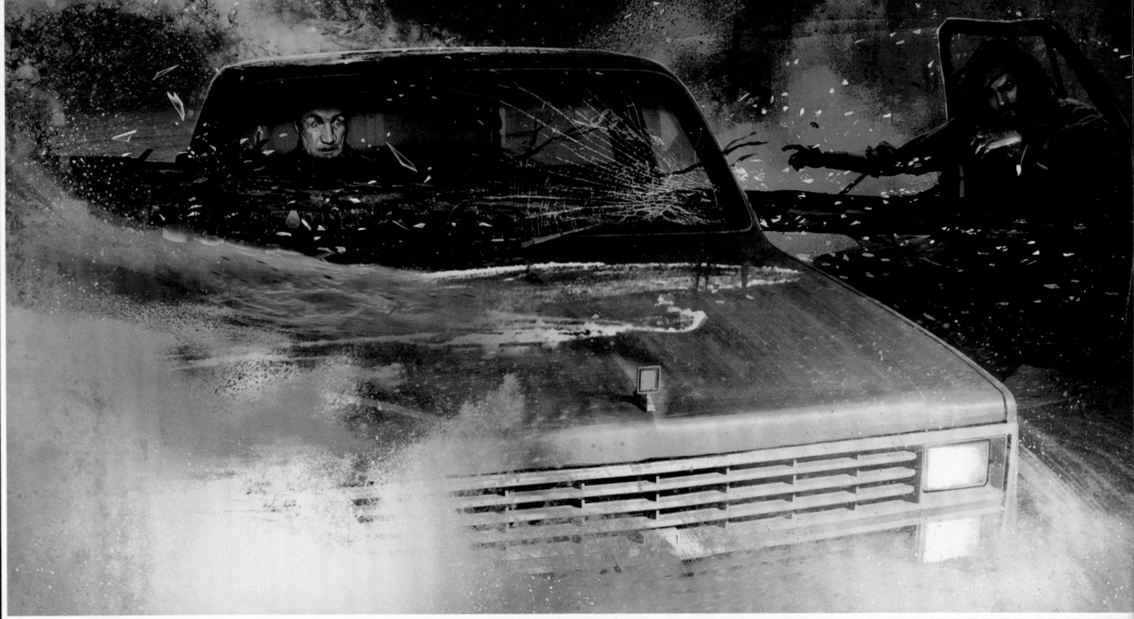
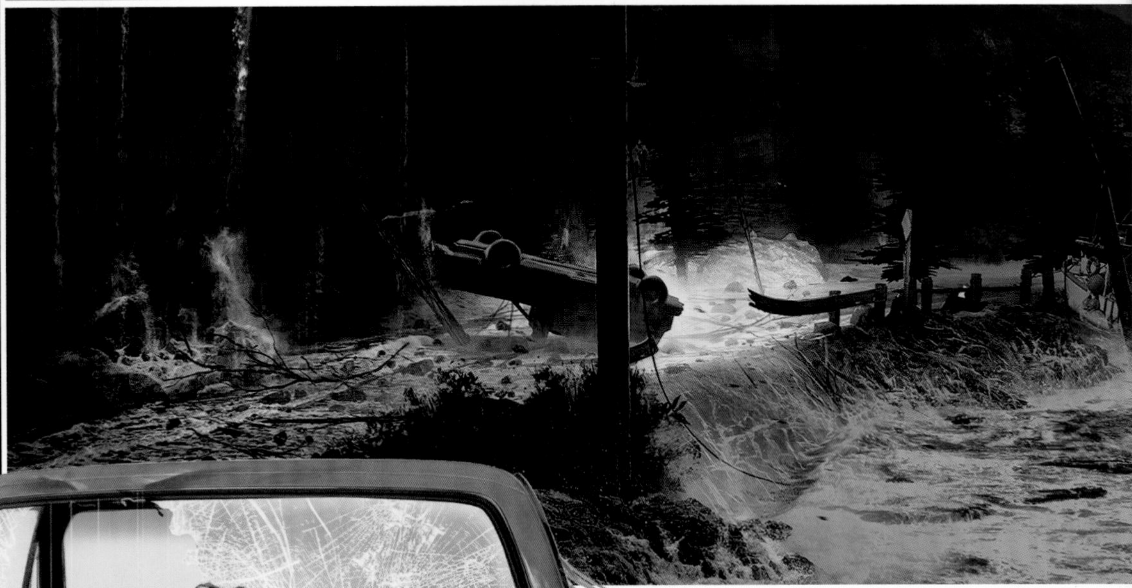
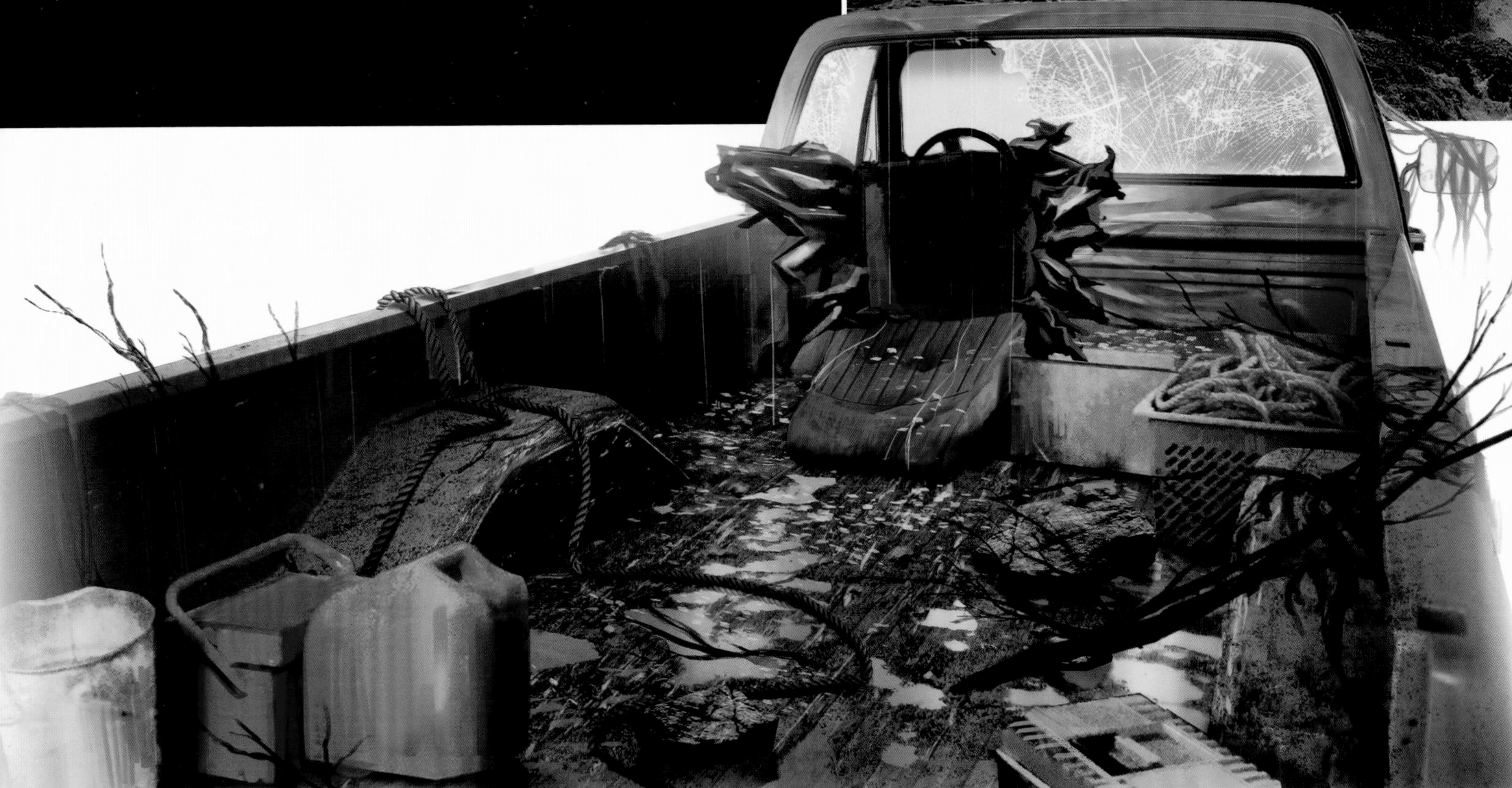

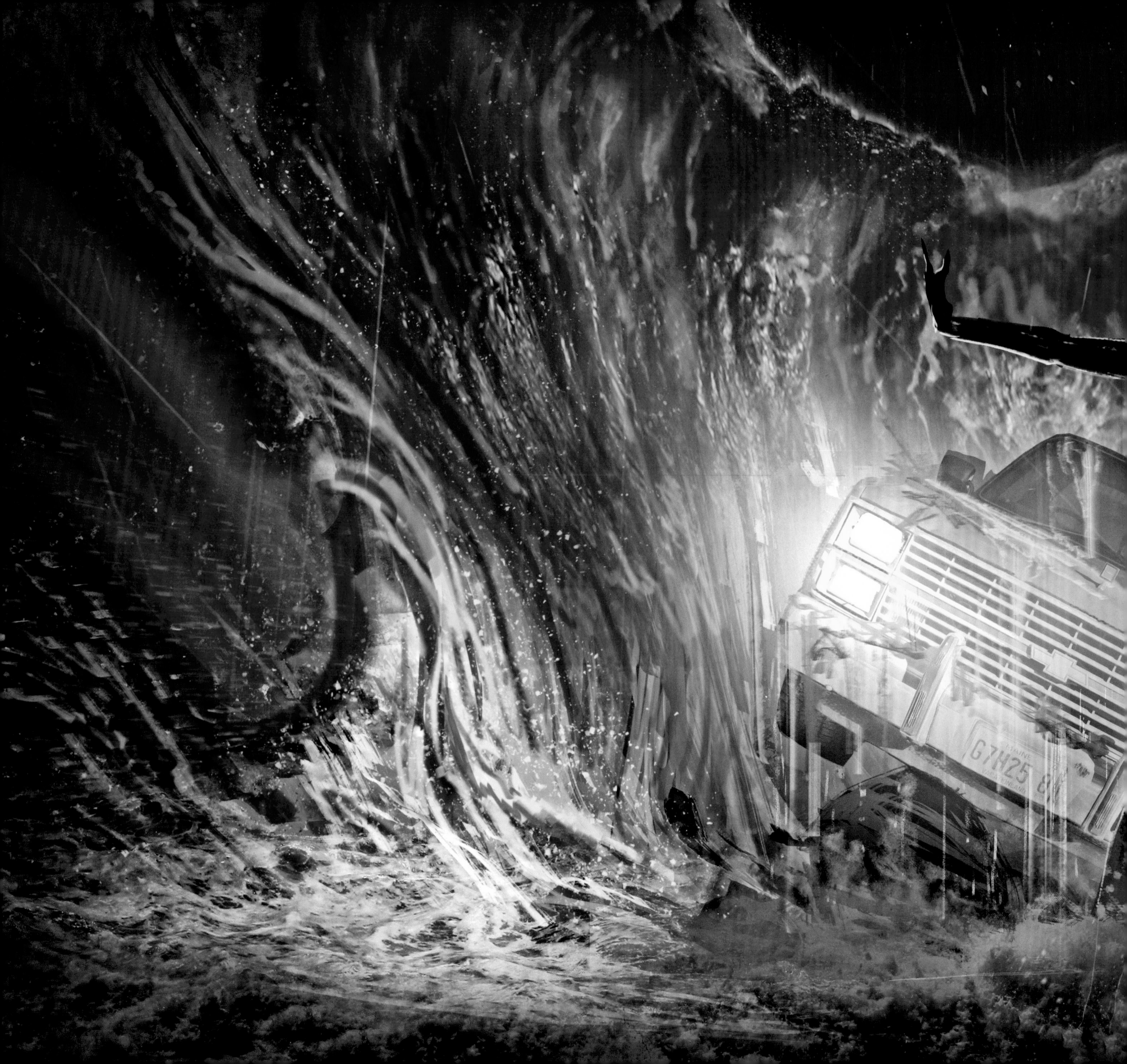
MAINE
G7H25

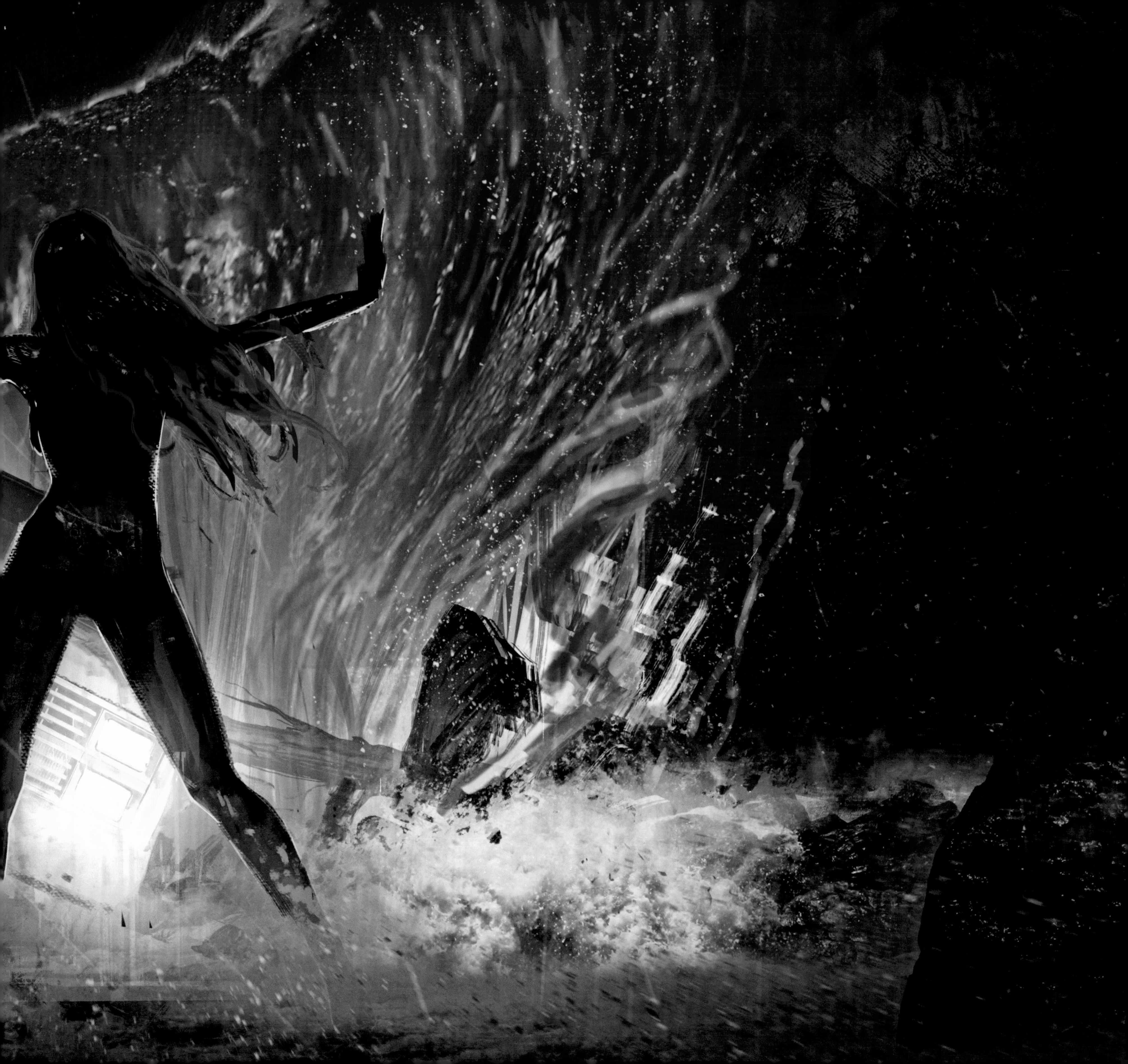

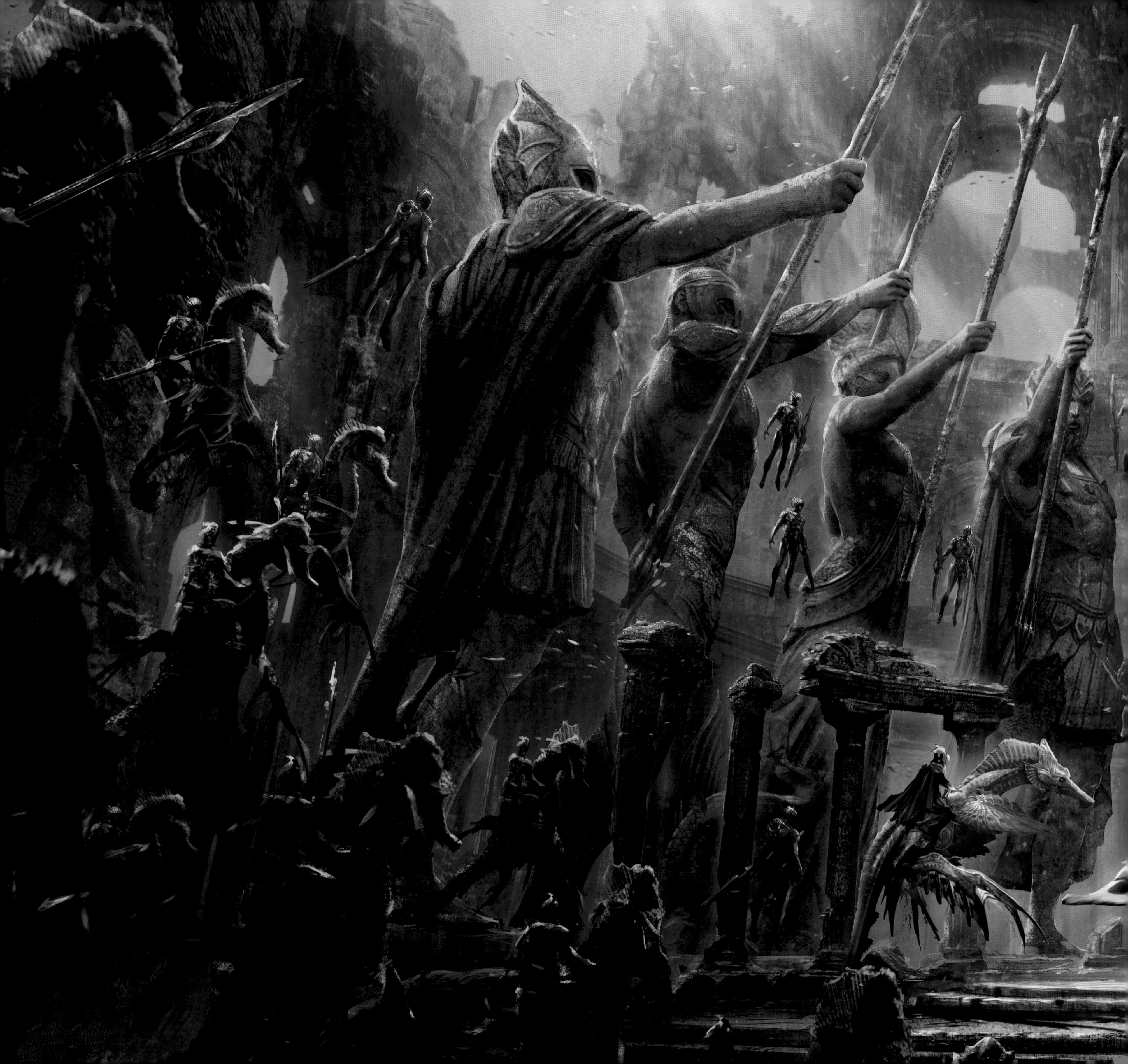

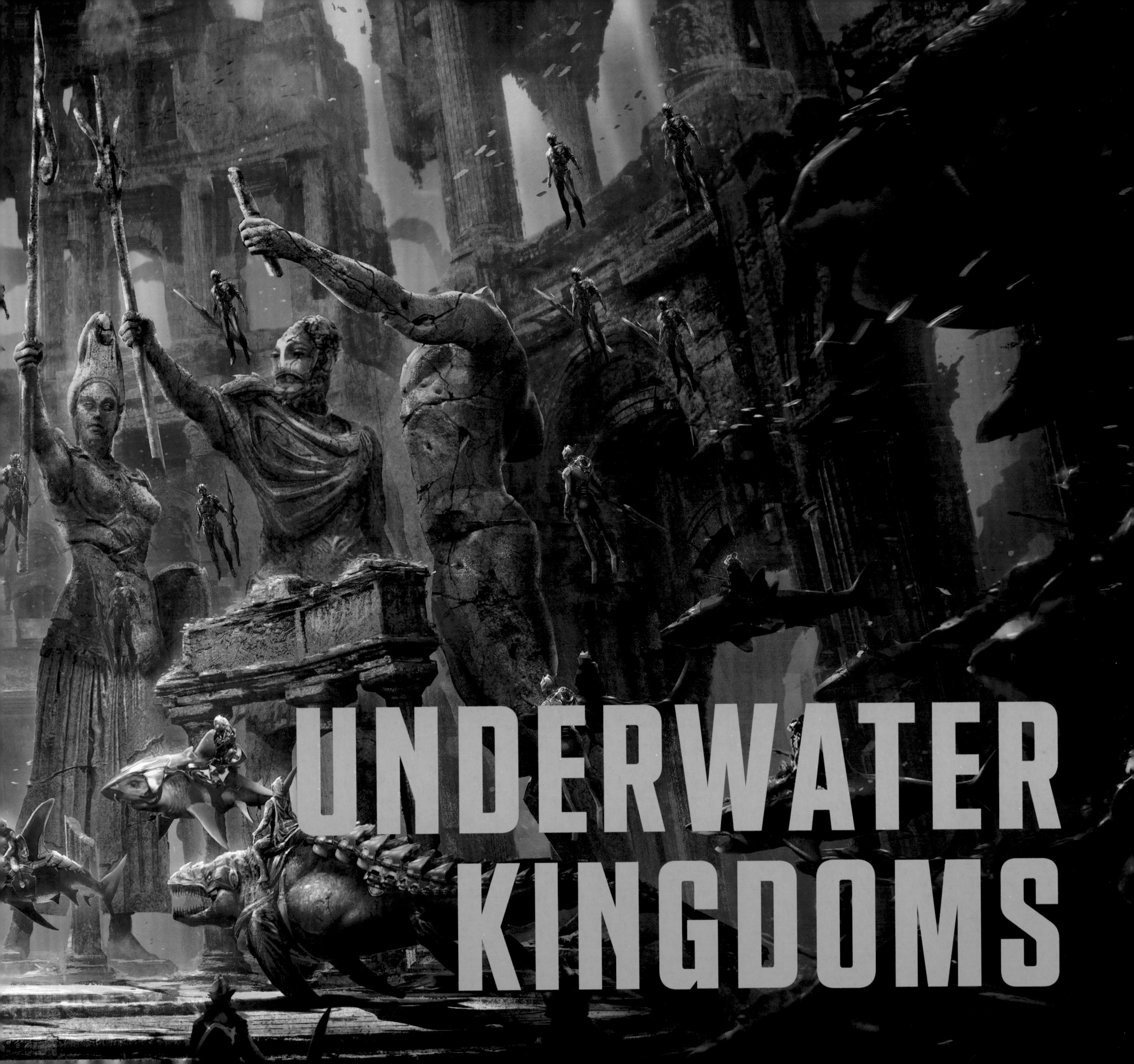

UNDERWATER KINGDOMS

BUILDING A WORLD WITHIN A WORLD

Aquaman is as much Atlantis's origin story as it is Aquaman's. The kingdoms that make up the world beneath the waves once existed in unison, as part of a larger kingdom of Ancient Atlantis that ruled the seas. An early scene at the ruins of the once mighty kingdom shows statues representing tribes that were once part of Ancient Atlantis, including Xebel, the Brine, the Fishermen, the Trench, and the Deserters. James Wan and an army of artists, designers, and prop masters welcomed the challenge of creating a universe from scratch. Very quickly imaginations ran wild with ideas on everything from weapons and ship designs to the types of materials to use to construct the cities and everything within them. "That was the trick and also part of the fun, designing a whole different world that we've never seen before that is so strikingly original," the director explains.

Brzeski and Wan spent much time discussing the ideology behind each culture and what made each one unique. "We tried to differentiate the types of kingdoms so that each stood out on their own," the production designer says. "It was fun trying to figure that out." For example, the Atlanteans are defined by their technological prowess. The Brine resemble crustacean soldiers, with shell-like armor and weaponry. If there is a peace-faring kingdom in the undersea realm, the Fishermen occupy that role; they believe educating humanity would be more productive than going to war with the surface world.

The director had some basic ground rules for the design aesthetic of Atlantis and how it worked. "We tried to have aspects that had to function. It couldn't just be a complete fantasy," says executive producer Rob Cowan. Brzeski adds, "We created this whole underwater way of doing things. We wanted to create reasonable explanations for how people live underwater."

Grounding fantasy in reality was the directive for each of the design departments, including props. "Once the characters had been defined by James Wan, I researched their respective origins as the roots of their inspiration," explains prop master Richie Dehne. "History is most certainly a major contributor of our concepts of Atlantis and the underwater world but our vision was to design a world that had never before been seen. We set out to reference elements of the past but with a distinctive new-world feel as one would concept sci-fi for say a distant planet. It was truly an exciting project."

PAGES 46–47: Ancient ruins of Atlantis concept art by Jeremy Love.
ABOVE: *Aquaman*, Vol. 7 #24 (December 2013) interior art by Paul Pelletier, Sam Parsons, and Rod Reis.
TOP RIGHT: Shark transport concept art by Howard Swindell.
BOTTOM RIGHT: In the ruins of Ancient Atlantis, Xebellian and Atlantean forces meet beneath statues representing the seven kingdoms.

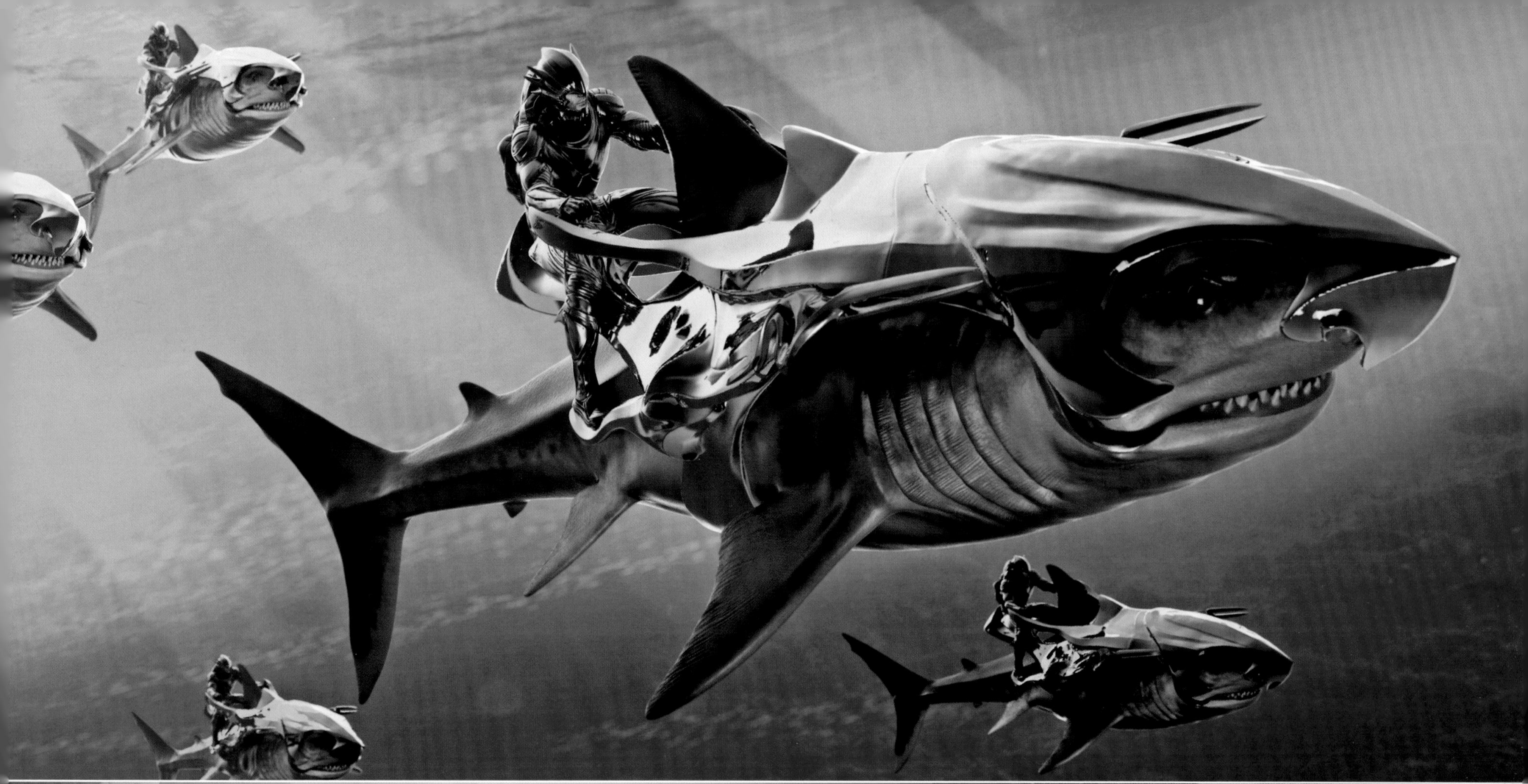
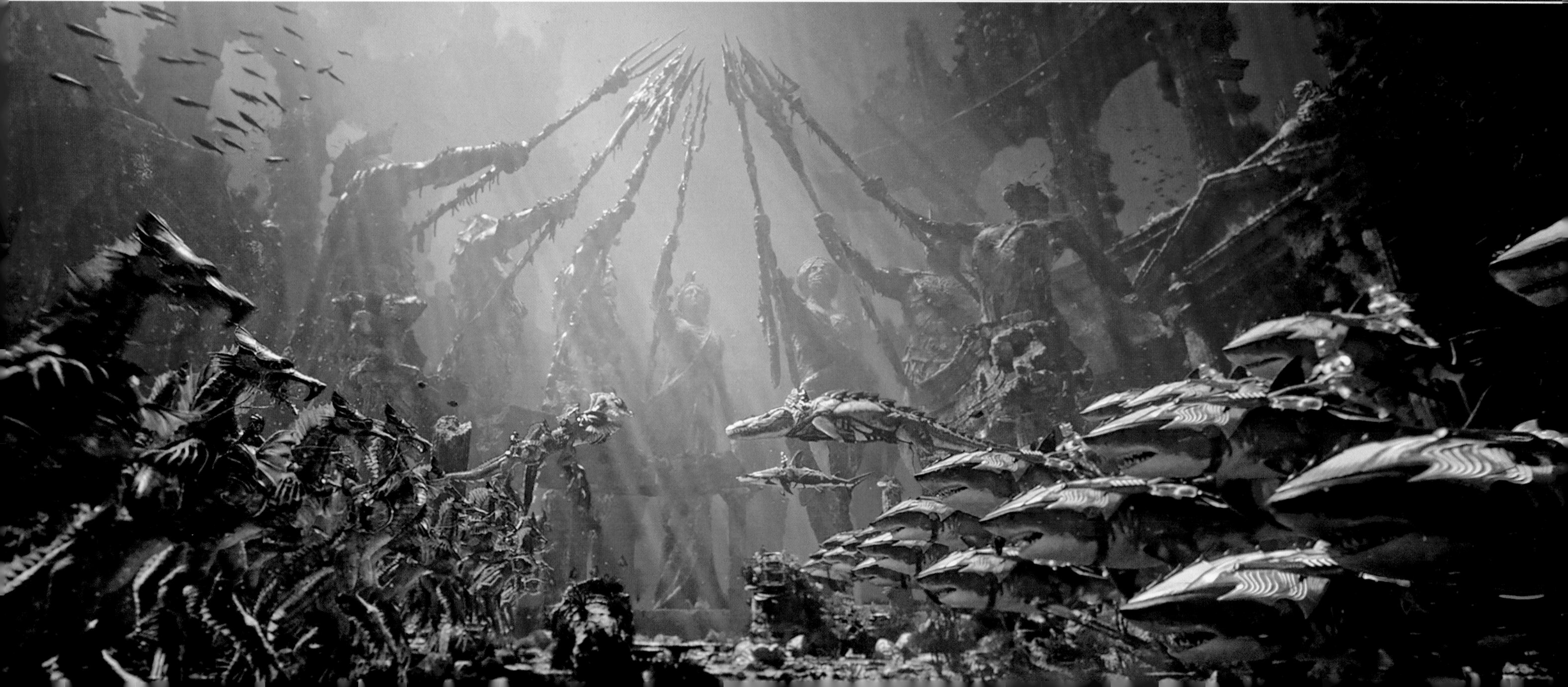

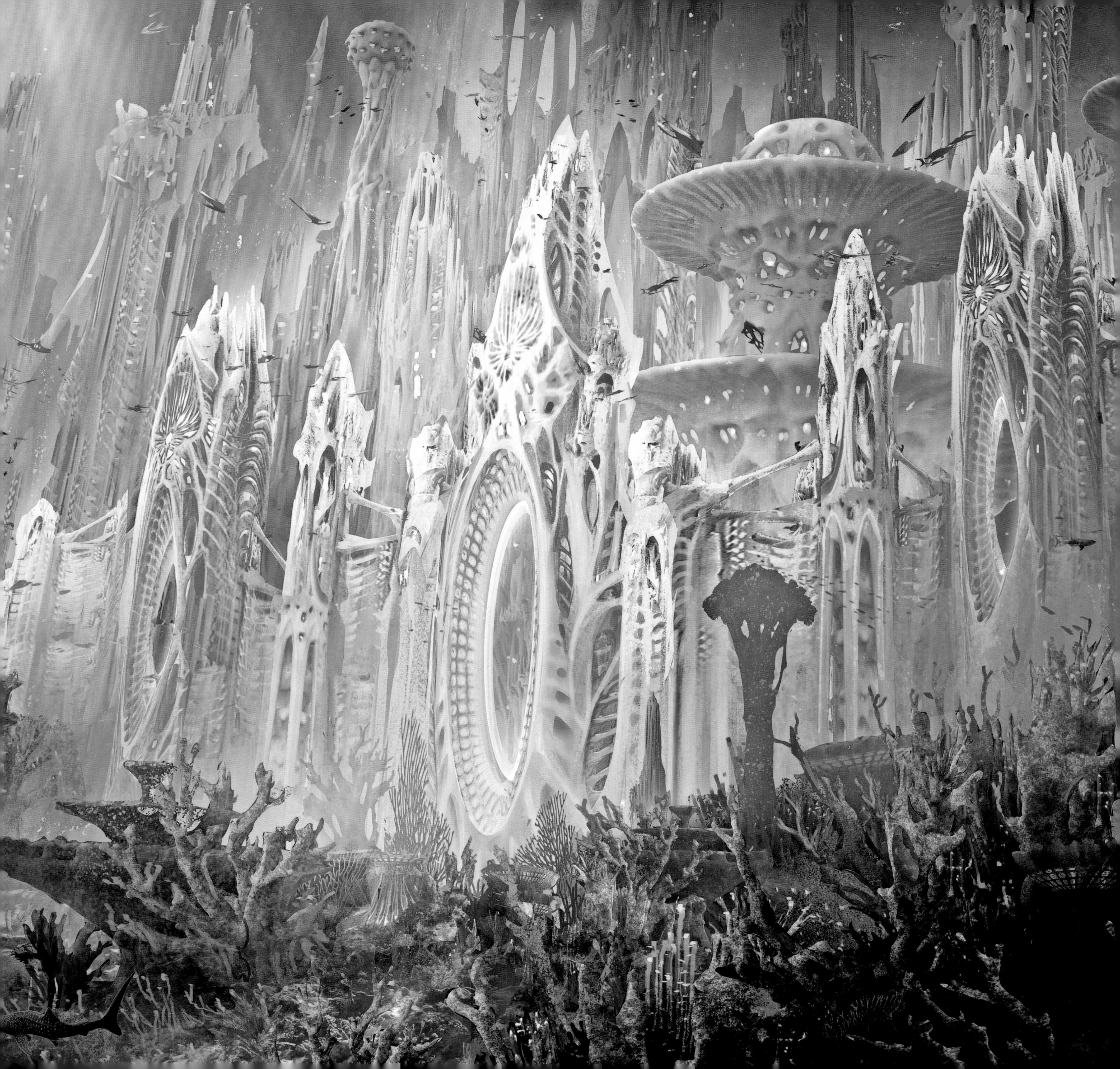

LEFT: Fishermen Kingdom concept art by Jeremy love.
ABOVE: Texture reference for construction materials in the undersea kingdoms.

Wan's insistence on plausibility inspired some creative engineering in the assembly of Atlantis and the other aquatic societies. The architecture of Atlantis is not made of steel or wood, but of an organic extension of coral, hardened sediments, and other ocean-found elements. Swords and other weapons are made of bone. As Brzeski describes it, the goal was to come up with a logical explanation for a society that lives underwater and that, over the course of seven thousand years, has evolved from breathing air to thriving—by various means—underwater.

There were many discussions on determining the types of building materials to use underwater. "How do you build things under the ocean?" Brzeski wondered as he approached his designs. Substances common in the surface world, such as brick, wood, and metal, wouldn't work beneath the sea. The filmmakers decided to take a more creative approach and establish their own rules of science and engineering. They determined that organic elements typically found in oceans, such as coral, would serve as the literal building blocks of the undersea kingdoms. The production staff found examples by artists who were using 3D printers to make items out of coral and extrapolated from there. The working thesis would be that the underwater kingdoms would grow the elements they needed to build their cities, structures, ships, and weapons. But of course, the most essential substance in the kingdoms is the one that covers more than seventy percent of the planet: water.

"Through water, the Atlanteans and the other cultures can create almost anything," Brzeski says. That includes power for their technology. The Atlanteans can communicate with surface dwellers through water holograms. Soldiers have hydroplasma rifles that transform water into powerful plasma beams. The trains of Atlantis are powered by water. "They had mastered the ability to use and transform water into almost anything," says the production designer.

Once they established parameters for the mechanics of life in Atlantis, the filmmakers, led by Wan, went to work on the other kingdoms and fleshing out the day-to-day lives of the residents. Not only does each realm have its own style, but within each kingdom a hierarchy was established to differentiate between the lives of the highborn and the commoners. This is largely seen in Atlantis as more time is spent in that kingdom than in any other. Location design divided the kingdom into a glistening underwater metropolis that was a playground for the wealthy, while the lower class was relegated to the ruins of Ancient Atlantis. They also incorporated the kingdom's rich history into the design. Atlanteans may pilot the most technologically advanced vessels, but the highborn also ride on fantastical sea creatures in pageantry for formal occasions.

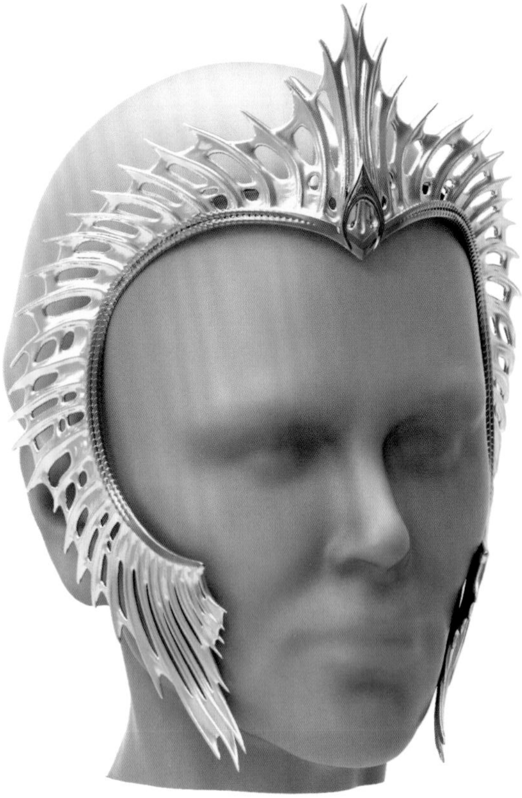

LEFT: Atlanna's crown.
BOTTOM LEFT: Close-up details of material from Atlanna's final costume in the film.
BOTTOM RIGHT: Close-up details of Orm's costume, worn beneath his gladiator armor.
OPPOSITE: Sea creatures move shipping materials through Atlantis in concept art by Ed Natividad.

Special effects are an obviously important element of any superhero film, on top of the practical sets. Despite the incredible visual effects needed to tell this story, *Aquaman* managed to roughly split the ratio of blue-screen backgrounds and practical sets. The reason for that is quite basic, according to the Brzeski: Practical sets give the actors something to play off and reference during their performances.

Still, with the numerous locations needed to tell the story, the production design team had a difficult task ahead. "Bill Brzeski did an incredible job on this film replicating so many different locations with phenomenal sets," according to Safran. "Our highest hopes for what our sets were going to look like have been dwarfed by what he's done."

Visual effects supervisor Kelvin McIlwain agrees that the blending of practical and visual effects sets was significant from a technical standpoint as well. "When the actors are wearing reflective costumes, like when Arthur and Orm have their armor on in the Ring of Fire sequence, the reflections you're getting are reflections of the set. Even though we may ultimately replace what's behind them—because we have to add all these different elements to the set, such as floating seaweed—the proxy sets were incredibly helpful in that regard too. It's just replaced with something that was built off the actual set, but then it allows us to do all of our effects work to it."

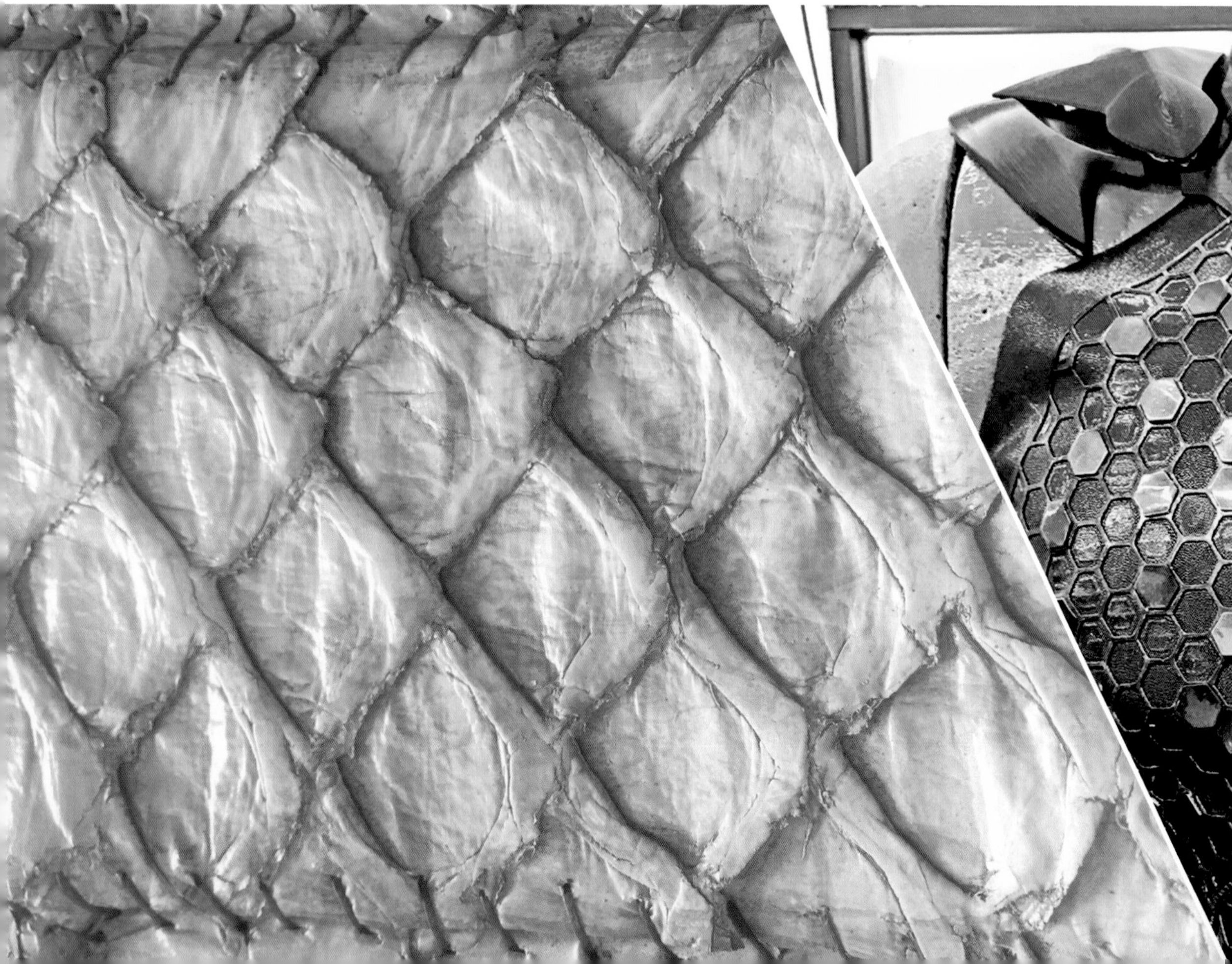

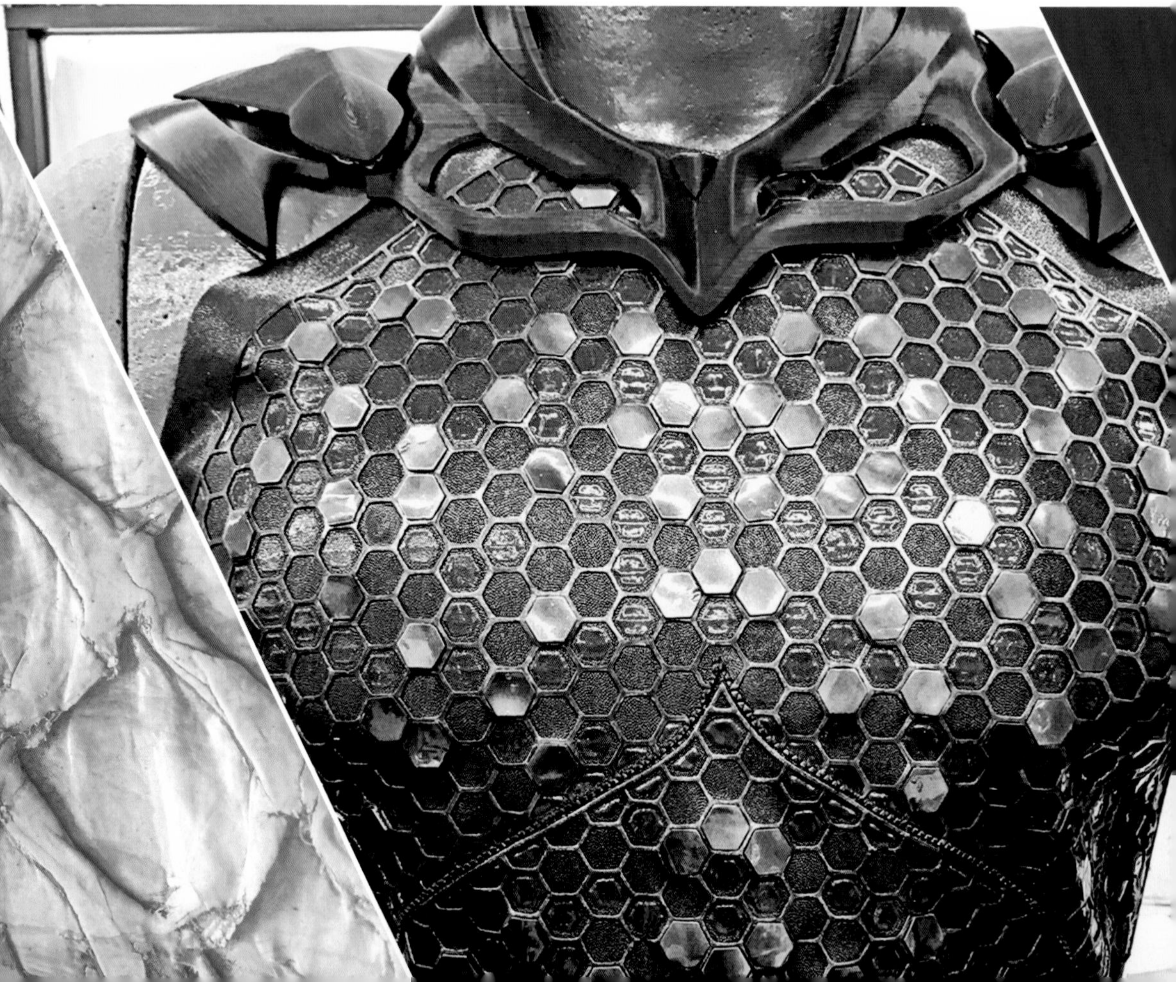

Award-winning costume designer Kym Barrett also played a key role in helping establish distinct identities for the fractured underwater kingdoms. The filmmakers knew they needed radical creative vision to accomplish this, and Barrett—who created the memorable costume designs for the *Matrix* trilogy, *Speed Racer*, *The Amazing Spider-Man*, and *Cloud Atlas*—was the person for the job. "It's not just creating Atlantis," explains Safran. "There are different kingdoms; each one has to be distinct. Kym is such a creative person and she worked so beautifully with James [Wan] to create a whole new world." Brzeski echoes the sentiment: "Kym Barrett, our costume designer, was essential to helping make each kingdom its own separate entity."

"I started my discussions with Bill [Brzeski] and we decided we wanted to present ten rules to James about living underwater, and what does that mean?" Barrett explains. "We figured if everyone stuck to the rules, we'd have a cohesive vision to present to James. One of those rules was that because Atlantis was so technologically advanced, they had conceived breathable, cellular fabrics that could keep someone warm. You have to remember, Atlantis is thousands and thousands of feet underwater and it's very cold at the bottom of the ocean."

Each kingdom demanded different requirements. For example, Atlantis was viewed as a cosmopolitan city of advancement, a submerged version of New York City. Those costumes called for various levels of sophistication. Barrett also turned to the ocean for inspiration to create the outfits the people of the undersea kingdoms wear.

"I had photographed beautiful fish and enlarged them greatly to see the different patterns on them so that you got beautiful, abstract prints on the body stockings of the Atlanteans," she says. "I did all of the people in the undersea kingdoms in a print that was iridescent."

Wan had a vivid and specific vision for the underwater world. He'd already laid the groundwork to give the production team the freedom to establish their rules when he successfully lobbied against including Atlantis in *Justice League* so that audiences would be introduced to the aquatic realm in *Aquaman*. "I want the audience to experience Atlantis the first time my lead character, Aquaman, experiences it as well," Wan explains, "because you share that same emotionality with our hero. What that allows you to do is to relate to this guy even more. You get to experience it with him. You get to see all this weird stuff—wonderful, magical things—as he's seeing it for the first time."

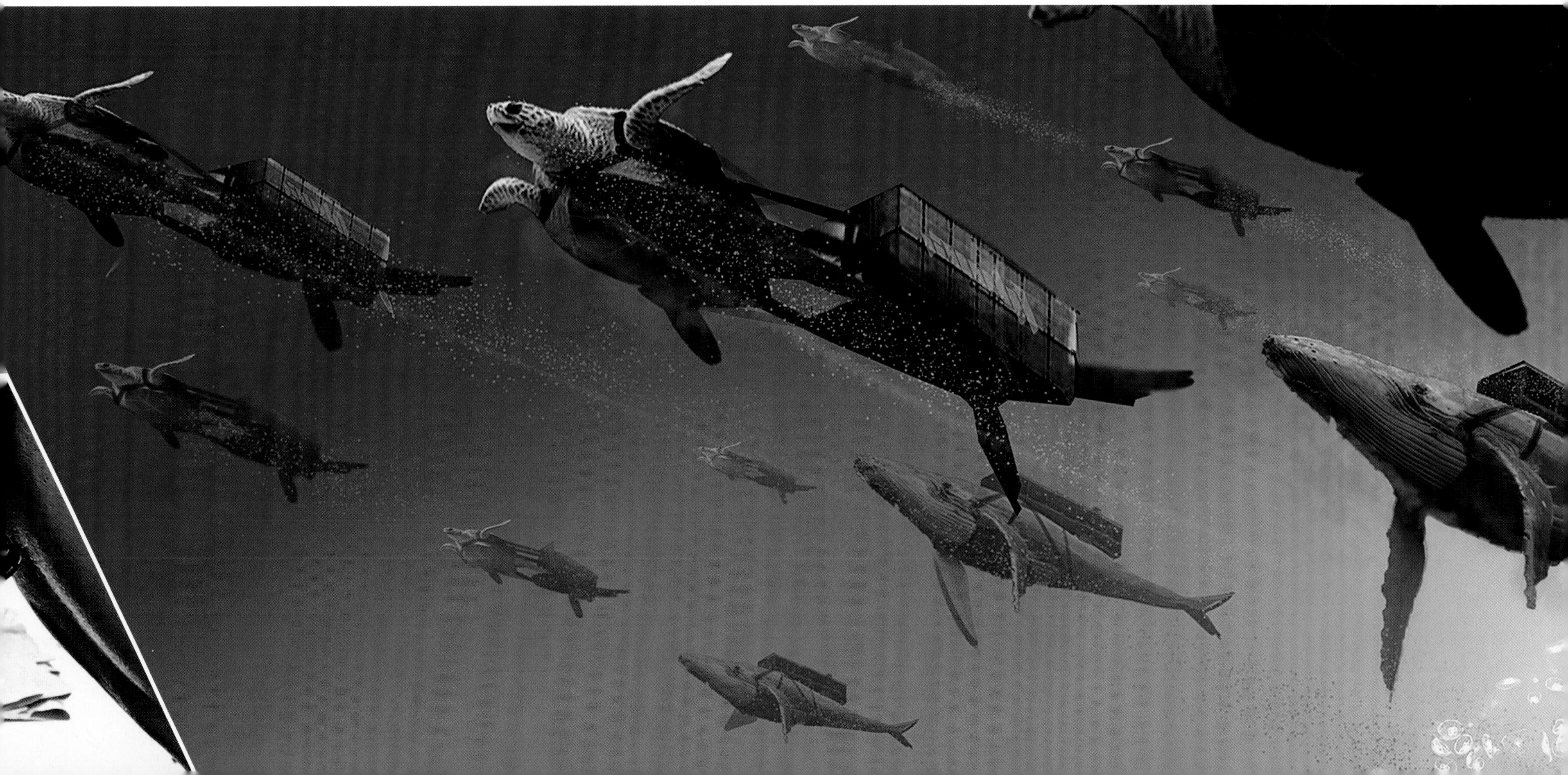

MERA

PRINCESS OF XEBEL

The film may be titled *Aquaman*, but it has a strong buddy-action-adventure feel with a little old-school, Hepburn-Tracy romantic comedy thrown in. The reason for that is the multifaceted character of Princess Mera of Xebel. In the comics, she has been around since the 1960s, but it wasn't until Geoff Johns reimagined her for the New 52 *Aquaman* relaunch that the character truly came into her own. She is now an equal partner for Arthur, not just a secondary character. That partnership carries through the film and was the primary reason Amber Heard signed on to play her. "They kind of sold me on this character by saying she gets both the sword and a crown," recalls Heard. "I don't know if they knew how much that would appeal to me, but it won me over."

All it took for Wan to realize he had found his Mera was to watch Heard's initial read with Jason Momoa. "One of the things that struck me when I first met Amber was just how charismatic and charming she is," says Wan. "Here's someone that can really sink into this role of Mera. Young girls can really look up to this character because Mera is so strong." The actress wholeheartedly agrees with that description of her character. "Mera is in many ways someone I can relate to and that I identify with. I like to connect with characters that are strong, empowered women, who are very much their own characters," Heard says. "And this is no exception. Mera is very much her own superhero."

OPPOSITE: Amber Heard as Mera using her power of hydrokinesis.

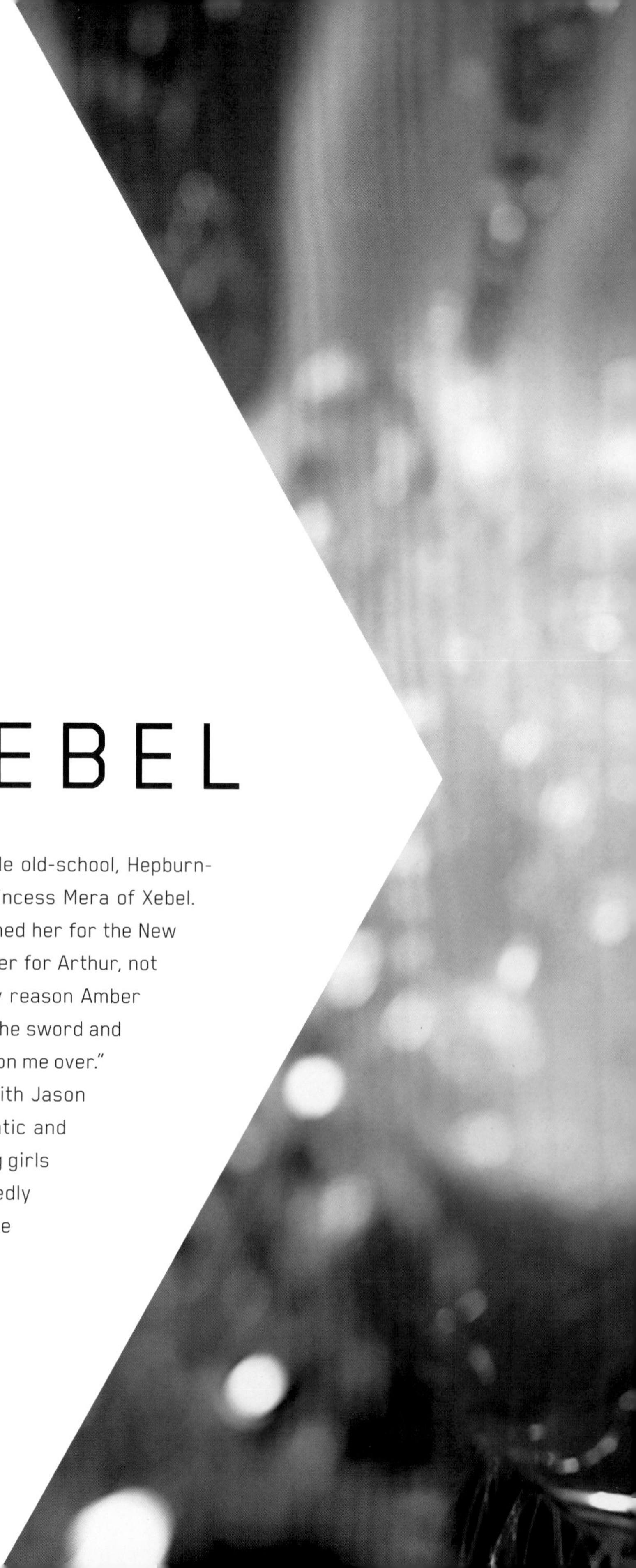

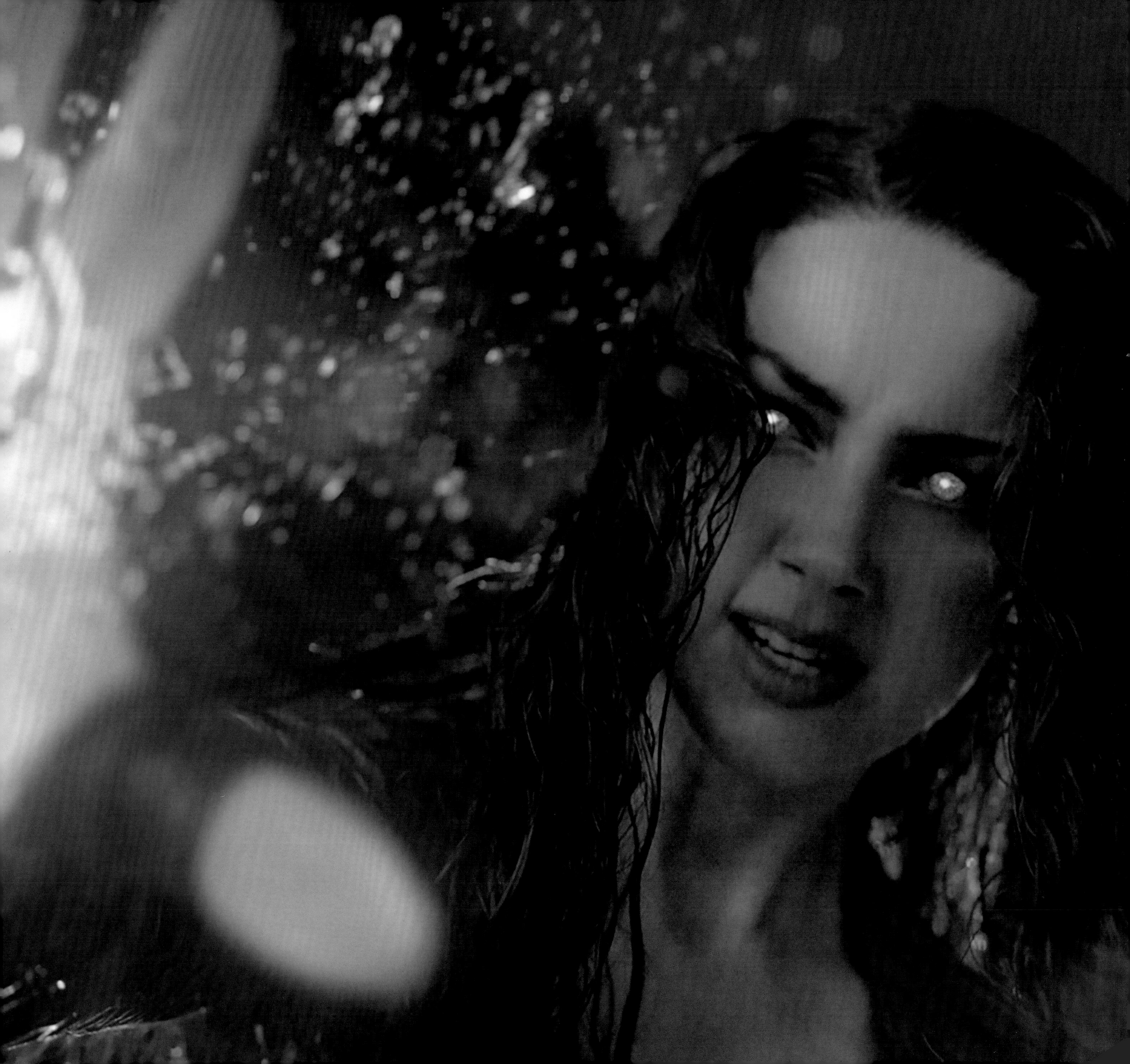

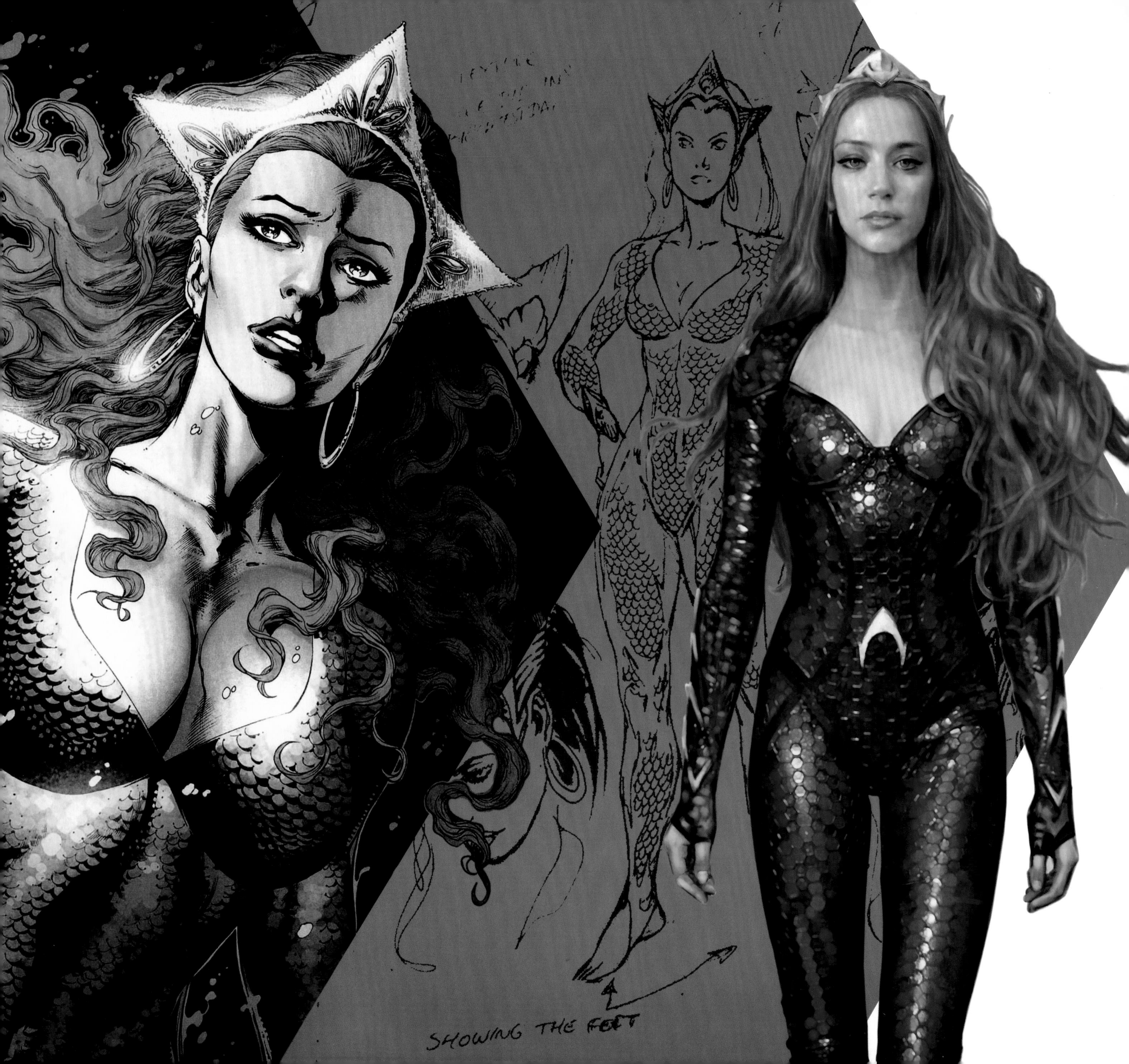
SHOWING THE FEET

Wan reinforces her point by recalling that in the comics Mera is at least as powerful as Arthur. Her powers in the film are no different. "She does as much ass kicking in this film as Arthur does. She is fun and funny, takes no prisoners and no crap," says producer Peter Safran. In one of her earliest scenes in the film, Mera saves Arthur and his father from being swept away by a tsunami that hits Amnesty Bay. It isn't the last time she rescues Arthur.

Mera's situation is complicated by the fact that her father, King Nereus, has arranged for her to marry Orm to maintain the delicate peace with Atlantis. The arrangement only strengthens her resolve to convince Arthur that he must return to Atlantis and prevent Orm from launching a strike against the surface dwellers. Mera's role in this movie is quite different from the types of roles that women often find themselves playing in superhero movies. "Typically women occupy much more passive positions in terms of driving the plot and function of the story," Heard says. "One thing I love about *Aquaman* is that it reflects the modern audience's desire to see women occupy more proactive, stronger roles. While it's about Aquaman, it's very much a two-hander, where the other half of the story—Mera's half— is just as proactive and strong, and very much a part of the driving force of this story."

The relationship between Mera and Arthur is vital to the film because it delivers energy—a bounce—that is different from other superhero films. "We always felt that in making this movie, it had to be fun. There's certainly been a period in DC films where there was a much darker edge," Safran acknowledges. "We never felt that that is what *Aquaman* should be."

Momoa calls Heard his Bonnie, a reference to a classic film about a memorable pair, *Bonnie and Clyde*. "We had a ball together," Momoa says of their work on the picture. "We shared each other's pain and are very supportive. She's like family."

OPPOSITE LEFT: *Brightest Day* #5 interior art by Ivan Reis, Vicente Cifuentes, and Peter Steigerwald.
OPPOSITE RIGHT: Mera comic book character sketches by Ivan Reis from the graphic novel *Aquaman: The Trench* (September 2012) (*left*); Mera costume concept art by Oksana Nedavniaya (*right*).
LEFT: Amber Heard takes a defiant stance in Mera's hero costume.

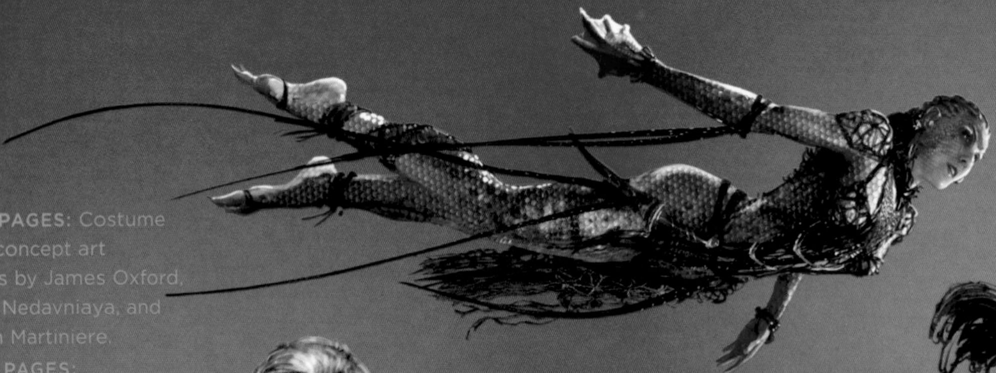

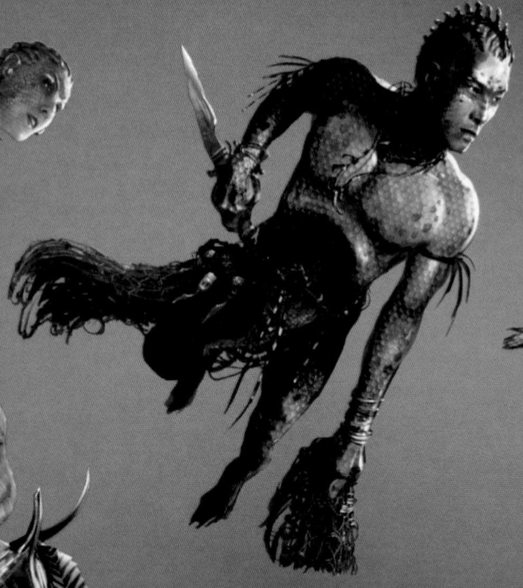

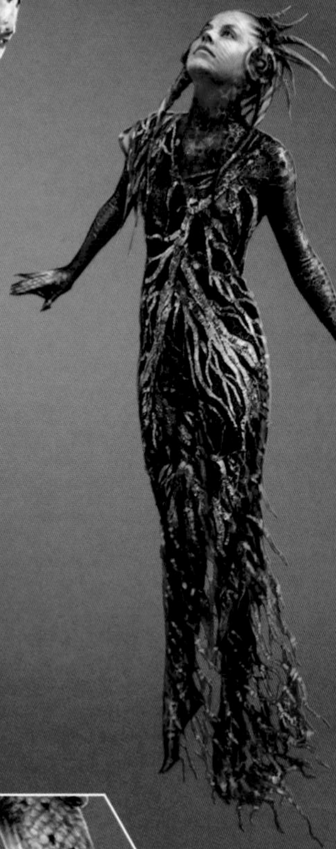

THESE PAGES: Costume design concept art sketches by James Oxford, Oksana Nedavniaya, and Stephan Martiniere.
OUTER PAGES: Closeup image of Mera's hero costume (*left*); hair and makeup test image for her ceremonial outfit (*right*).

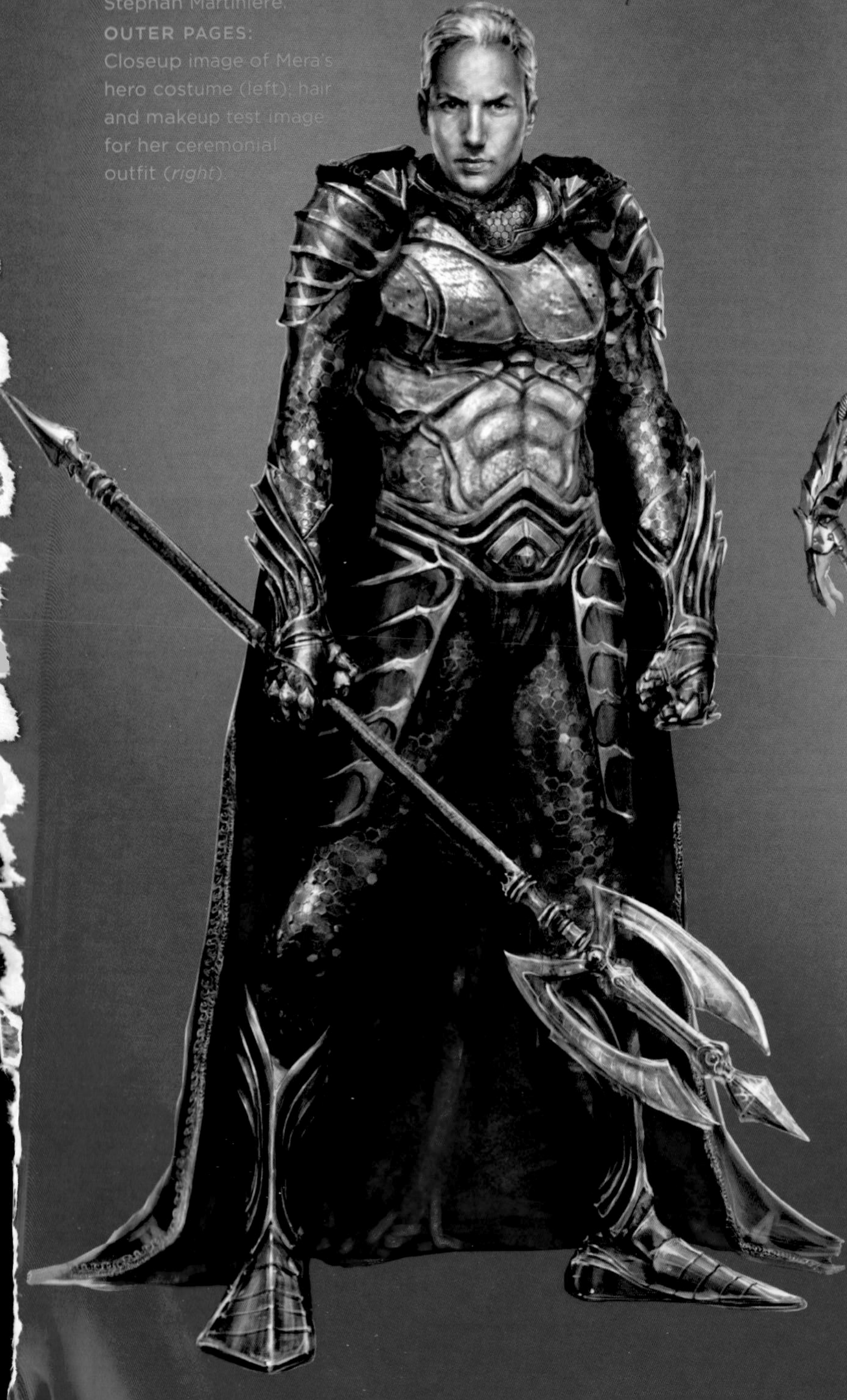

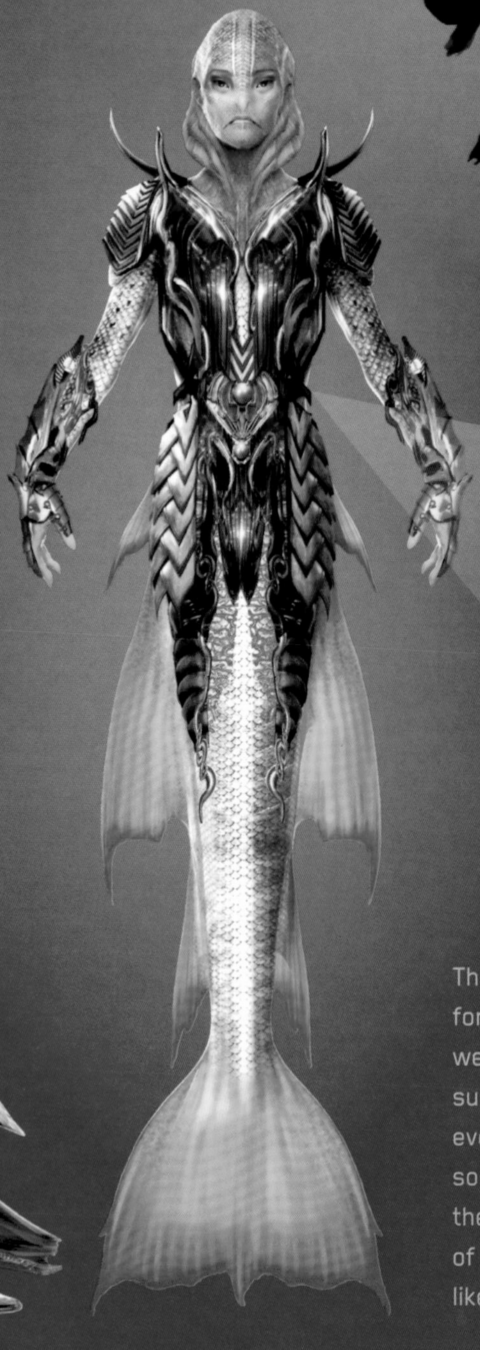

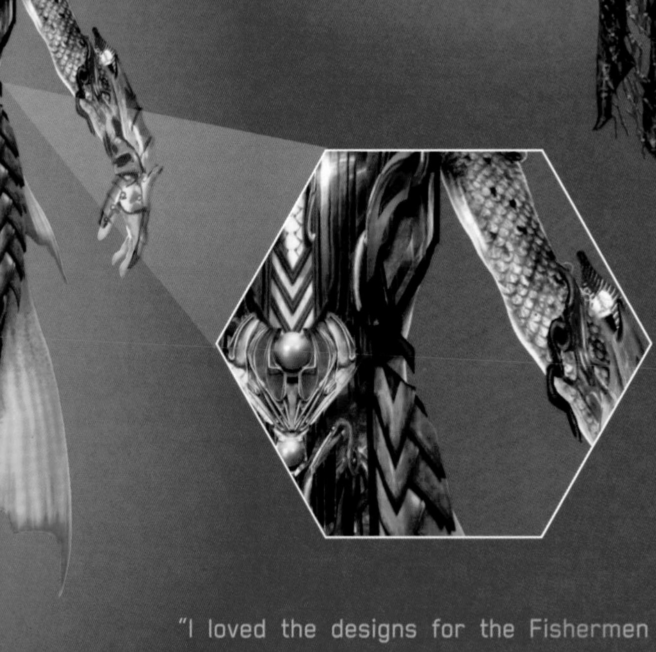

"I loved the designs for the Fishermen Kingdom. They incorporate a lot of our rules that we established for continuity in this undersea world. They're the ones we won't see much of in the movie, but I feel they were super successful because they captured the plausible evolution of that race of creatures. I got a chance to do some great characters with that sequence. Some, like the Fishermen Queen and Princess, had their own type of camouflage, like skin that was much more colorful, like a coral reef or the colors of a tropical fish."

DRESSING AN UNDERWATER WORLD

As the rules were established for the mechanics of life in the undersea kingdoms, costume designer Kym Barrett used them as parameters for her work. She shares her thoughts on the creative process:

"The production design team and I spent a lot of time working things out, like what kind of textures could they use on their sets, and whether I could use certain materials for my outfits. I would ask if I could steal texture off their walls so I could re-create it on my costumes. It was a great job for artistic collaboration. It was a lot of fun in that regard."

Again, adopting and following a set of rules was very important to Barrett's costuming process. "If you devolved from an air-breathing human into a water-breathing Atlantean over twenty thousand years," Barrett explains, "and you devolved really fast compared to normal evolution—you would lose all your body hair, your eyes would become rounder and bulbous, more fishlike, so you can see in all directions; you would be ribless. So we talked about the reality of what would actually happen and walked it back into what would be an acceptable version of reality, and what people would be happy to look at it.

"For example, we thought most people wouldn't have much body hair. Everyone who lives in Atlantis has a skin, like a wetsuit, but breathable water skin. Just like we do as humans, they decorate it and pattern it in accordance to what they see around them."

"James was keen on having characters like King Orm using capes. I asked, 'Well, can we forgo the capes?' Because a cape under the water won't do anything except create drag. Then we thought, 'What if they only wear capes for ceremonial purposes?' Like how a member of a royal family might wear a cape to a coronation, or the royal guardsmen. In Atlantis, we determined the capes would be part of any ceremonial function or meetings of dignitaries."

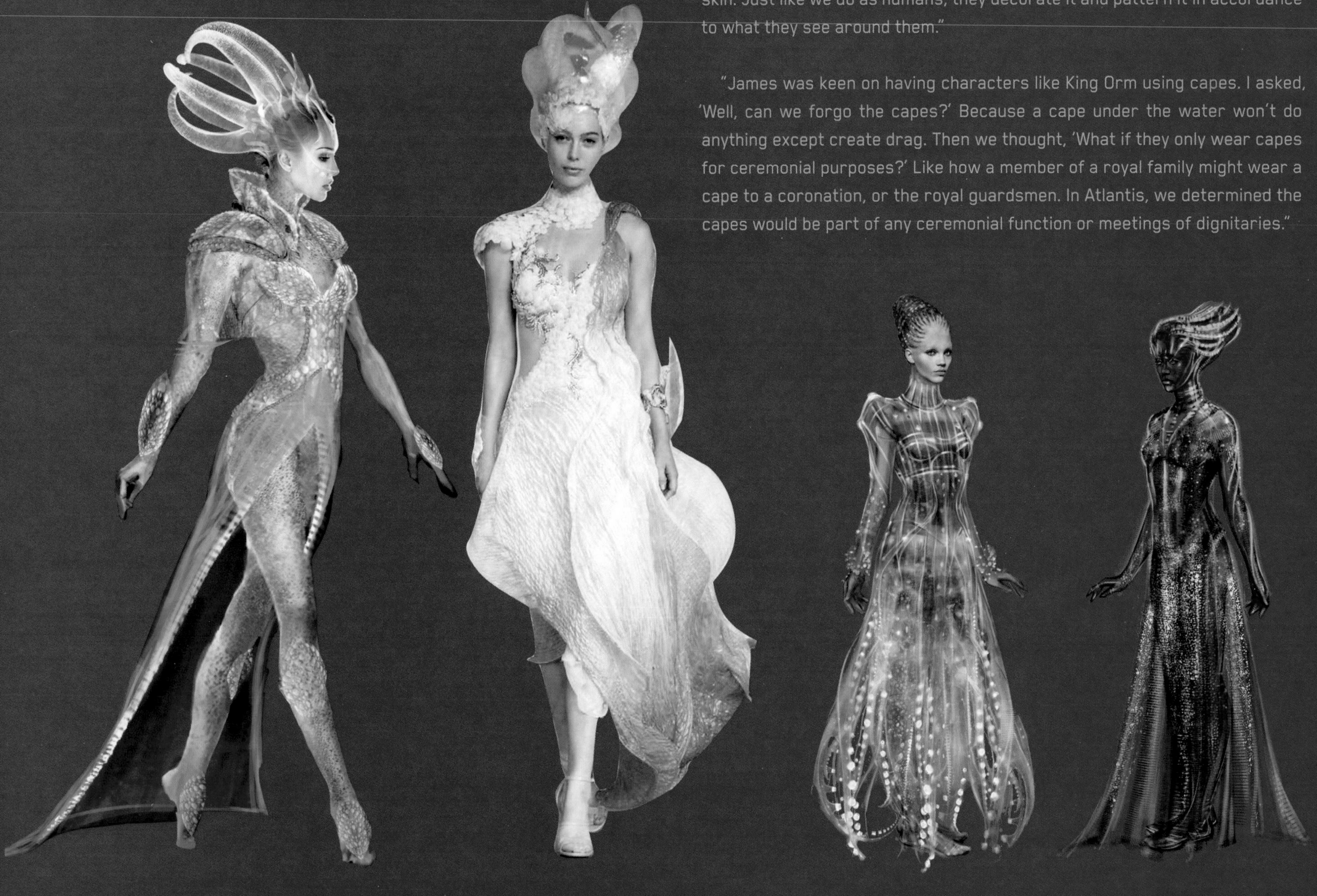

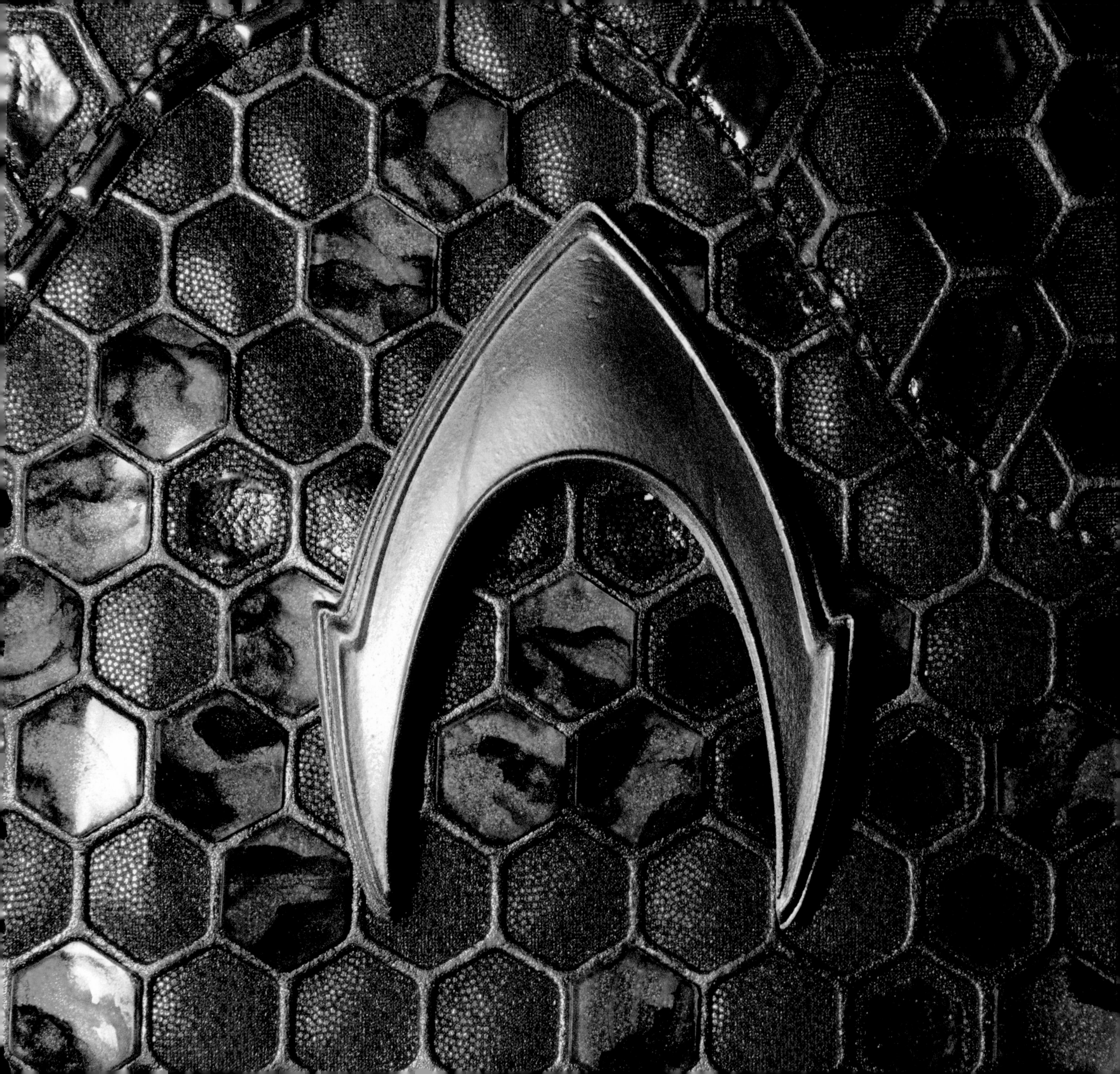

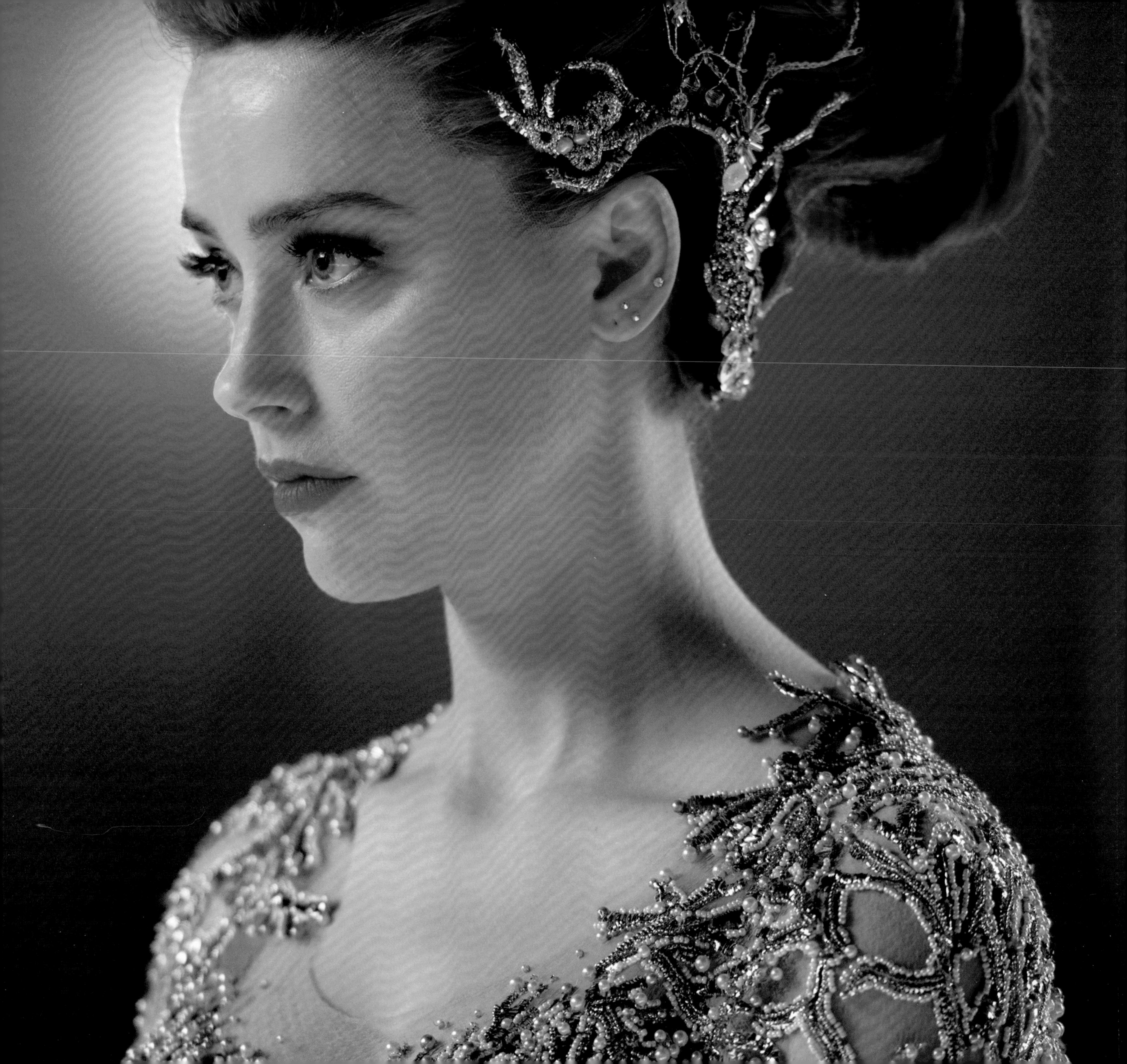

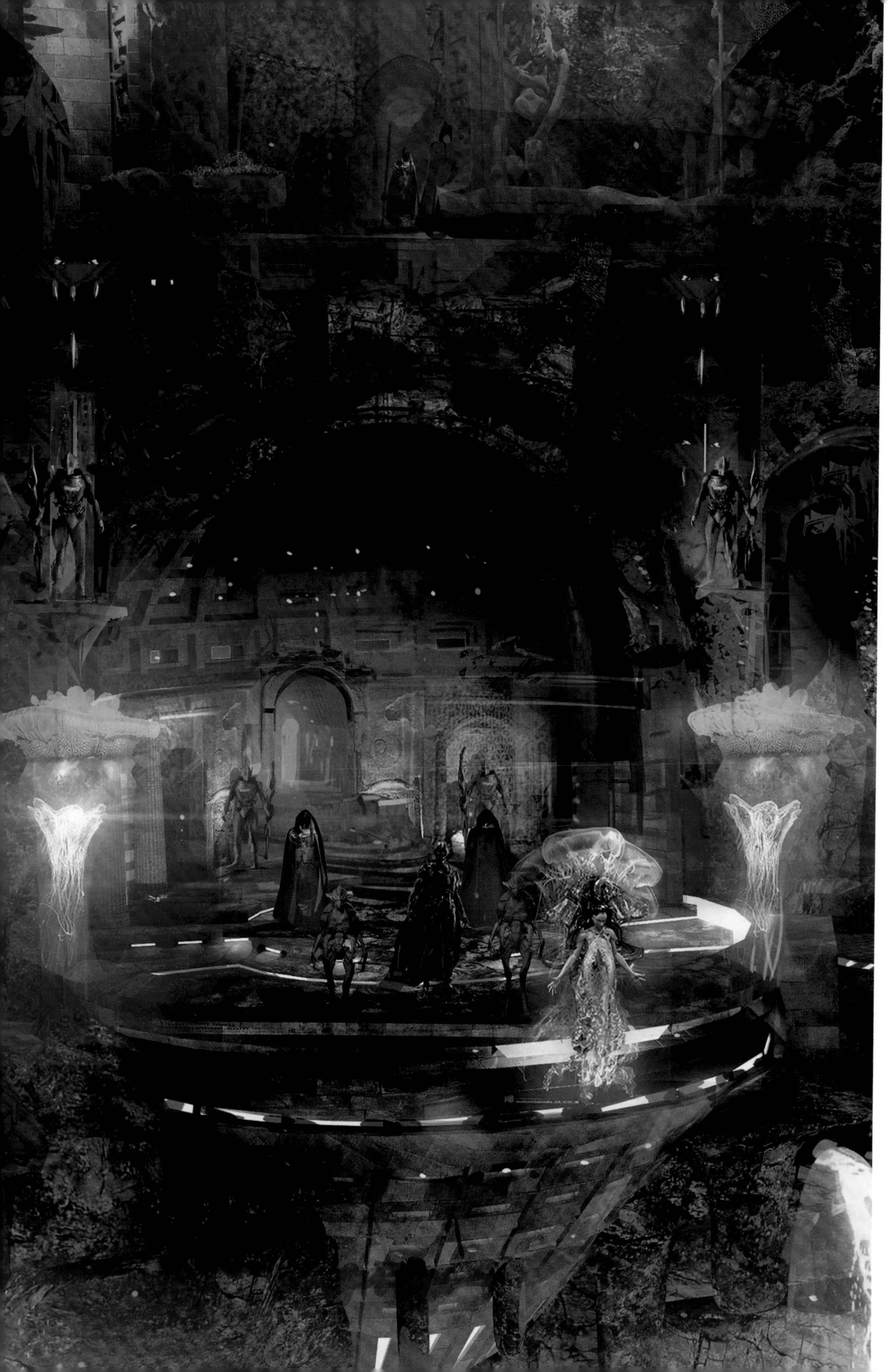

Peter Safran credits screenwriter David Leslie Johnson-McGoldrick with injecting the humor that runs through the film. As Arthur and Mera go off on their quest to find the lost trident of King Atlan, the pair clearly doesn't get along. Heard notes, "Arthur and Mera have a playful banter that evolves throughout the course of their relationship." They eventually come to see they are both burdened by vulnerability. Like Arthur, Mera does not yet understand her place in the world. Her journey in the film is about discovering where she fits into the bigger picture. "Both our lead characters, Arthur and Mera, go on this crazy fun journey. It's like a rite of passage story, where they learn who they are and what they're meant to be," says Wan.

After spending the better part of two years on this film, Heard is happy to finally get to see the finished product. "I don't think we've seen anything like what James Wan has created," she says. "The sets have been amazing and incredibly complex, but they are only a few feet deep. Then it's all blue screen. So I'm excited to see what it all looks like together when all the effects have been added." Working on a movie about a civilization of deep-sea dwellers, shot primarily with blue screen and partially constructed sets, can be jarring, to put it mildly. Occasionally, even a professional like Heard can feel a bit lost. "Sometimes I found myself asking James, 'Like so, are we . . . is this the lava over here, or . . .' You know what I mean? It's really weird, a weird process, but it has been a lot of fun."

"THE FORMAL OUTFIT MERA wears in the royal box during the Ring of Fire sequence underscores the importance of formality for Atlanteans and Xebellians."

—Kym Barrett, Costume Designer

OPPOSITE: Coliseum concept art by Christian Scheurer.

THIS PAGE: Mera jellyfish dress and hair design concept art pieces by Oksana Nedavniaya.

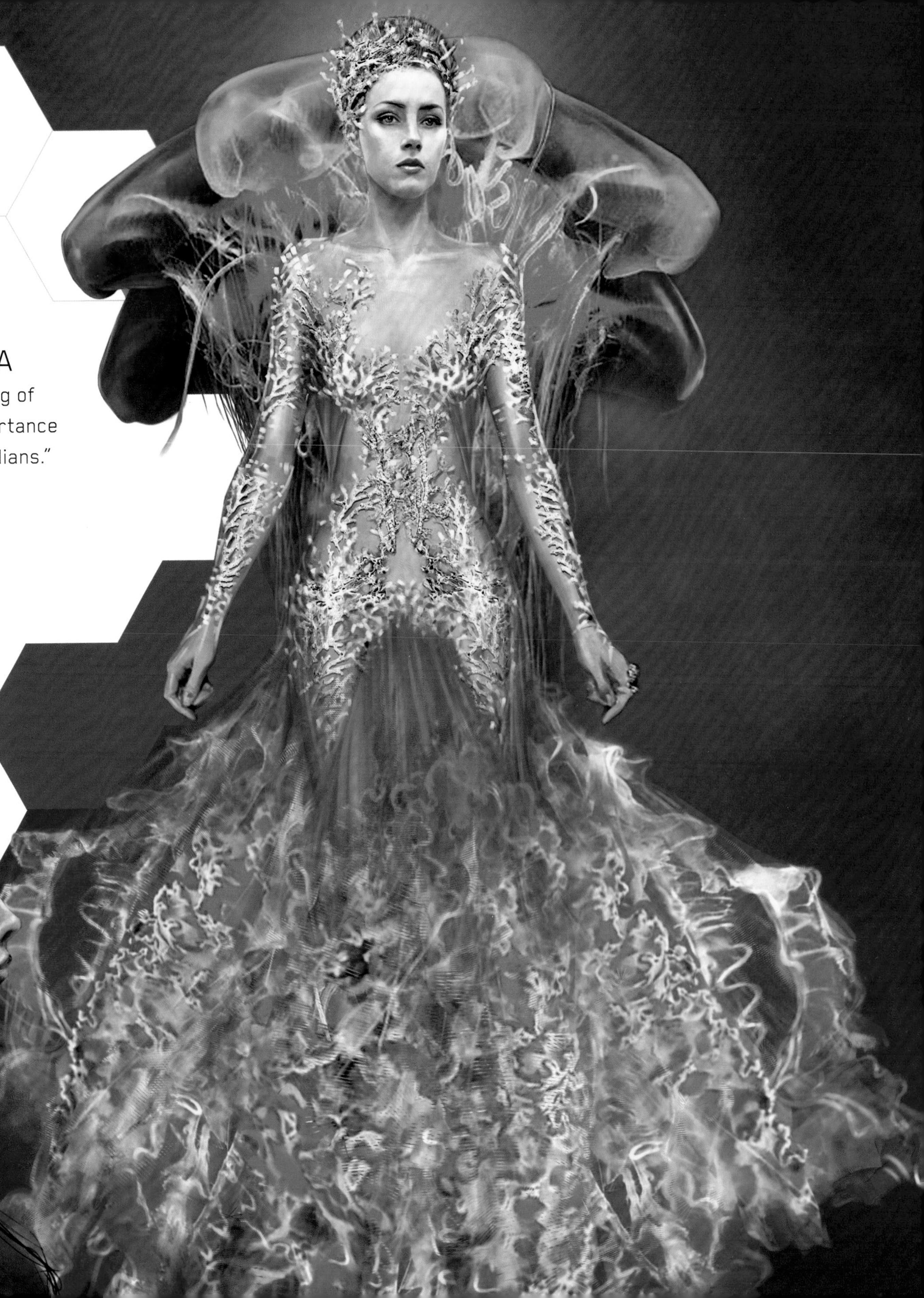

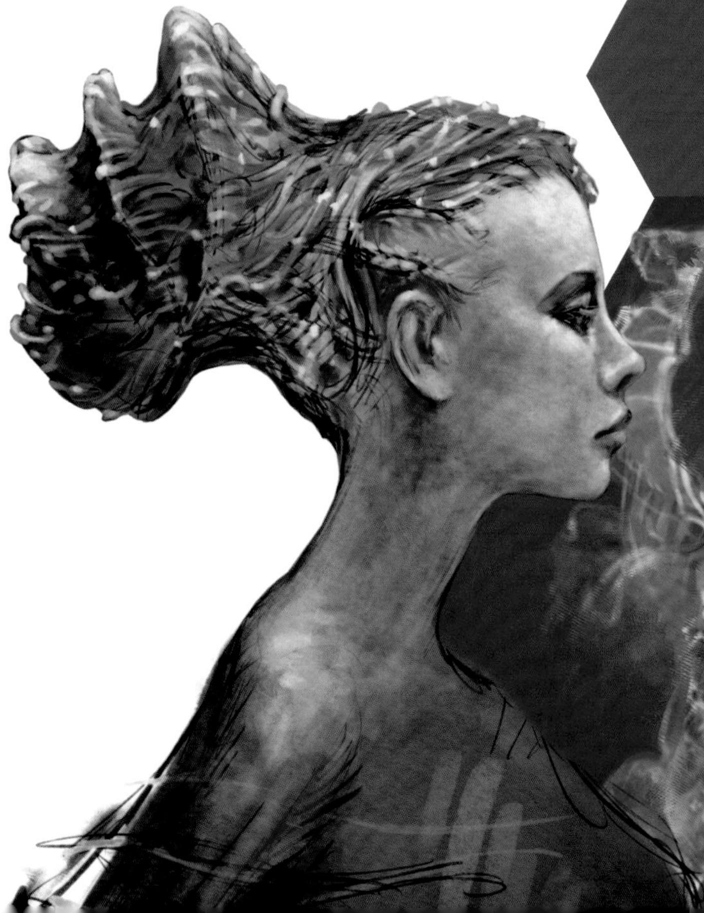

ORM

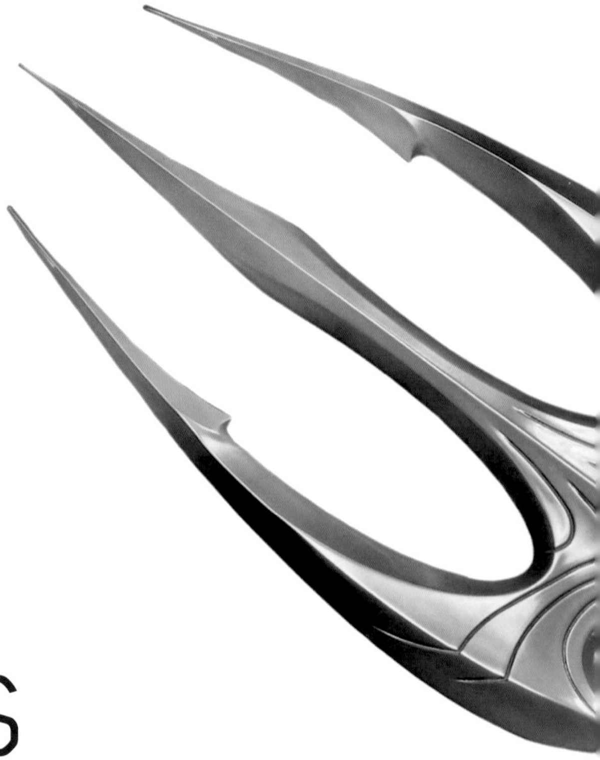

KING OF ATLANTIS

Almost immediately upon discovering he was going to be Arthur Curry's half-brother and the main nemesis in *Aquaman*, Patrick Wilson knew one thing for certain: He had better hit the gym. It's not that the actor wasn't physically fit already. But to face Jason Momoa, Wilson—of *The Conjuring*, *Insidious*, and TV's *Fargo*—felt compelled to bulk up.

"Jason is a big dude," Wilson points out. "And I'm barely six feet. In the comics, too, Orm is a big dude. I wanted to be a formidable opponent. I've always been in shape, but I wanted to be . . . I wanted to get bigger." Wilson went through a rigorous training program that helped him pack on fifteen pounds of muscle before he even arrived in Australia to begin filming. That's when the actor discovered that Orm's on-screen costume had significantly less exposure than he expected. "What was on-screen, it literally comes down to about one arm," the actor jokingly observed. "I did like five months of working out for nothing!"

There was nothing lighthearted about portraying the movie's central antagonist. Informed largely by the character's iteration in Geoff Johns's *Aquaman* comic series from the New 52, Orm is the ruler of Atlantis, with even grander ambitions. "Part of our journey in this movie is him becoming Ocean Master," Wilson says. "In order to do that, I have to get the kingdoms underwater to align with me. I feel like I am the rightful heir to the throne of the undersea kingdoms."

OPPOSITE: Patrick Wilson as Orm.

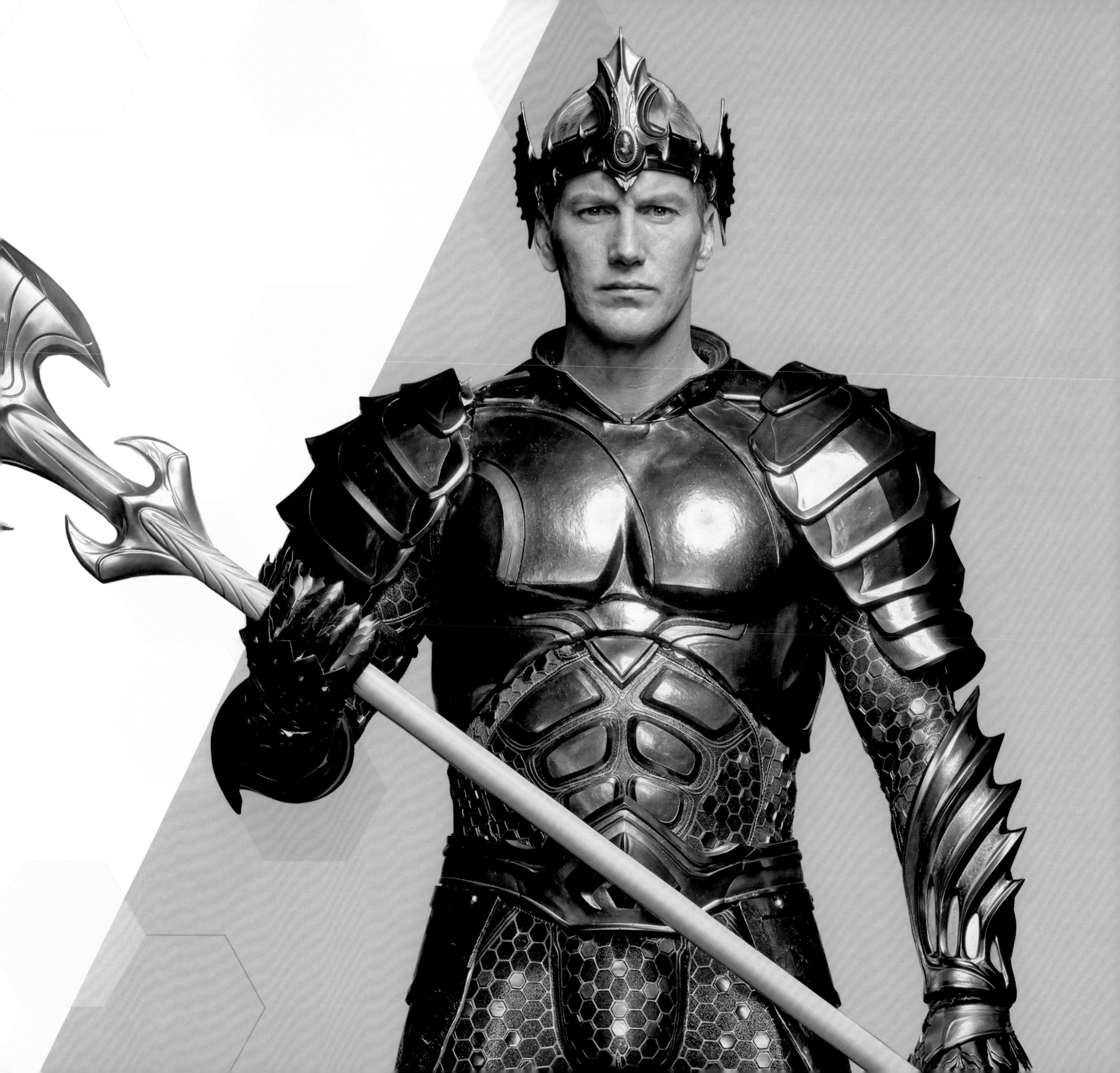

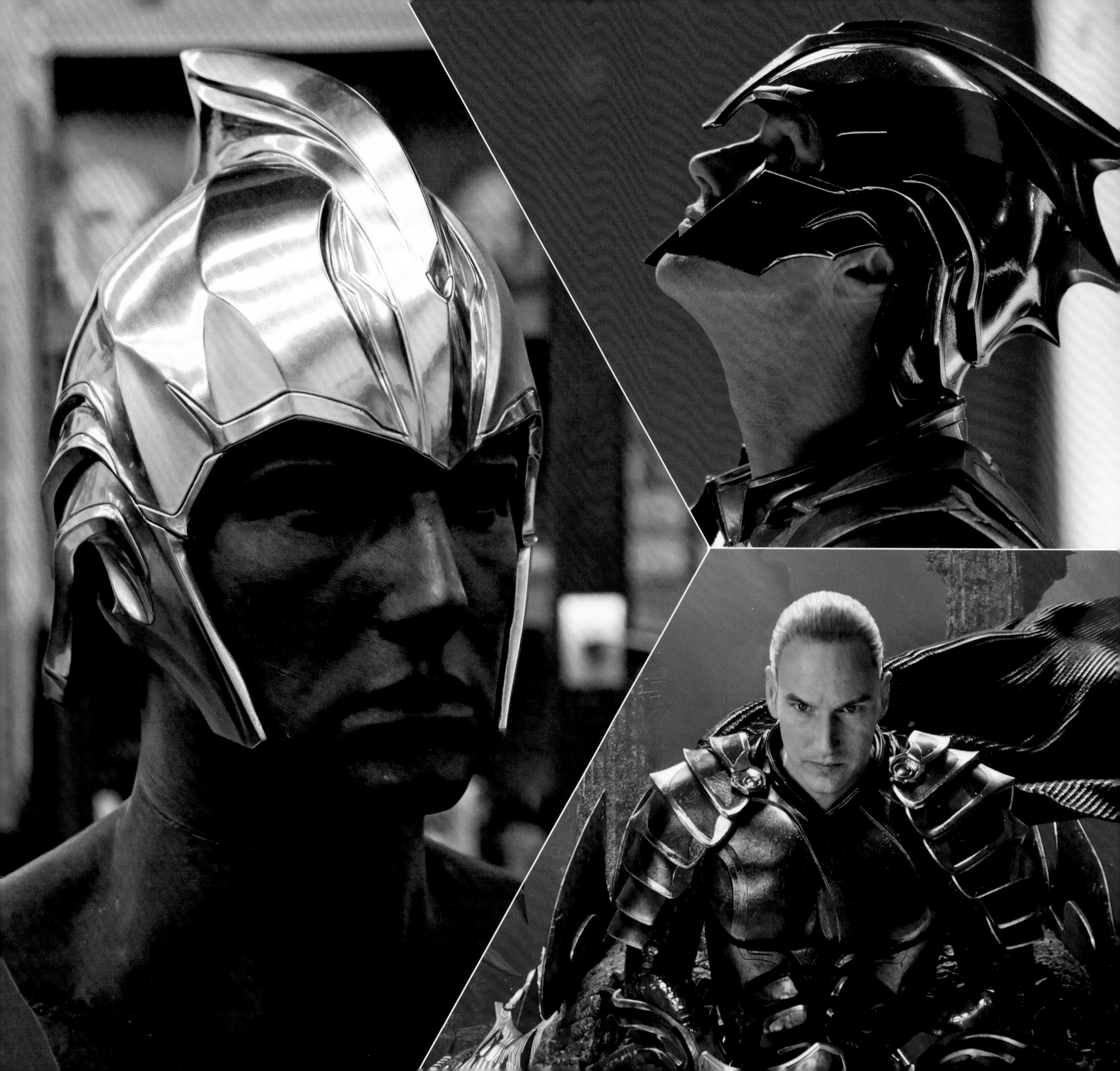

To achieve his goal, Orm must forge new alliances. That requires deft manipulation on his part, because the undersea civilizations have been fractured for millennia. By Atlantean law, to become Ocean Master and wage war on humanity, Orm must convince four of the kingdoms to join his cause. The first step in Orm's plan is to persuade the Xebellian King Nereus. He does so by staging an attack during a meeting of the Council of the Kings at the Ancient Ruins—using a submarine so that the council would suspect humans were behind the unwarranted act. To Orm, a just end will always justify ruthless means.

Wilson was attracted to the role because Orm is not your standard movie villain. "For centuries, humans have been polluting the oceans and ruining his world. Which is true," he points out. "How he goes about dealing with this, we can certainly discuss." The actor adds that there is a method to Orm's madness. The only way to defeat the surface world is to have the ocean's kingdoms align with him, so his plan will unify the undersea realm. And the Atlantean ruler cleverly uses Aquaman's very public heroics of late to paint him as a threat to the underwater kingdoms. By revealing himself to the surface world, Orm warns, Arthur has put all of the undersea races at risk.

This is Wilson's fifth movie with Wan (including the *Conjuring* films and the first two chapters of *Insidious*). As a result, the director kept envisioning Wilson as King Orm as he was working on the *Aquaman* script. "To me, he is an amazing character actor trapped in the body of a leading man," Wan says. "But what I love about Patrick is just how much he disappears into his character." Their working relationship is such that Cowan just assumed Wilson would be joining the cast. "He's in every one of James's movies already. No matter what James does, Patrick is going to come along," Cowan says. "He's a guy who just always delivers, and this was a fun role for him because he's playing a bad guy of sorts, but he's also bringing a lot of humanity to the part."

Orm's conflict with his half brother comes into play when Aquaman shows up. Orm realizes that Arthur, as the first-born son of the former queen, has a legitimate claim to the crown. The fact that others, such as King Nereus, are aware of the existence of another royal offspring is also not lost on Orm. Arthur's very presence is a threat to Orm's place as ruler of Atlantis and to his ambitions of becoming Ocean Master. There is another reason why Orm despises the brother he's never known. Much like Arthur feels he was abandoned by his mother, so too does Orm. In his eyes, Atlanna betrayed him and the Atlantean people by having a son with a human. Those feelings of betrayal have warped Orm's mindset, and he's turned his anger on Arthur.

Momoa calls Wilson "a phenomenal actor" to work with and says their fiery on-screen rivalry is the result of two performers pushing each other to the very limit. There are many facets to the conflict between the two estranged siblings. The relationship is expressed through intense physical battles as well as emotional conflicts. Orm does not believe Arthur is worthy of leading Atlantis. In his view, Arthur is not a true Atlantean and therefore has no legitimate claim to the throne. In addition, Orm knows Arthur does not aspire to be king. "I think that's what makes it very interesting," Wilson notes. "Arthur doesn't want it, either."

OPPOSITE LEFT AND TOP RIGHT: Orm's battle helmet, unpainted and in battle.
OPPOSITE BOTTOM RIGHT: Orm in battle armor without helmet.
RIGHT: *Mera: Queen of Atlantis* #2 (May 2018) interior art by Lan Medina, Norm Rapmund, and Veronica Gandini.

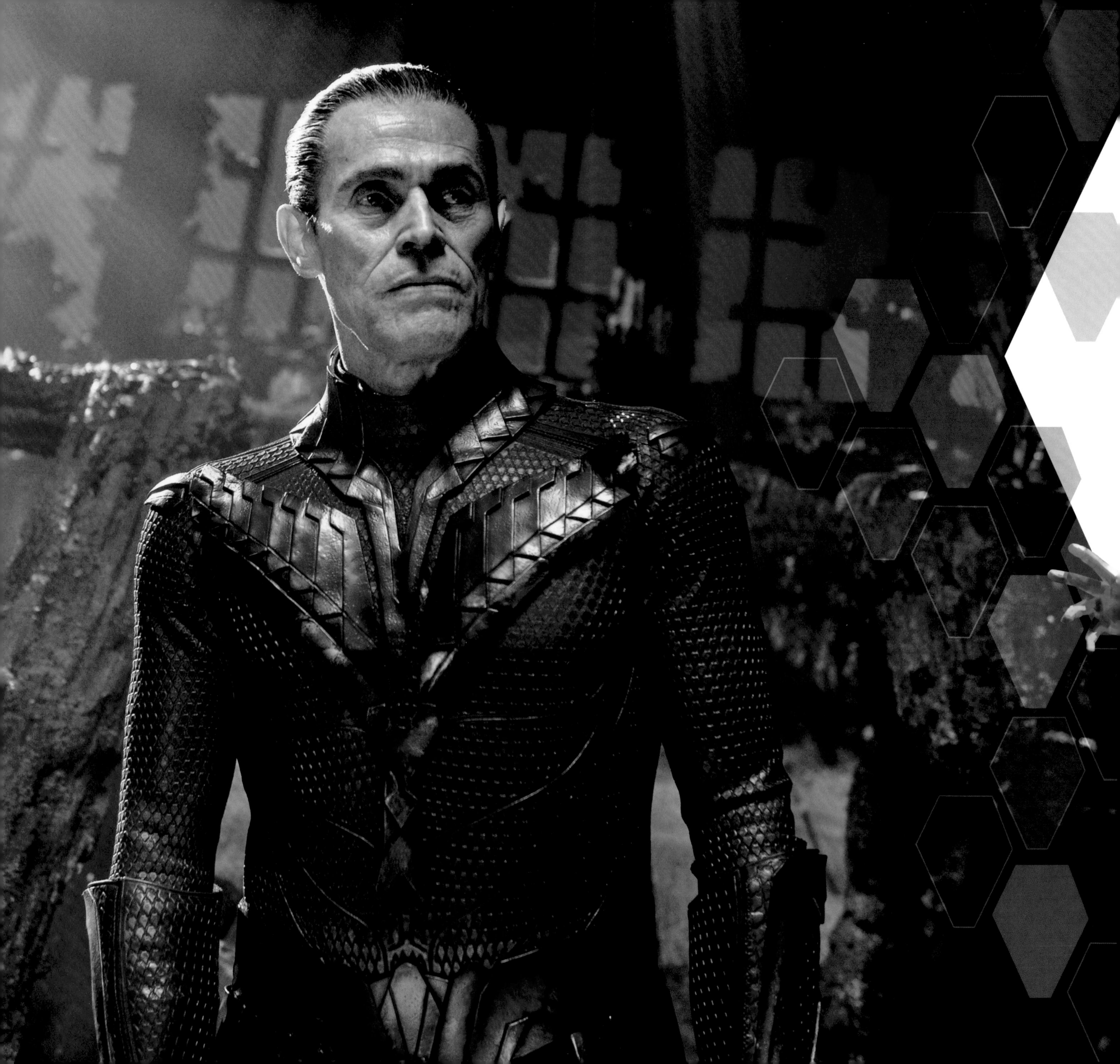

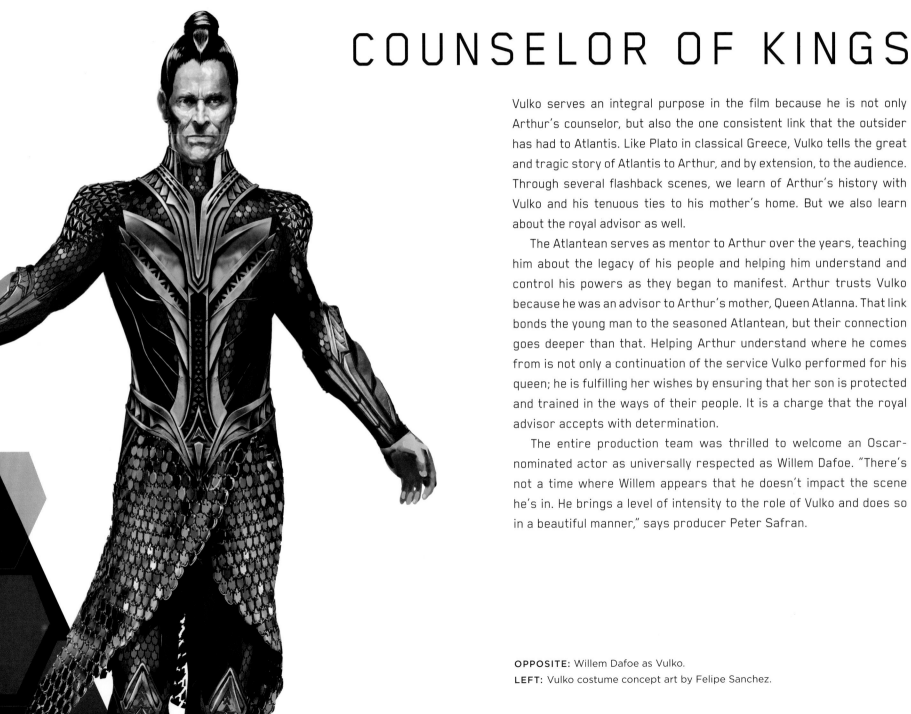

NUIDIS VULKO

COUNSELOR OF KINGS

Vulko serves an integral purpose in the film because he is not only Arthur's counselor, but also the one consistent link that the outsider has had to Atlantis. Like Plato in classical Greece, Vulko tells the great and tragic story of Atlantis to Arthur, and by extension, to the audience. Through several flashback scenes, we learn of Arthur's history with Vulko and his tenuous ties to his mother's home. But we also learn about the royal advisor as well.

The Atlantean serves as mentor to Arthur over the years, teaching him about the legacy of his people and helping him understand and control his powers as they began to manifest. Arthur trusts Vulko because he was an advisor to Arthur's mother, Queen Atlanna. That link bonds the young man to the seasoned Atlantean, but their connection goes deeper than that. Helping Arthur understand where he comes from is not only a continuation of the service Vulko performed for his queen; he is fulfilling her wishes by ensuring that her son is protected and trained in the ways of their people. It is a charge that the royal advisor accepts with determination.

The entire production team was thrilled to welcome an Oscar-nominated actor as universally respected as Willem Dafoe. "There's not a time where Willem appears that he doesn't impact the scene he's in. He brings a level of intensity to the role of Vulko and does so in a beautiful manner," says producer Peter Safran.

OPPOSITE: Willem Dafoe as Vulko.
LEFT: Vulko costume concept art by Felipe Sanchez.

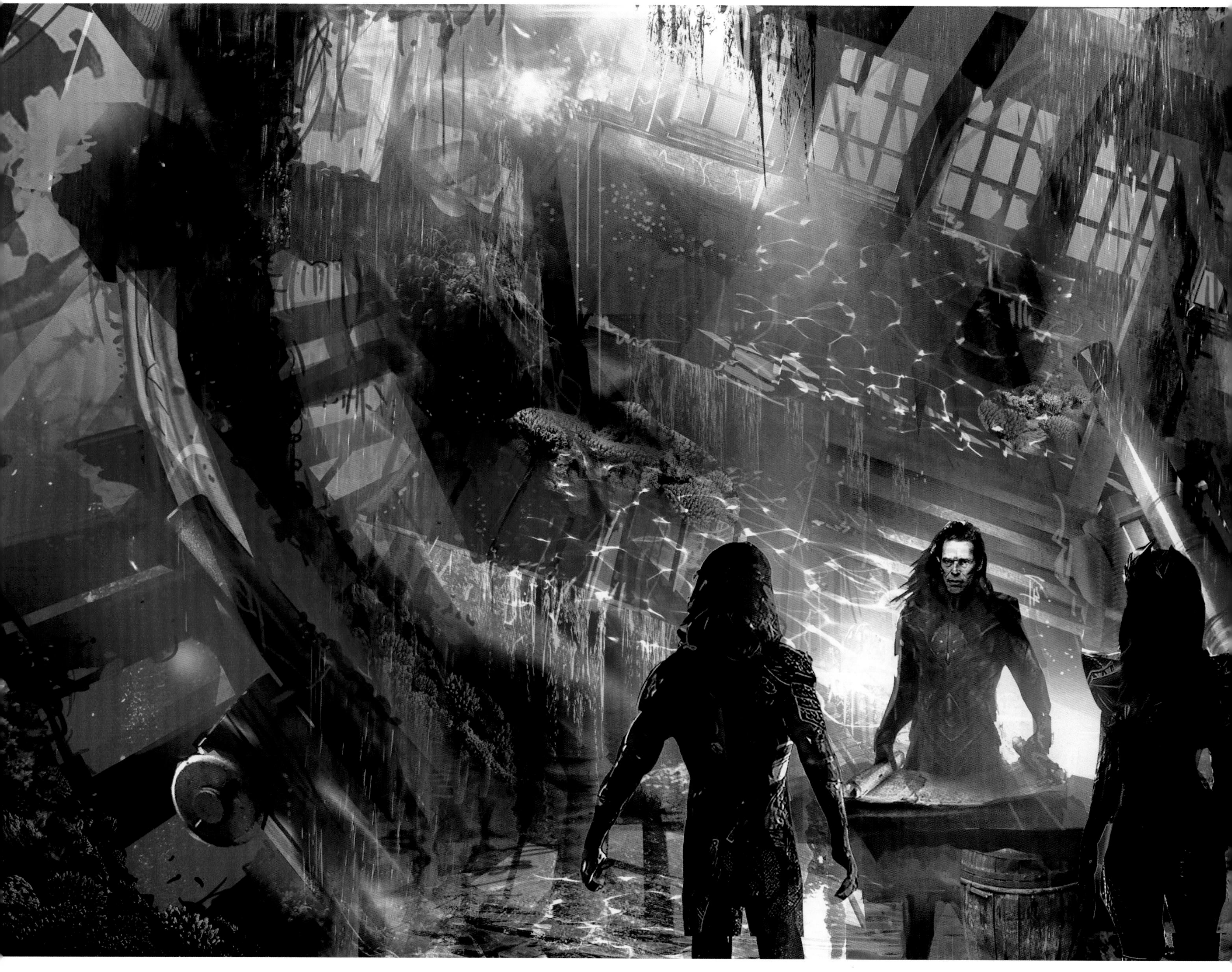

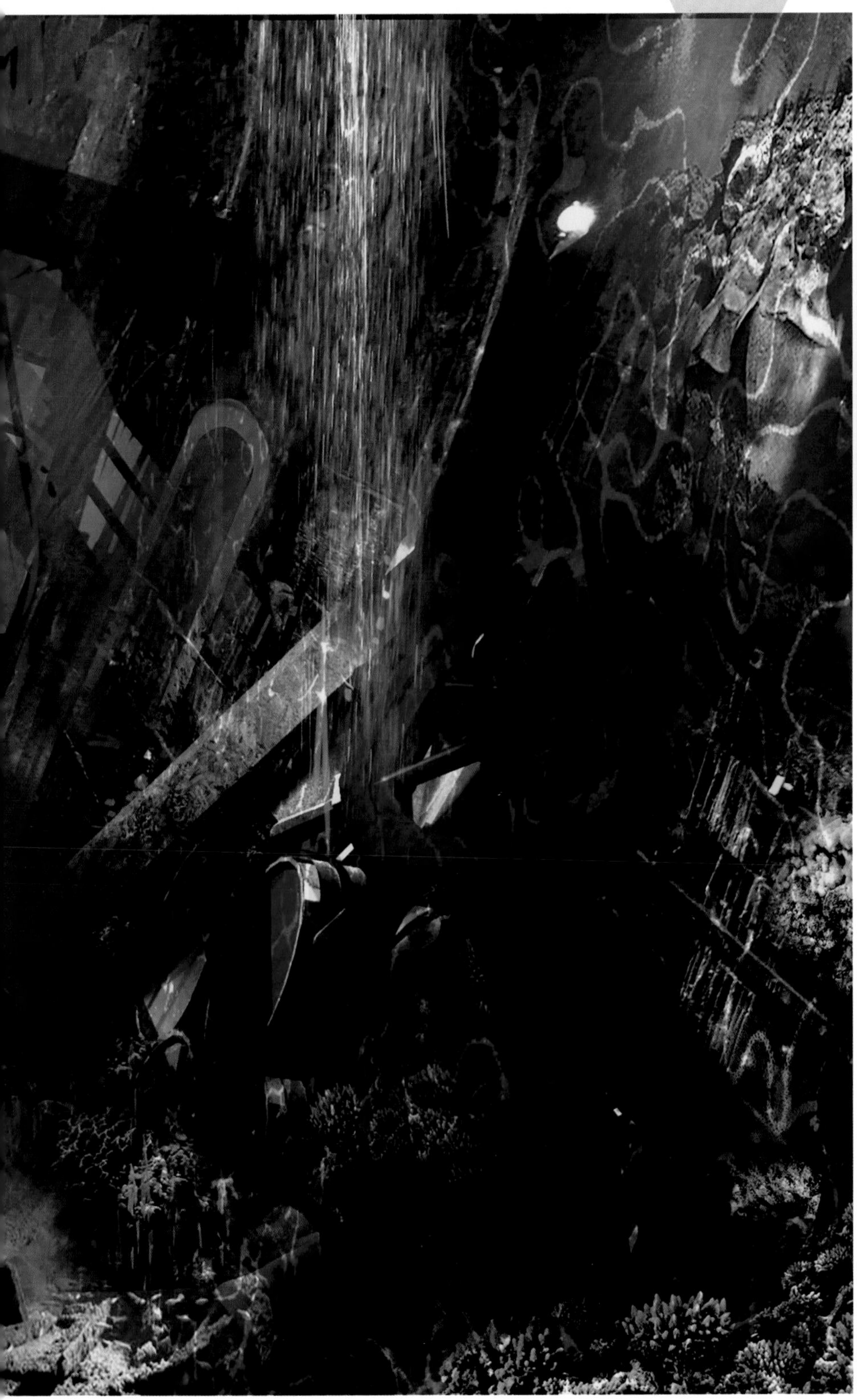

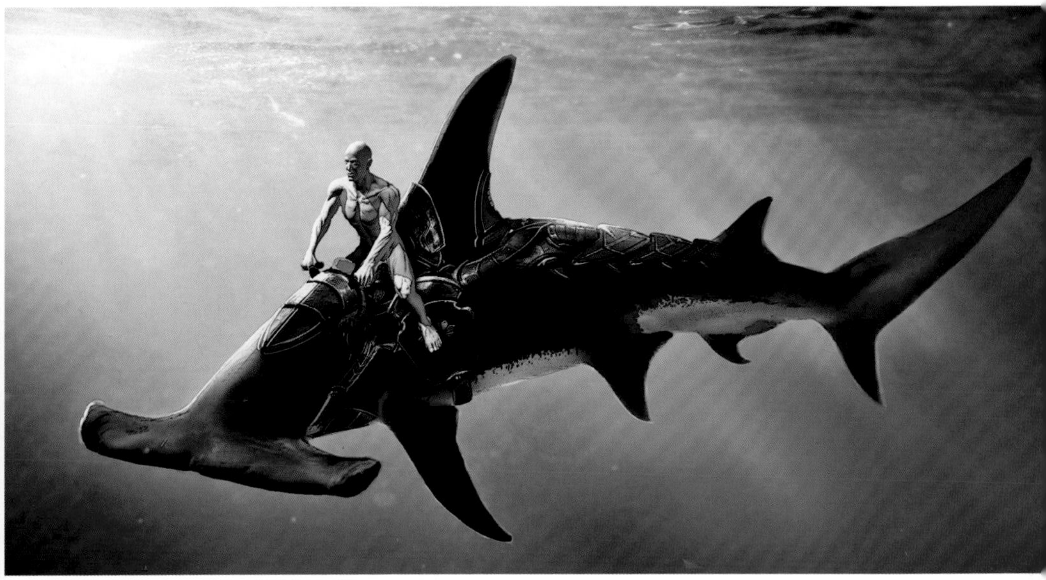

Vulko is also the one who lights the fuse of the quest at the heart of *Aquaman*. He sends Mera to the surface world to convince Arthur that finding King Atlan's trident is the key to stopping the war Orm wants to incite with humanity. When the three meet later in the Sunken Galleon, it is Vulko who introduces the journey that Arthur and Mera must undertake to prevent a war. He has uncovered a sharkskin map that identifies the first step in the quest to retrieve the lost trident. While Vulko is aiding Mera and Arthur on their mission, he must also maintain appearances as Orm's trusted lieutenant—his duty to the throne at odds with his loyalty to his queen and her oldest son. Vulko truly believes that Arthur, despite never having stepped foot in Atlantis, is better suited to rule than Orm.

The actor, with multiple Academy Award nominations (including his 2018 best supporting actor nomination for *The Florida Project*), has a special affinity for the more rugged aspects of working on *Aquaman*. Wan particularly enjoyed filming with Dafoe after finding out how excited the actor was about getting involved in whatever action set pieces he could. "Here is this really highly regarded thespian and he's talking to me about doing this crazy action stuff. He told me that's why he signed up to do this role in the first place. He did not want to just be relegated to the sideline as the older, wiser guy. He wanted to get in there. He wanted to be like Obi-Wan Kenobi, this old samurai guy."

LEFT: Sunken Galleon interior concept art by Christian Scheurer.
ABOVE: Vulko's mount concept art by Sebastian Meyer.

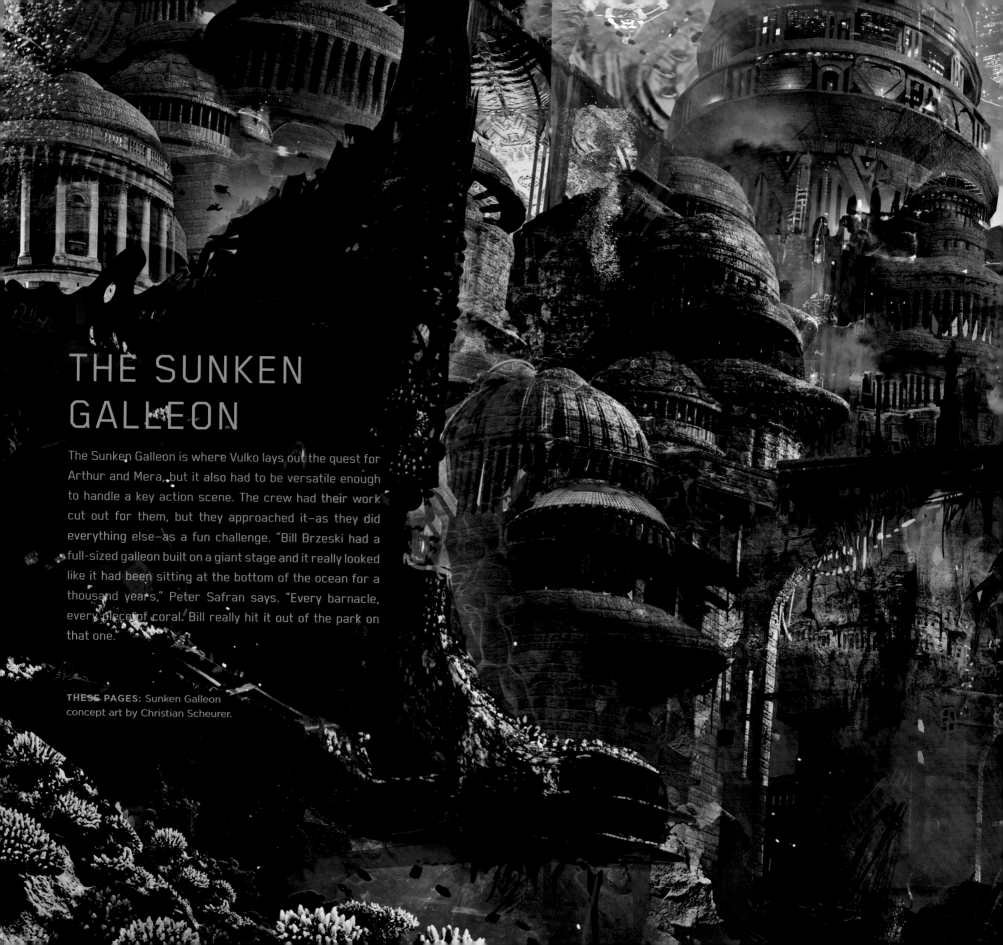

THE SUNKEN GALLEON

The Sunken Galleon is where Vulko lays out the quest for Arthur and Mera, but it also had to be versatile enough to handle a key action scene. The crew had their work cut out for them, but they approached it—as they did everything else—as a fun challenge. "Bill Brzeski had a full-sized galleon built on a giant stage and it really looked like it had been sitting at the bottom of the ocean for a thousand years," Peter Safran says. "Every barnacle, every piece of coral. Bill really hit it out of the park on that one."

THESE PAGES: Sunken Galleon concept art by Christian Scheurer.

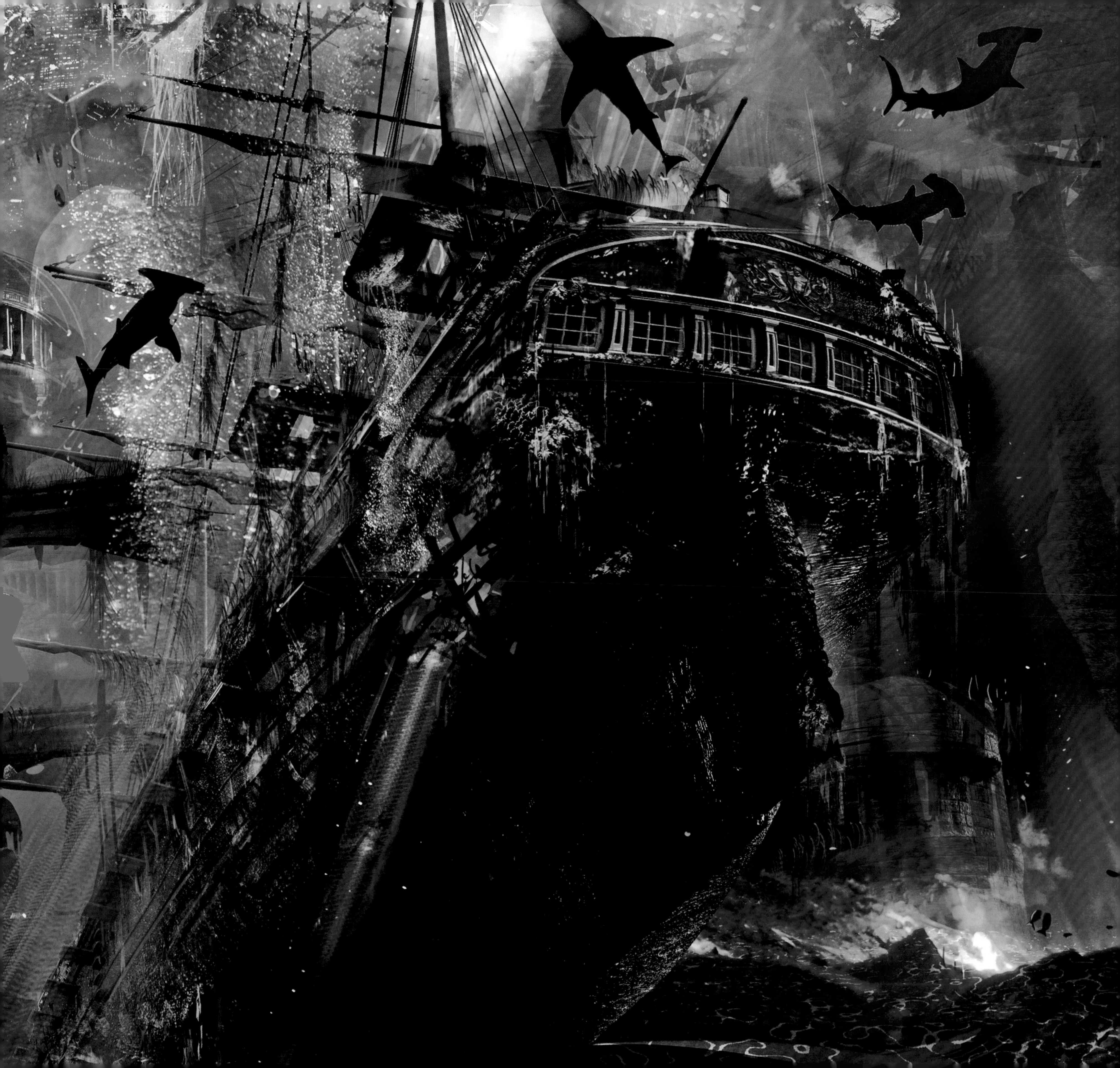

KING NEREUS

MASTER OF POLITICS

King Nereus is in a precarious position. The protection of the citizens of Xebel is his primary concern as he joins Orm at the council meeting at the Ancient Ruins. Nereus does not necessarily agree with Orm that going to war with the humans is the right decision . . . or maybe he does. The king is secretive and guarded, but those are just the surface layers of this complex character. Maintaining a balance between the love for his daughter and the needs of his people is a constant battle for the king. With every scene in which he appears, it's impossible to say which side of an argument his character will come down on.

Dolph Lundgren cuts an imposing figure as the Xebellian leader. In Lundgren's view, Nereus is a savvy political player who is playing both sides for his, and Xebel's, ultimate benefit. "What I thought was cool is my character hasn't made up his mind, and he makes some decisions that maybe aren't really good ones, but they come from a good point of view. He wants the best for his people," the actor observes. "The way I see the character is that anything kind of negative, I just do it out of necessity."

The submarine attack at the old ruins ultimately convinces the king to make an uneasy alliance with Atlantis against humanity, further straining Nereus's relationship with his daughter Mera. This comes on top of the existing Shakespearean conflict of Mera and Orm's arranged marriage, an Atlantean tradition that the Xebellian princess openly criticizes. The father-daughter bond is tested following the Ring of Fire sequence, where Mera helps Arthur escape from Atlantis. Mera questions her father's judgment and his reasons for siding with Orm, but that doesn't stop him from working alongside his new ally. Even so, Lundgren admits that those questions hit Nereus particularly hard: "She has a lot of good points. It's very painful to me to realize that she looks at me as the enemy now."

As Wan was developing *Aquaman* and fleshing out the characters, he imagined Lundgren for the role of the Xebellian ruler. Just like they did with Nicole Kidman and Atlanna, the design team incorporated Lundgren's face into the concept art before he had even been approached about joining the cast. Once the phone call was made, it was an easy decision for Lundgren. The veteran star of *Rocky IV* and *The Expendables*—and recurring character on the hit DC Comics television adaptation *Arrow*—was happy to play against type and be less involved in action sequences than usual. "It was cool for me," he says, when speaking of the strategic player whose moves are mental rather than physical. "It was different and challenging to mainly be a political figure in the movie."

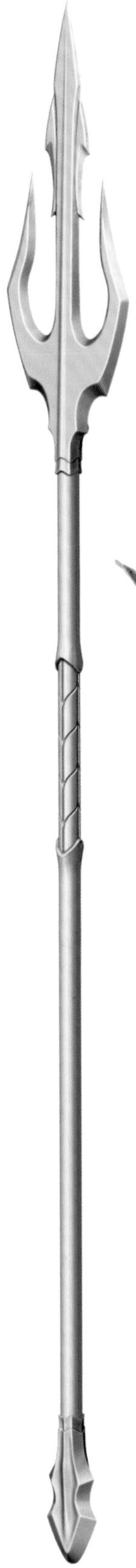

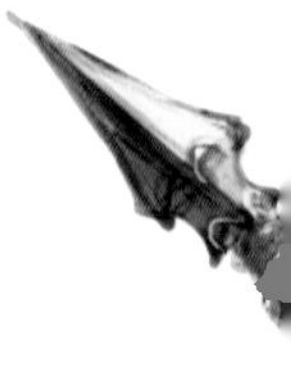

RIGHT: The trident of King Nereus, unpainted prop.
OPPOSITE LEFT: King Nereus costume concept art by James Oxford.
OPPOSITE RIGHT: Dolph Lundgren as King Nereus.
PAGES 76–77: Ruins of Ancient Atlantis concept art by Sebastian Meyer.

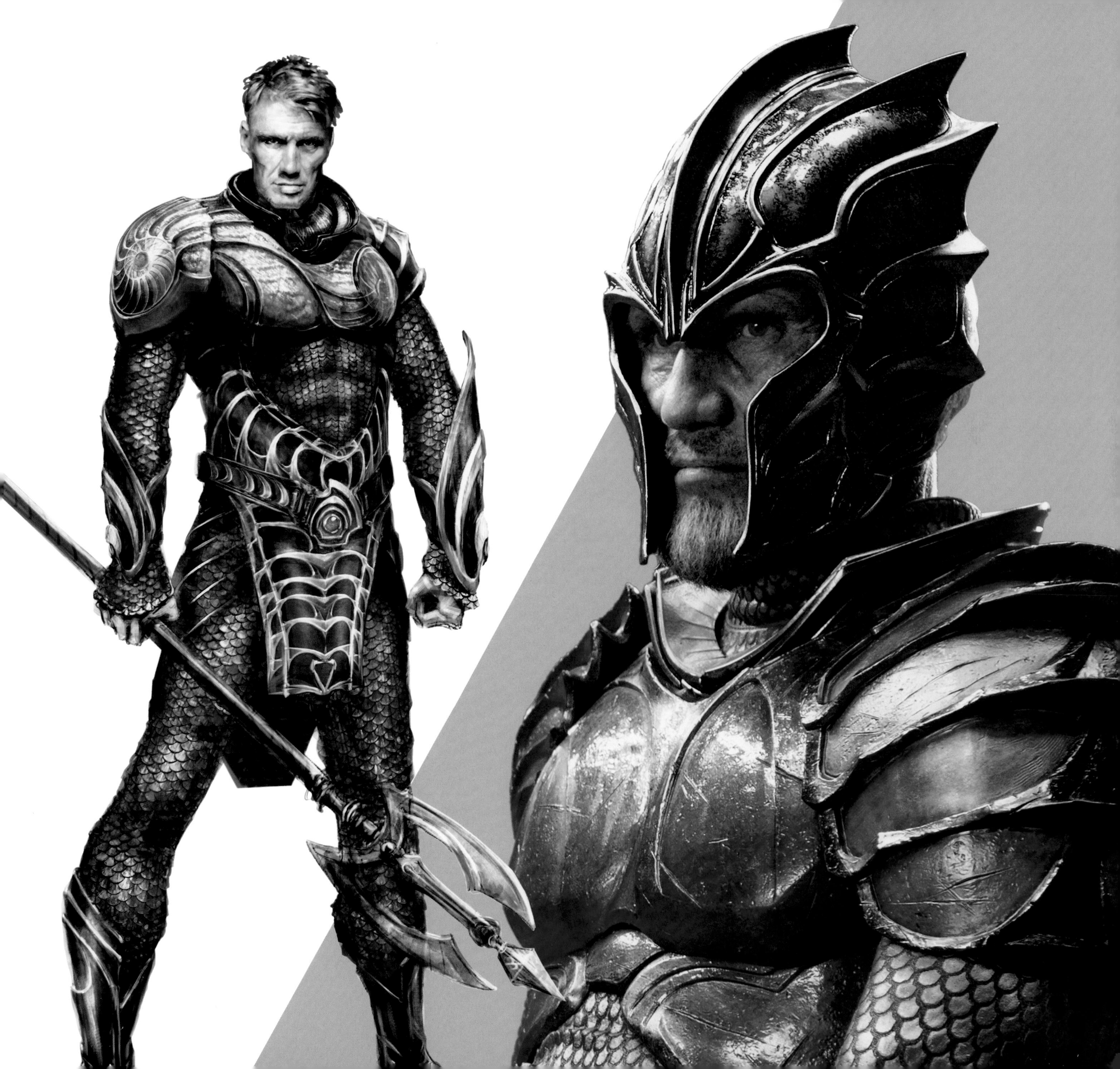

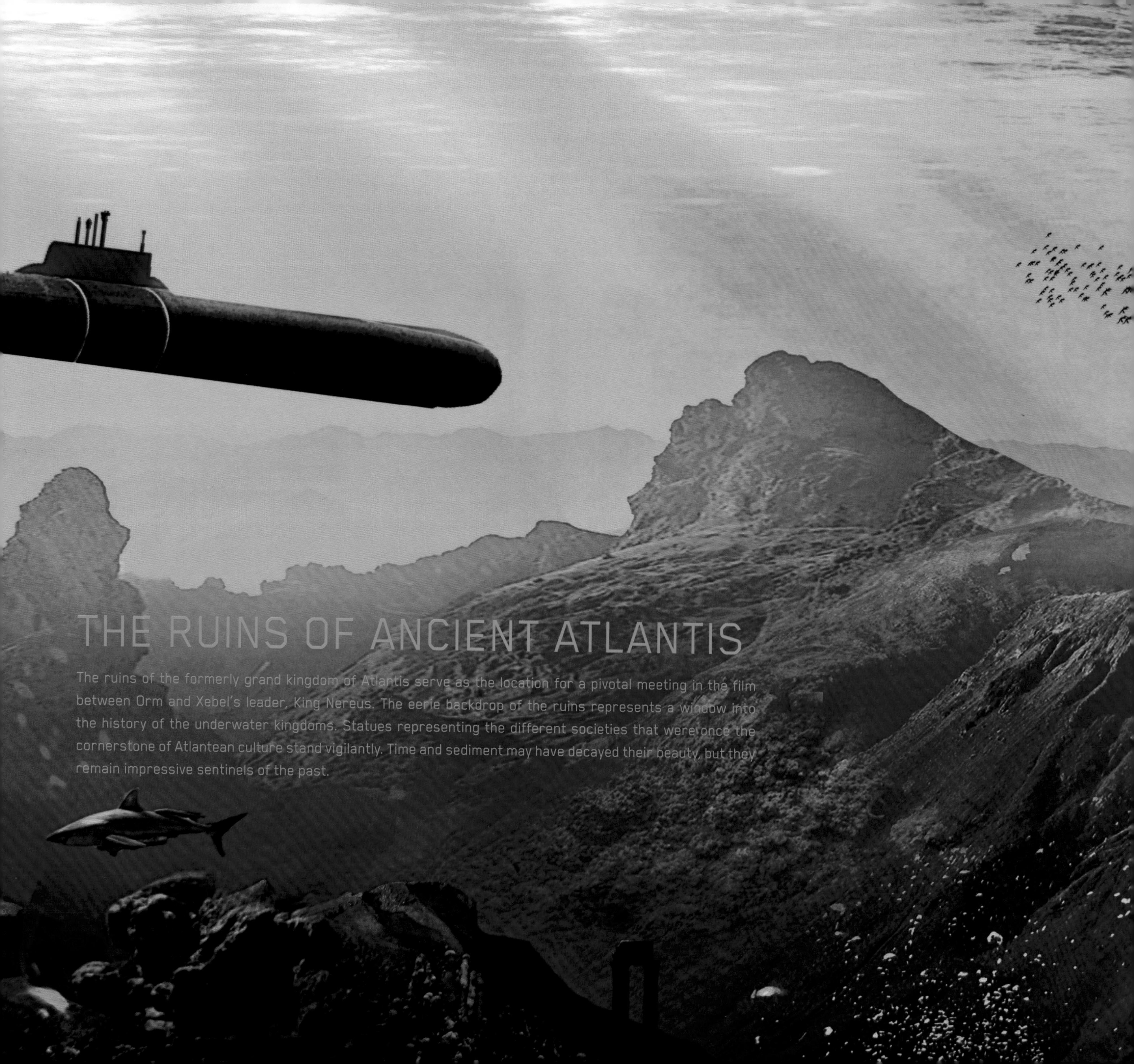

THE RUINS OF ANCIENT ATLANTIS

The ruins of the formerly grand kingdom of Atlantis serve as the location for a pivotal meeting in the film between Orm and Xebel's leader, King Nereus. The eerie backdrop of the ruins represents a window into the history of the underwater kingdoms. Statues representing the different societies that were once the cornerstone of Atlantean culture stand vigilantly. Time and sediment may have decayed their beauty, but they remain impressive sentinels of the past.

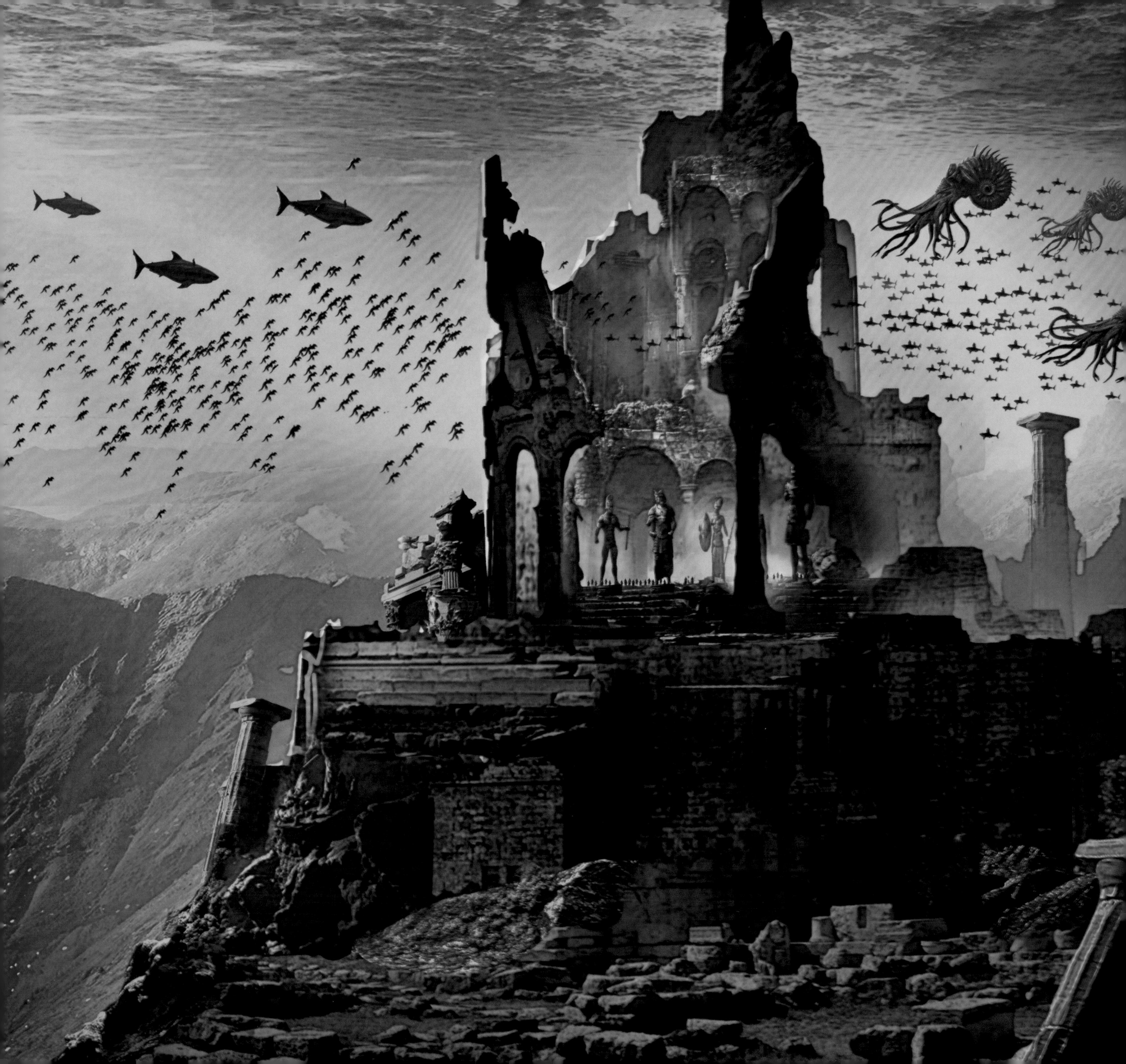

ATLANTIS

The opportunity to birth an entirely new underwater realm is a goal not many filmmakers get the chance to tackle. In making *Aquaman*, James Wan realized one of his filmmaking dreams. "I'm a big fan of world creation. I want this, in some ways, to be like my *Star Wars* in that you're creating really interesting characters," the director says. "You're creating really interesting scenarios and these huge, huge worlds, from a design standpoint. You're only limited by your own imagination."

How does one go about creating a civilization beneath the waves? For Wan and his production crew, it was a matter of arriving at the intersection of untethered imagination and plausible functionality. As Rob Cowan explains, the entire production team, led by visual effects supervisors Charlie Gibson and Kelvin McIlwain, embraced the challenge of creating a fully realized world through a combination of cutting-edge technology, material sets, and pure imagination. "A great aspect for everybody in this movie is that the production designer and the props people and the costume people, they all got to kind of let their imaginations go wild," Cowan says.

Their imaginations are on display from the first view of Atlantis, a sprawling sunken island city that provides a rare speechless moment from Arthur Curry: the first time his eyes fall upon his mother's home. The capital city is a grand masterpiece of technological sheen draped over neoclassical architecture that reveals the kingdom's ties to the past. Natural undersea mountain ranges serve as a protective wall around the city. A gleaming gateway bridge is the only entrance point, a relic of the old Atlantis before it sank beneath the waves, back when the population walked on two feet. Modern-day Atlantis is a three-dimensional city unbound from gravity. There are no stairs or roads beyond that lone bridge. Water powers vertical subway-like trains—organic technological marvels. Bioluminescence from enormous Portuguese men-of-war bathes the metropolis in natural light, while a massive power wheel pumps organic light throughout Atlantis. "As a result, everything in Atlantis shimmers and glows," Brzeski explains. That wheel helped create what amounts to night and day below the surface, giving Atlanteans and the other undersea cultures a circadian rhythm, a natural sleep-wake cycle. Meanwhile, Atlantean soldiers on armored sharks and other sea creatures maintain patrol, with hydrocannons positioned by the bridge to protect against invaders.

Wan and the production team established parameters for how Atlantis should function. Functionality was as important as visual flair. Wan emphasized that his job as director included understanding what life is like for the Atlantean people: "How do they eat? How do they sleep? How do they use the bathroom? You have to think about all that stuff. All of it affects the world you're trying to create." That thought process extended beyond Atlantis to the creation of the other kingdoms, but Atlantis was the epicenter of the design process. Once the production knew how Atlantis worked, that knowledge helped them build out the infrastructure of the rest of the kingdoms.

RIGHT: Atlantis gateway bridge concept art by Christian Scheurer.
PAGES 80-81: City of Atlantis concept art by Christian Scheurer.

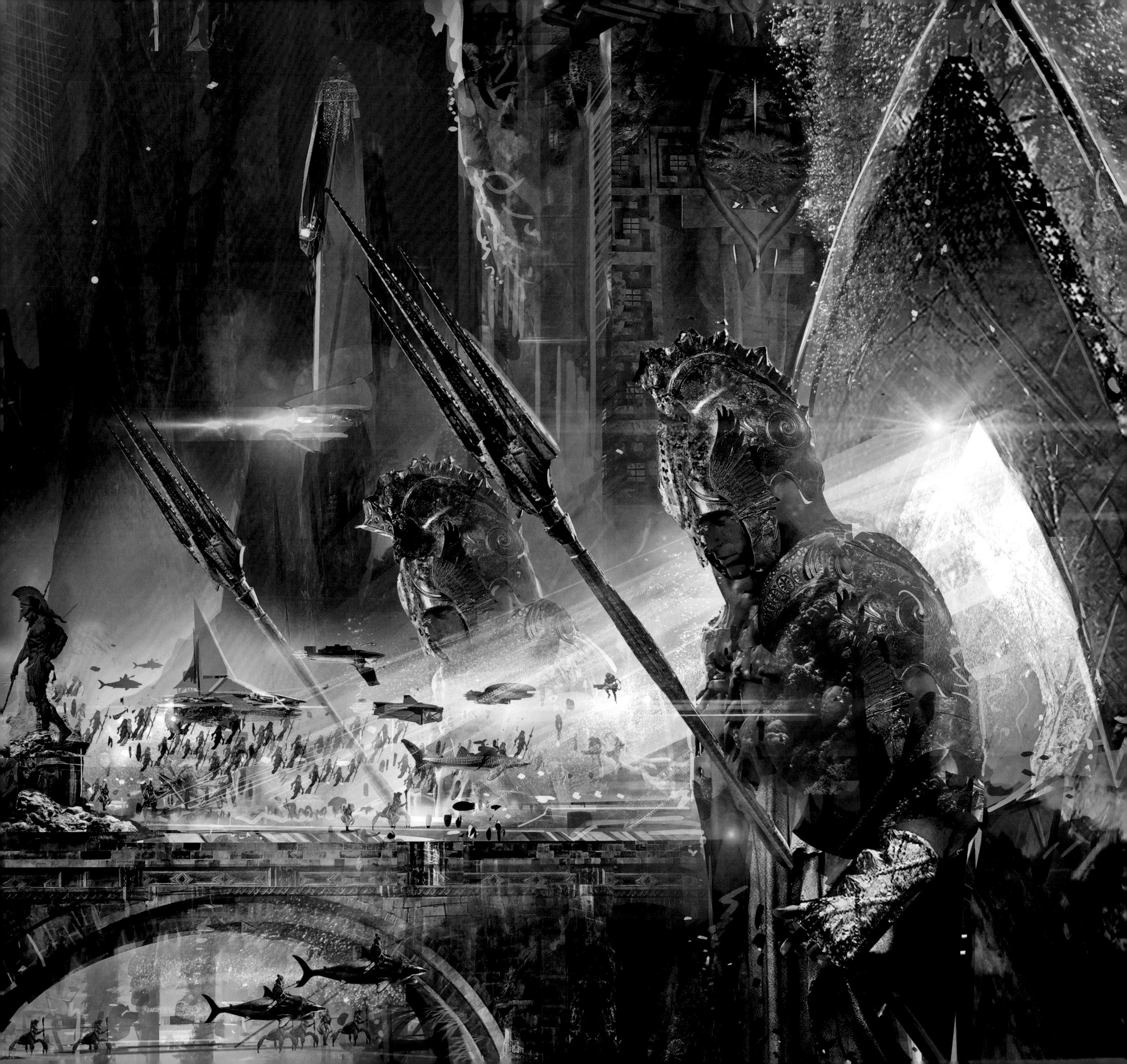

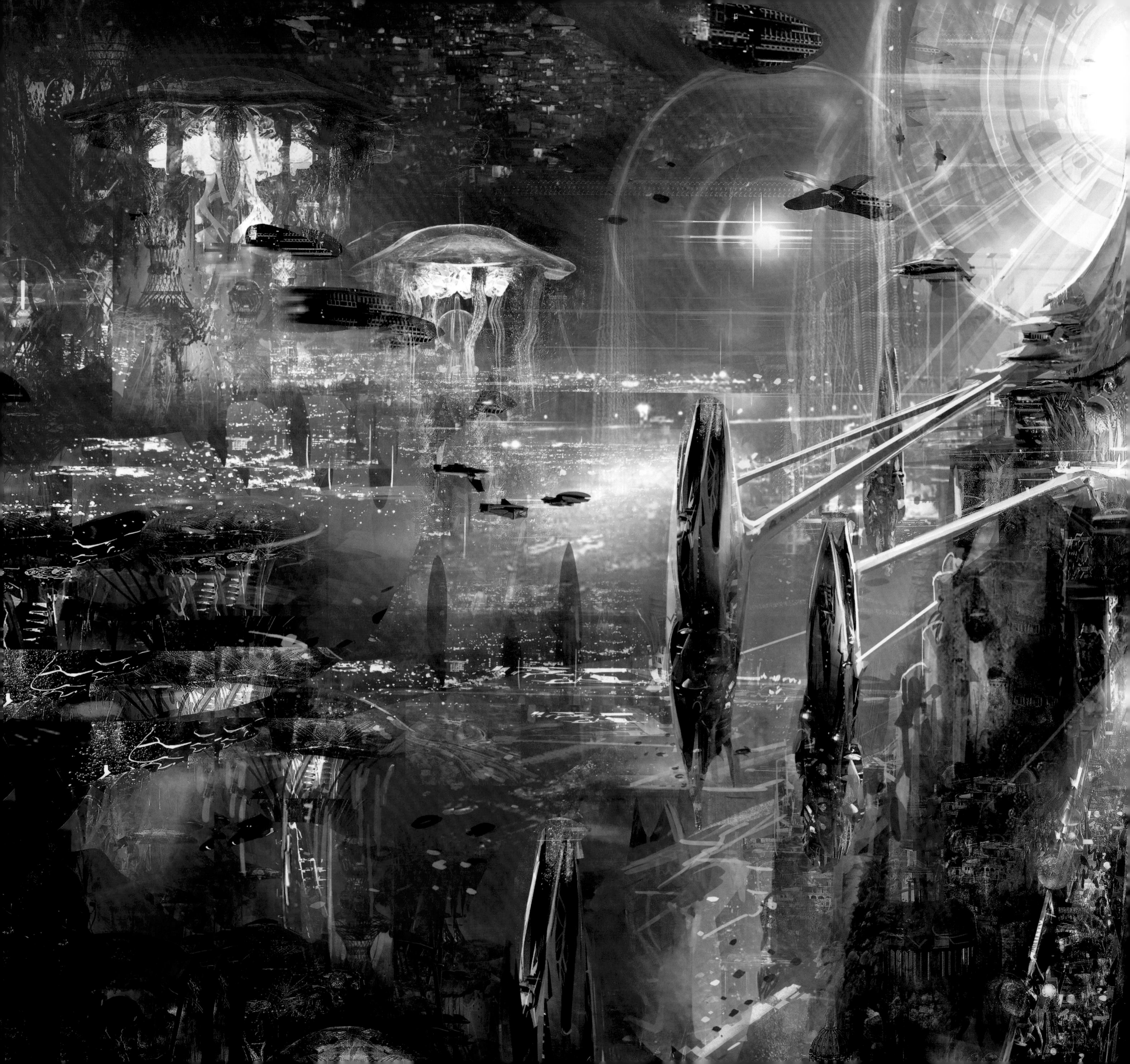

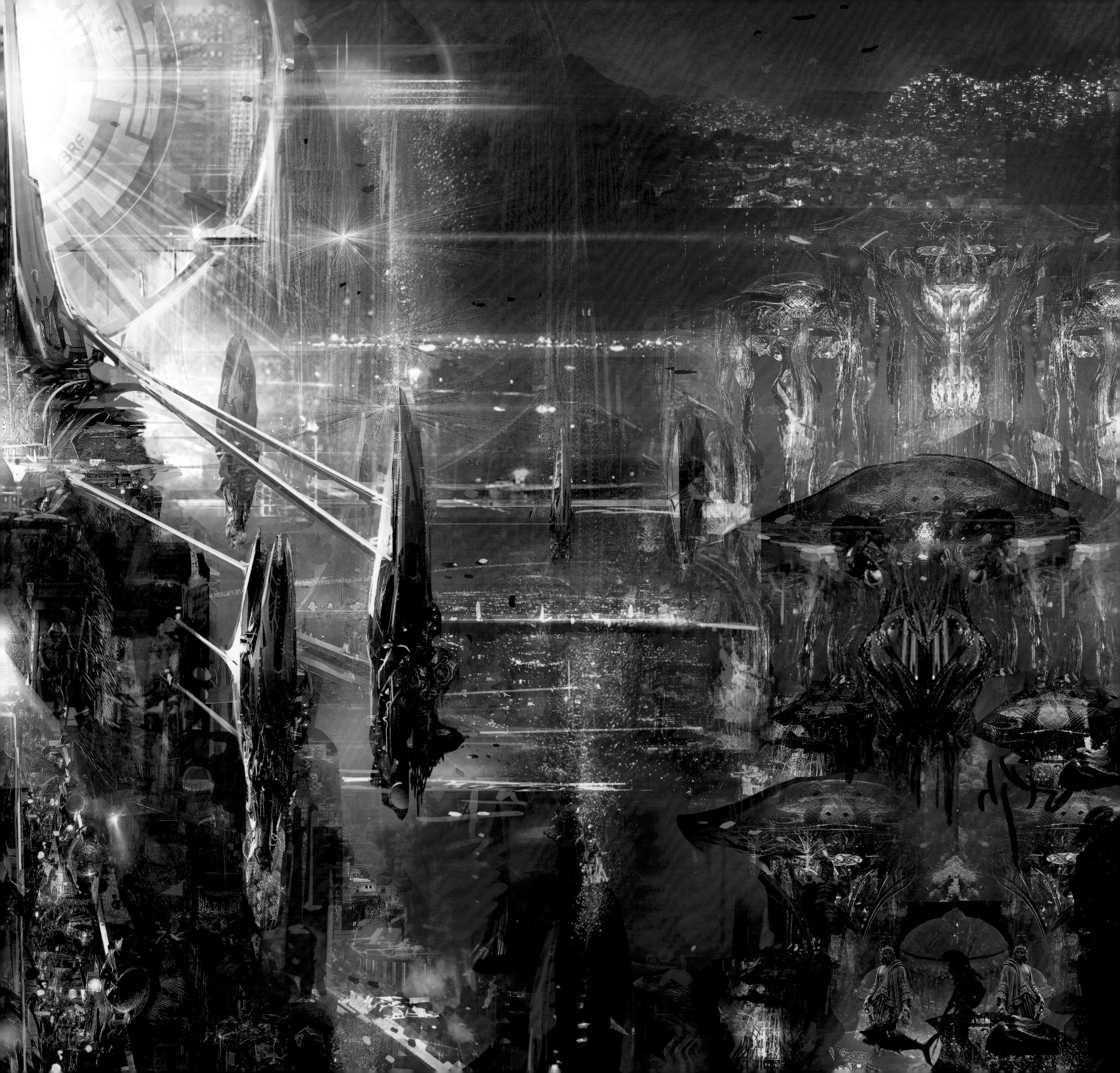

ATLANTEAN ARMOR

"The design of the armor for the elite Atlantean soldier shows a much bulkier, more militaristic design than other armors in the film.

"James really wanted to have people fighting in suits of armor. I said to myself, 'If they did have suits of armor, they would be made from really tough, engineered fish scales.' They would look metallic, and James said just to make it as macho as we could.

"We came up with scenarios that would suggest that the Atlantean armor would almost serve as camouflage as they neared the surface. If humans would see a school of dolphins or sharks, they wouldn't notice the Atlantean soldiers swimming alongside because the water-based armor would change colors to resemble the water at the surface point."

—Kym Barrett, Costume Designer

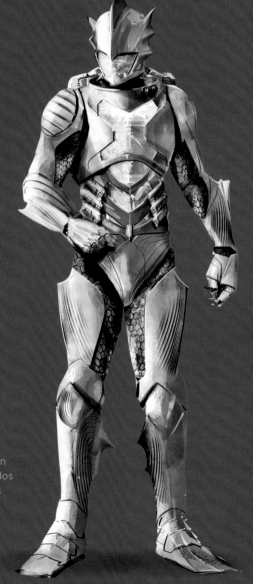
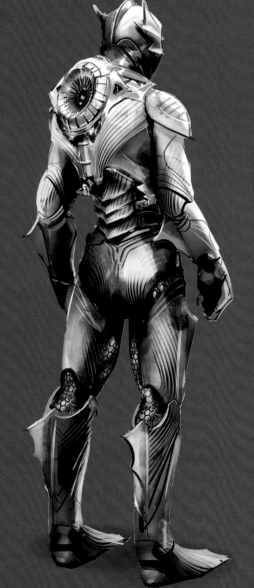

THESE PAGES: Atlantean armor for elite commandos (*left*), traditional soldiers (*right*), and ship digital renders by Ed Natividad.

ATLANTEAN VESSELS

ATLANTEAN WATER BALLISTIC STUDY

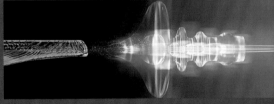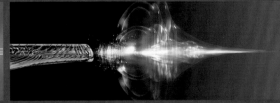

"The guns were our ultimate design challenge. The guards had very bulky armor so it was important to factor in having an ergonomic shape. The Atlantean guards' guns are know as 'hydropulse rifles' and are obviously water powered as usual firepower was never going to fly down there. I initially collected a bunch of sample shells to show James potential finishes and with the Atlantean guards he was instantly sold on a mother-of-pearl finish. So began our long process of designing, cutting silhouettes, then our first prototypes. I think we had about ten show-and-tells before we produced what we see on-screen. Then there was the lighting for the guns that was a very complicated first, which was controlled through the mixing desk. Our inspiration for the lighting was the strange bioluminescent deep-sea creatures that light up the deepest parts of the sea. It certainly gave us more intensity, which was an important selling point."

—Richie Dehne, Prop Master

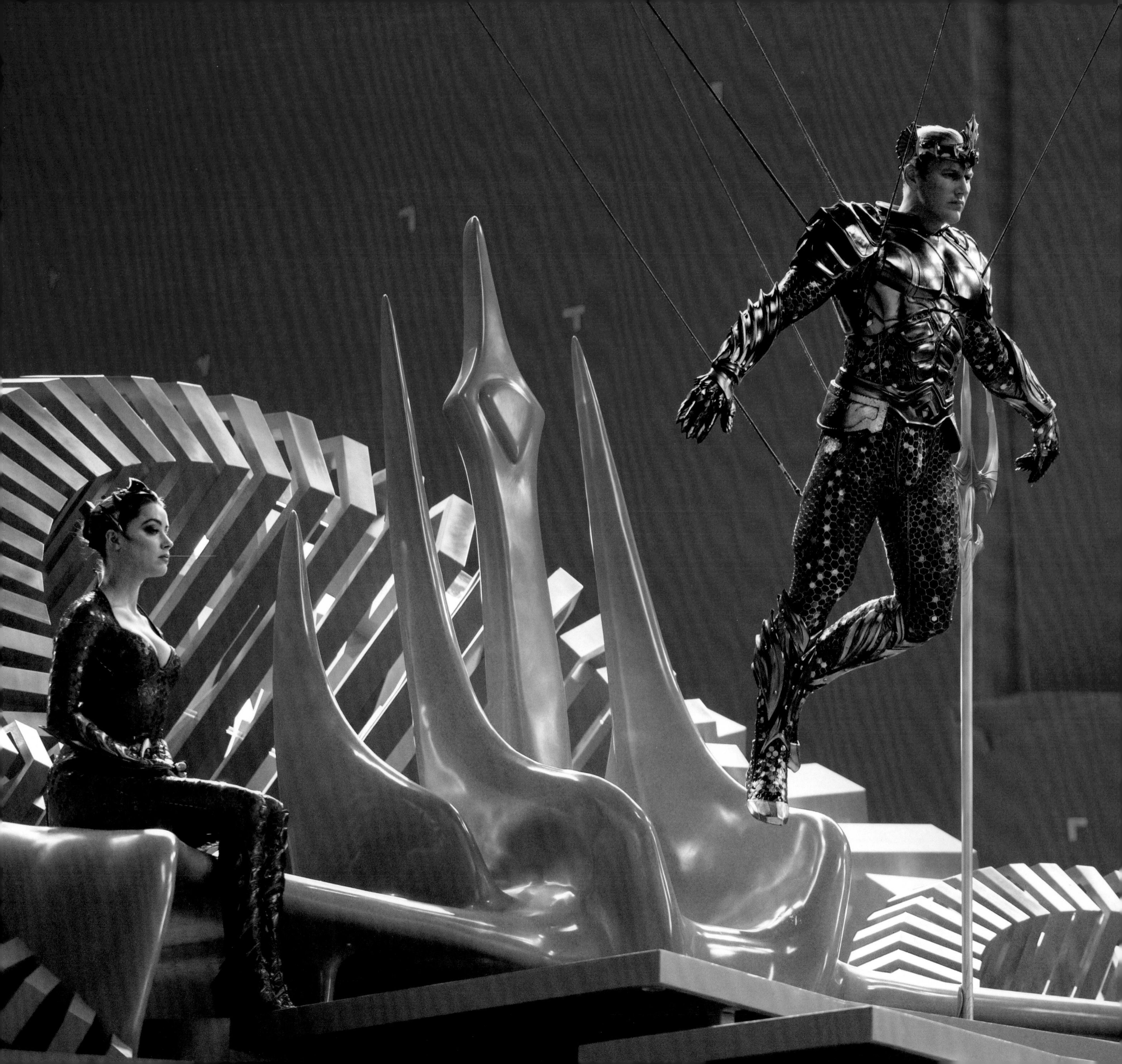

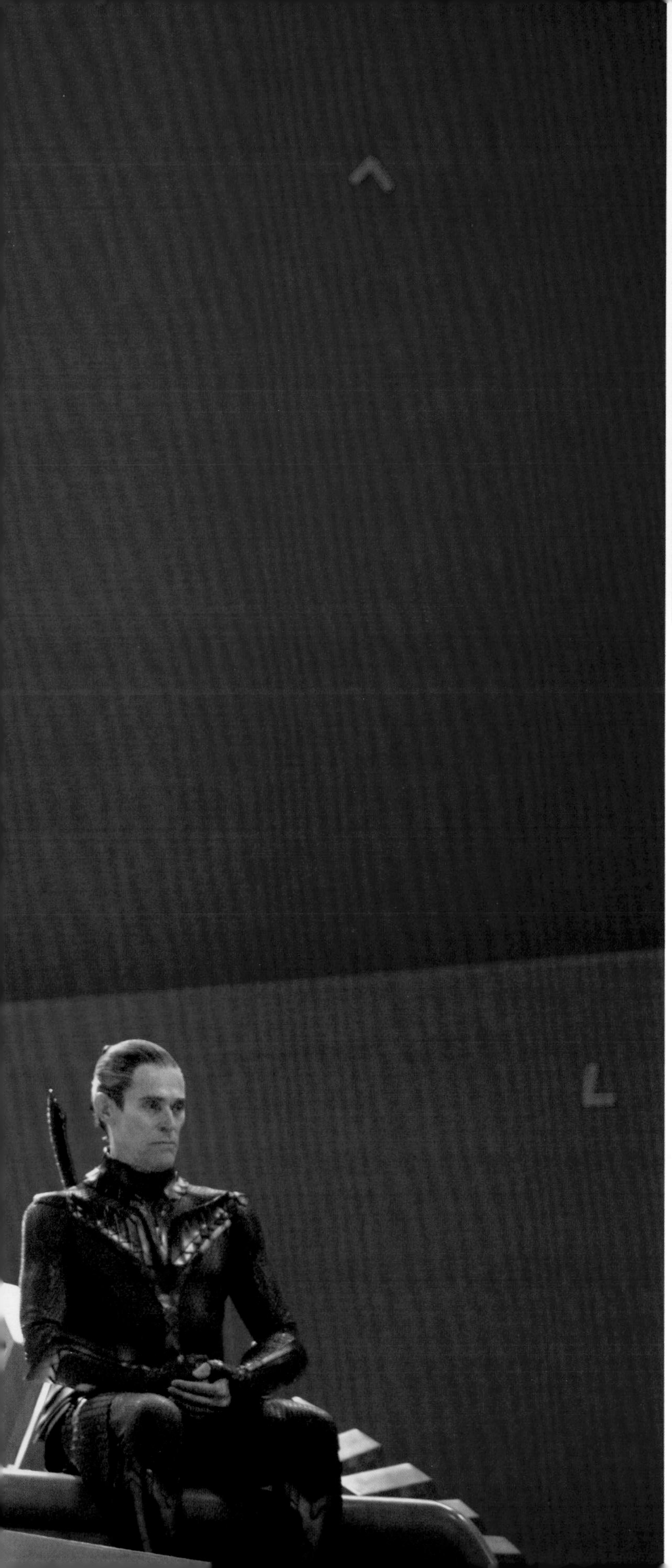

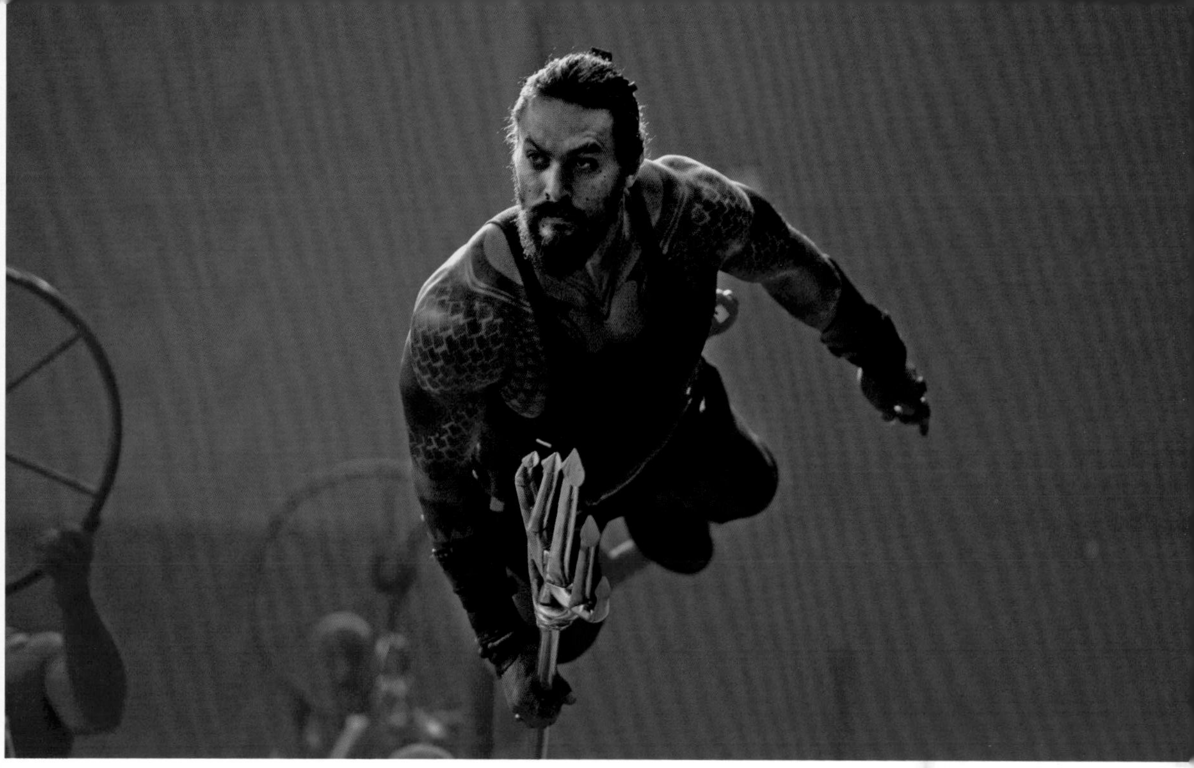

DRY FOR WET: MAKING AN AQUATIC FILM

In moviemaking circles, shooting a water-based motion picture is known to be a filmmaker's folly. It's an immense logistical challenge filled with unpredictability. Hollywood history is dotted with stories of productions that have witnessed firsthand the fickle nature of the oceans. There is no getting around that particular obstacle when you're filming a movie called *Aquaman*. How do you shoot a movie set in an underwater kingdom and properly capture the actors having conversations, extended fight scenes, and so forth? The answer, it turned out, was on dry land.

A surprisingly small amount of time was actually spent shooting in water. James Wan took the bold step of shooting many of the film's underwater scenes in dry-for-wet style. Essentially, that means the scene is filmed with the actor against a blue screen, and then the volume of water is digitally added to the scene in postproduction. The actors' hair was tied back and reentered via CGI later to capture the movement of the hair. The process also involved complex wirework for the action scenes, and camera rigs such as the mambo and gimbal rides were specifically designed for the production to capture certain sequences. As producer Peter Safran notes, this movie most likely couldn't have been made a decade or even five years earlier because of the massive technological work required. "If two-thirds of your movie is set under the water, but we're shooting it dry, how do you give the actors a natural sense of buoyancy?" Safran asks, running through the challenges they faced in filming. "How do

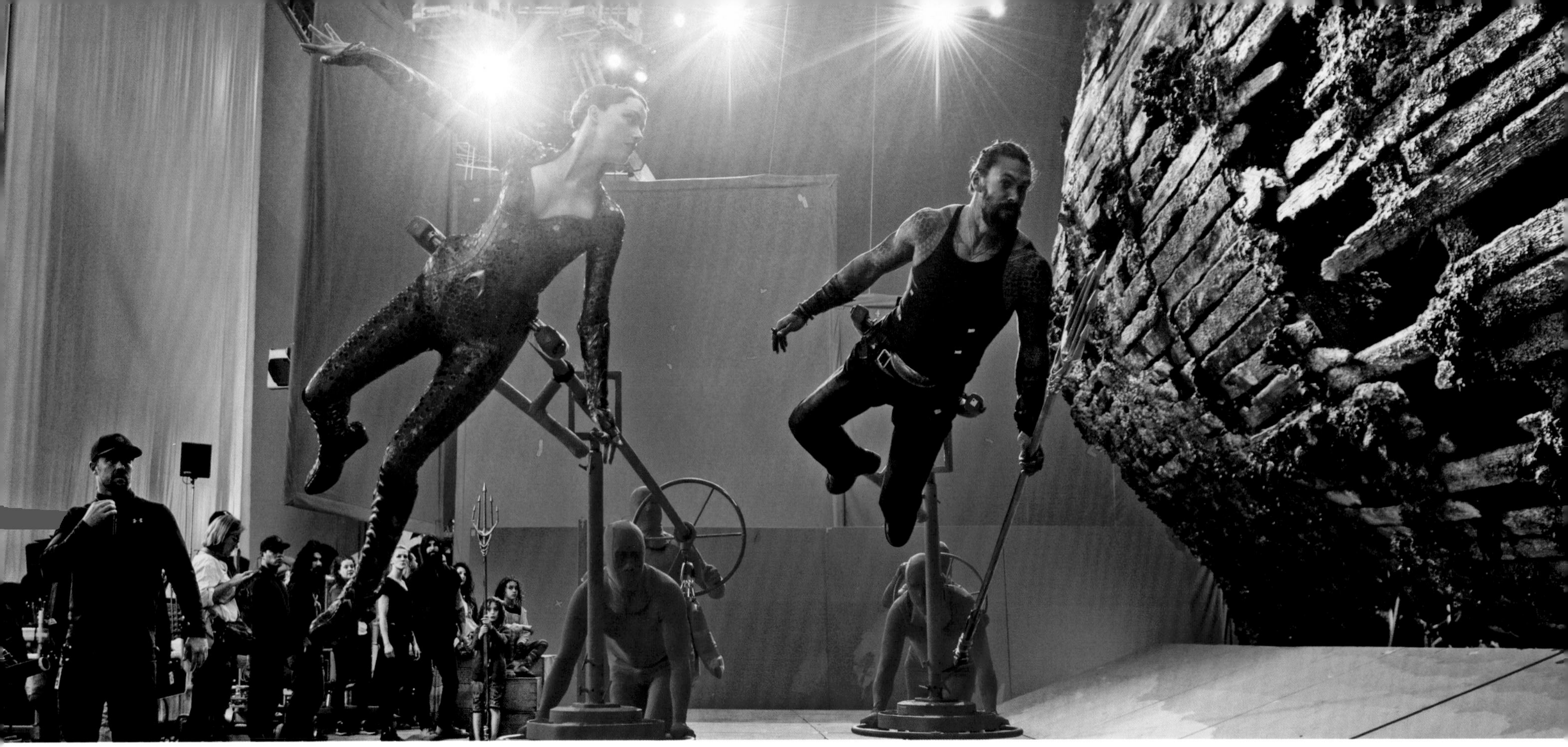

you give them the movement they would have underwater so it's not just people standing on the surface?"

These were difficult questions to answer. To properly capture the natural buoyancy of the zero-gravity world of Atlantis, many different production workarounds came into play. A harness system the crew called a "tuning fork" was used to help maintain consistency in the buoyancy of the actors. It was placed at the actors' hips for balance. Amber Heard, who plays Mera, says the device is exactly what it sounds like: "Imagine you're in between the prongs of a giant fork. What you do is hold your body into a position. It's a bit like doing a plank at the gym. It's a bit strange because I had to appear as if I was underwater in the middle of an empty studio."

"We used a number of variations on the tuning fork," explains visual effects supervisor Kelvin McIlwain. "We had one that was called 'the mambo.' Essentially, you have a rolling base that acts like the fulcrum and so your actor is on one end of the tuning fork, which is literally just a steel pole that bifurcates and is attached to the actors' hips. On the other end of the fulcrum, you have a counterweight, and a couple of stunt guys who are manipulating it. They can take the actor up and down, and because the fulcrum is on wheels, they can glide them around and puppeteer them through space. That was probably the preferred method, because it allowed us to get the actors in and out of the rigs relatively quickly. It also allowed you to manipulate them over and drop them down onto the ground so they could rest when the cameras weren't rolling." The crew also had tuning forks that hung from the ceiling that allowed them to do the larger moves as well as spin harnesses that provided 360 degrees of movement. "It's a hoop that goes around the actor's waist that has bearings in it," McIlwain continues. "It allows them to spin freely within the tuning fork. This was particularly useful in fight sequences where the actors needed to turn their bodies around in quick motion."

Other times, old-style studio camera pedestals like those used on sitcom productions were brought in because they

PAGES 84–86: A system of wires and devices the crew called tuning forks allowed the production to create underwater movement on land.

OPPOSITE: Postproduction added in the undersea environment, even re-creating actors' hair to mimic flowing underwater.

have air-pressure canisters that let operators raise and lower them. The crew put mounts on them so actors wearing blue-screen motion-capture suits could be wheeled around to simulate movement in the deep ocean waters. Another tool was a new bit of technology the crew called the "fancy cam." When the fancy cam is pointed at the blue screen on a particular monitor, the filmmakers can see the background that will ultimately fill in that shot, or at least a version of it. As Safran explains, it's incredibly helpful because it allows the director, the effects people, and even the actors to adjust and compensate for the scope and scale of the environment they are occupying in that scene.

Another adjustment, of a different sort, was made when the production team decided to film the proxy sets on a blue screen rather than the more common green. This was done for a few reasons. "When you're in a world of color and you're going to be in it for a good amount of time, blue screen is just much easier to deal with, psychologically, than green," explains visual effects supervisor Kelvin McIlwain. "The last movie I worked on that was shot on film was *Fast & Furious 6*. Green screen was used because it allowed for better usage of mattes, and provided better quality edges from the green emulsion layer of film than you do with blue. With film, blue screen tended to be grainier and give rougher edges than you wanted. Since *Aquaman* is all shot digitally, the blue channels now are very clean and not noisy, so it's easier to use blue now."

Relying on blue screen helped for other reasons, McIlwain continues: "A lot of our environments tend to be blue based, so when you're shooting the actors in a blue-screen world, a lot of color gets cast on them. Now if I needed to put them in a different environment, then I have to process out a lot of that light spill. But because they're in an underwater, very blue-tinted environment, I can leave a lot of that blue spill from the screen in their skin tones because it's something that we already need to be there."

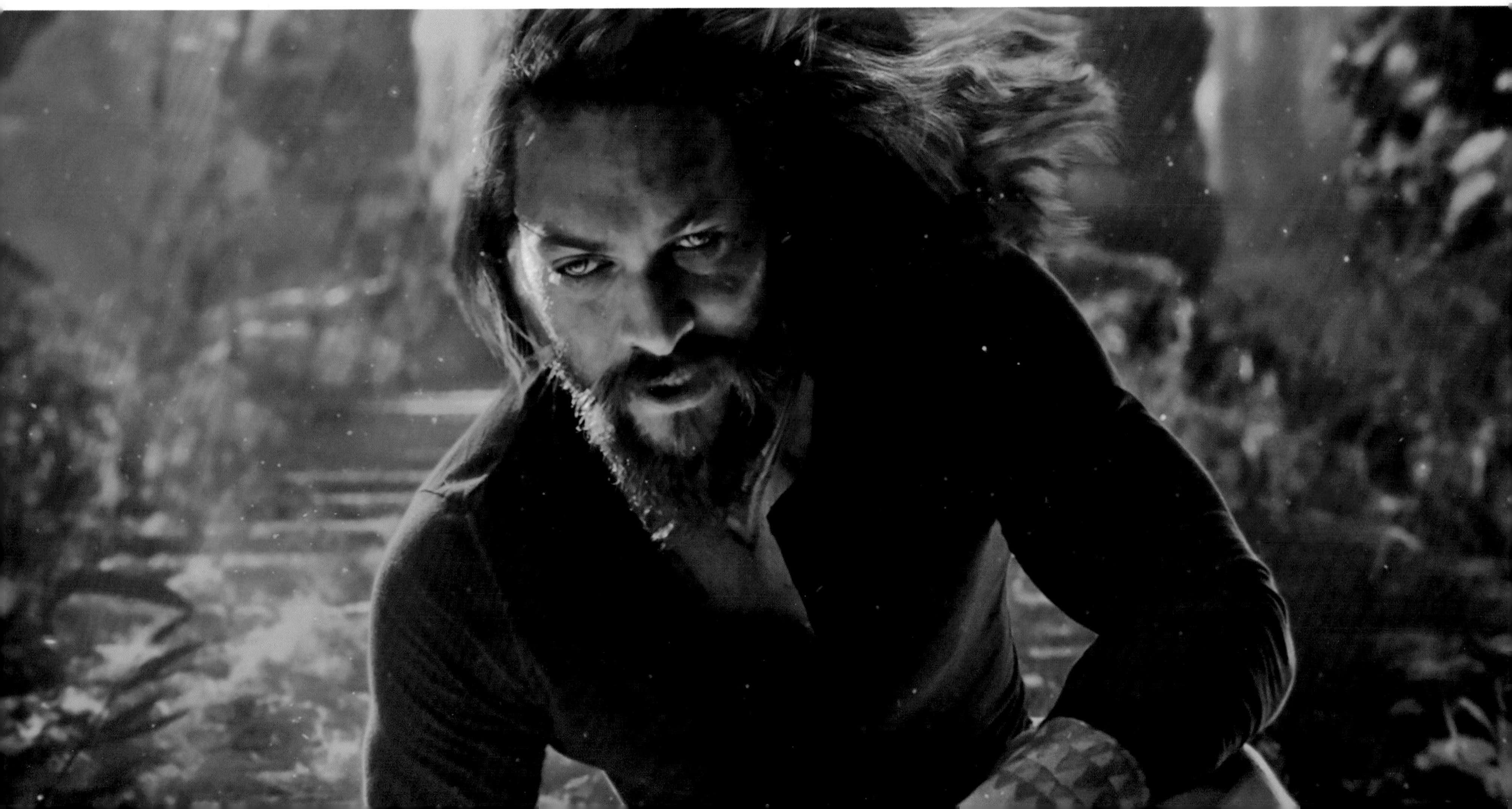

THE RING OF FIRE

One of the standout set pieces in the film is the Ring of Fire sequence, after Arthur is baited into accepting a challenge to fight Orm in a ritual combat. Although the battle comes relatively early in the film, it's also something of a culmination to the years of tension between the half brothers who only just met. All this time, Orm has blamed Arthur for their mother's death simply because of Arthur's mixed-heritage existence. This formal Atlantean battle takes place in the cone of a bubbling undersea volcano, and it is the perfect opportunity for Orm to take his revenge.

It's a dramatic showdown with both combatants in battle armor, squaring off in an arena with thousands of Atlanteans in attendance, including Mera, Vulko, and other luminaries watching from the royal box. The influence of Roman and Greek architecture is evident in the grand and dramatic landscape of Atlantis. And just as it was for the Romans, the coliseum is the epicenter of entertainment for Atlanteans.

Despite the intermittent training in proper Atlantean combat that Arthur received from Vulko over the years, he is outclassed in this fight by his more disciplined half brother. As Patrick Wilson observes, "This is Orm's world. Arthur has to come fight on my turf. It's what makes this part of the movie so dynamic, that [Arthur] is uncomfortable. This is my world and things move a little differently here. It's definitely a great equalizer between us in the fight."

The staging of this scene once again shows the alchemy of practical set builds and cutting-edge visual effects technology. The hand-to-hand fight sequence between Momoa and Wilson involved traditional stunt wirework—with stunt doubles stepping in for the more difficult elements— shot against a blue screen on a small soundstage in Australia. But other challenges were unique to this project. Because this is a fight between water breathers at the bottom of the ocean, the tuning forks were used again to hoist the actors (and stunt doubles) in the air and replicate how they would float underwater. "Within the tuning forks, we sometimes had the spin harness as well," explains Kelvin McIlwain, the film's visual effects supervisor. As he described earlier, the harness locked around the waist of the actor or stunt person, permitting them to spin freely within the tuning fork. This opened up the fight choreography, allowing performers to move more fluidly than they would if they were earthbound or strung up on wires.

ABOVE: Arthur's gladiator costume concept art by James Oxford.
RIGHT: Ring of Fire concept art by Christian Scheurer.

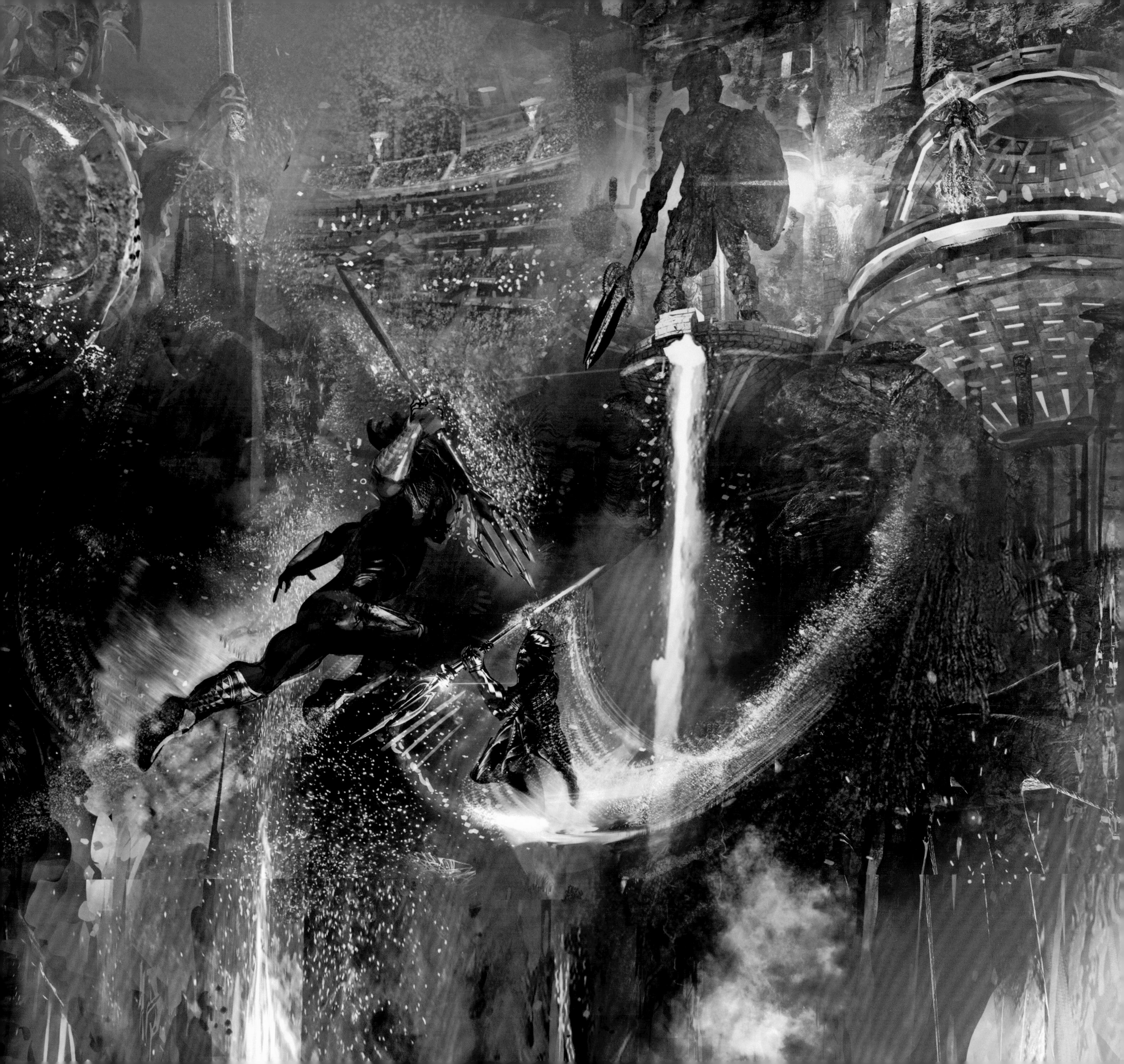

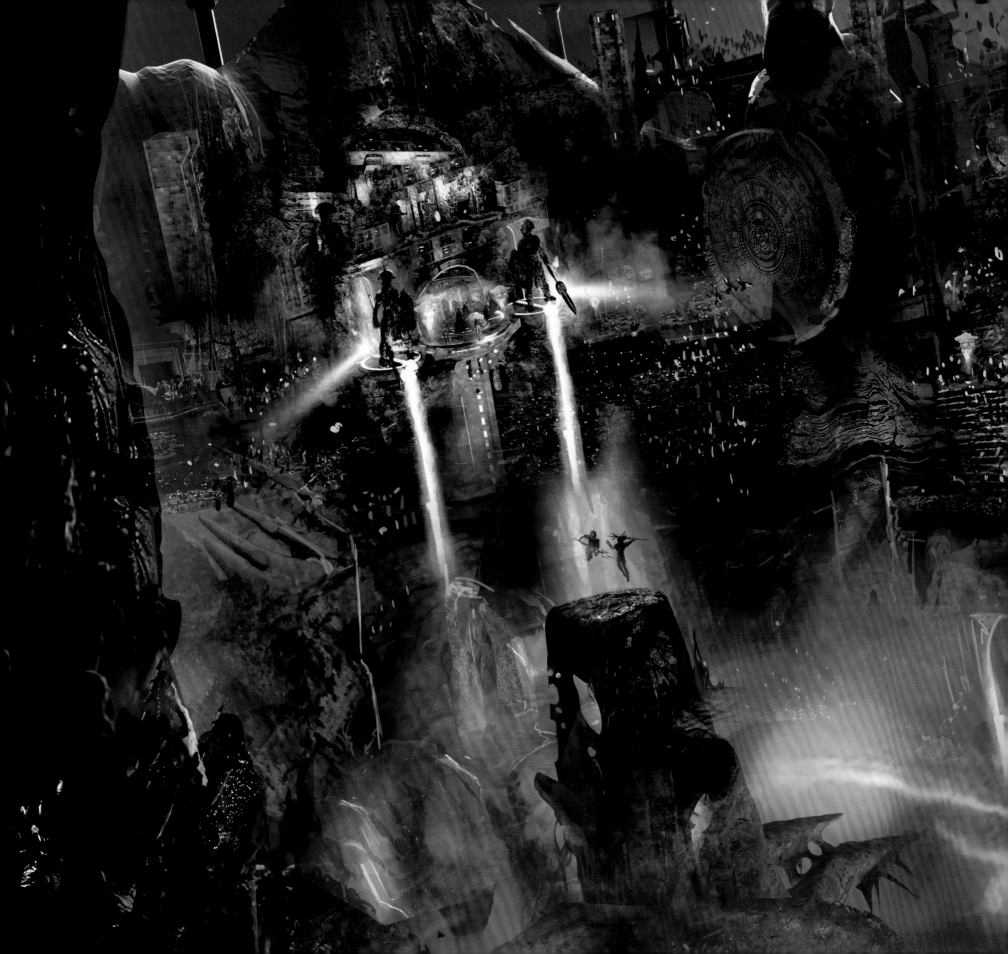

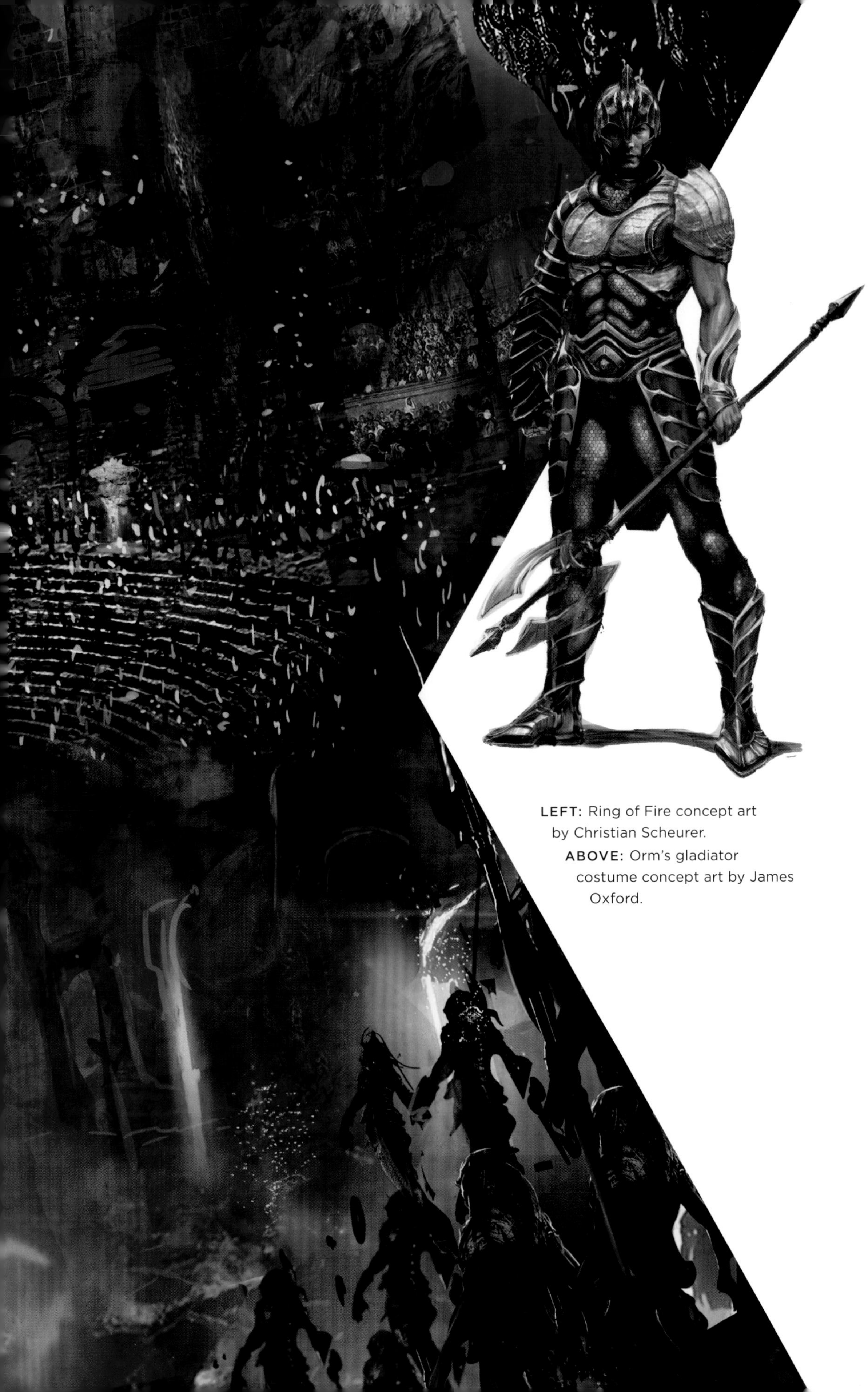

LEFT: Ring of Fire concept art by Christian Scheurer.
ABOVE: Orm's gladiator costume concept art by James Oxford.

On a set so separated from reality, Wilson found it helpful to walk through the storyboarded sequence, see the rudimentary concept designs, and view the scenes on the real background. All this helped him envision where Orm and Aquaman's battle fits in to the greater landscape. "You've got to imagine that stuff," Wilson explains. "'Wait, so what are those? Oh, that's lava. But I'm underwater! Okay, all right.' It's just trying to understand what the scene is because there is so much blue screen. Thank God we have that technology that we can at least see a little video of what we're about to be a part of."

The visual effects team turned the footage into a finished product that placed the battle in a majestic arena with an elevated rock platform, surrounded by a ring of volcanic fire. "That's what we do with our scenery now, we call it 'proxy scenery,'" Bill Brzeski explains. "It's useful for visual effects because what they do is, they texture it and they use the light reference from it." The result is a sequence that resembles a subaquatic Roman gladiator showdown. The physical battle chamber set provided Momoa and Wilson with the proxy markers they needed to understand how the choreography of the scene would play out. "We put up walls and painted them, along with plastic tubes with LED lights in them to effectively be stand-ins for the bolts of lava," Brzeski said. "That helped the actors know where they would be moving past, and also helps with the lighting."

The staging of this scene, shot over two days with as many as ten cameras in use, once again exemplified the helpful alchemy of practical set builds and cutting-edge visual effects technology. As McIlwain pointed out earlier, the proxy sets the production used created reflections that played off the shiny surfaces of the gladiator costumes, which helped ground the scenes in the location. The proxy sets also built out that location by providing makeshift bleachers for a few dozen extras to fill. Those extras in the bleachers were repeated digitally, growing them into a huge viewing audience that enhanced the battle scene, building it into a major moment in the film.

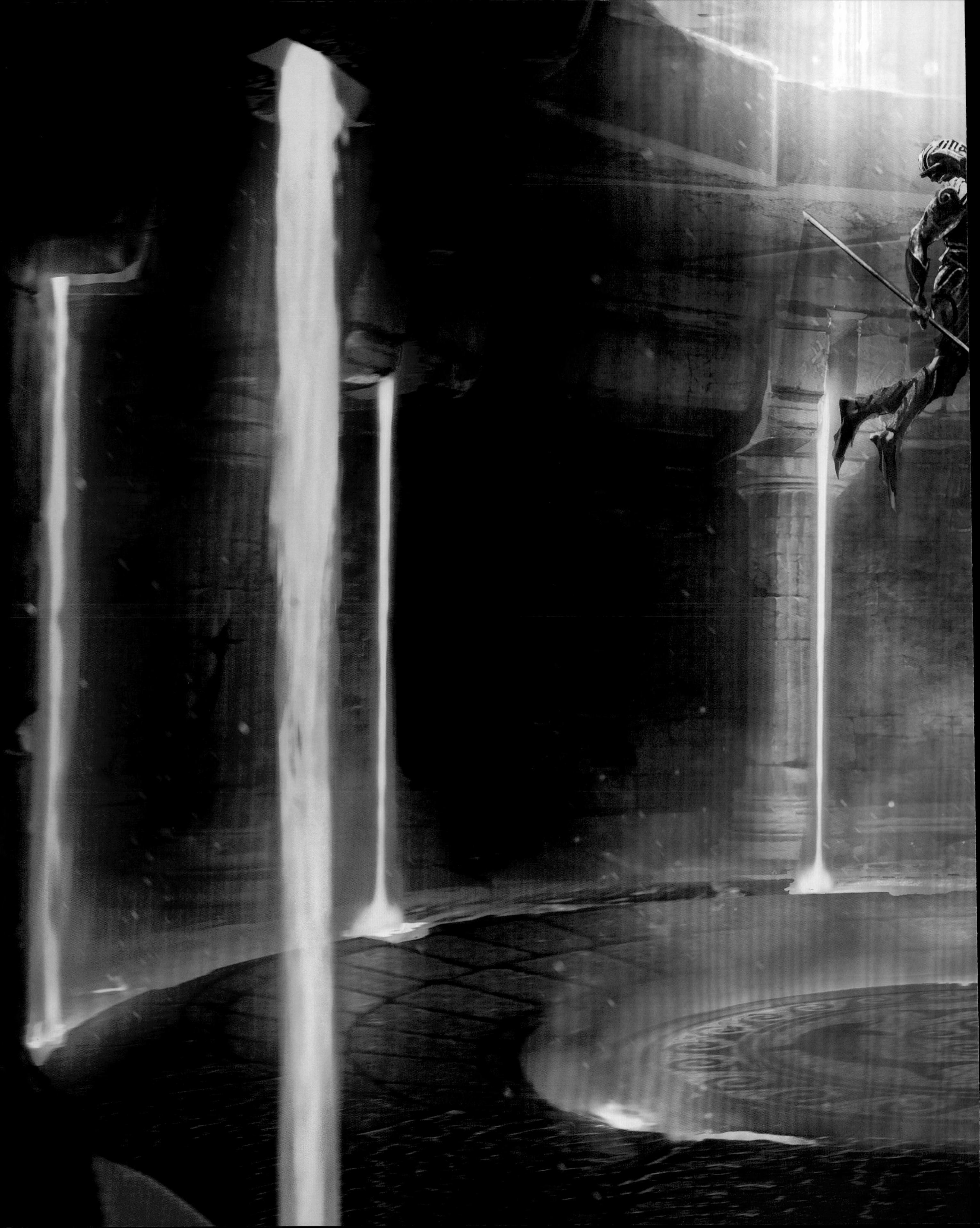

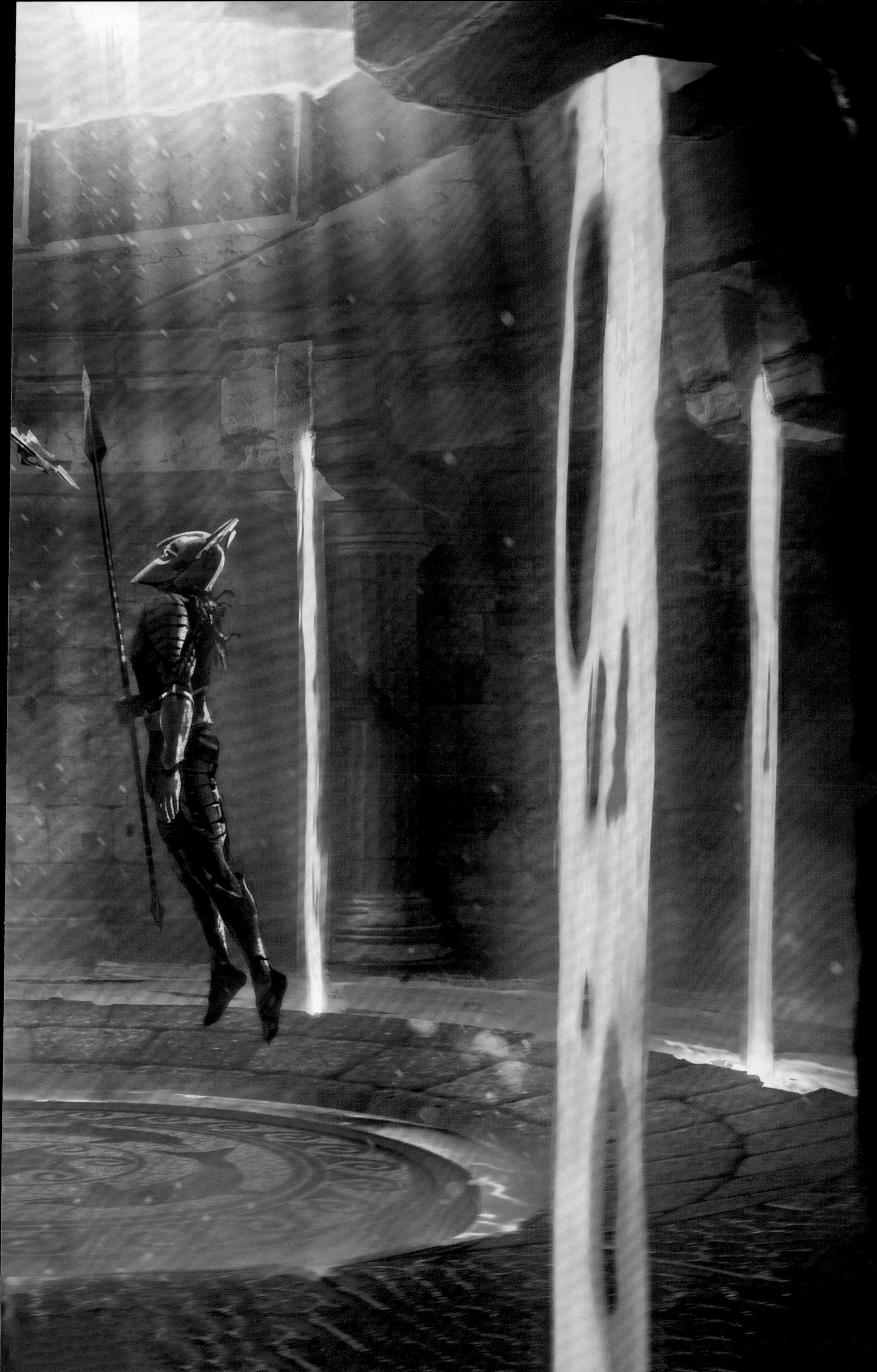

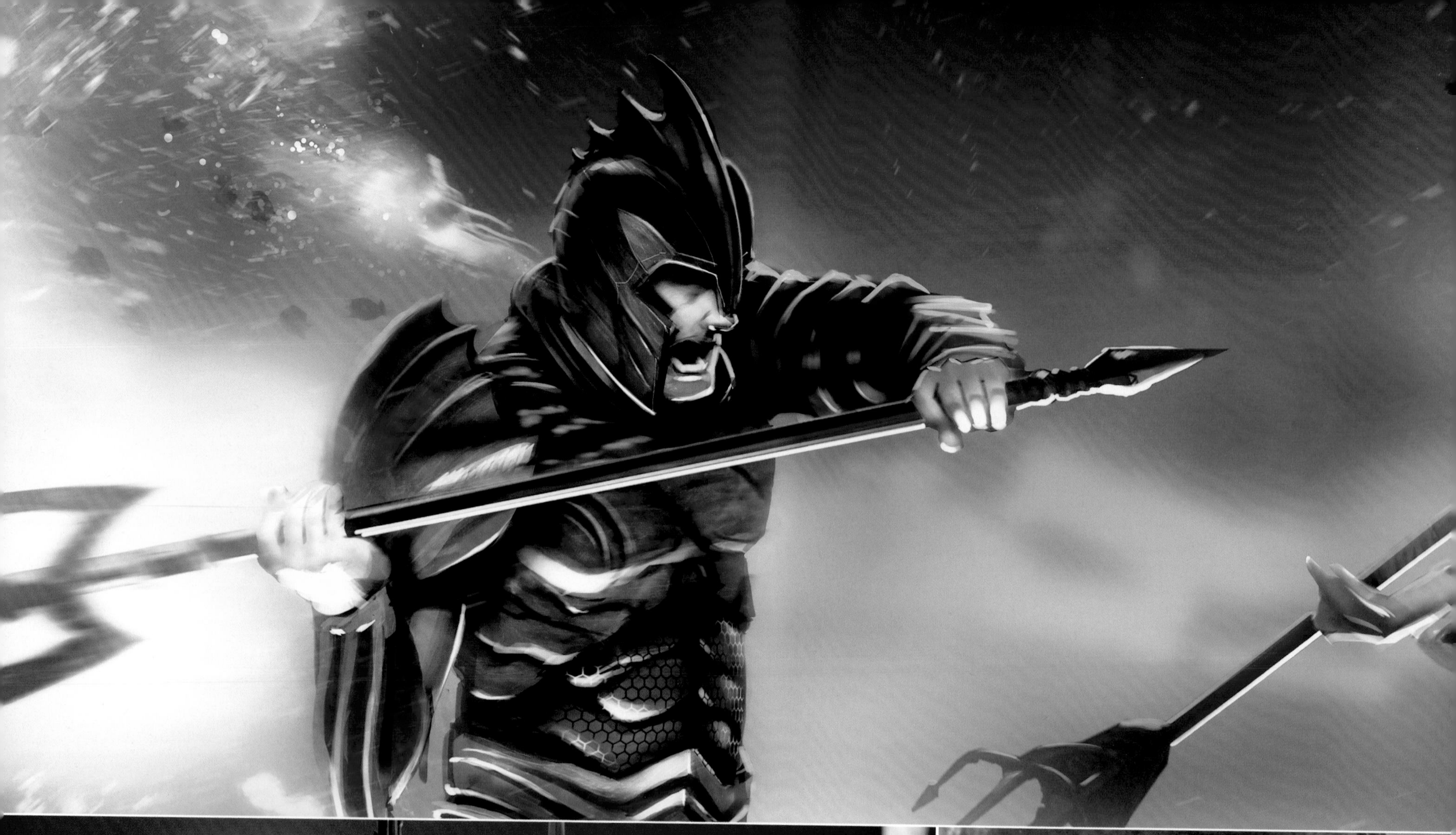
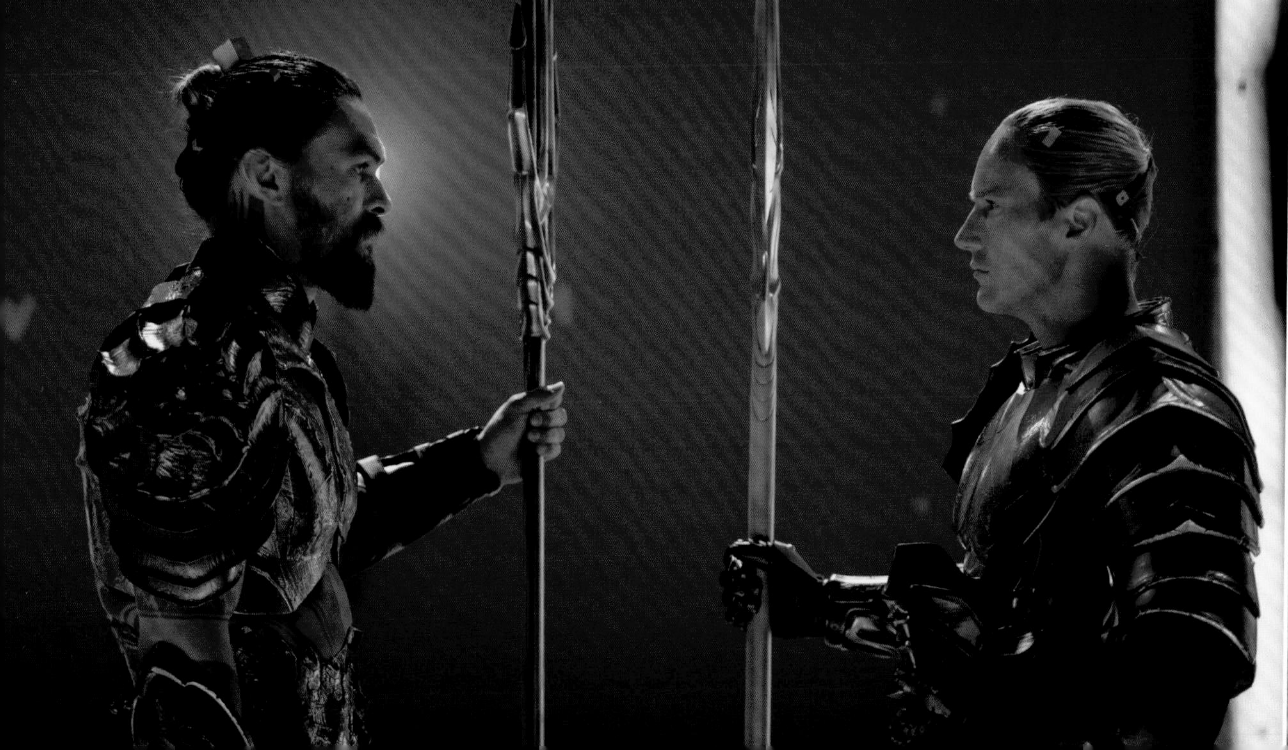
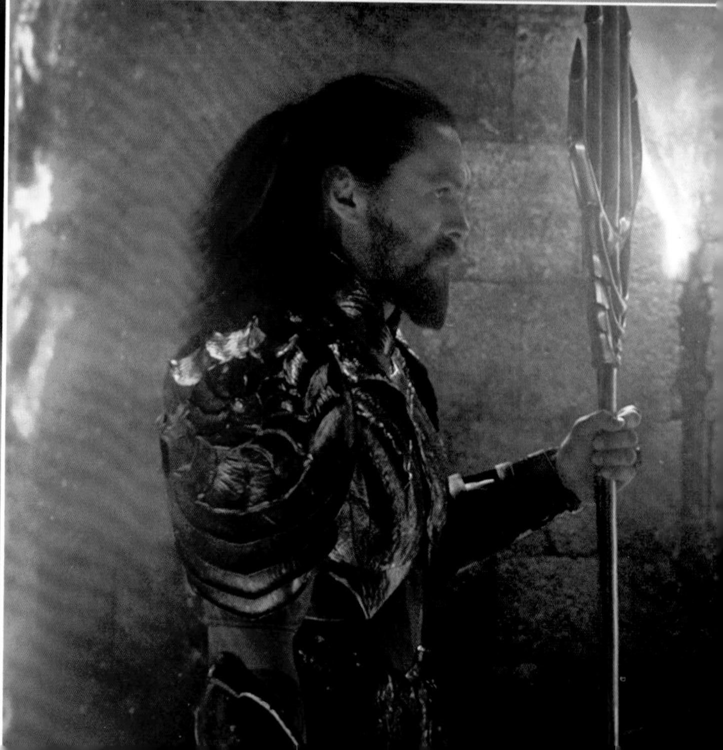

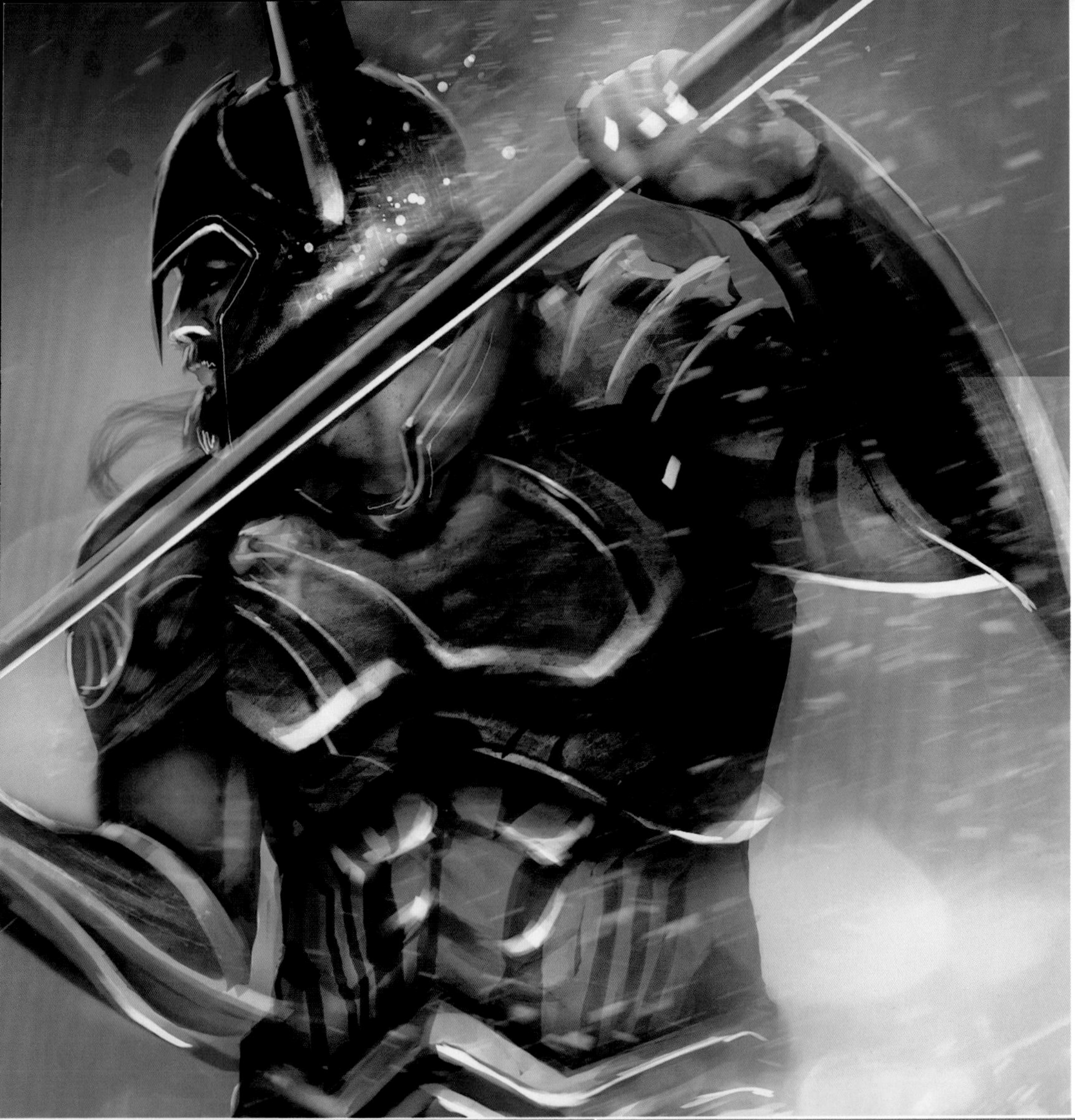

Breakthroughs in modern CGI have benefited high-concept productions like *Aquaman* because they allow filmmakers to save several steps. "We don't actually have to build a whole spaceship anymore. We don't have to build a whole throne room," says Brzeski. "We just have to build the parts that human beings interact with." But the Hollywood veteran is quick to offer up that modern technology, despite all its advantages, doesn't make moviemaking easier. The concept artists still have to draw every tiny nuance, every background image. The computer graphics don't create the design; they just execute the vision of the filmmakers. And Brzeski's team still had to build dozens of practical sets during the production, including the arena stage. "It doesn't let you off the hook in terms of designing anything. The digital world never lets you off the hook," he said. "Actually, it gets more complicated."

PAGES 92–93: Ring of Fire concept art by Jeremy Love.
LEFT: Gladiator battle concept art by Brad Nielsen.
OPPOSITE BOTTOM LEFT AND RIGHT: Arthur and Orm face off beneath the coliseum in unit photography and VFX shot revealing the changes made during postproduction.
BELOW: Arthur and Orm prepare for battle in the arena, with a large audience digitally added in the background.

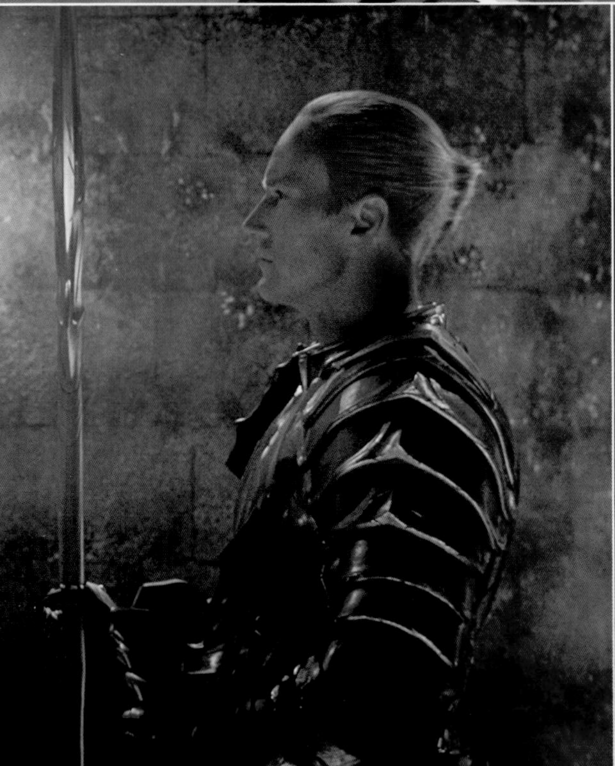

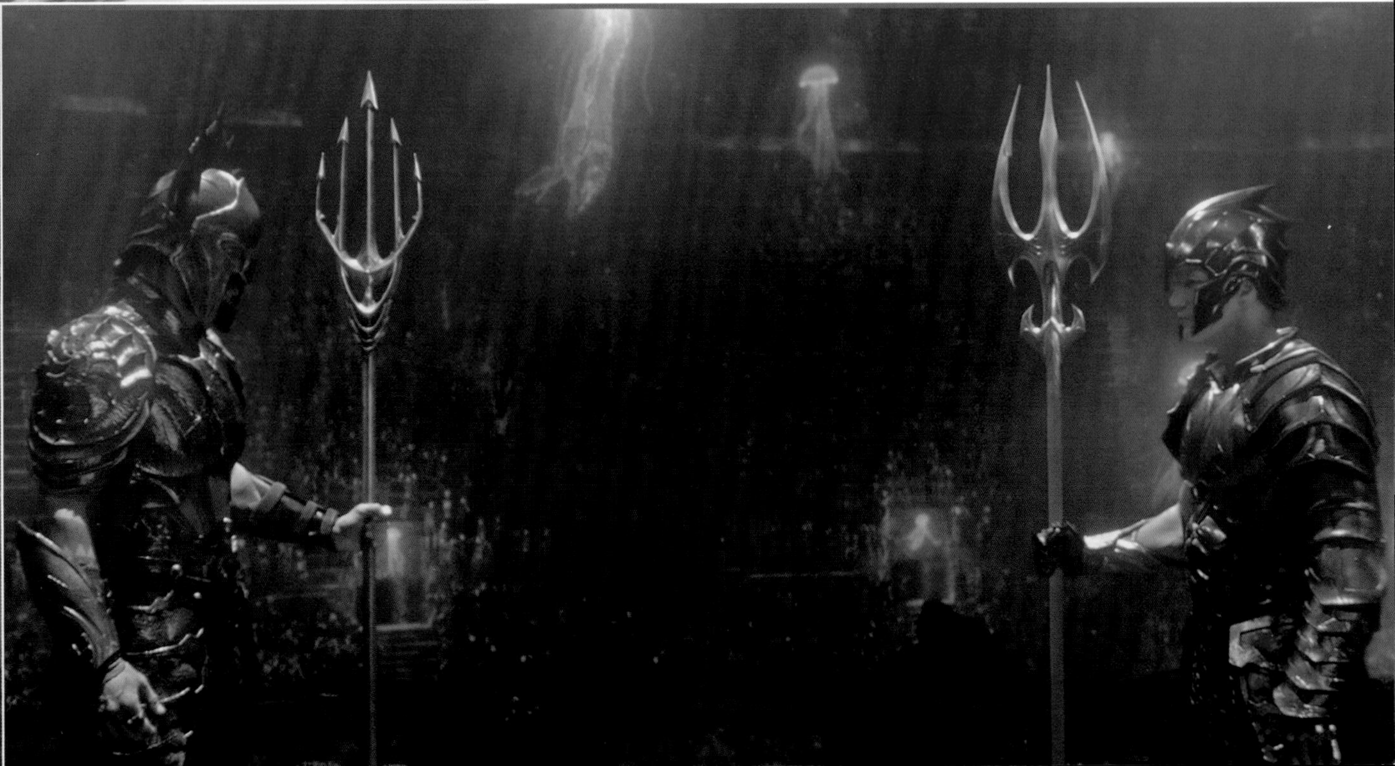

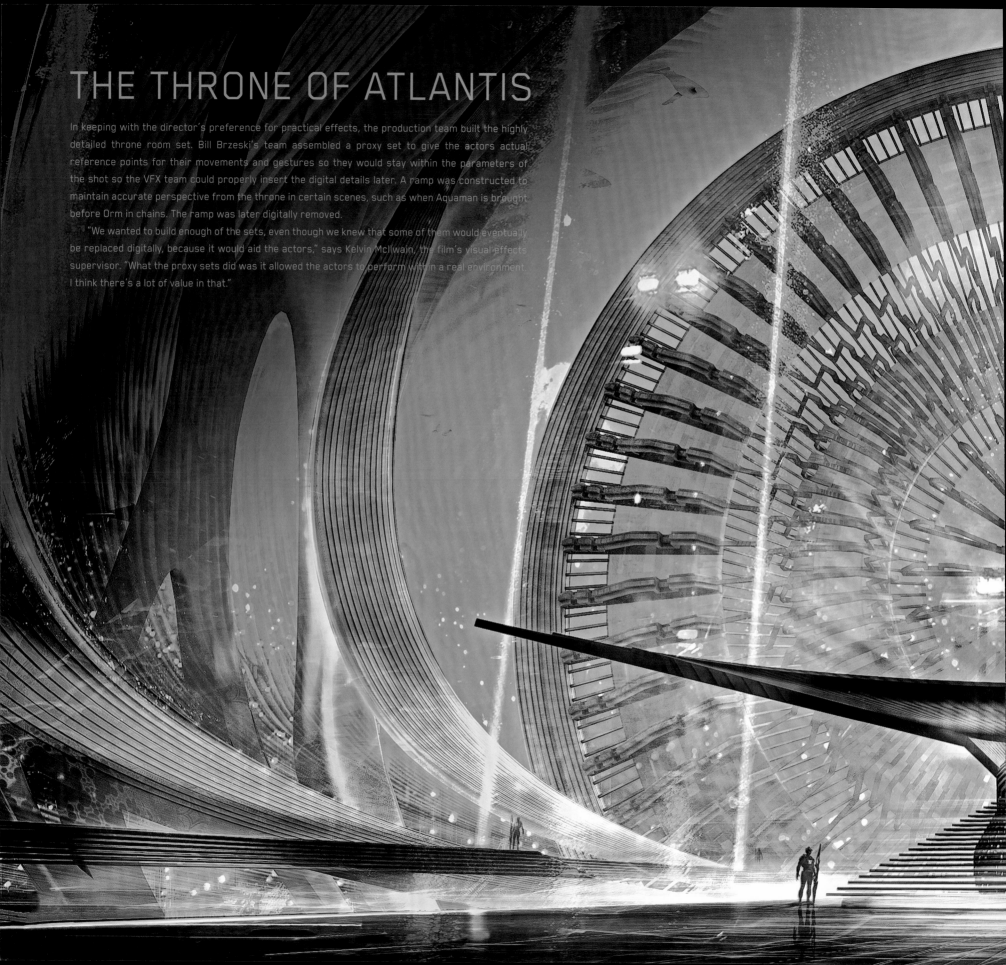

THE THRONE OF ATLANTIS

In keeping with the director's preference for practical effects, the production team built the highly detailed throne room set. Bill Brzeski's team assembled a proxy set to give the actors actual reference points for their movements and gestures so they would stay within the parameters of the shot so the VFX team could properly insert the digital details later. A ramp was constructed to maintain accurate perspective from the throne in certain scenes, such as when Aquaman is brought before Orm in chains. The ramp was later digitally removed.

"We wanted to build enough of the sets, even though we knew that some of them would eventually be replaced digitally, because it would aid the actors," says Kelvin McIlwain, the film's visual effects supervisor. "What the proxy sets did was it allowed the actors to perform within a real environment. I think there's a lot of value in that."

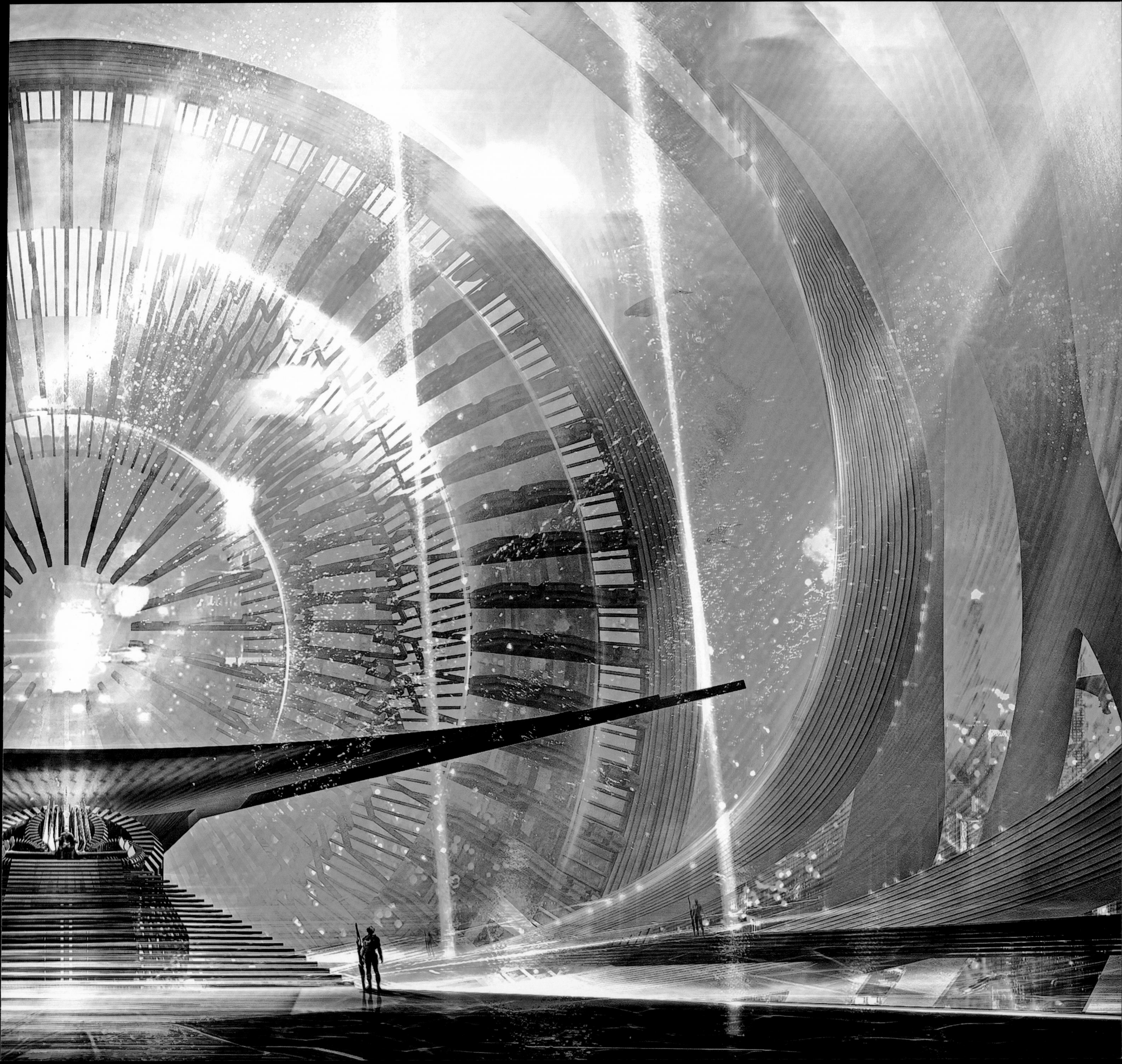

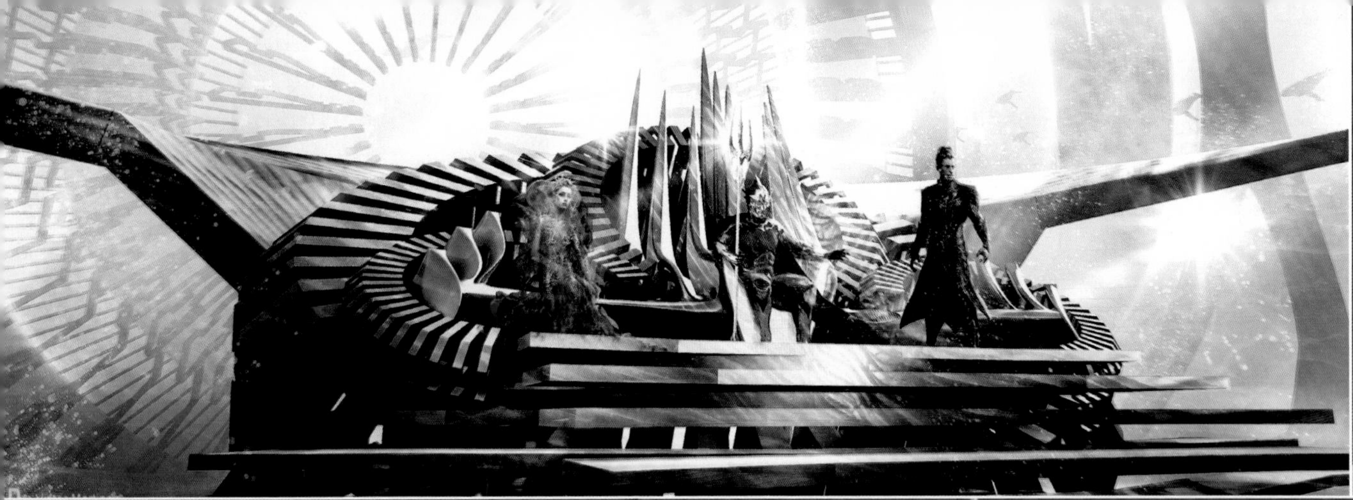
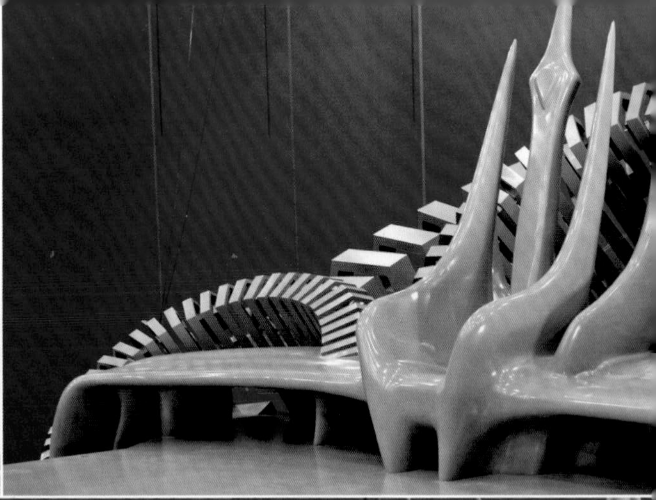
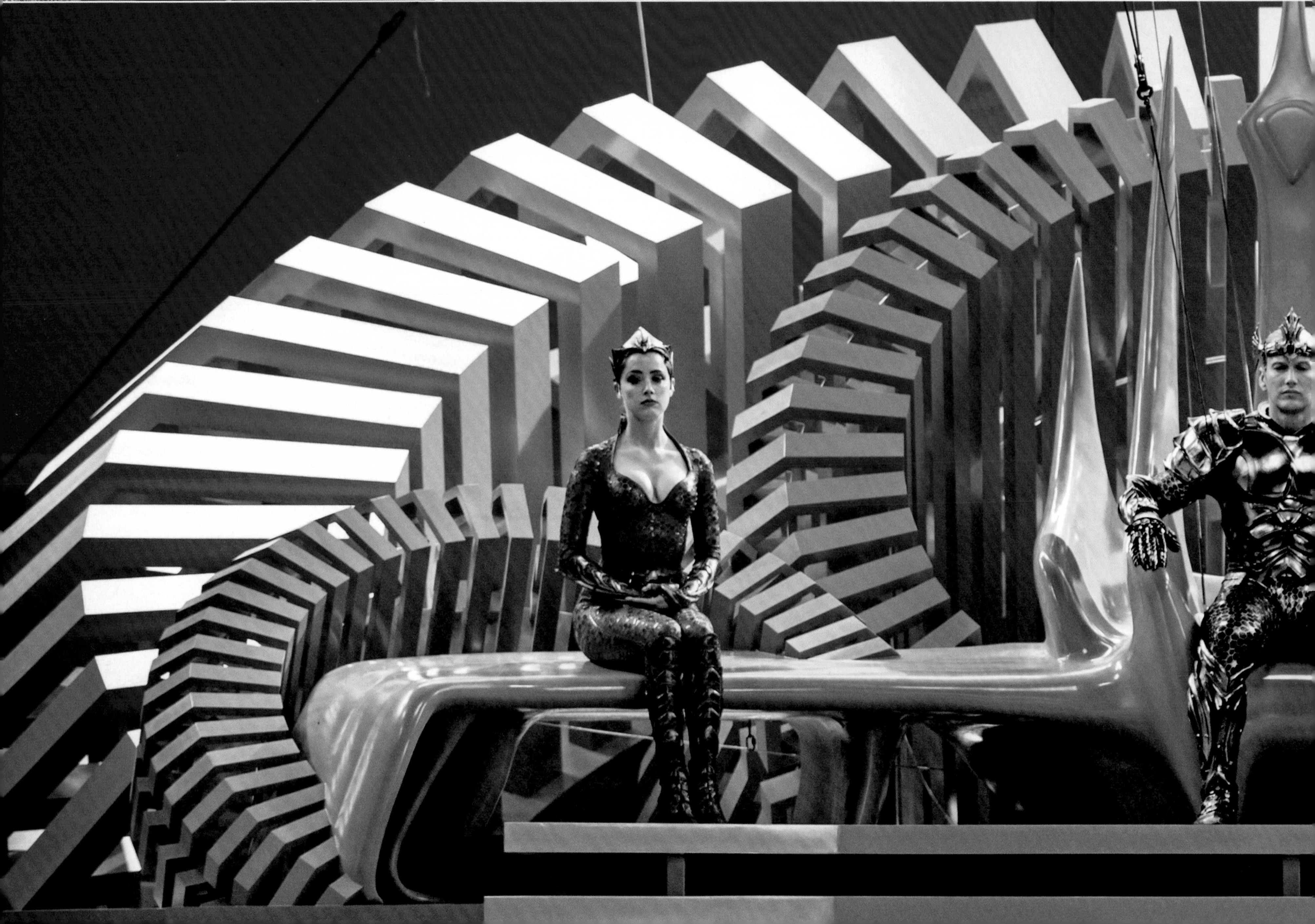

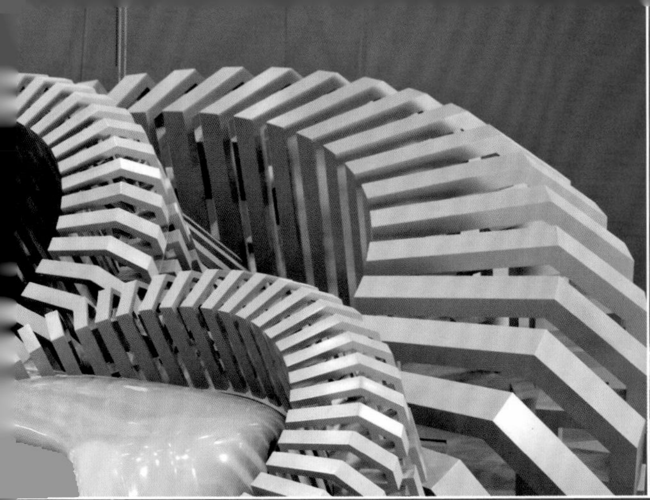

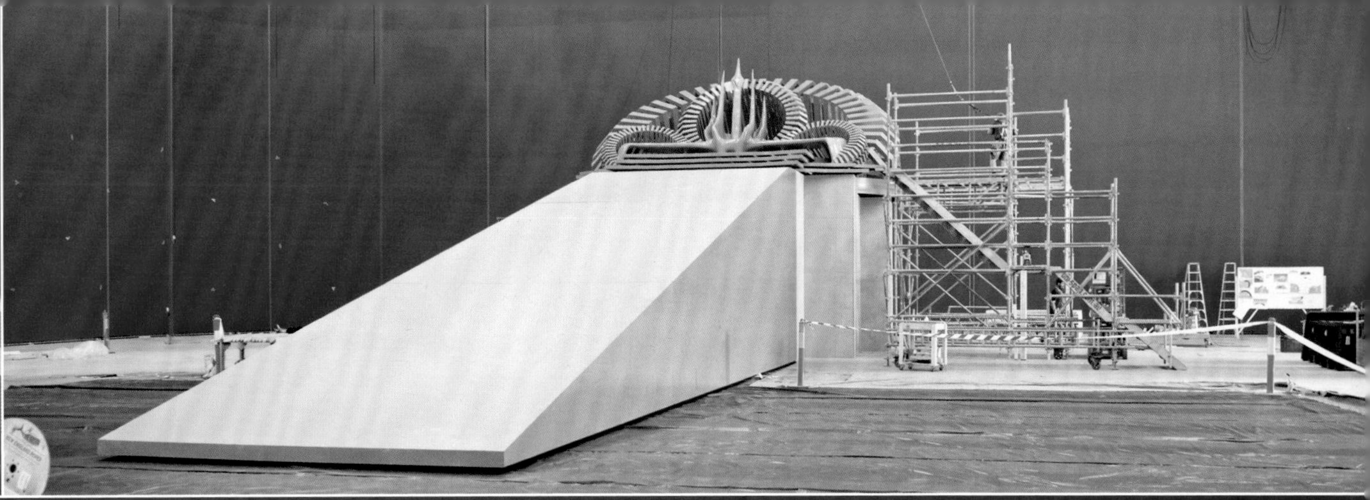

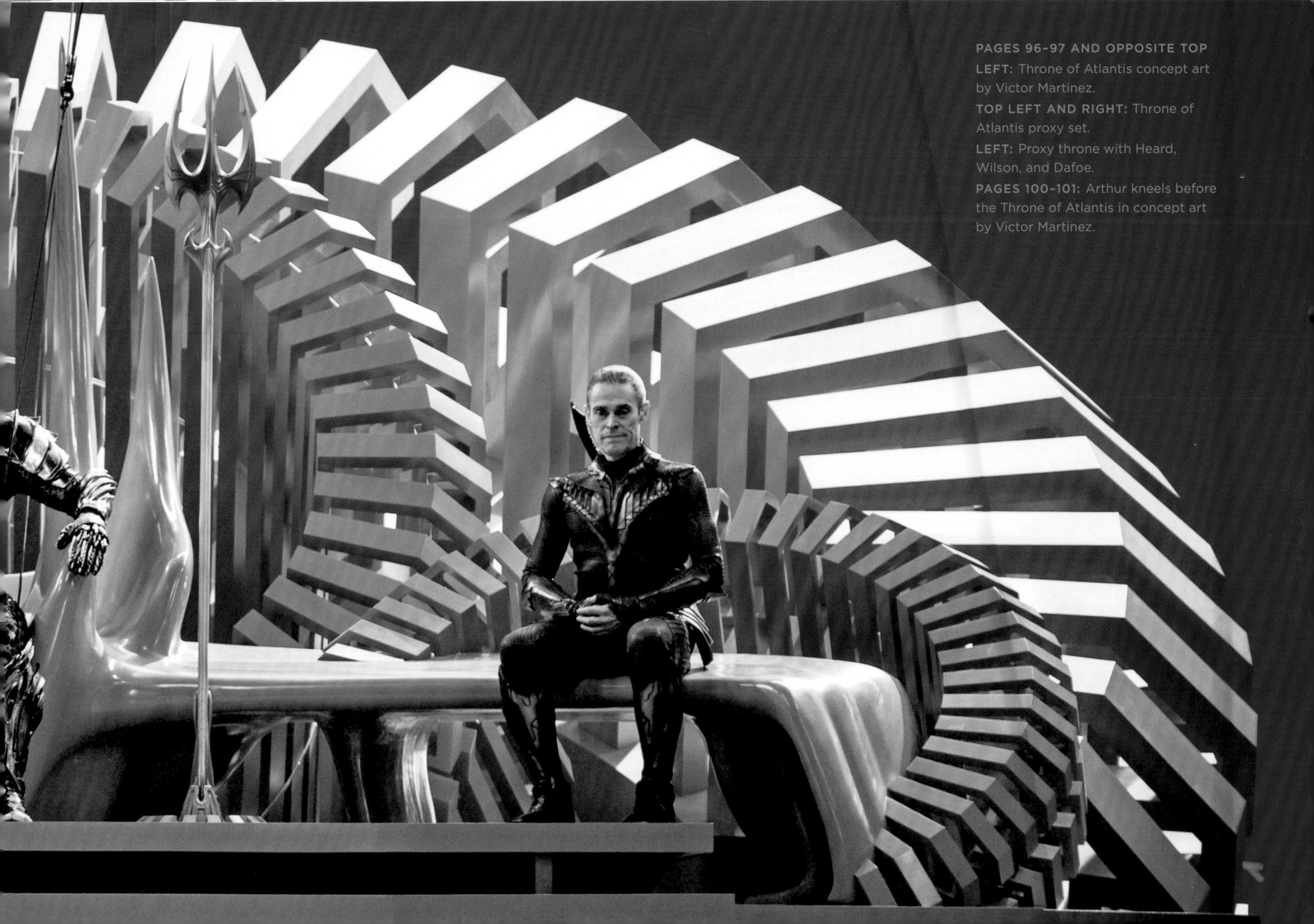

PAGES 96–97 AND OPPOSITE TOP LEFT: Throne of Atlantis concept art by Victor Martinez.

TOP LEFT AND RIGHT: Throne of Atlantis proxy set.

LEFT: Proxy throne with Heard, Wilson, and Dafoe.

PAGES 100–101: Arthur kneels before the Throne of Atlantis in concept art by Victor Martinez.

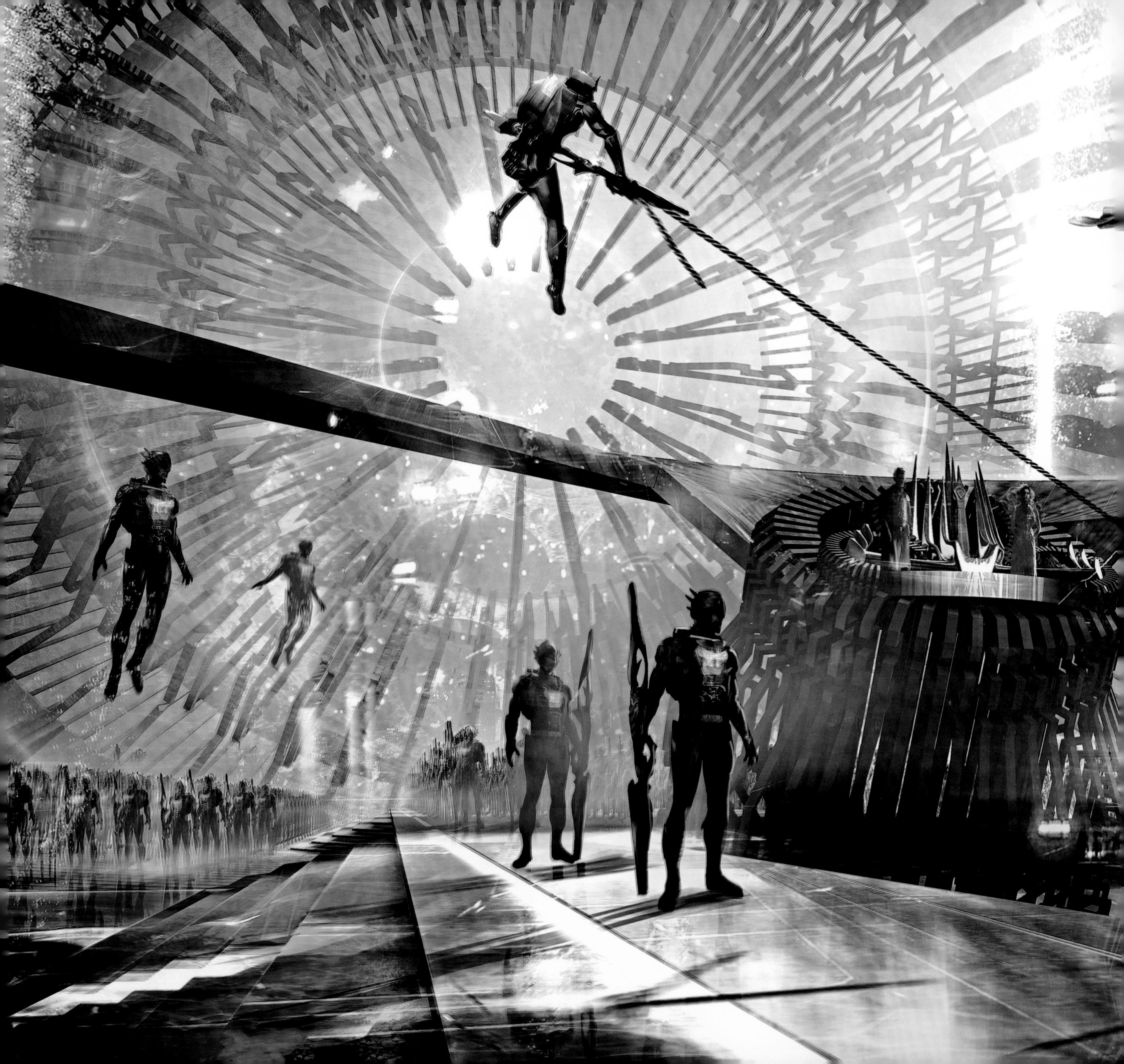

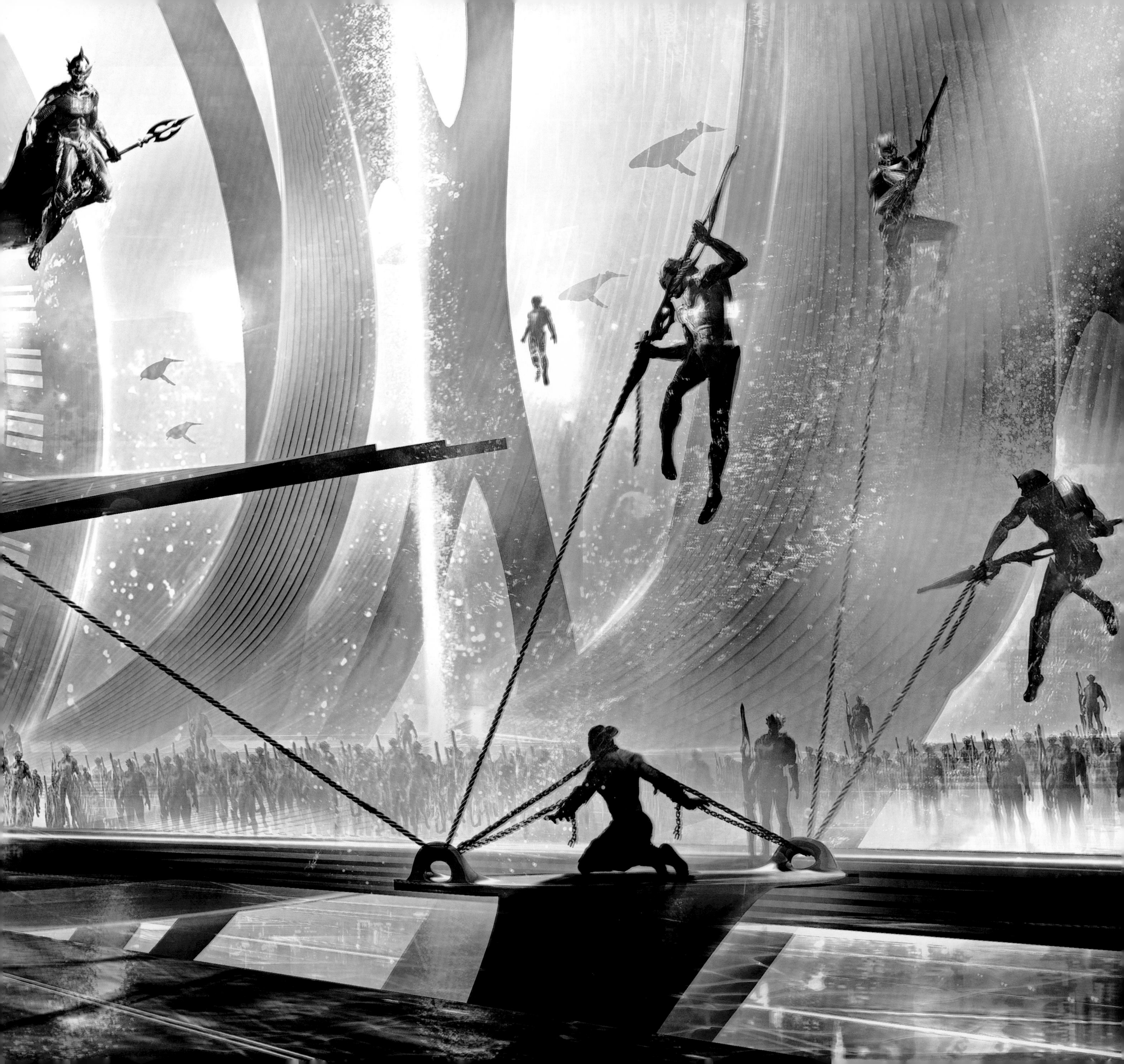

ANCIENT ATLANTIS

Aquaman is, at its core, a movie about identity and family. Arthur Curry has struggled to understand both for most of his life. As the filmmakers were figuring out the story, they determined that the best way for Arthur to get the answers he needed was for him to understand the past. To give him that historical context, they would need to flash back to a significant period in the history of Ancient Atlantis and create the kingdom as it appeared during what was effectively its golden age.

With nearly eighty years of comic book mythology to work from, the filmmakers certainly had a lot of material to inspire them. They took creative license with some of the mythos past creators established around Atlantis in the comics, and they used historical influences to build the city and its glorious history. Without a rigid plan of adaptation, the production team—from Wan and the producers to the writers and concept artists—could freely devise the backstory of Atlantis. "One of my goals that I wanted to do with this film is to create a very magical world that we have never kind of seen before," Wan explains. That magic shines through on the screen thanks to the crew's impressive work, beginning with the earliest concept designs.

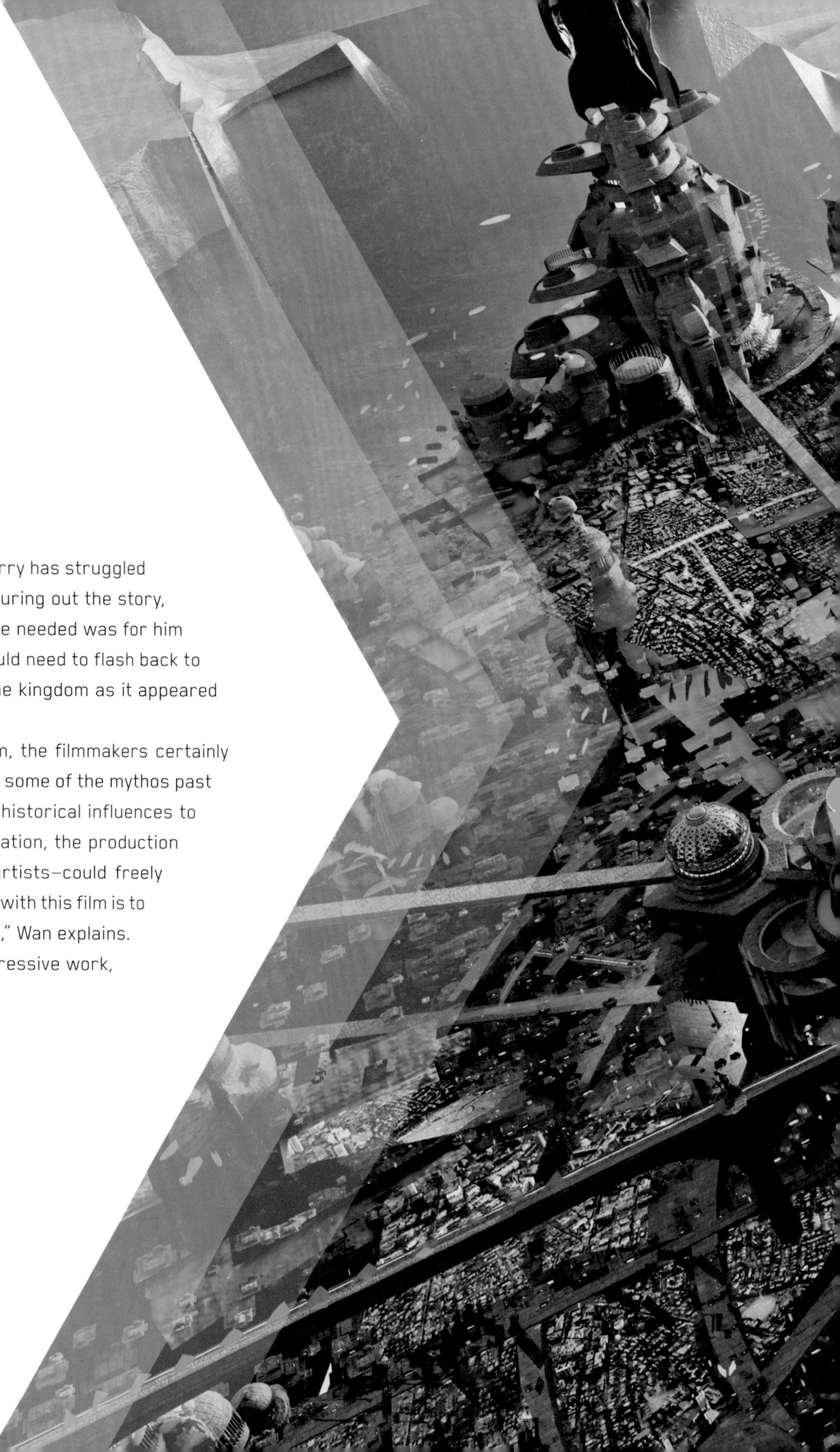

RIGHT: Ancient Atlantis concept art by Christian Scheurer.
PAGES 104–105: Ancient Atlantis concept art by Christian Scheurer.

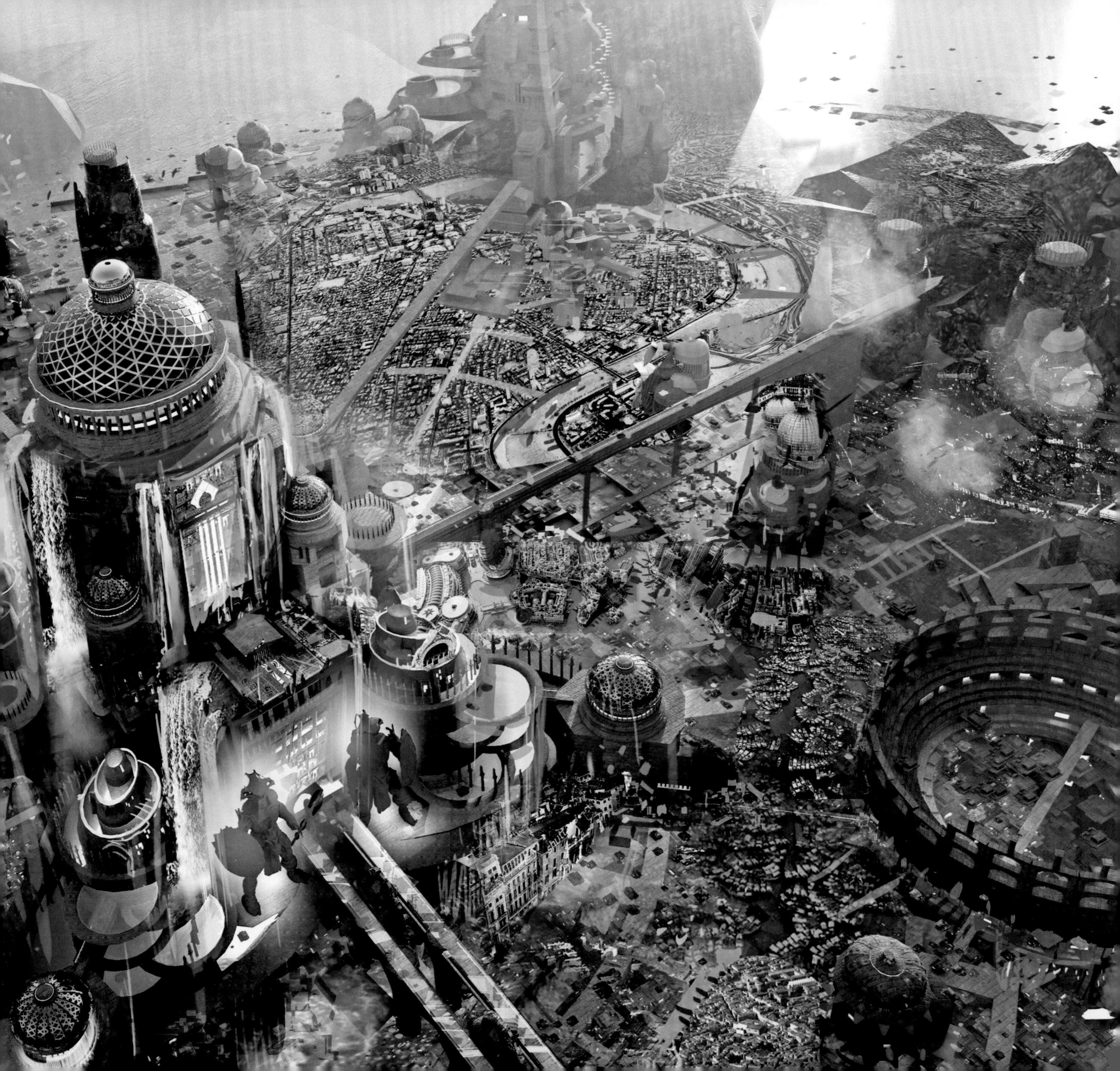

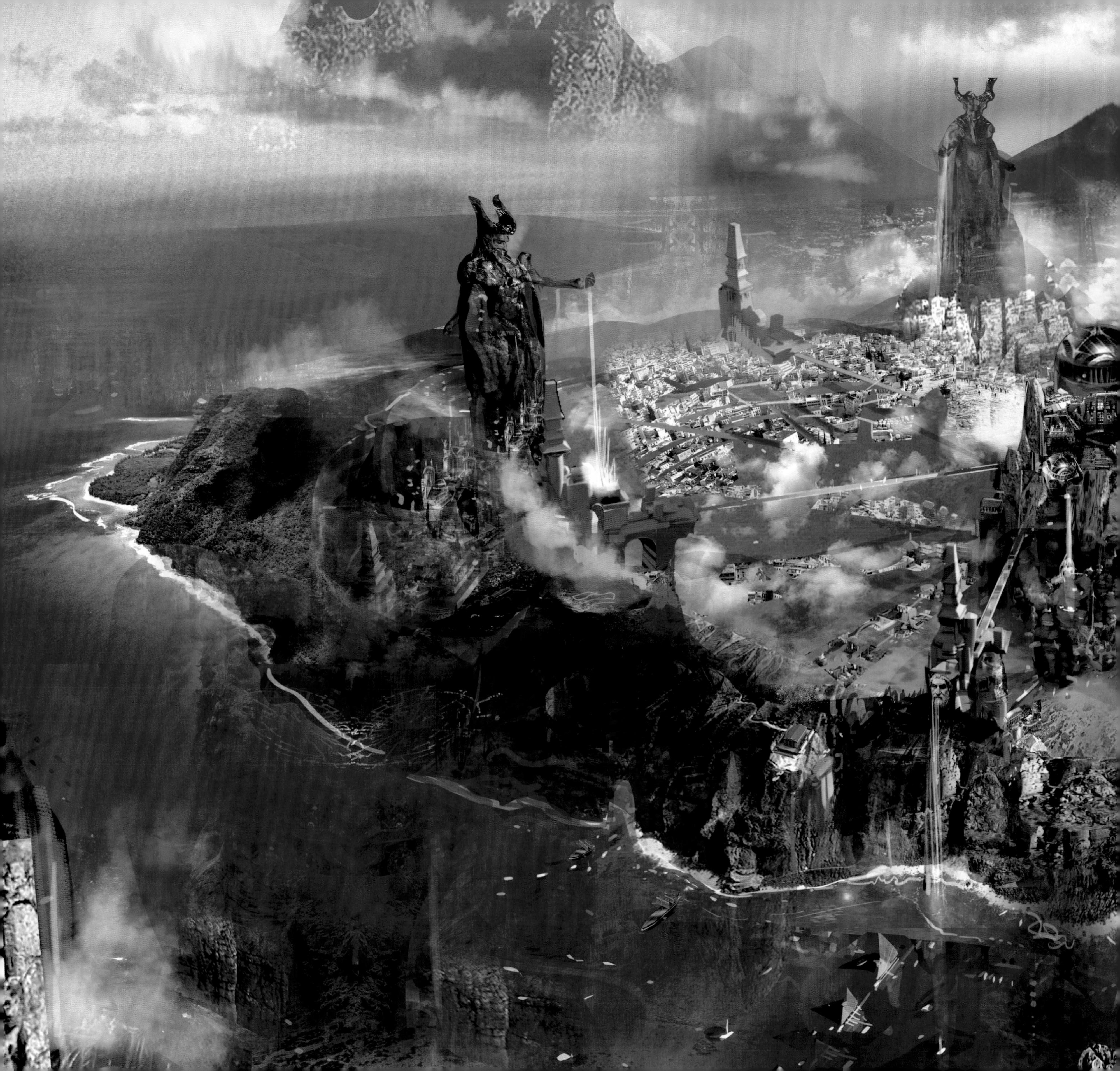

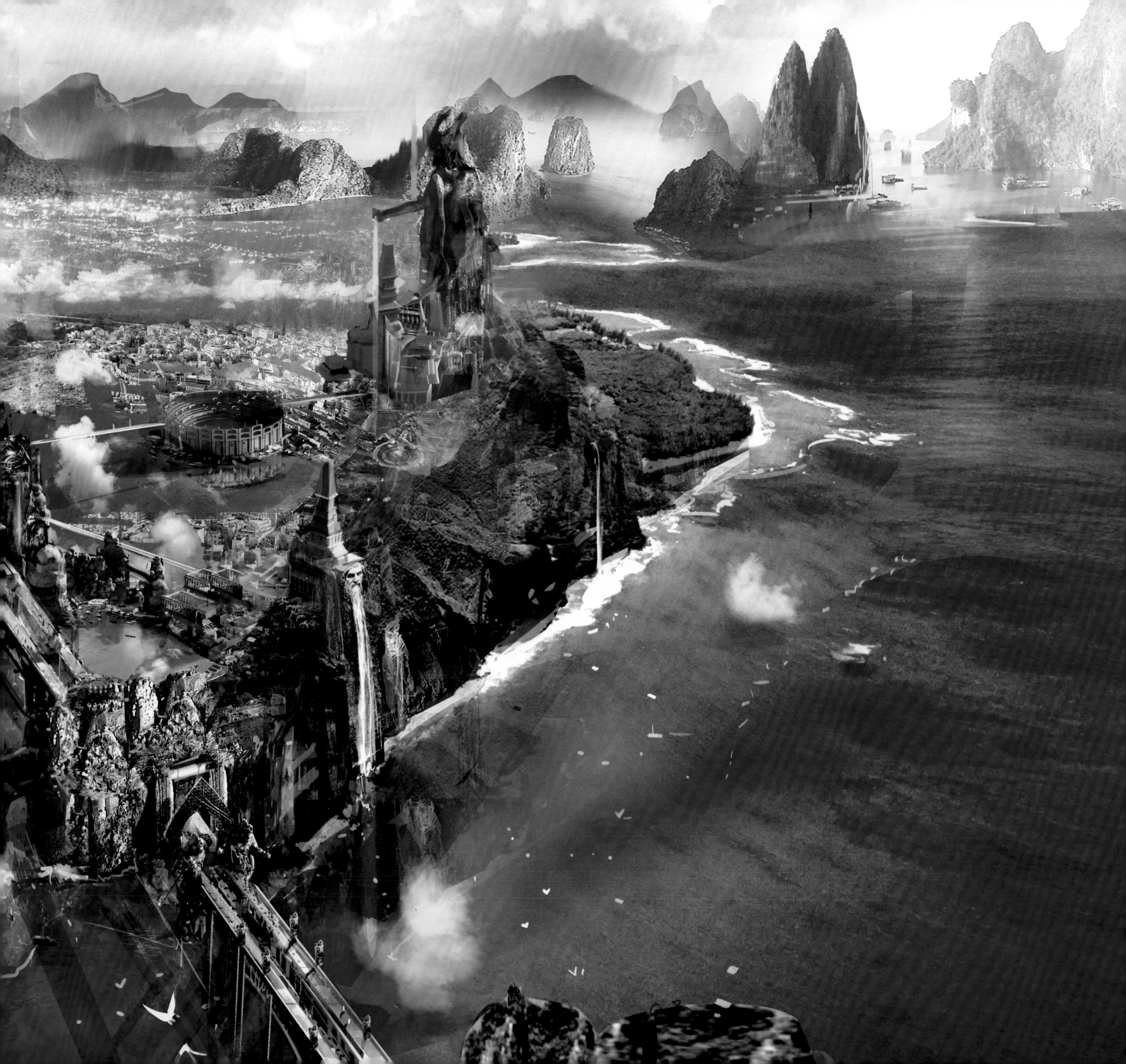

THESE PAGES: Ancient Atlantis throne room (*right*) and Atlantis exterior (*opposite*) concept art by Christian Scheurer.

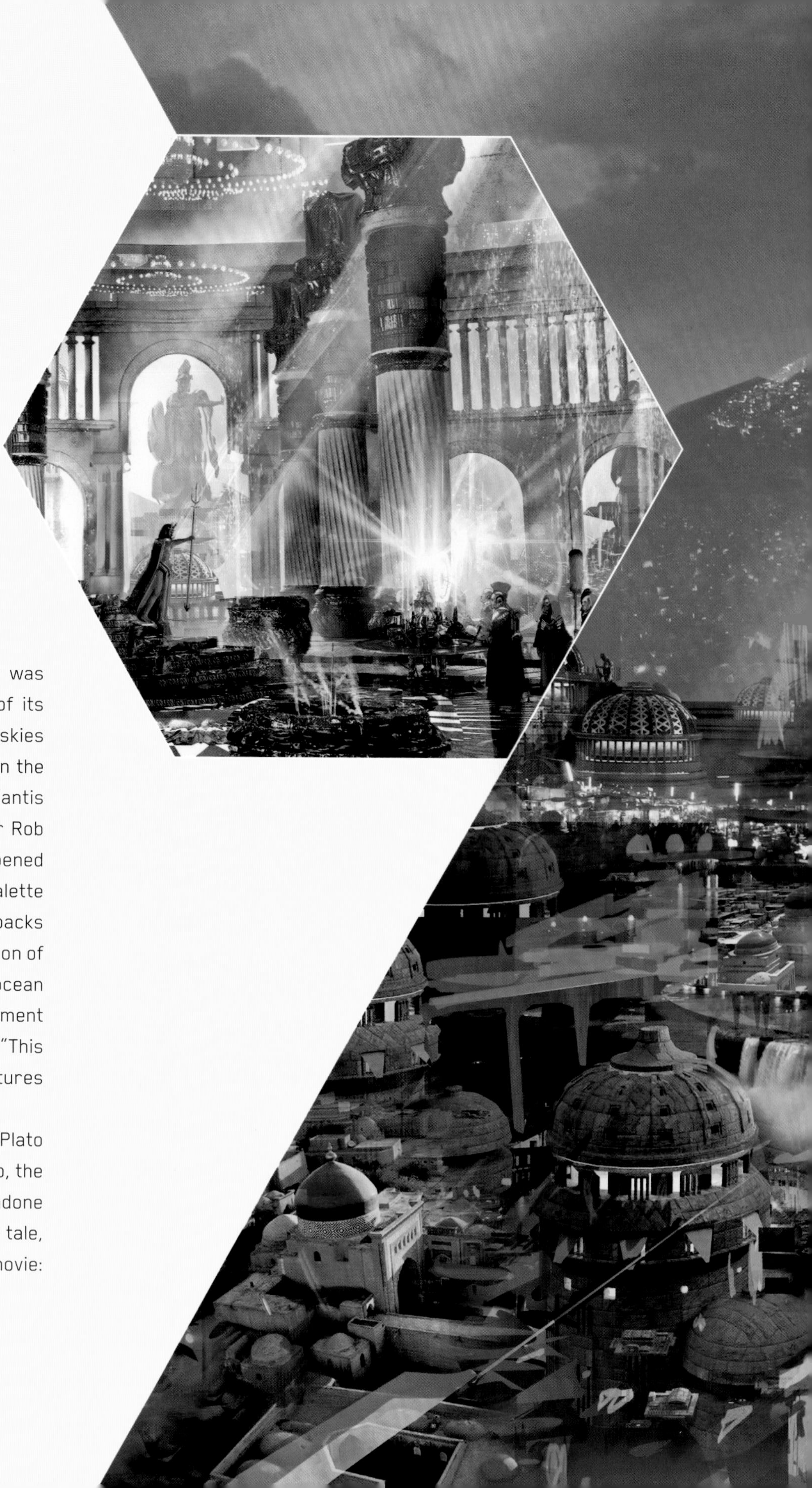

The surface-dwelling city of Atlantis that has been lost to history was a glittering steampunk rendition of Ancient Rome. The size and scale of its structures were staggering. Massive statues of the gods pierced the skies above, while the gateway bridge seemed to span most of the ocean. When the production team's rich reproduction of the ancient surface city of Atlantis was complete, it opened up the film for the crew. As executive producer Rob Cowan explains, "We were able to travel back in time and see what happened and how [Atlantis] got to be where it is today, so it gave us a really wide palette to be able to paint a picture with and be able to tell a full story." The flashbacks offer a compelling contrast between past and present, showing the evolution of Atlantis from its days as an open-air metropolis to its current place in the ocean depths. Just as important, the flashbacks show the technological advancement of the Atlantean culture and the majesty and wonder of its achievements. "This particular nation, this civilization, was so far advanced beyond other cultures before it sank," explains Wan.

While the Atlantis in the Aquaman canon differs quite a bit from the city Plato first mentioned in his Timaeus dialogue more than two thousand years ago, the similarities are clear. Both were gleaming, magnificent cities eventually undone from within, victims of their own hubris and corruption. That cautionary tale, Wan recalls, inspired a moral foundation for the Atlantis shown in the movie: "They grew too powerful for their own good."

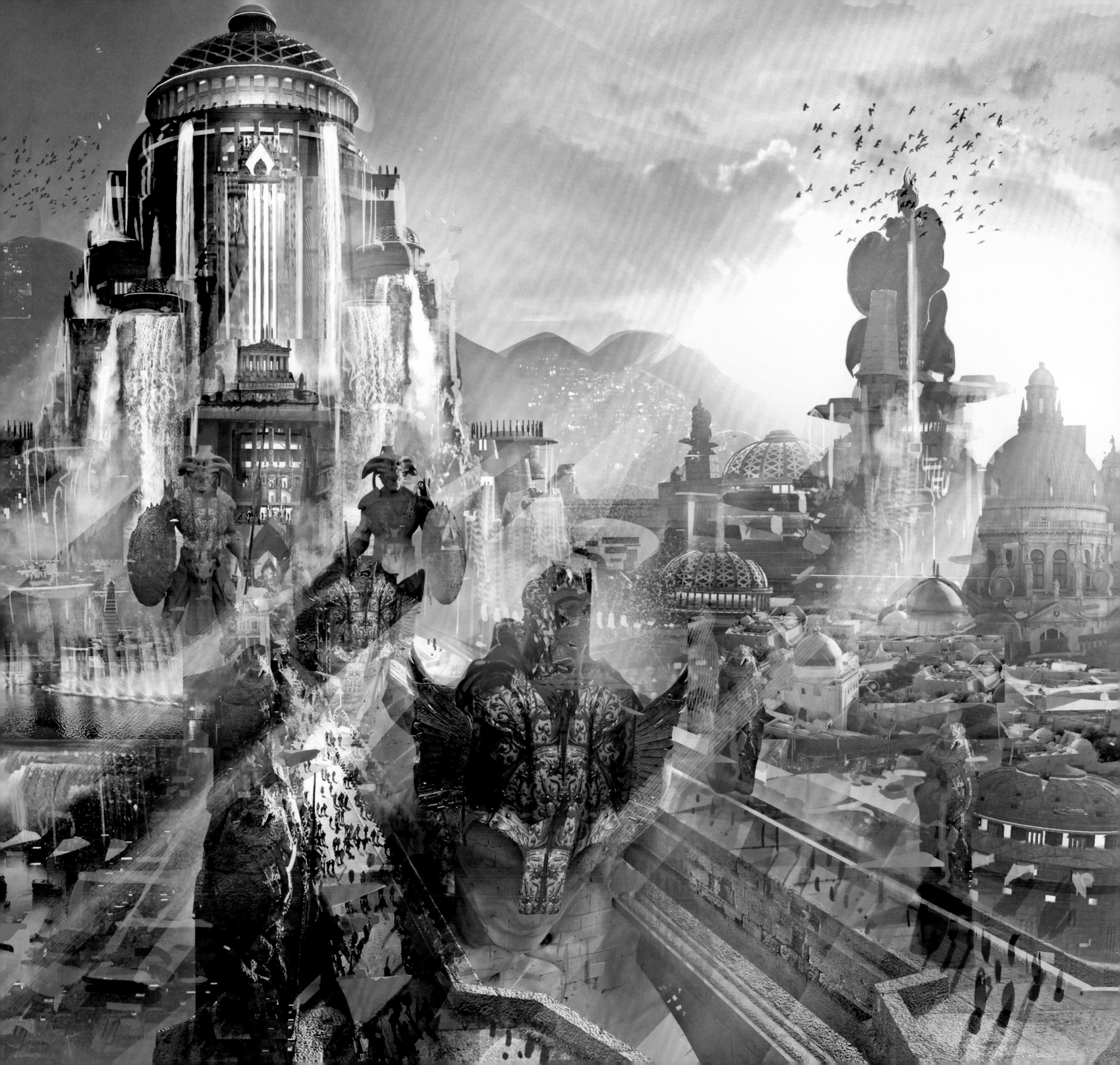

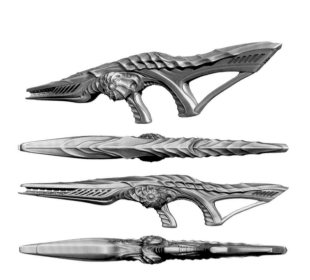

XEBEL KINGDOM

Once seated at the right hand of Atlantis in all political matters, the kingdom of Xebel is now an independent realm and the near equal of its former ally. Although the relationship between Xebel and Atlantis is strained, the leaders of both kingdoms recognize that there is strength in unity. Together, they plan to unite the remaining undersea kingdoms to bring power to the oceans once more.

"Each kingdom had its own distinct look," explains prop master Richie Dehne. "These design parameters were established by Bill Brzeski, so I took my lead from the elements used from his Xebellian world. The costumes also had distinctive lines so the guns again needed to blend ergonomically. I remember James mentioned Xebellians could have echoes of Asian '60s sci-fi art. I ran with that."

ABOVE: Xebellian rifle prop concept designs.
RIGHT: Xebellian guard armor costume concept art by James Oxford.
OPPOSITE: Xebellian Electrocutioner concept art and Mera's sub concept art by Ed Natividad.

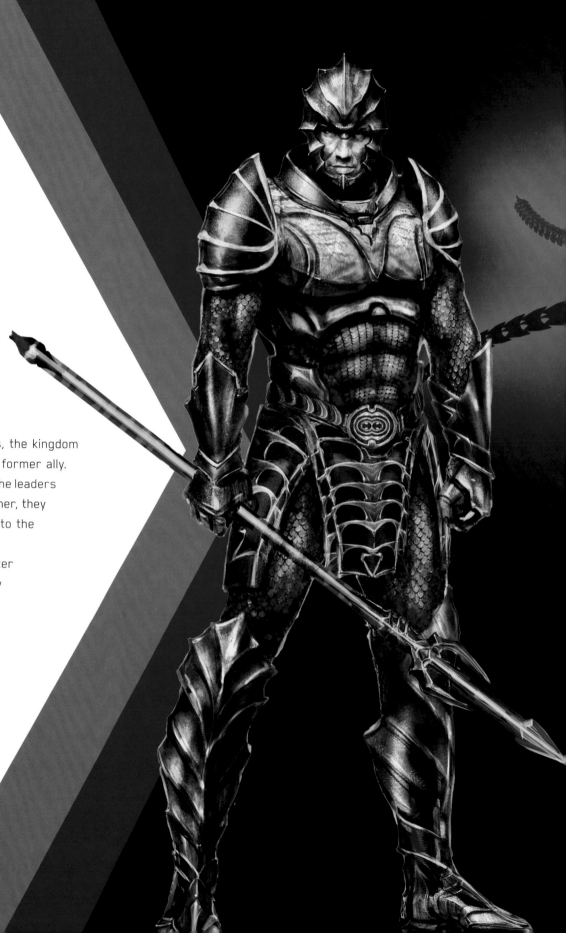

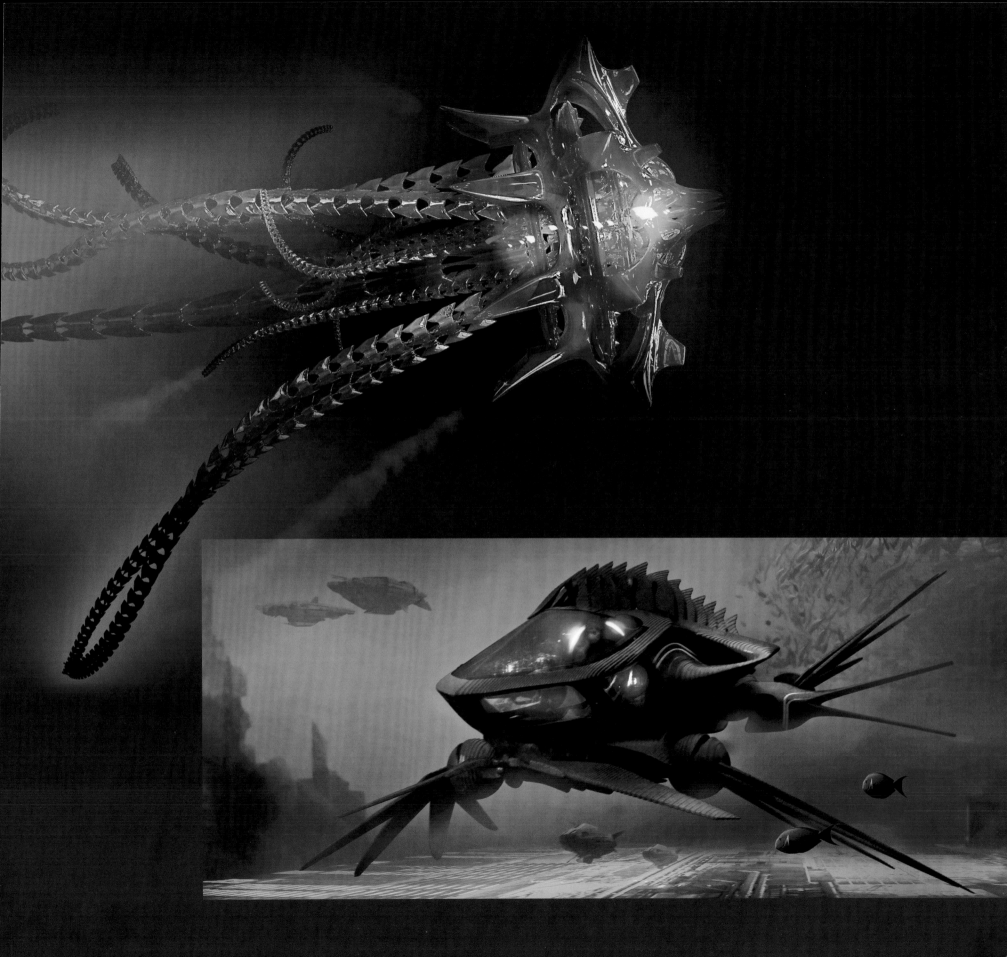

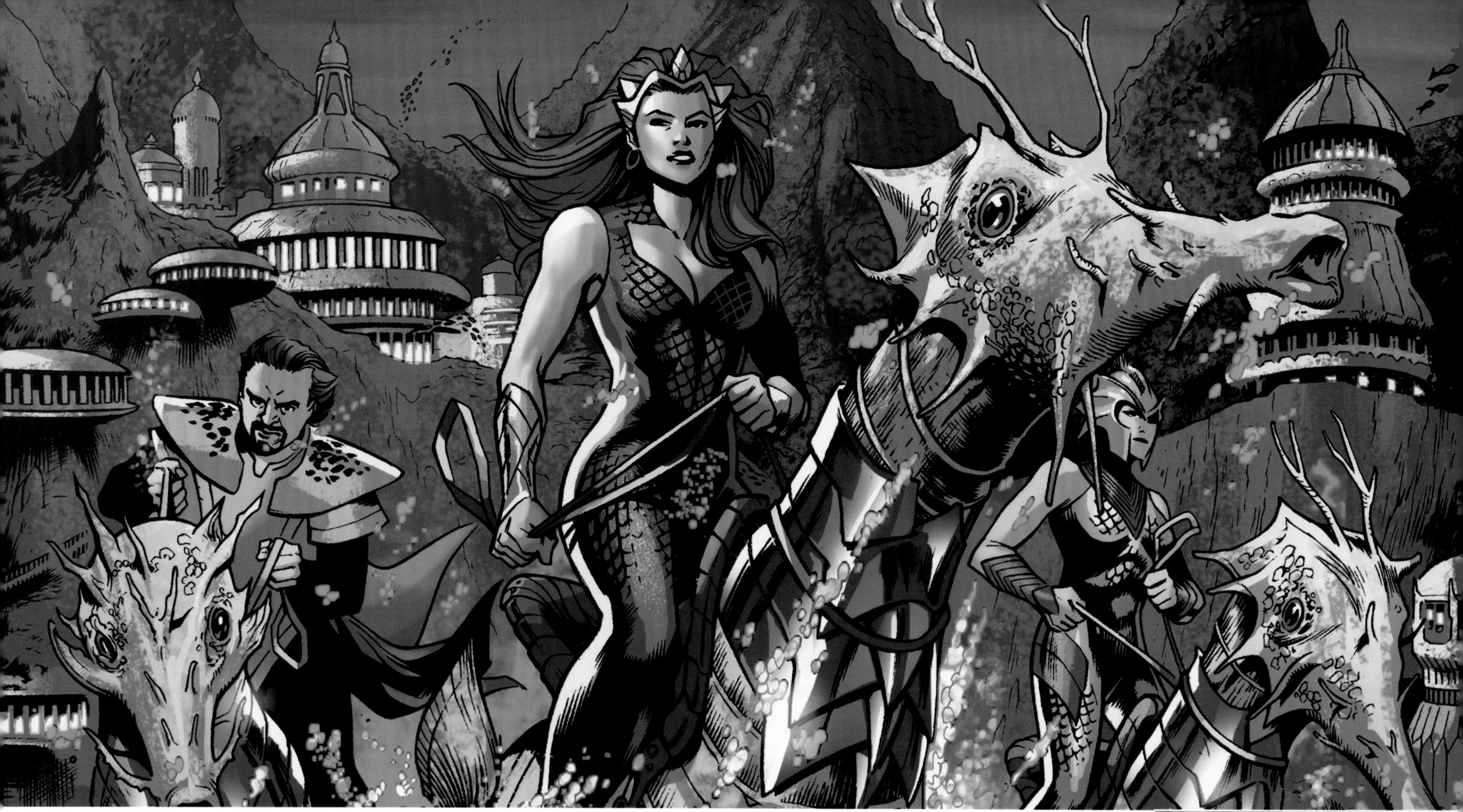

SEA DRAGONS

"The Sea Dragons concept was worked out ages ago. James settled on a design very early in the process, which made it easier for us. When the visual effects team actually started building the creatures, we had a lot of great representative artwork to work from. Of course, we're always trying to make things better, and embellish designs. We also have to make it look real. But James really had some very strong ideas about what he wanted this film to look like, and that included the creatures and the underwater structures. From my perspective, it makes my job a heckuva lot easier. Because we're not trying to fish around for the solution, or come up with a lot of ideas and presenting them to James to try and figure out what he responds to. He knows what he wants. There are always refinements and tweaks that happen, but 90 percent of the time, he knew what he was after."

—Kelvin McIlwain, Visual Effects Supervisor

TOP: Seahorses from the graphic novel *Aquaman: Sea of Storms.* The comics' seahorses inspired the movie's Sea Dragons.
RIGHT: The Xebel army sits atop their Sea Dragon steeds.
OPPOSITE: Sea Dragon concept art by Sebastian Meyer.

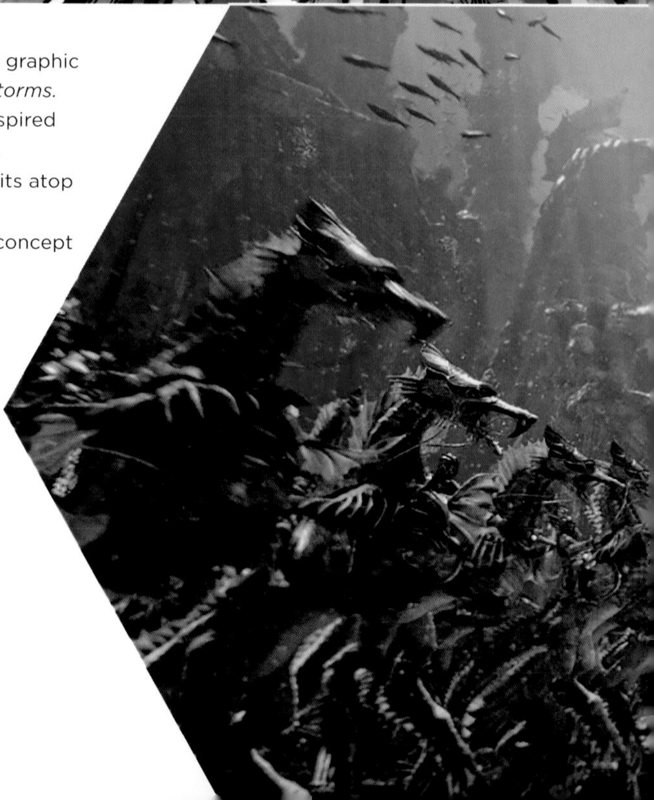

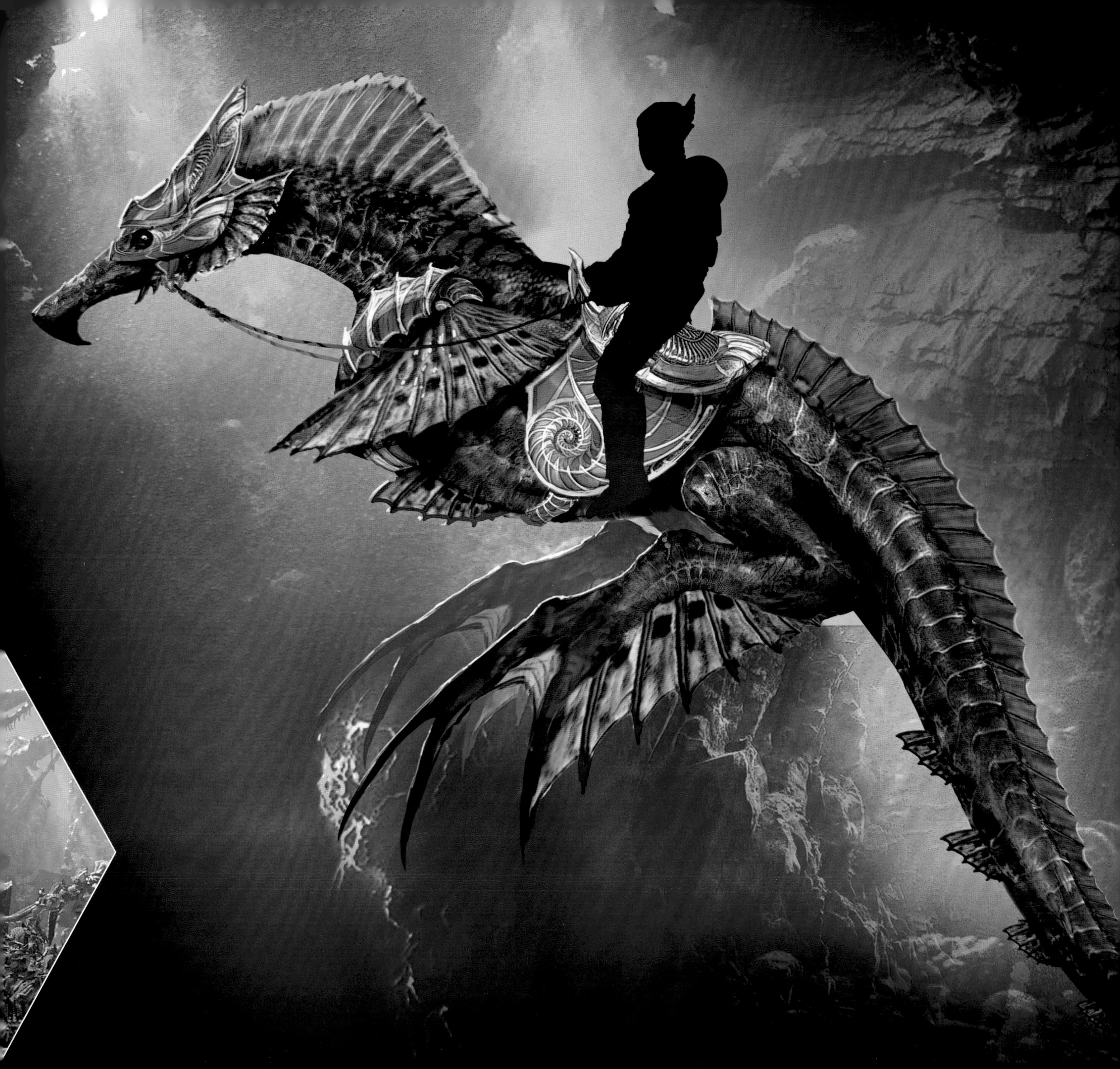

MERA'S SUB

"Ultimately the design of Mera's ship was a very iterative process. Our production designer Bill Brzeski came up with the initial concept based off sea creatures. James, knowing that the final finished design would not be realized until postproduction, reserved the right to make the finishing touches late in the schedule. He brought back our vehicle designer Ed Natividad after principal photography to polish the final look as well as make military variations of the design. Ed finished up the design and look concepts for the vehicle and then we passed those off to our VFX team at Industrial Light and Magic. Jeff White, the VFX Supervisor at ILM, took those designs and created animatable photorealistic realizations of James's imagination. ILM helped James realize a ship that moved organically and referenced aquatic creature locomotion at the same time that it utilized advanced technology for propulsion."

—Kelvin McIlwain, Visual Effects Supervisor

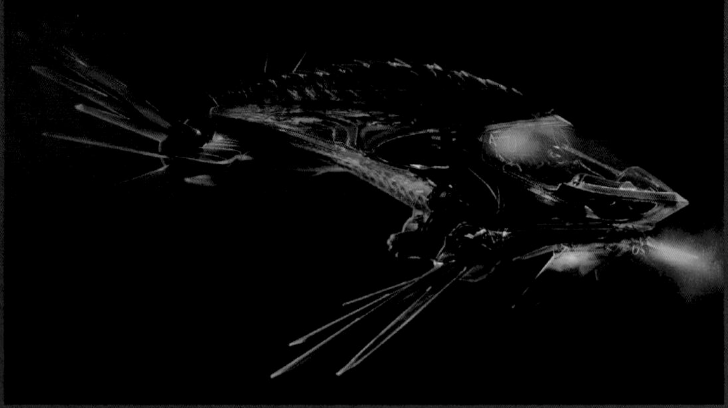

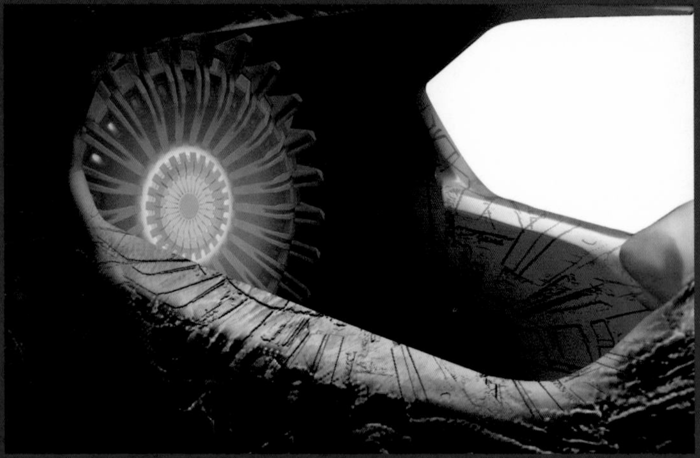

THESE PAGES: Xebel ships concept art by Ed Natividad.

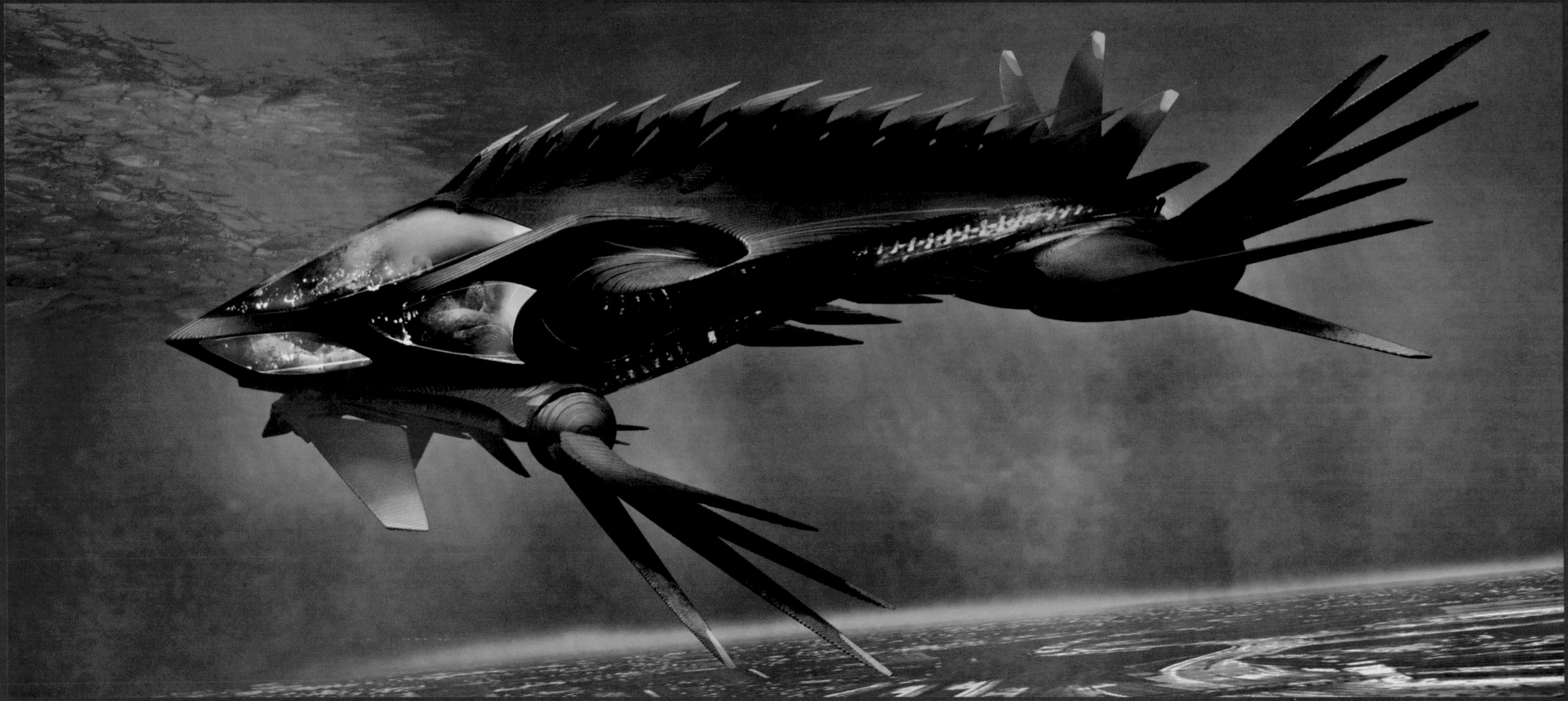

XEBELLIAN VESSELS

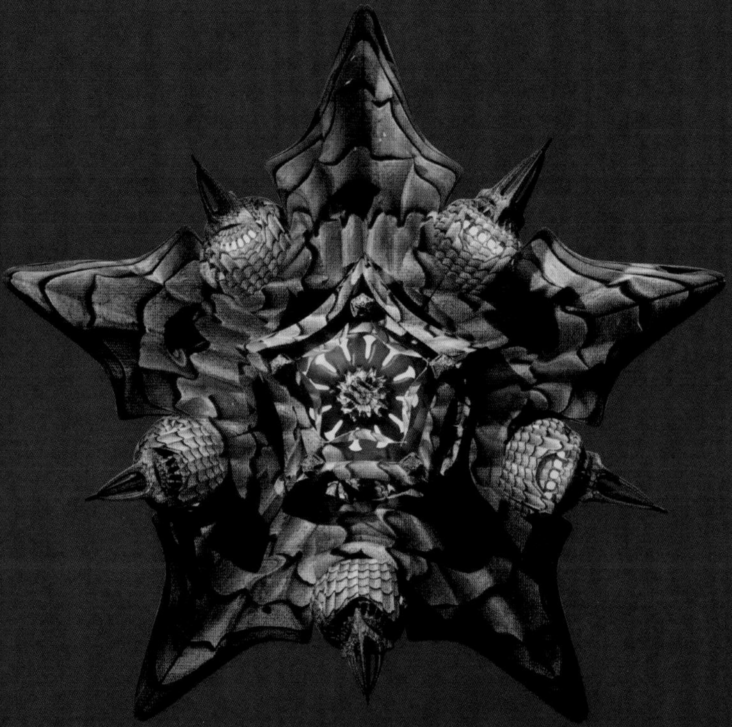

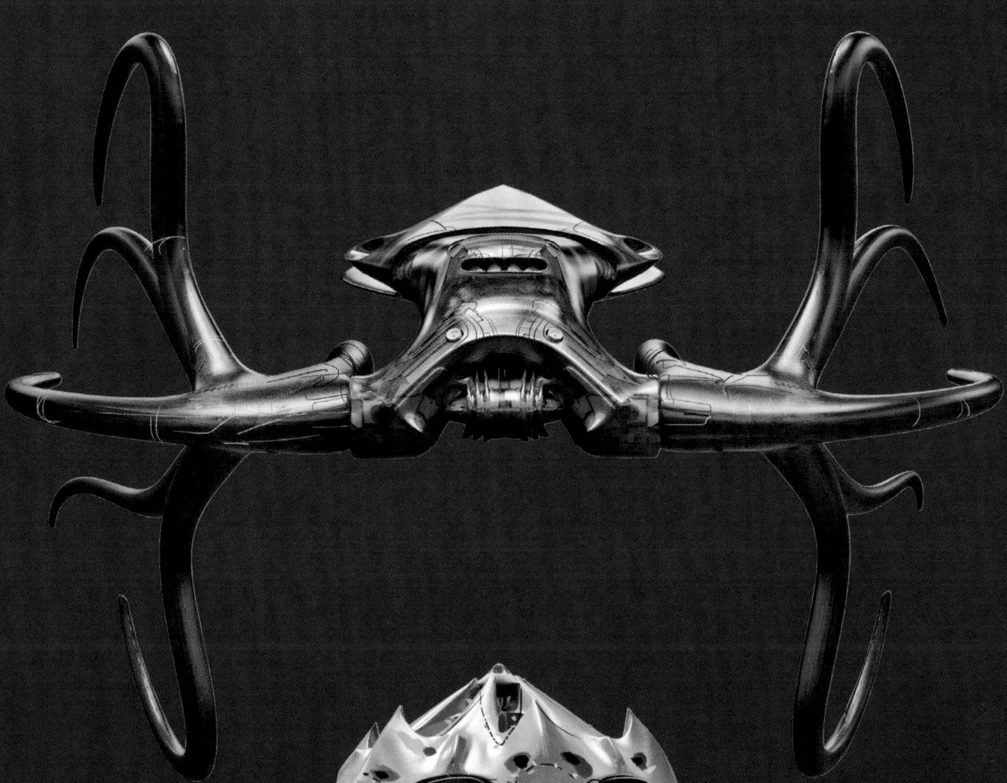

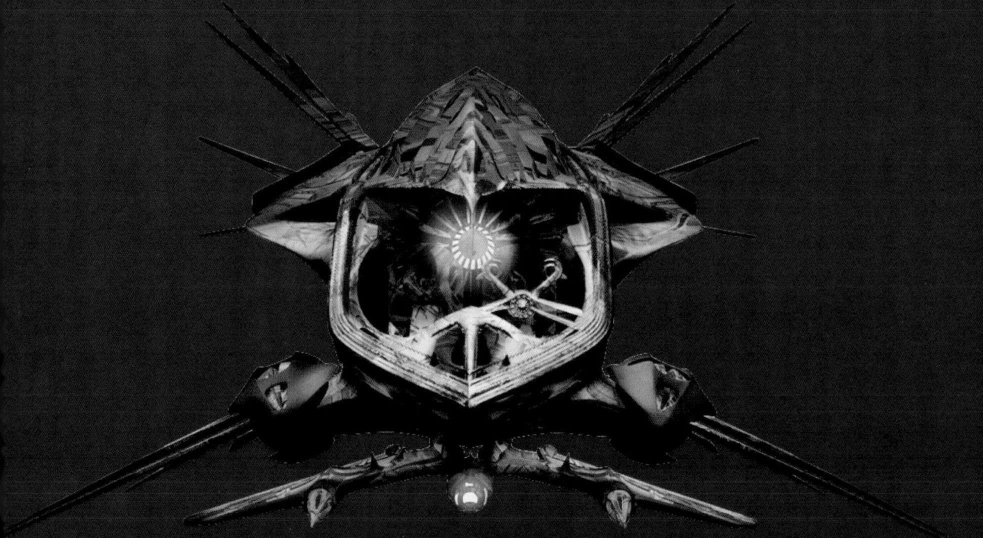

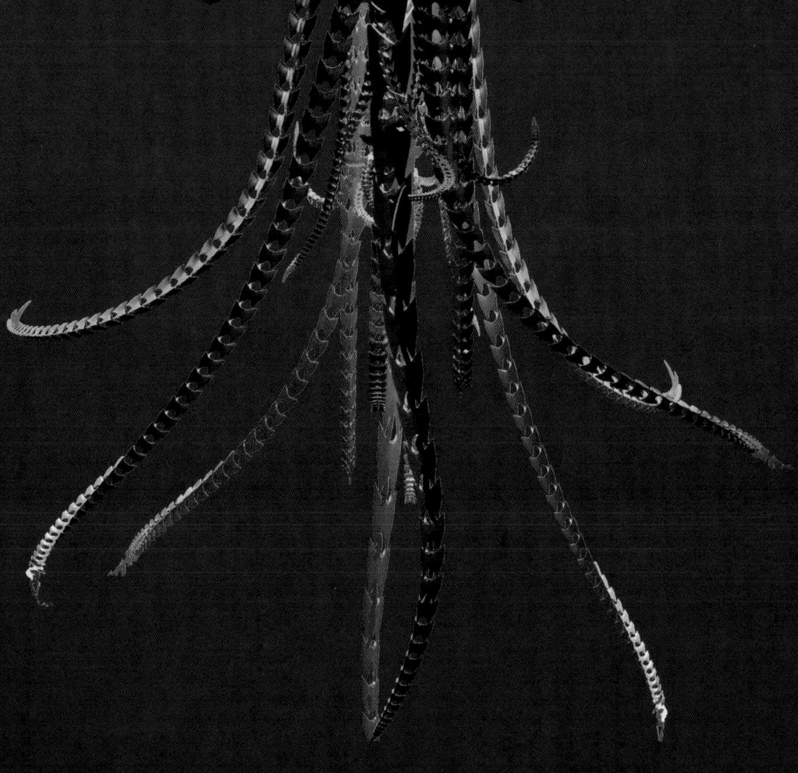

FISHERMEN KINGDOM

Peace can be found in even the roughest seas, and the people of the Fishermen Kingdom are proof. These poets and philosophers have evolved beyond their human forms to become one with the creatures of the seas. Though they prefer to remain separate from the politics of Atlantis, events conspire to bring them into the conflict between the realms of the land and the sea.

"The Fishermen Kingdom is very gothic. The interior design of their palace feels very art nouveau, with a touch of classic grandeur to it. It all feels like and references easily recognizable structural motifs of underwater life-forms, such as coral. Bill Brzeski pulled a lot of ideas from the nineteenth-century German marine biologist and artist Ernst Haeckel, who published several wonderful books on coralline structures and microscopic creatures in the sea. There are really some amazing design elements that they were inspired by and they riffed on to create the look of the Fishermen Kingdom."

–Kelvin McIlwain, Visual Effects Supervisor

RIGHT: Fishermen Kingdom concept art by Jeremy Love.

OPPOSITE: The Fishermen Queen design is a combination of practical makeup and visual effects.

PAGES 116–117: Fishermen throne room concept art by Jeremy Love. Fishermen King design by Stephan Martiniere beside a prop of the Fishermen King's trident (*right*).

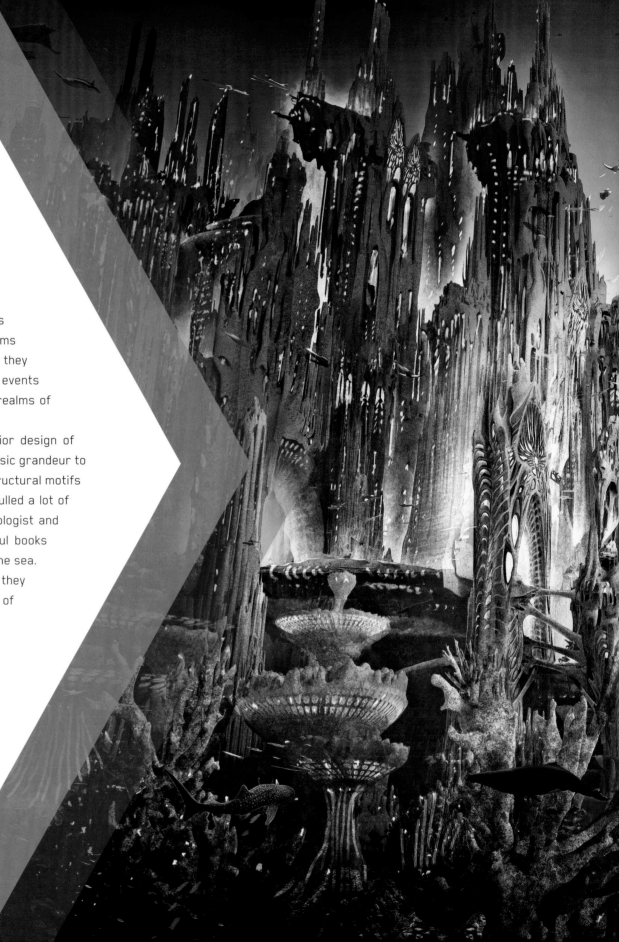

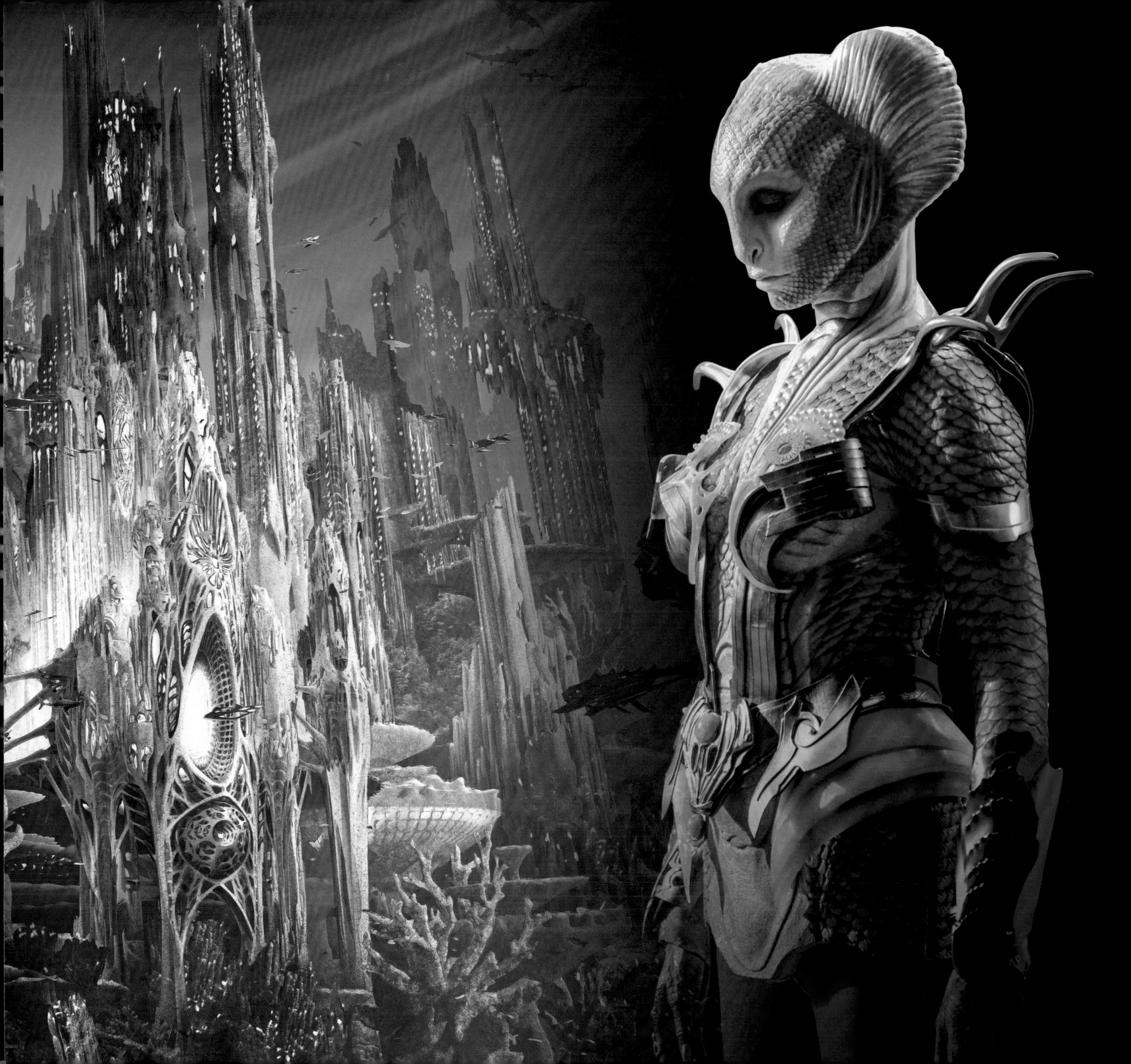

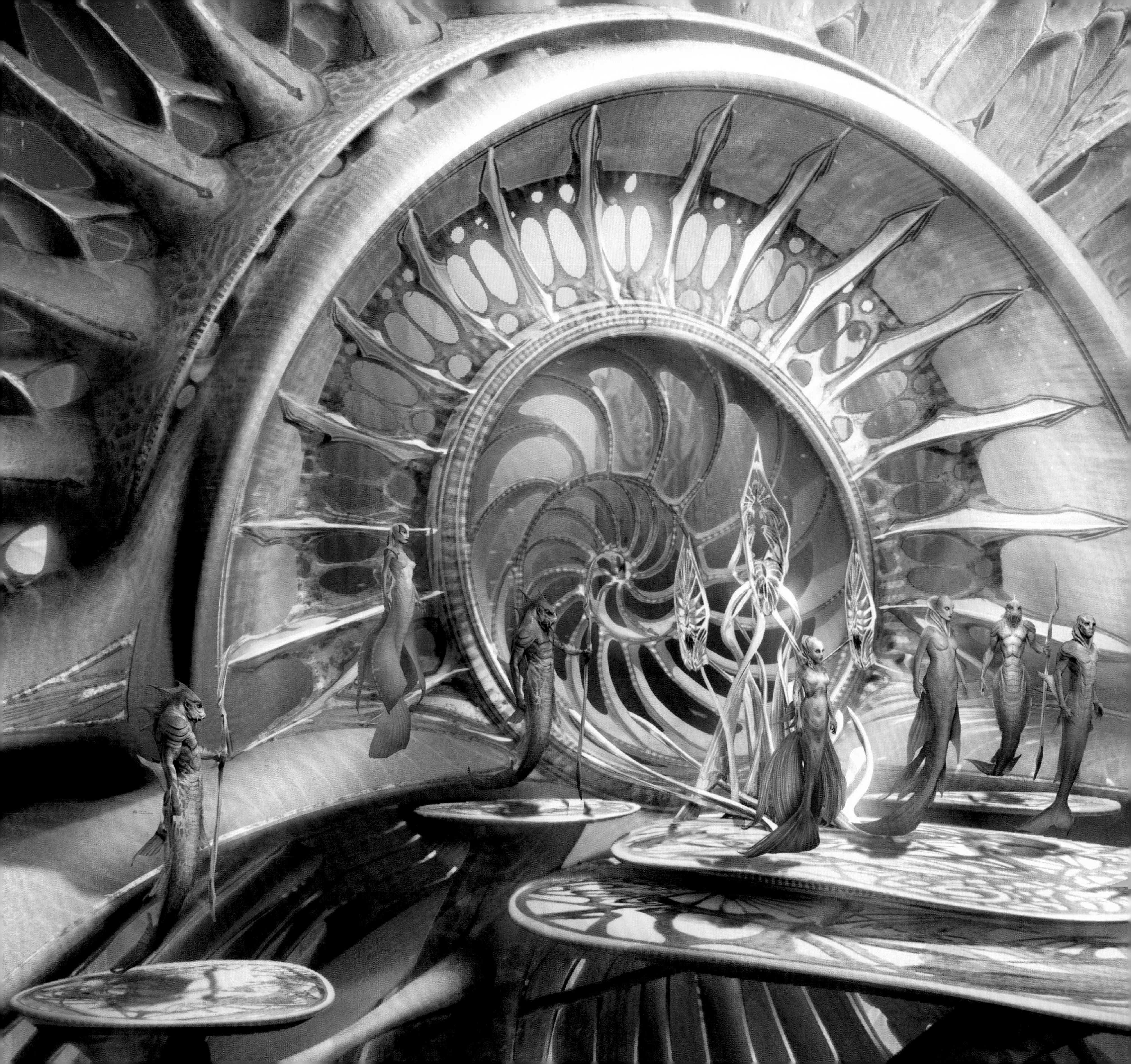

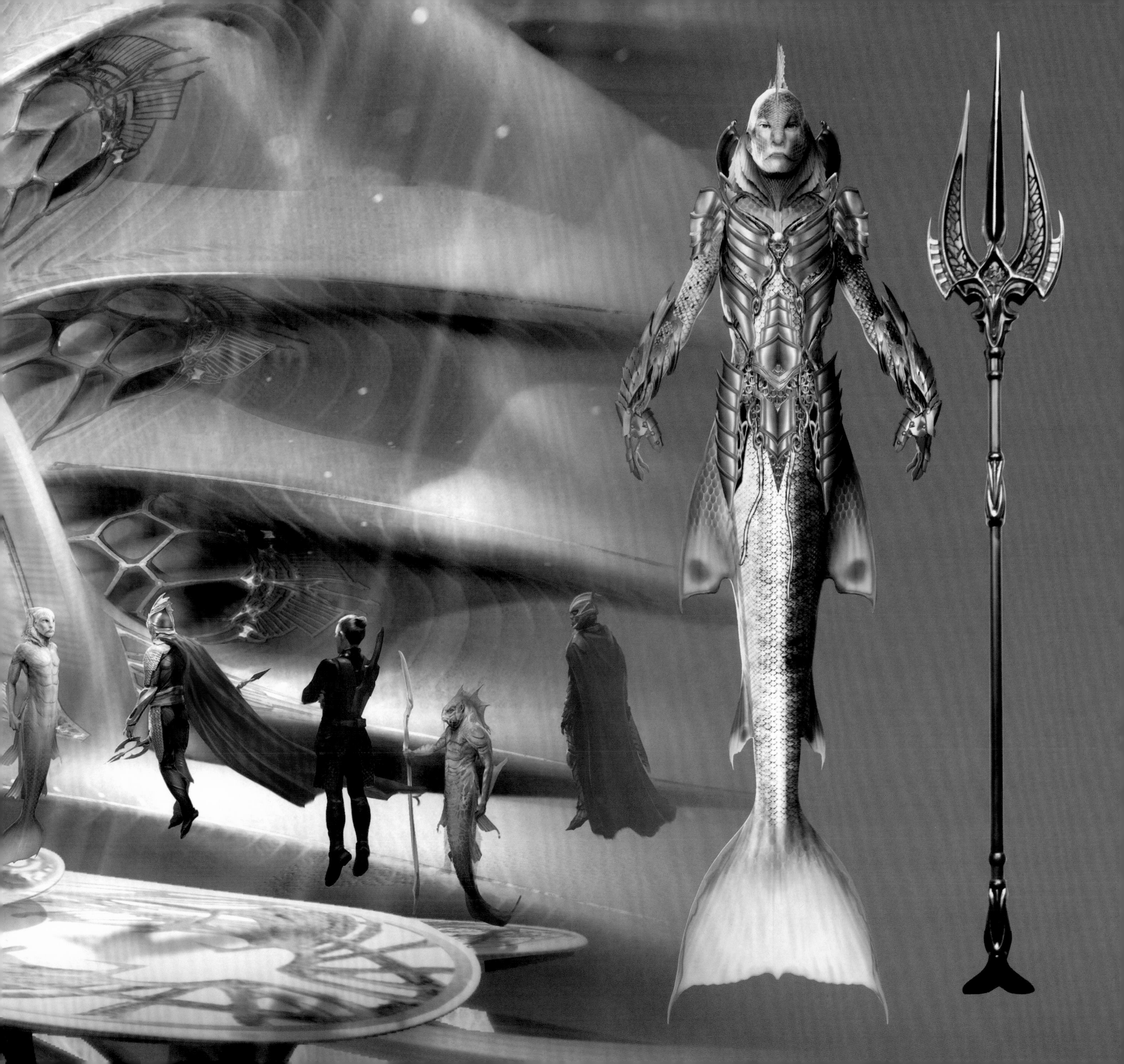

FISHERMEN VESSELS

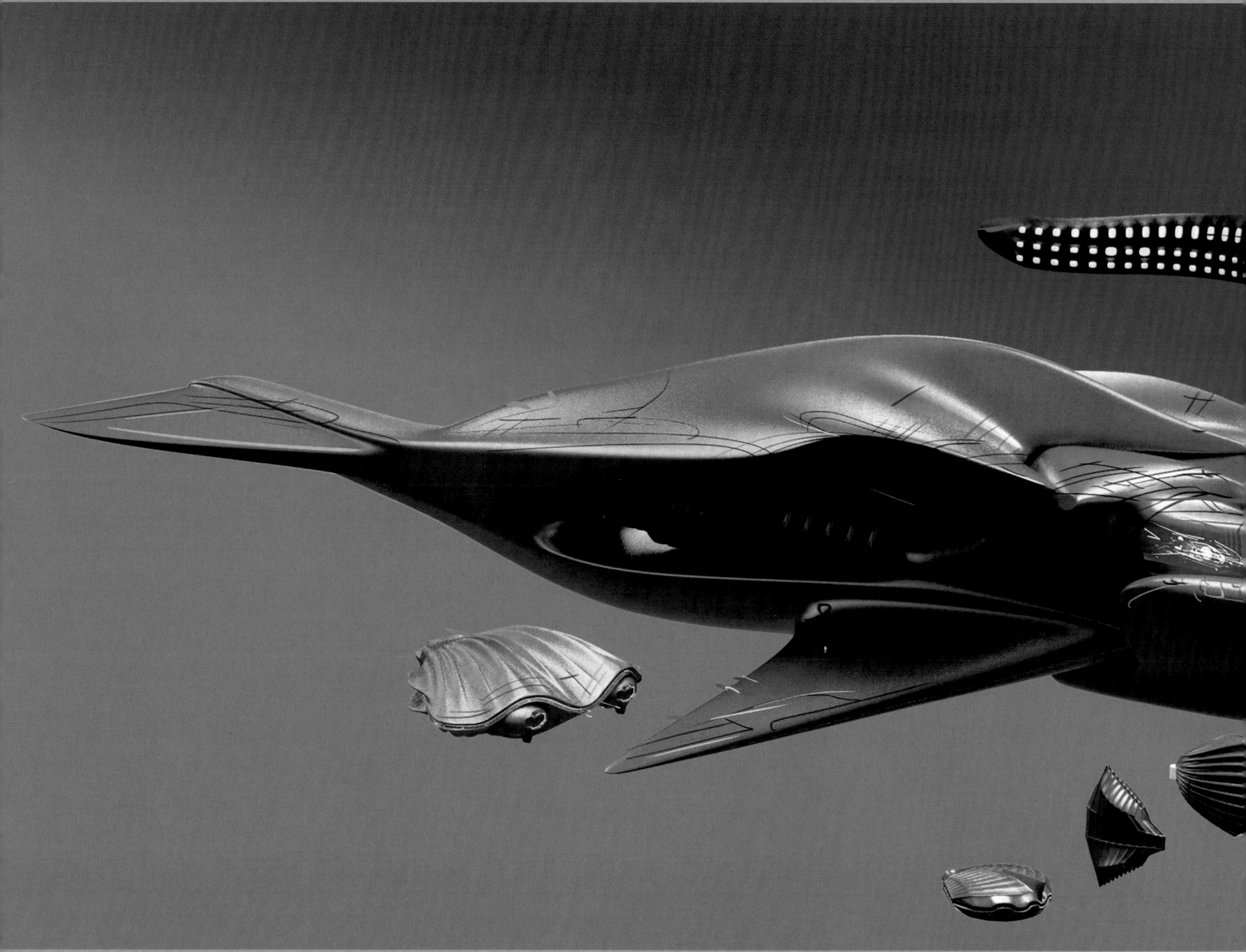

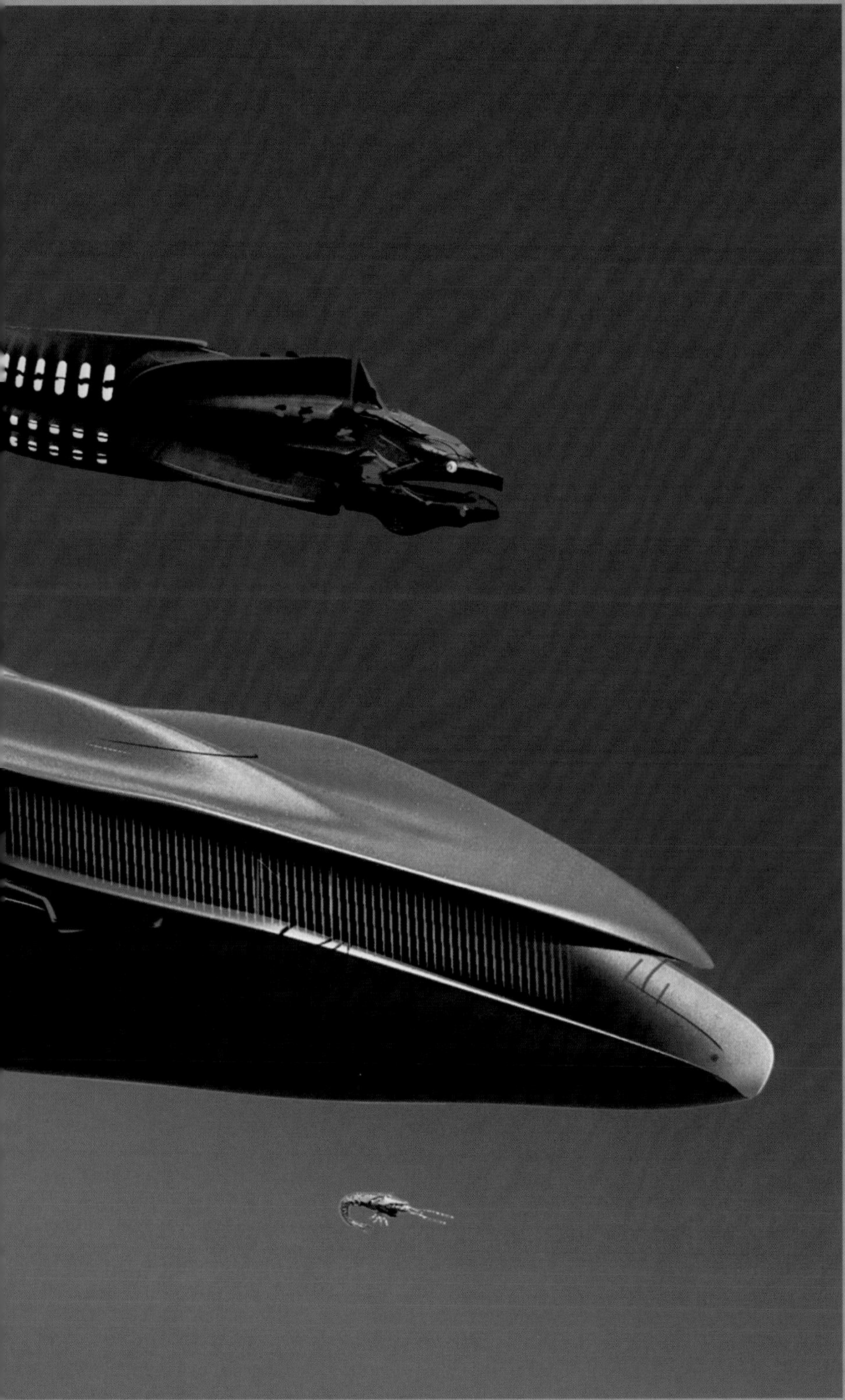

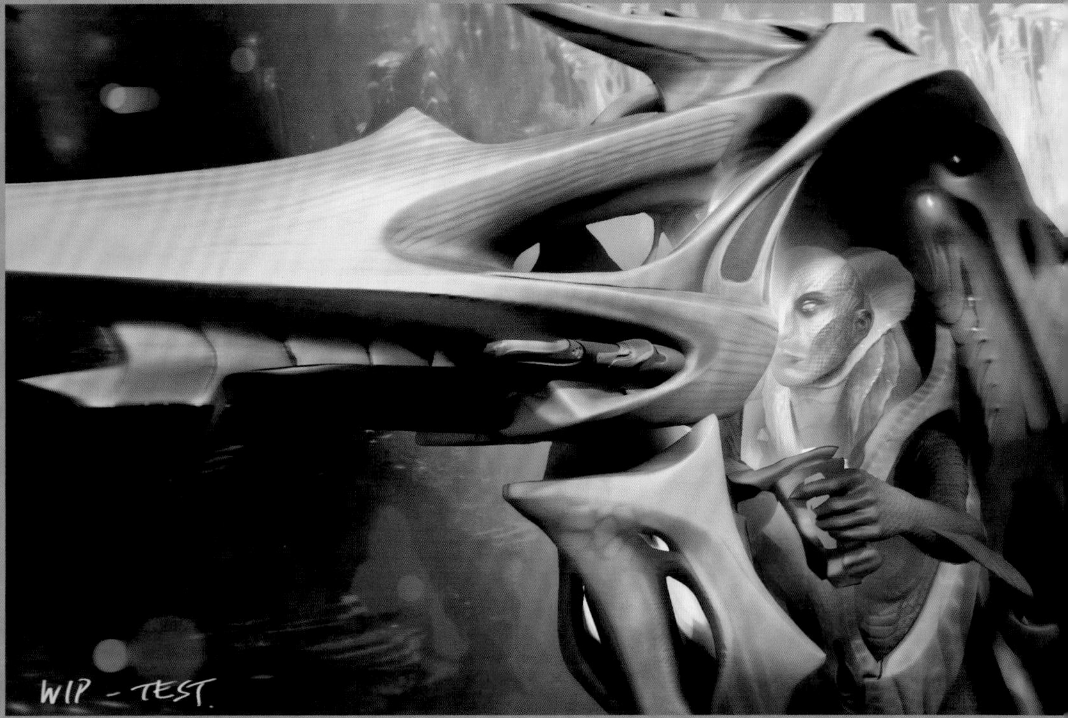
WIP - TEST

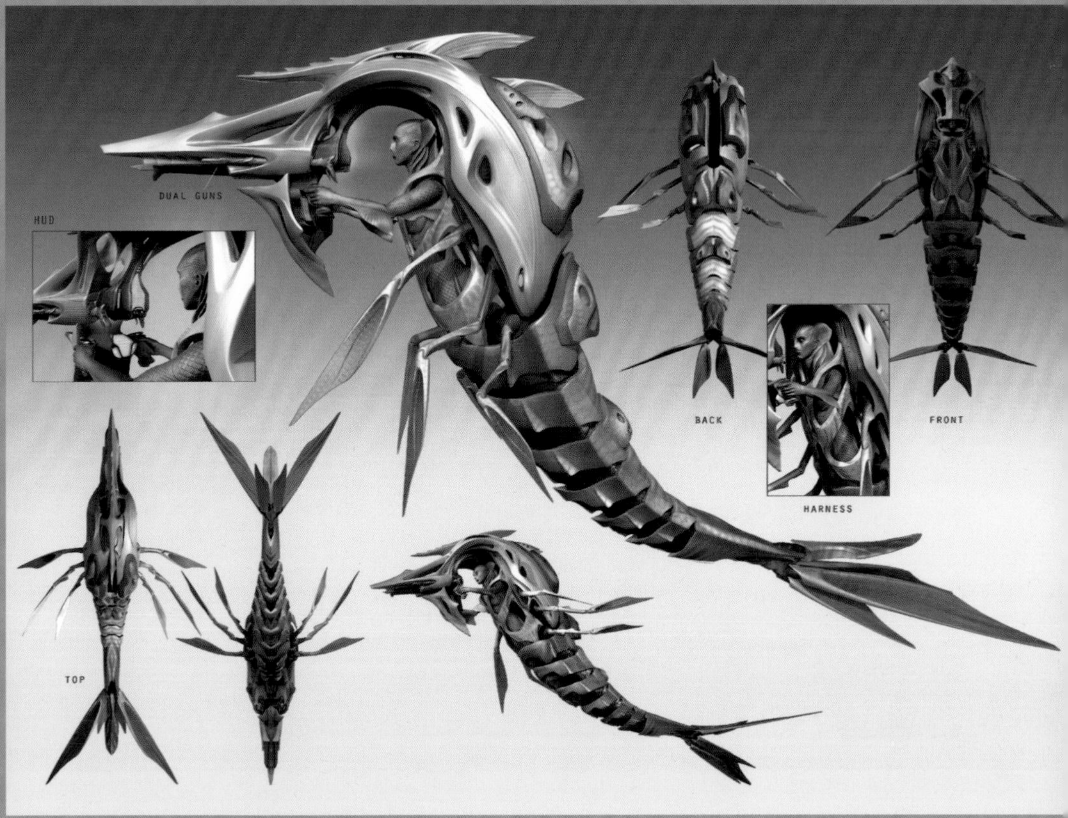
DUAL GUNS
HUD
BACK
FRONT
HARNESS
TOP

LEFT: Fishermen vessels concept art by Ed Natividad.

ABOVE TOP AND BOTTOM: The Fishermen Princess's personal craft concept art by Jeremy Love.

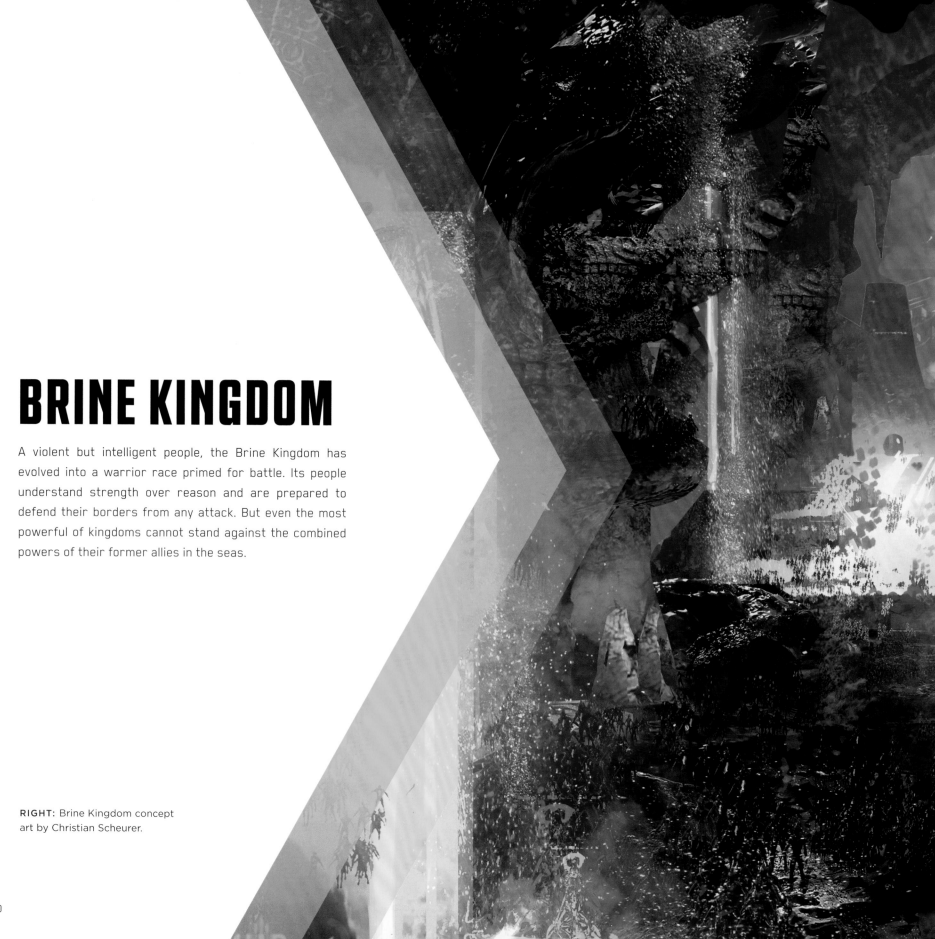

BRINE KINGDOM

A violent but intelligent people, the Brine Kingdom has evolved into a warrior race primed for battle. Its people understand strength over reason and are prepared to defend their borders from any attack. But even the most powerful of kingdoms cannot stand against the combined powers of their former allies in the seas.

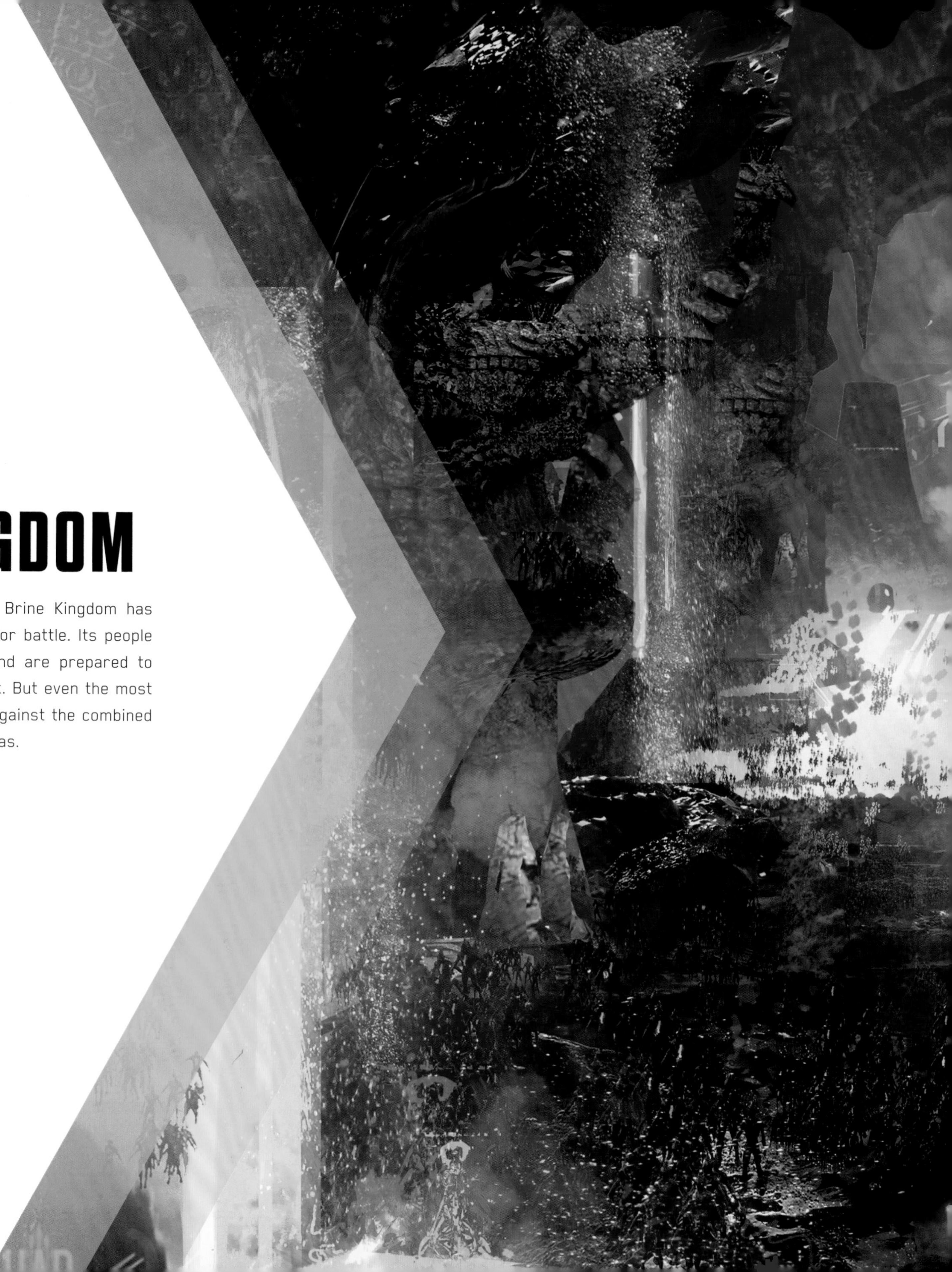

RIGHT: Brine Kingdom concept art by Christian Scheurer.

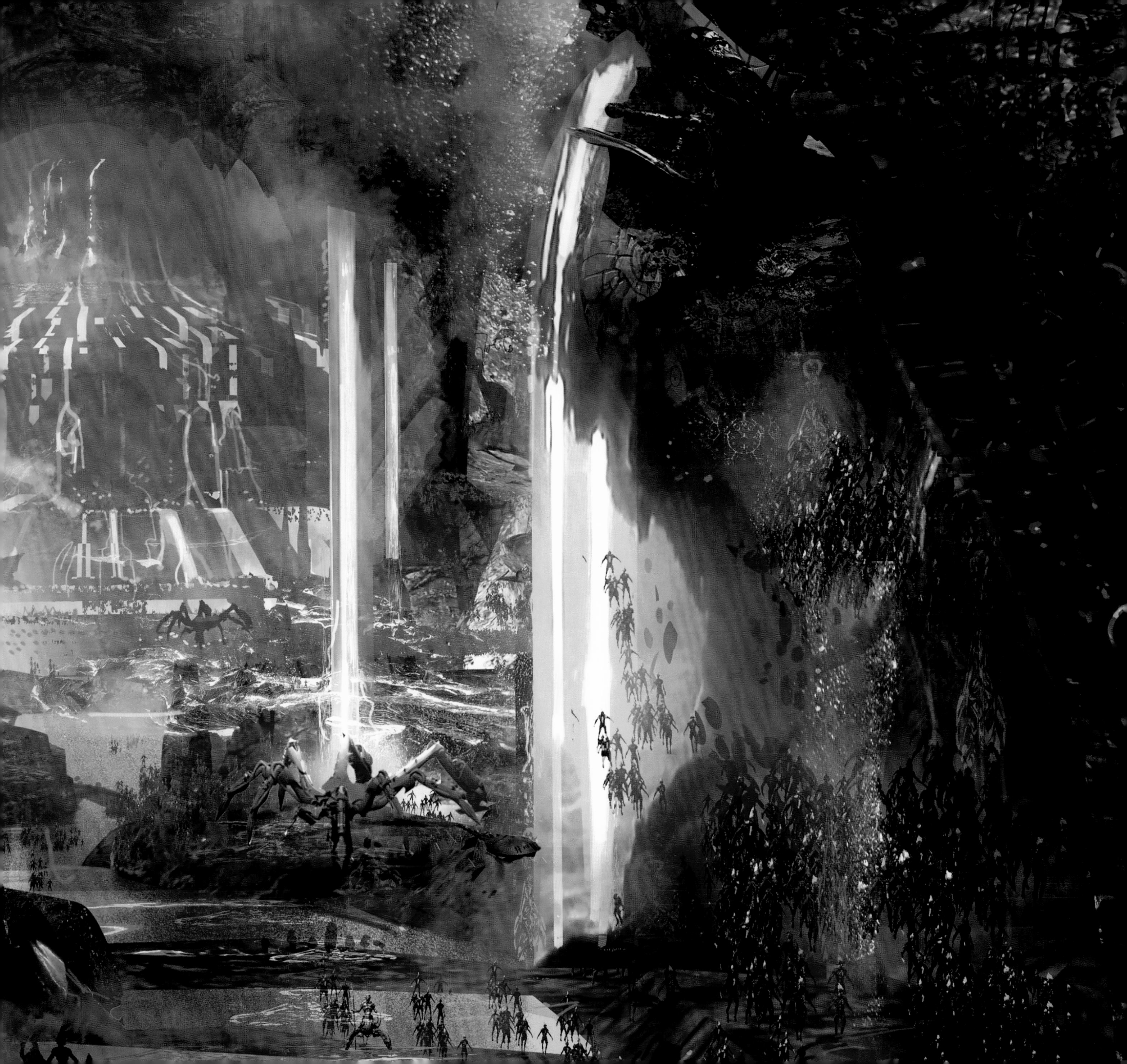

BRINE VESSELS

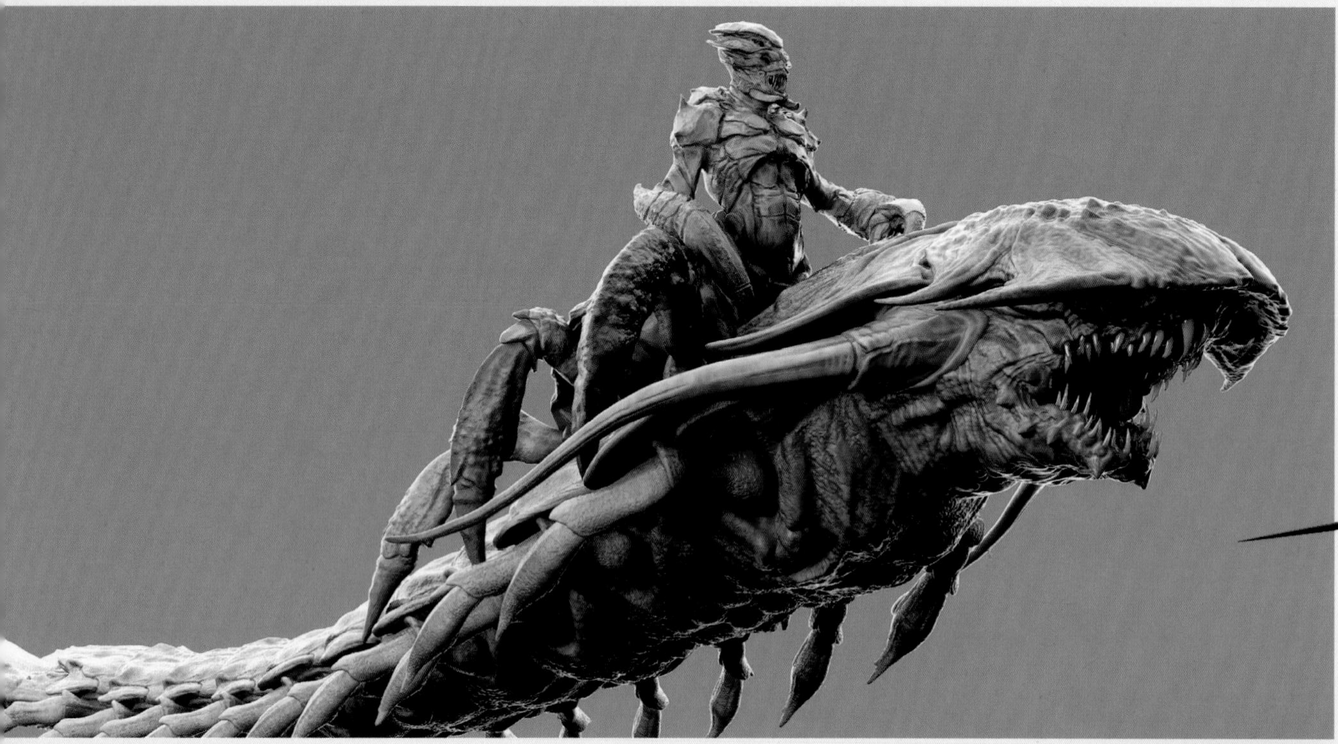

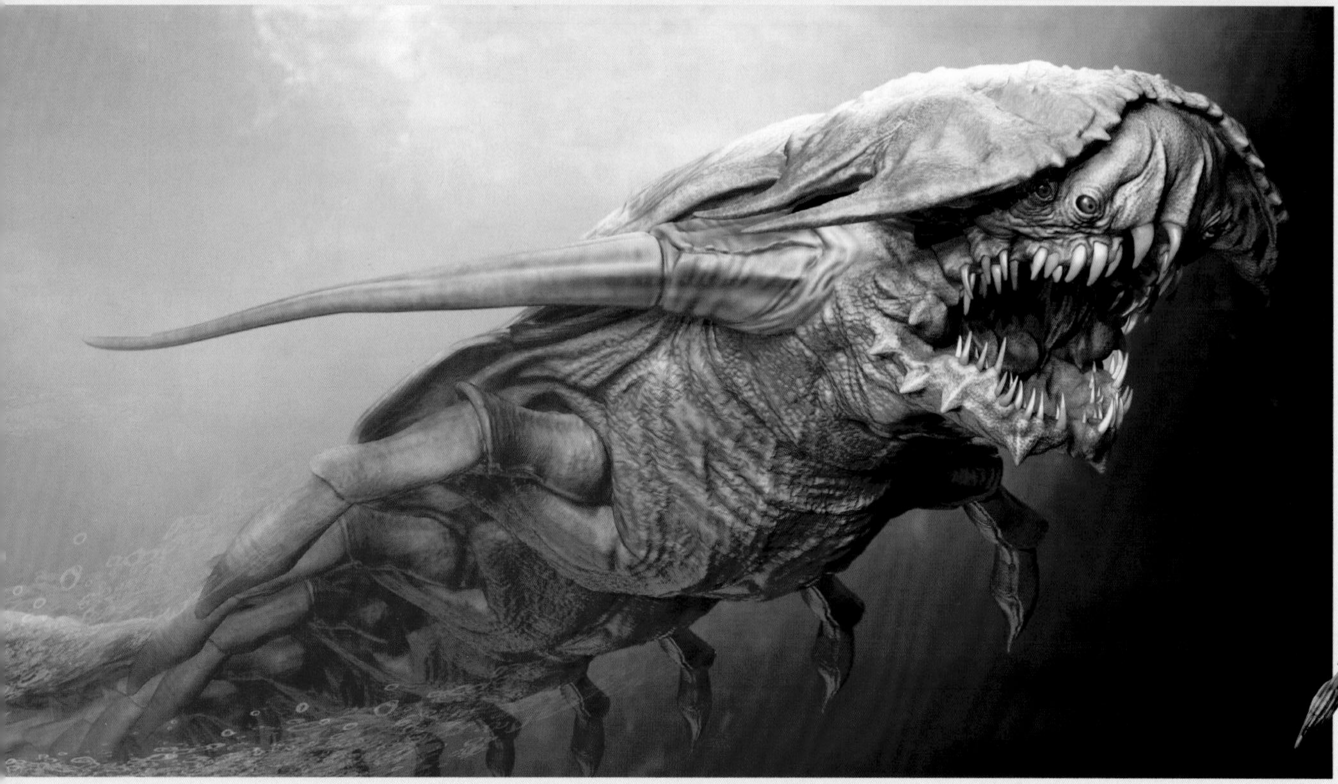

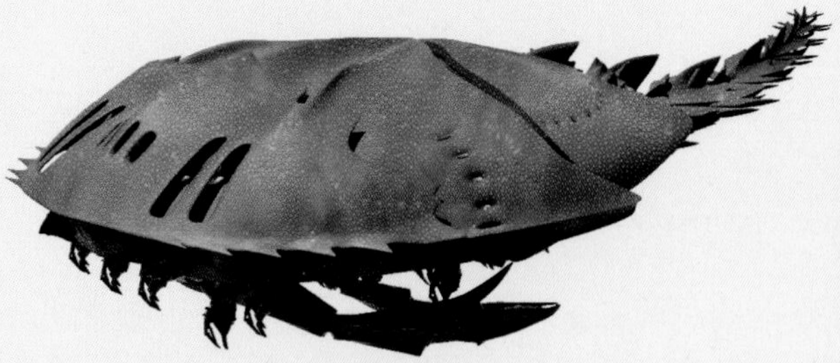

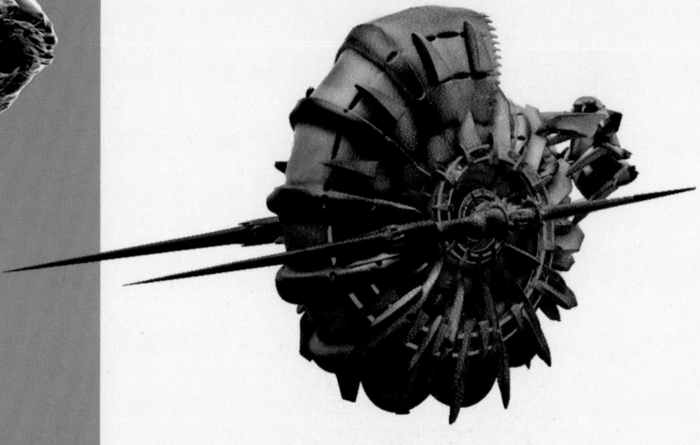

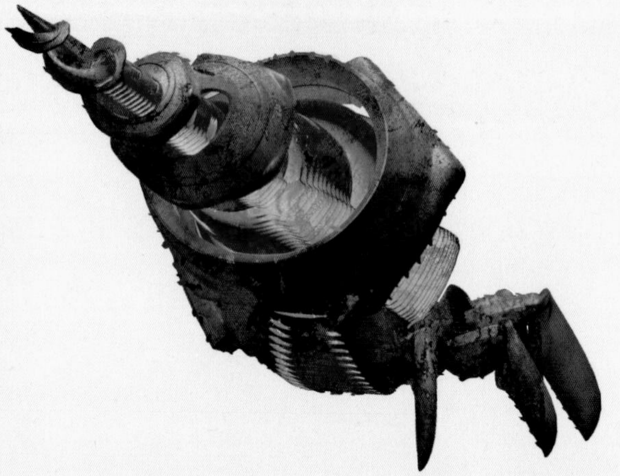

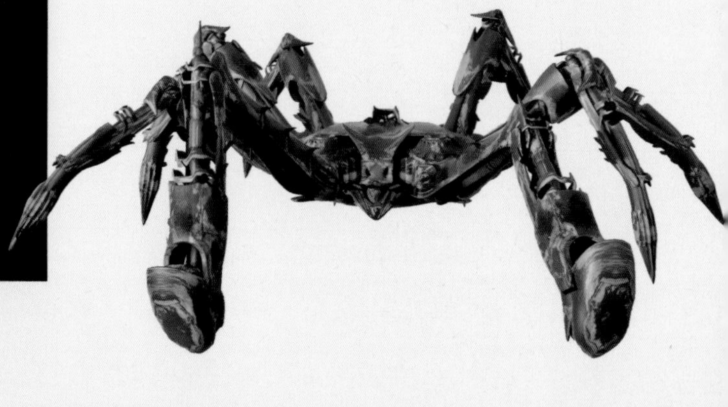

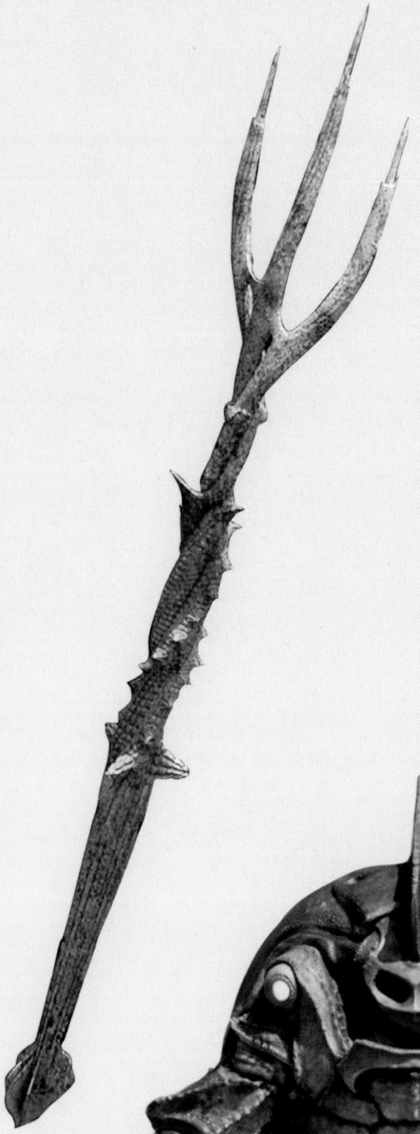

OPPOSITE LEFT: Two Brine creature troop carrier concept art pieces by Howard Swindell.
OPPOSITE RIGHT: Four Brine vessel concept art pieces by Ed Natividad.
THIS PAGE: The Brine King's trident (*left*); Brine King concept art by Ed Natividad (*right*); and Brine King final CGI revealing the minor enhancements made to the character after the art (*below*).

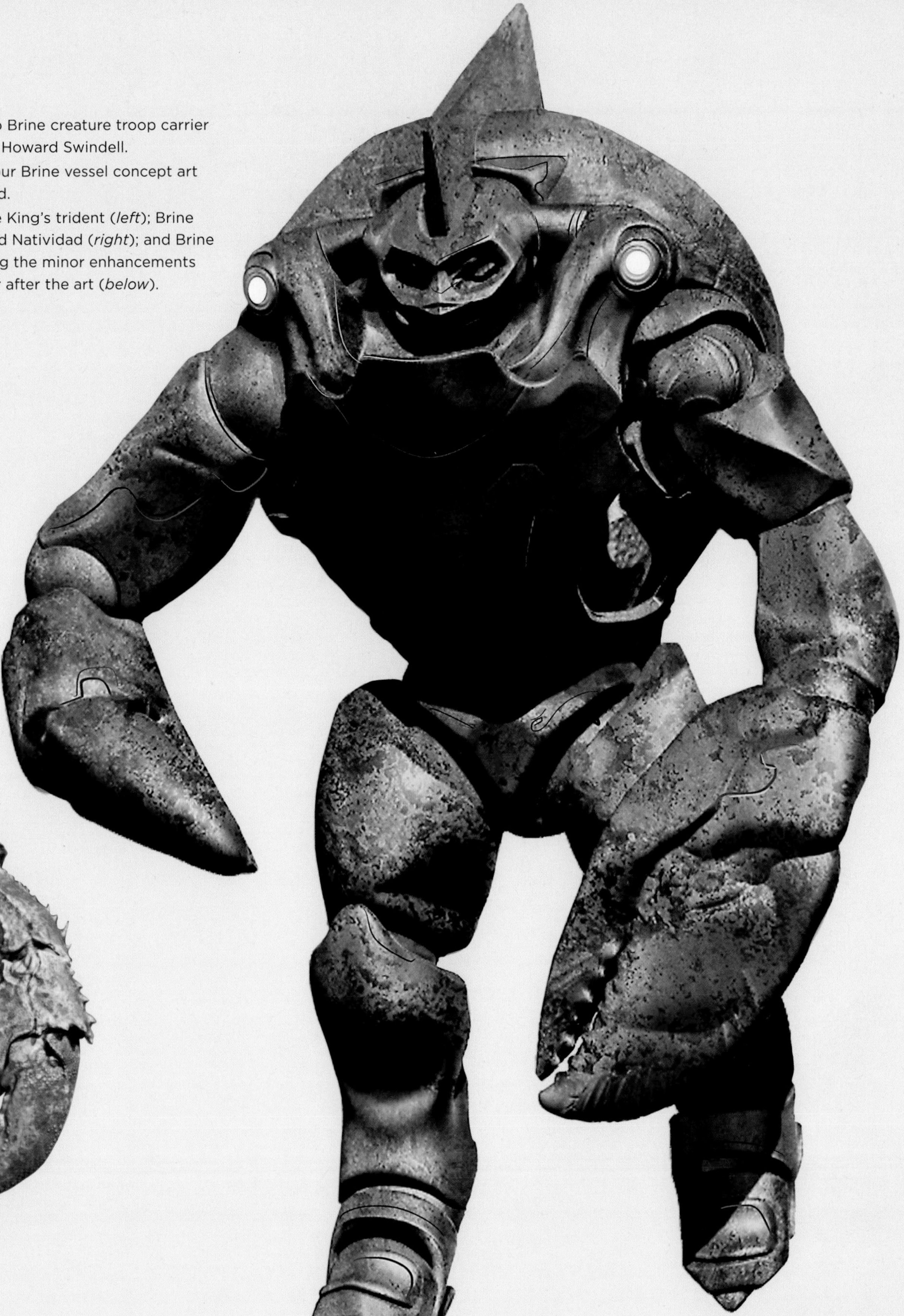

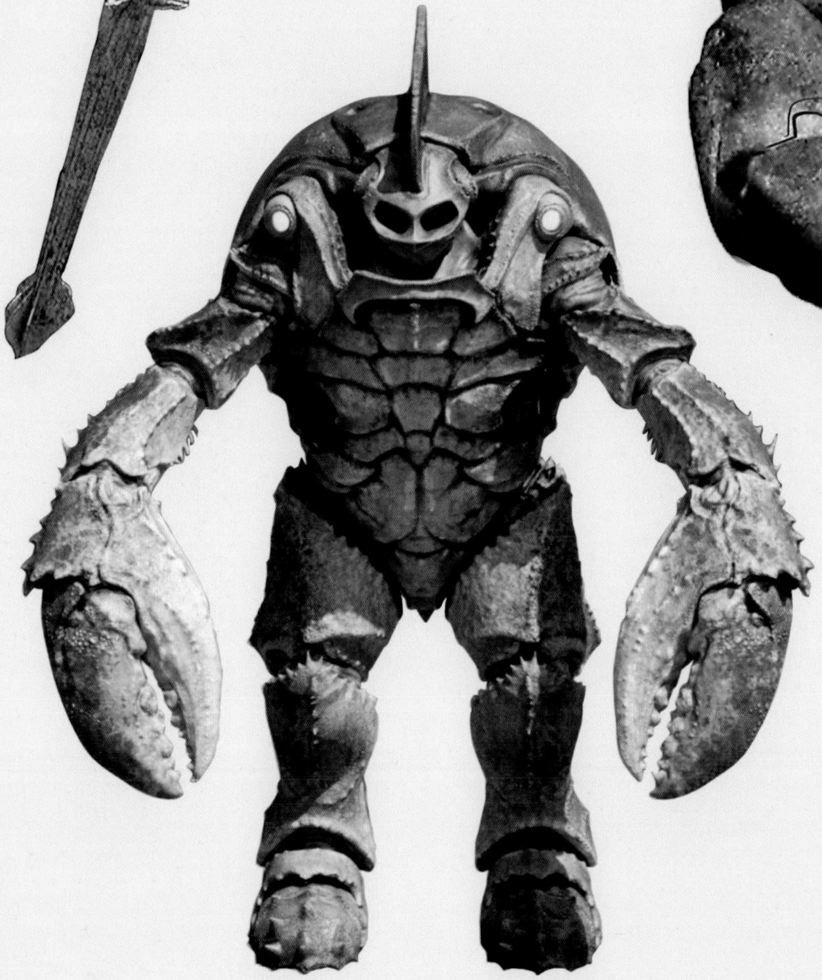

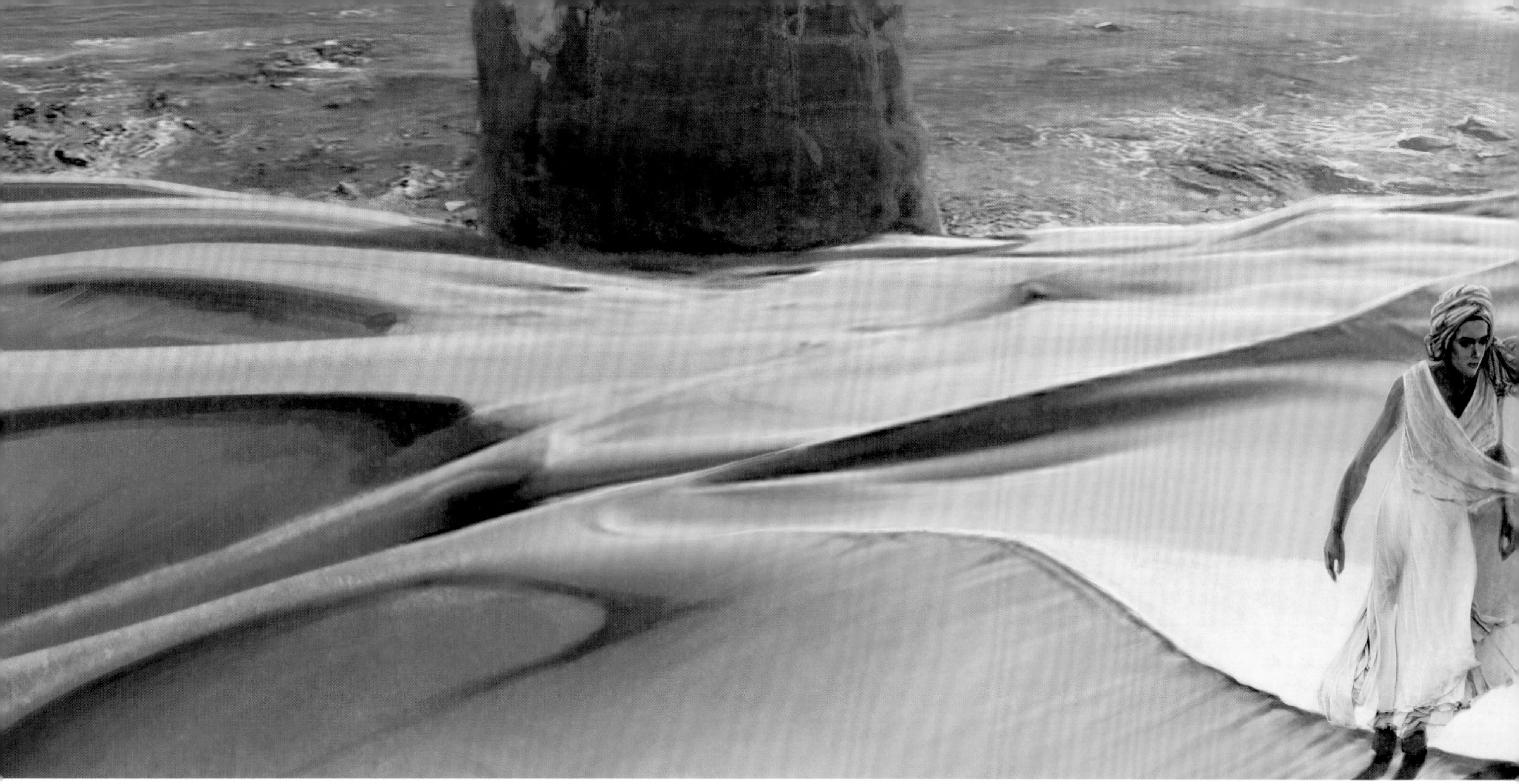

DESERTERS KINGDOM

The first kingdom to separate from Atlantis gave birth to the word that has come to represent a craven form of abandonment. The Deserters Kingdom is the most dramatically different of the kingdoms, and it is a significant location in Arthur and Mera's quest for the sacred trident. Once a strong ally and the formal armory of Atlantis, the kingdom has gone extinct, with its great hall and the intricate machinery therein lost for generations.

ABOVE: Sahara desert concept art by Jason Carson.
OPPOSITE BOTTOM: Deserters Kingdom concept art by Jason Carson.
PAGES 126–127: Deserters Kingdom flashback art by Christian Scheurer.

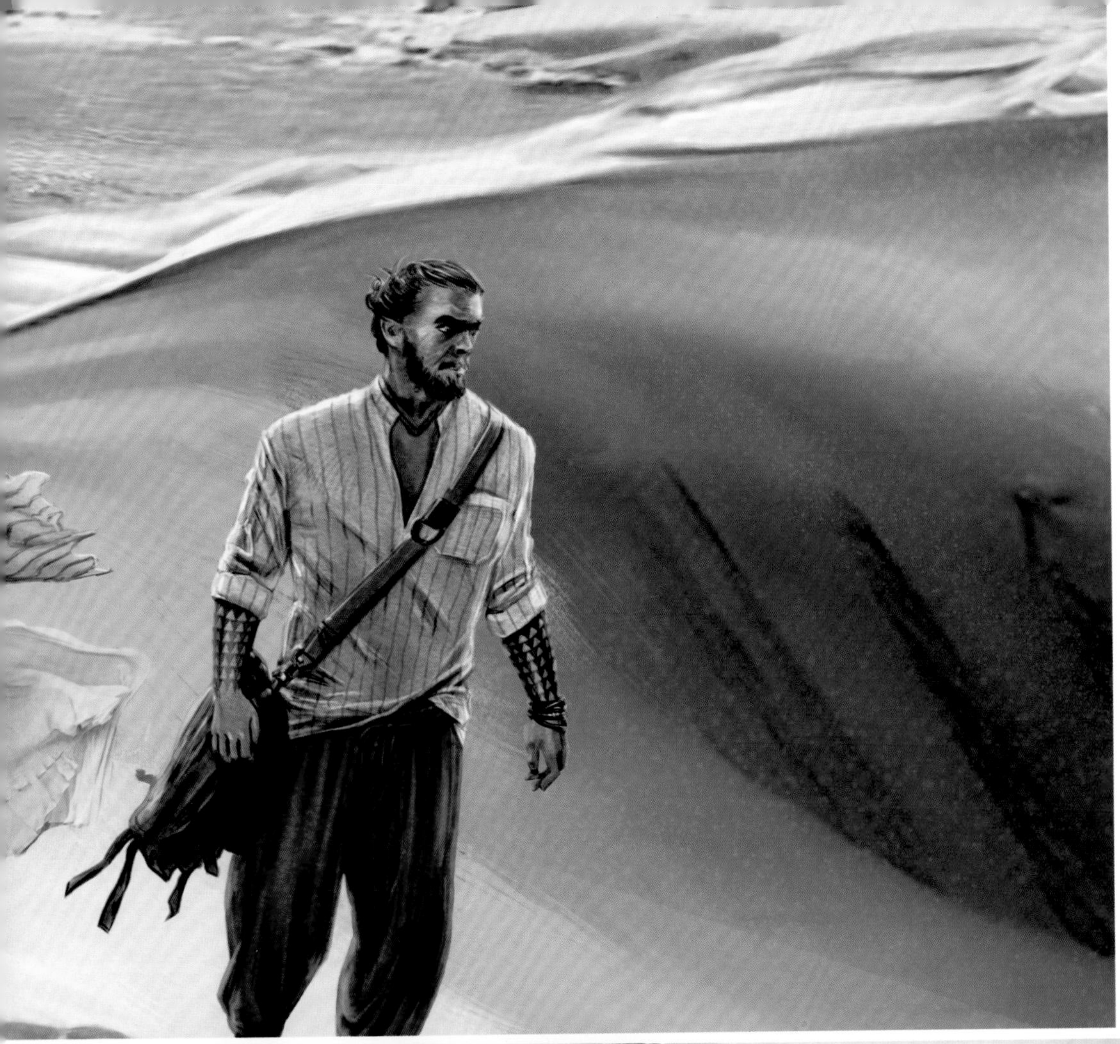

"THE DESERTERS KINGDOM WAS fun. We don't really know in this movie if any of the Deserter people are still alive, or if the race is completely extinct and gone. Their kingdom now is completely dried out. It's discovered underground in the middle of the Sahara desert. It has a wonderful, Indiana Jones-like quality to it."

—Kelvin McIlwain, Visual Effects Supervisor

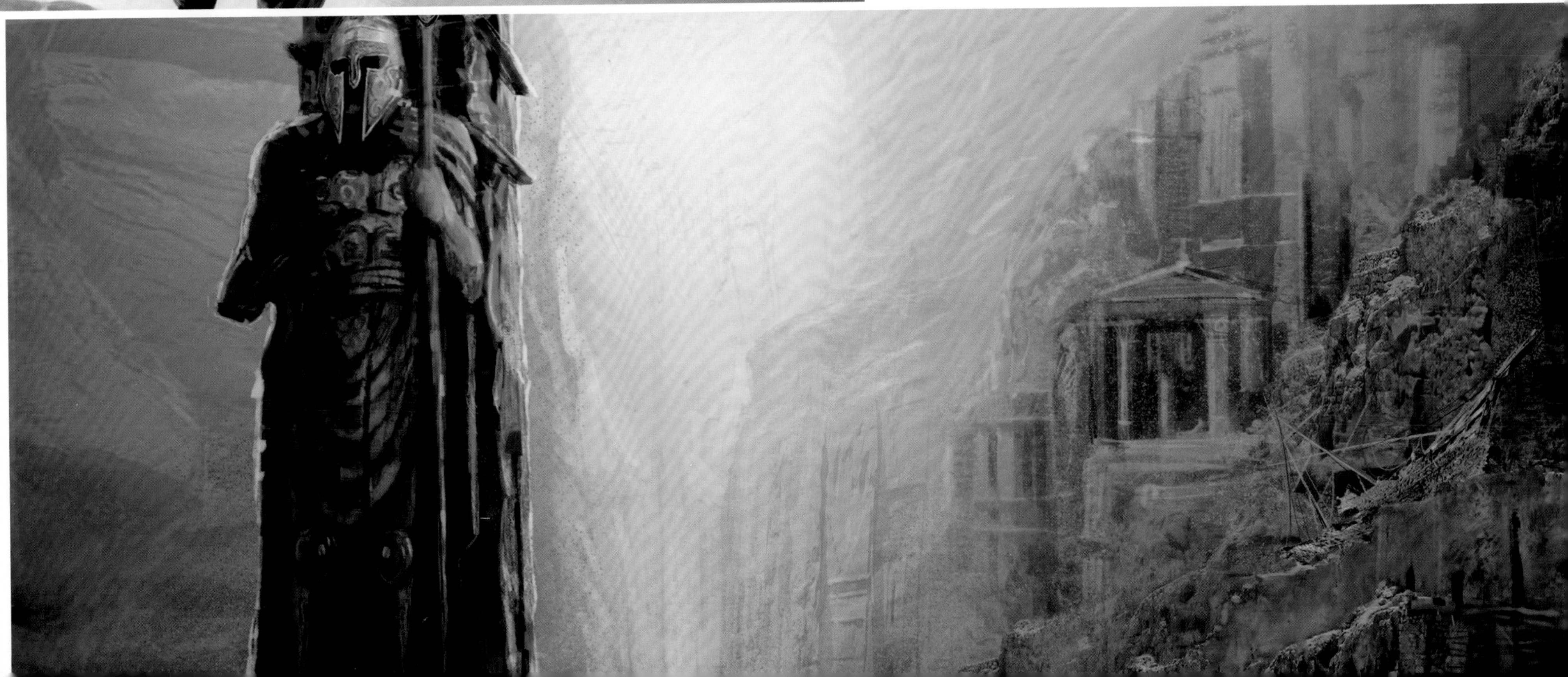

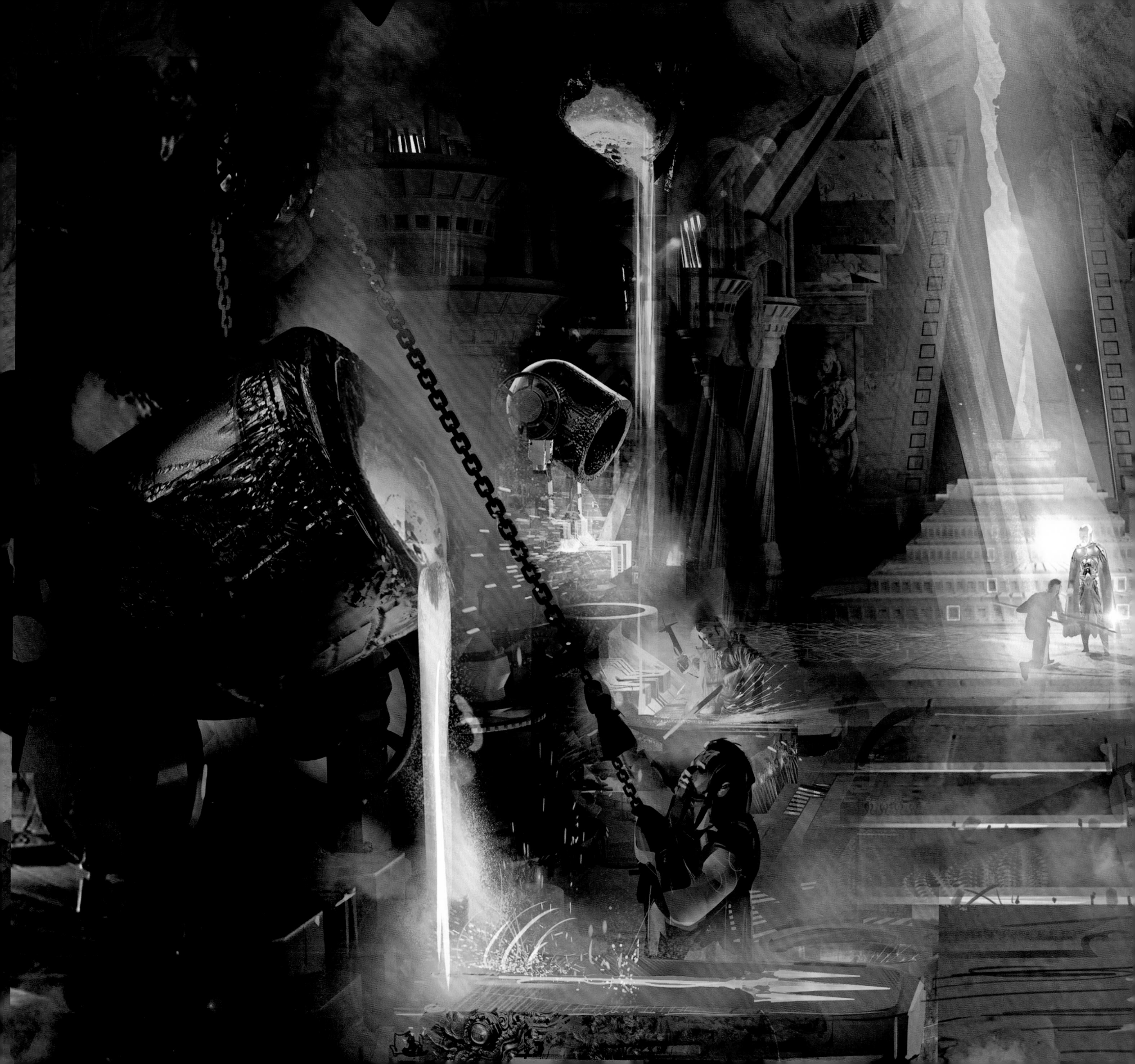

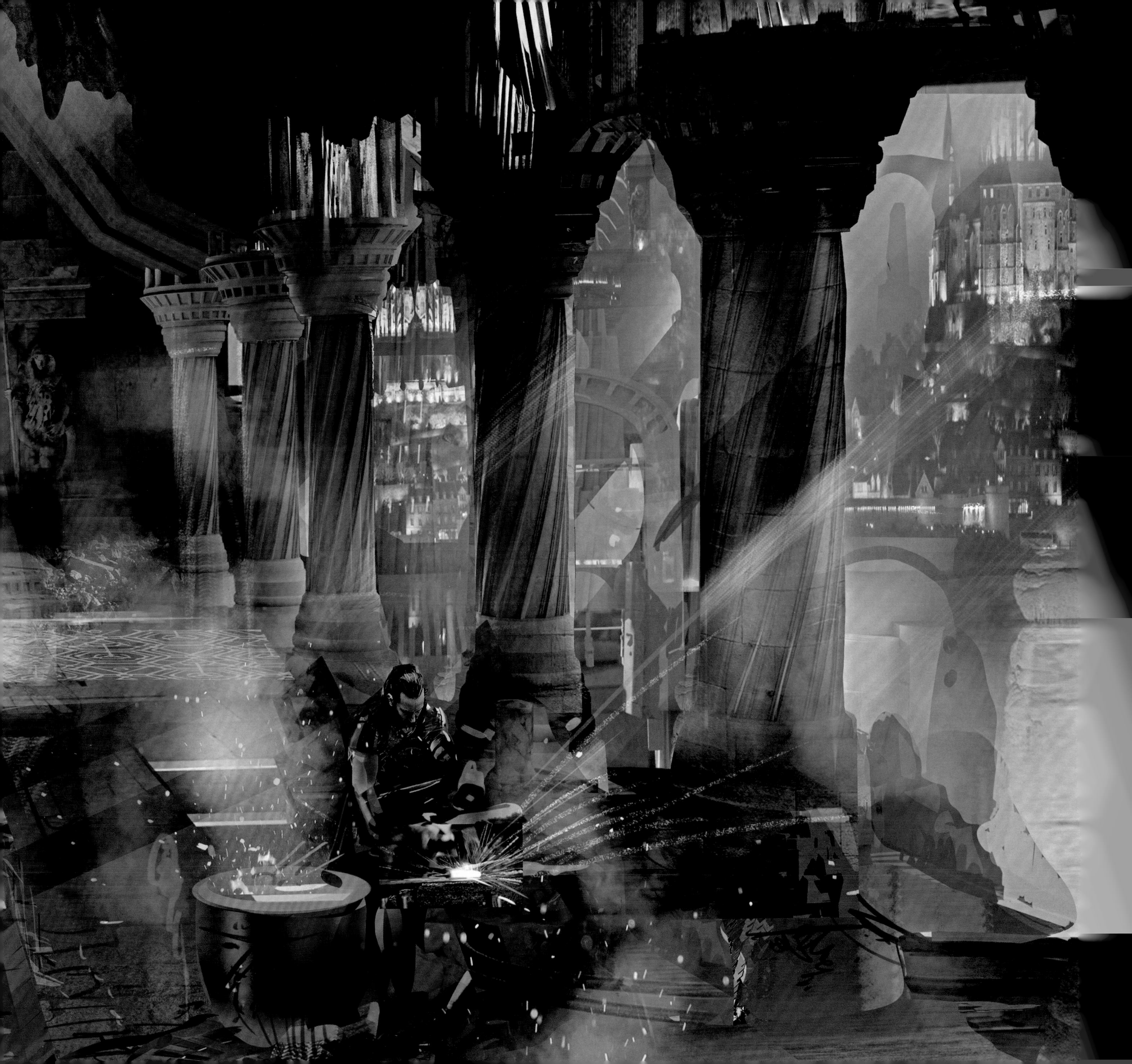

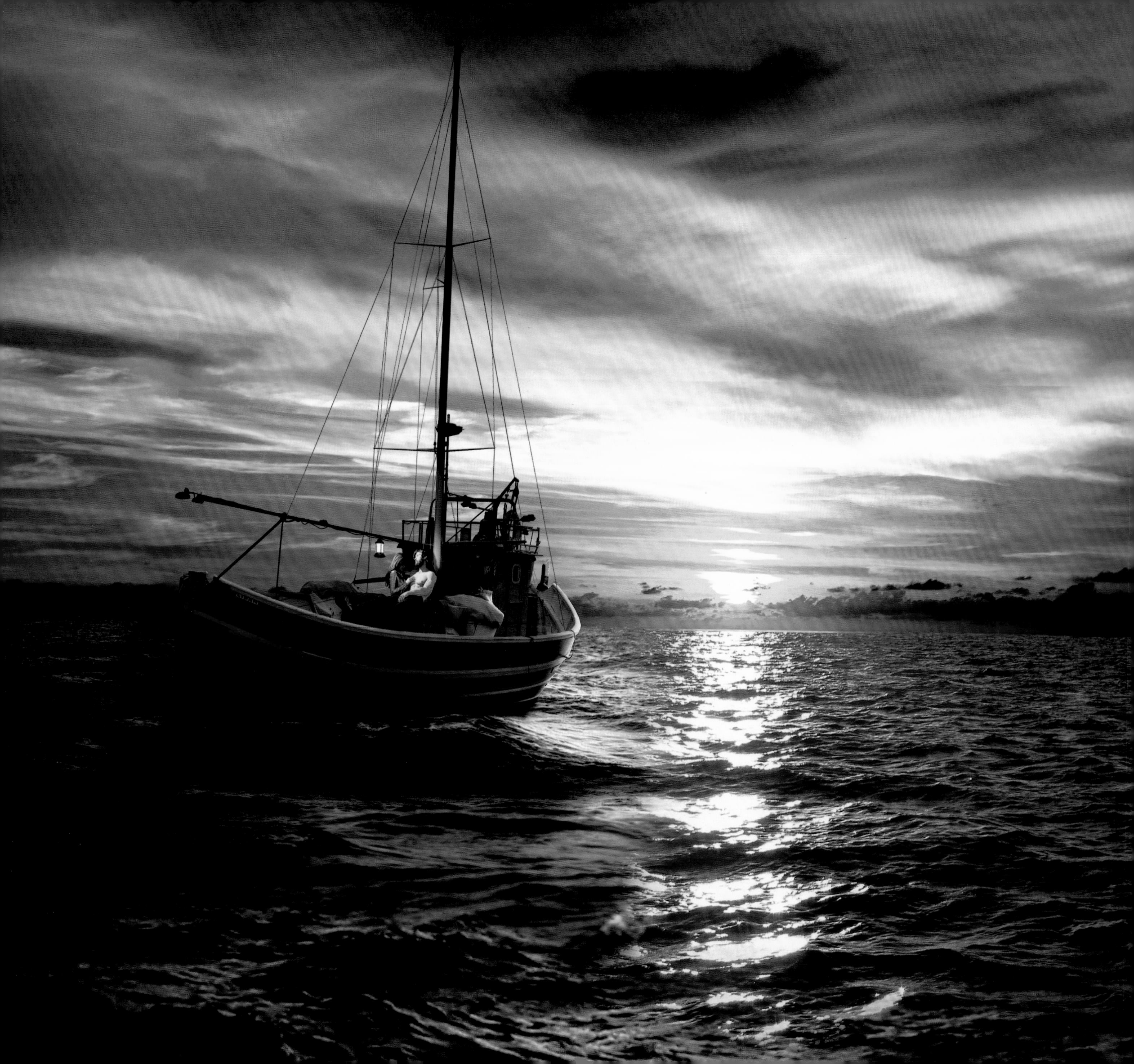

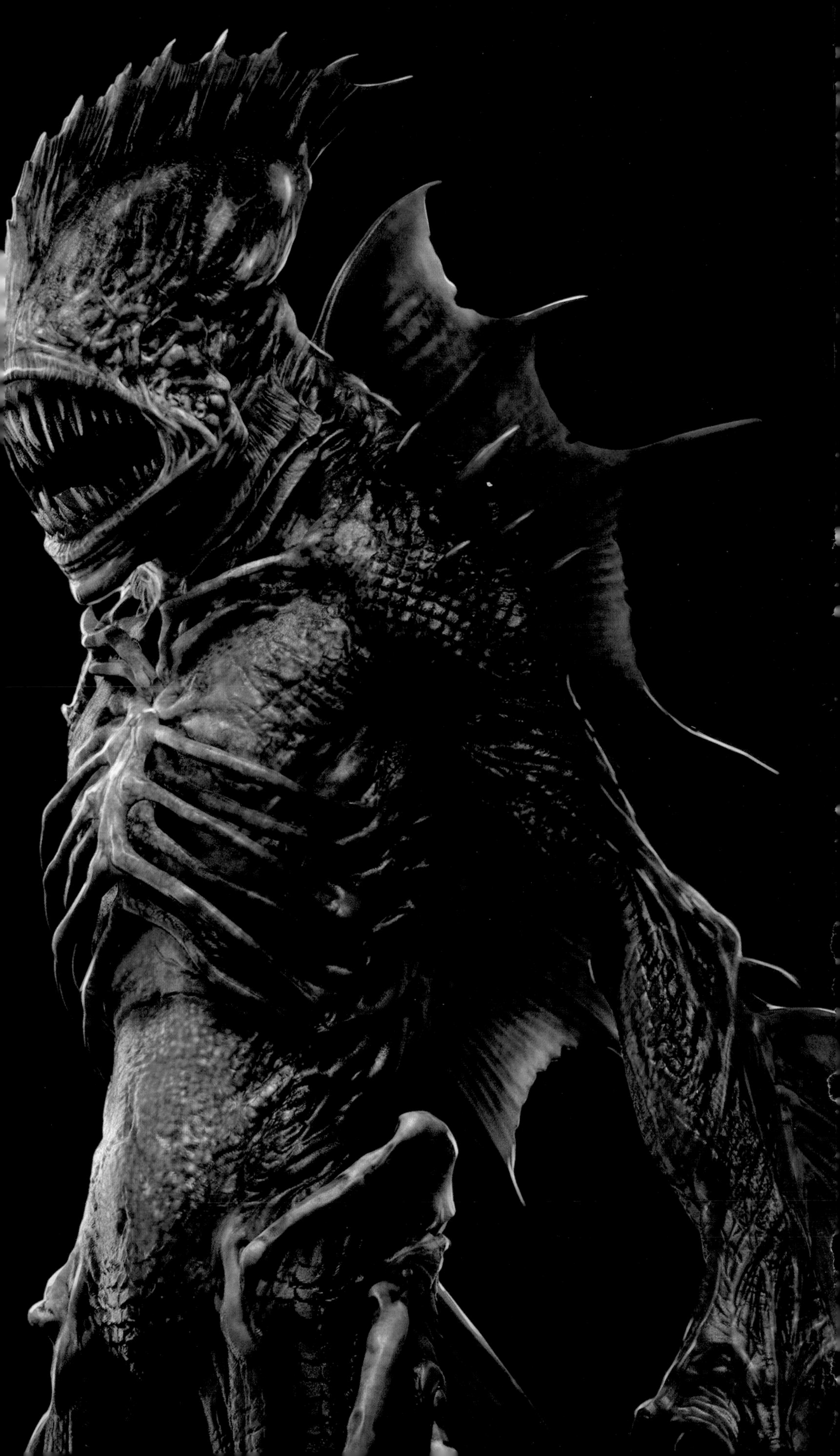

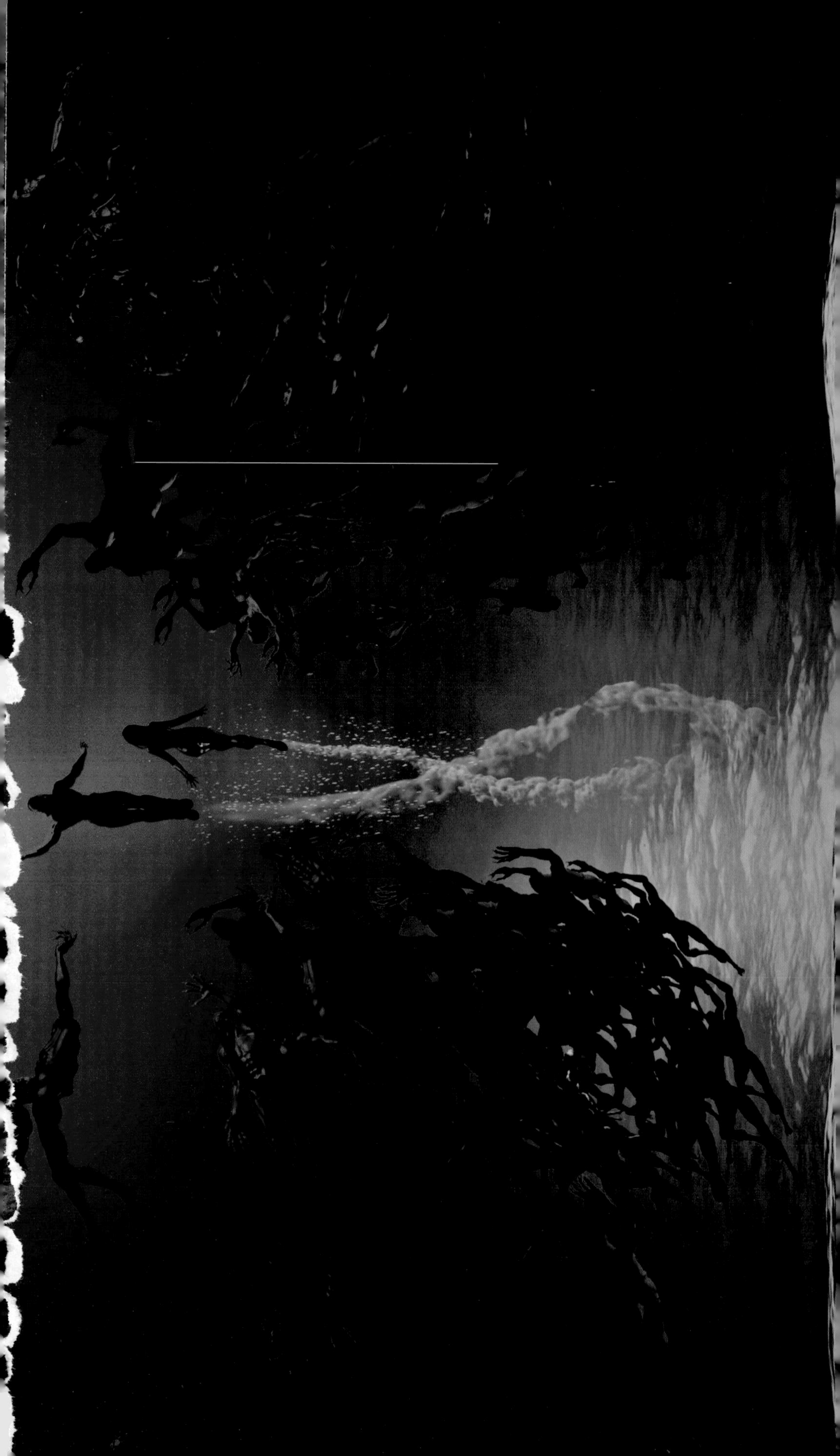

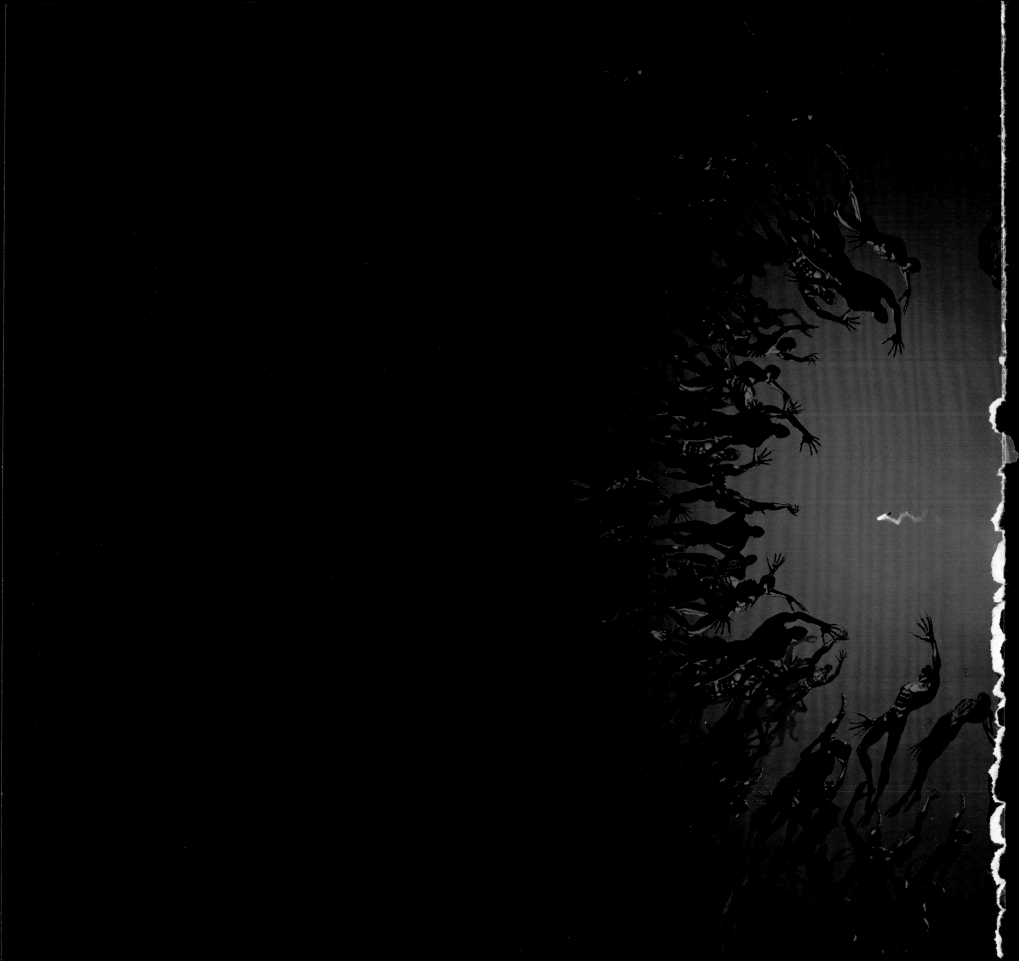

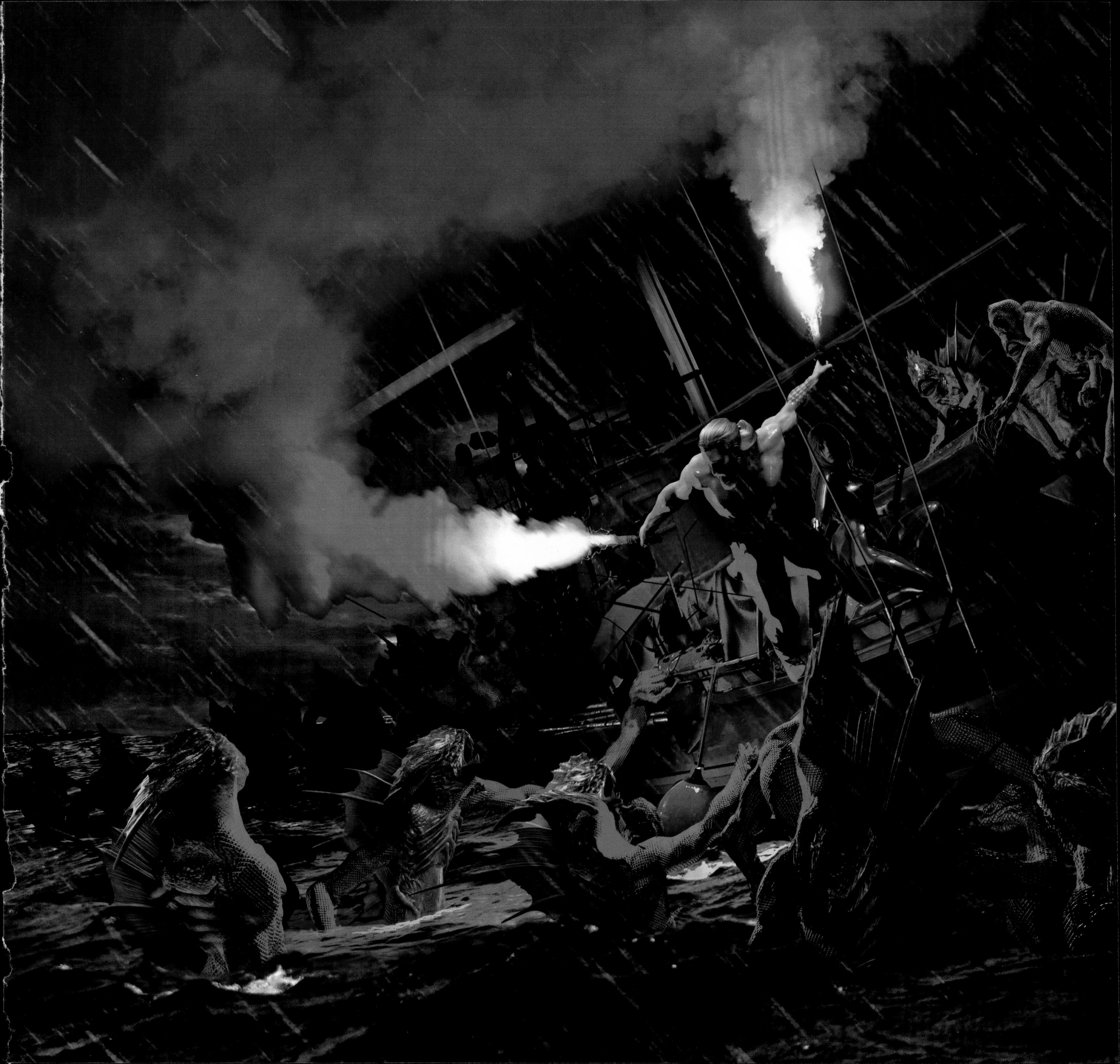

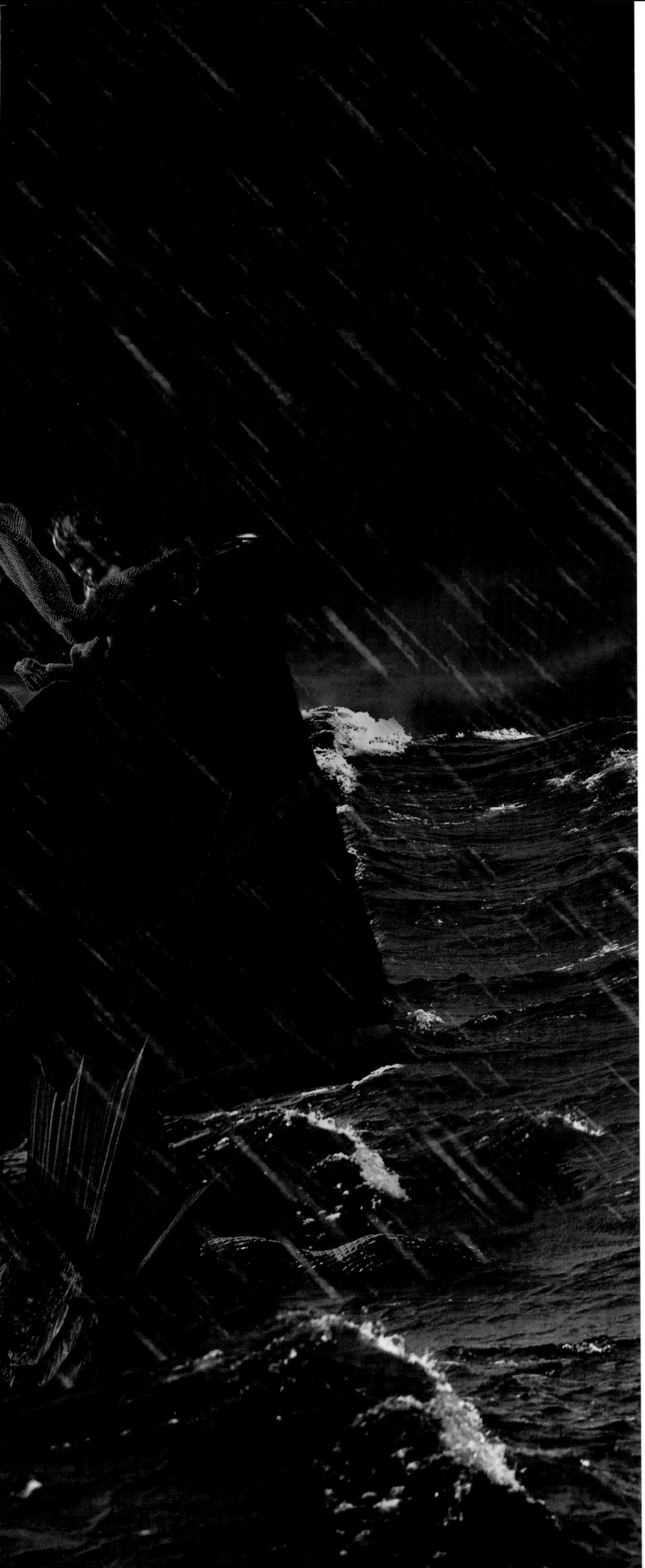

THE TRENCH ATTACK

Arthur and Mera are attacked by a horde of the Trench while on a fishing boat at night as they near the end of their quest for the lost trident. It is one of the most visually stunning moments in the movie. According to Peter Safran, a rudimentary mockup of that moment actually helped convince Warner Bros. to go ahead with the film. "We created an animatic version of that scene that we showed the studio, and it harkened back to James [Wan]'s pure horror days," says Safran. "It's like *Creature from the Black Lagoon*, but the 2018 version. It's pure horror, it's fantastic, and I think it's one of the things that really got the green light for the movie."

At one point during the Trench sequence, Arthur and Mera are swimming down into the Mariana Trench. The only light comes from a flare that Arthur fires to keep the Trench horde at bay. That's when the camera pulls back to reveal hundreds of creatures descending upon Arthur and Mera as they try to escape. It's a terrifying image that Wan crafted to encapsulate that, for all its majesty and natural beauty, the ocean can be a truly scary place. "James's bread and butter is horror. He really wanted to make that scene special and it meant quite a lot to him," Bill Brzeski says.

Wan had his team use real people inside temporary costumes for the close-up scenes when the Trench storm the fishing boat. Computer designers would add the final touches to the Trench creatures in postproduction, along with hundreds more CGI monsters, but the director wanted to take a practical approach to give the scene more authenticity. The Trench stunt team's unique challenge was to navigate their way around the fishing boat set on stilts while being pelted with rainwater.

The deck of the boat was larger than normal to accommodate camera coverage. "The Trench attack is a really detailed sequence, where the creatures get on the boat and then Arthur and Mera have to get flares and they have to fight these creatures," Brzeski says. "There needs to be enough room on the deck to do that." Even though it was performed on an Australian soundstage and not out in the open sea, this scene underscores the difficulty of filming any ocean-based scene. "Boats are never easy," Brzeski warns. "Water really adds a lot of complications to moviemaking."

It was a challenge the team fully embraced for a movie called *Aquaman*.

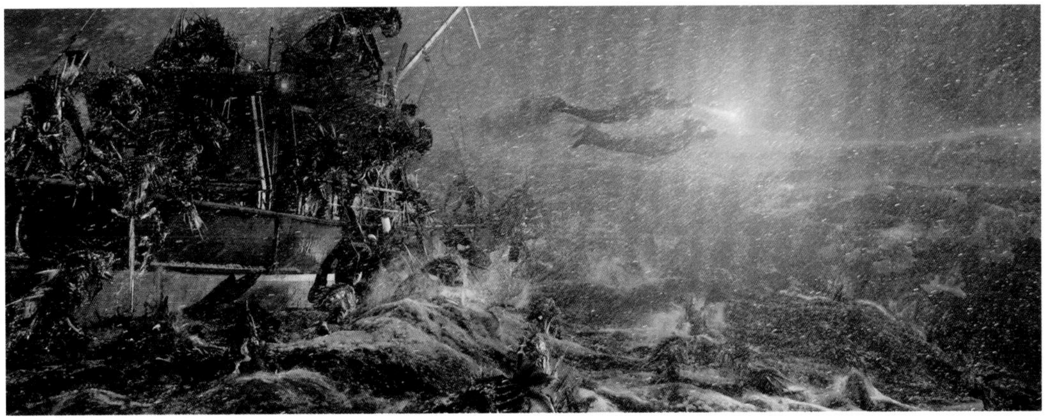

DEAD KING'S ISLAND

The oceans hold many secrets, and one of the deepest of these mysteries is the location of the sacred trident of Atlantis. Nestled away inside a hidden island, the trident sits in the final resting place of King Atlan, legendary ruler of Atlantis. A world of immense beauty populated by creatures as ancient as the seas, the Dead King's Island holds more than one surprising truth about Arthur's destiny.

PAGES 132-133: Trench attack concept art by Rob McKinnon (*left*) and final VFX shot of the scene (*right*).
RIGHT: Dead King's Island concept art by Sebastian Meyer.

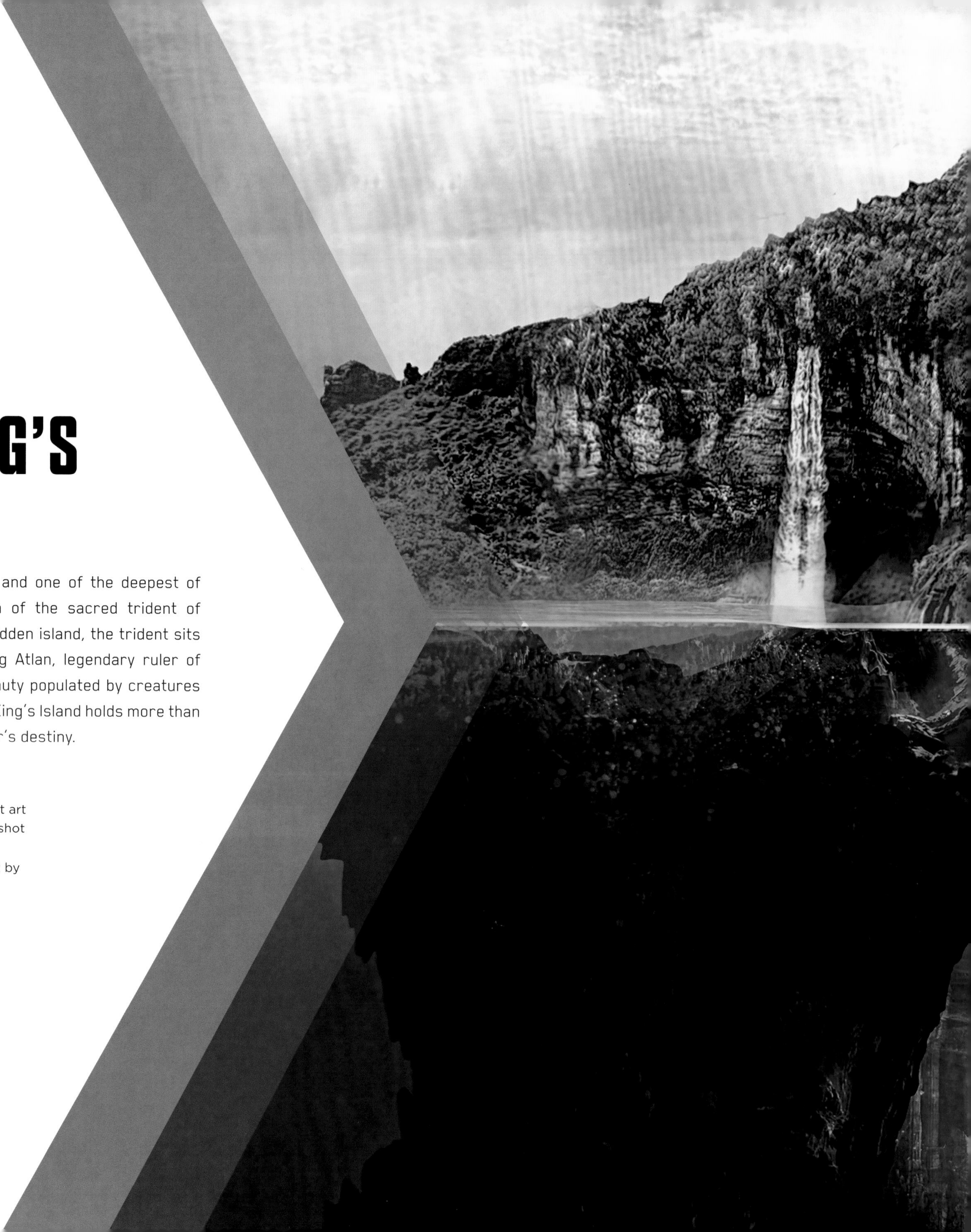

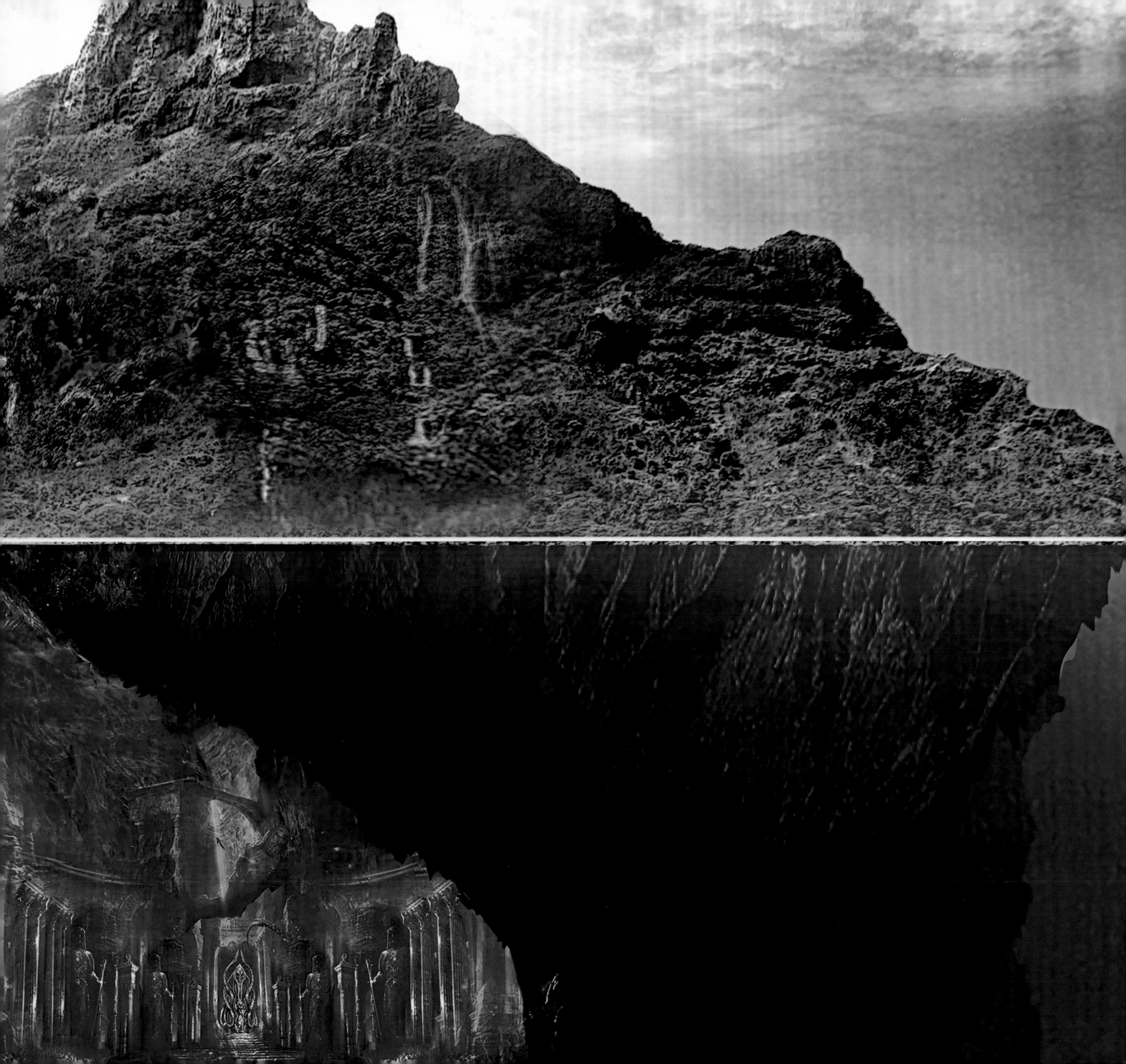

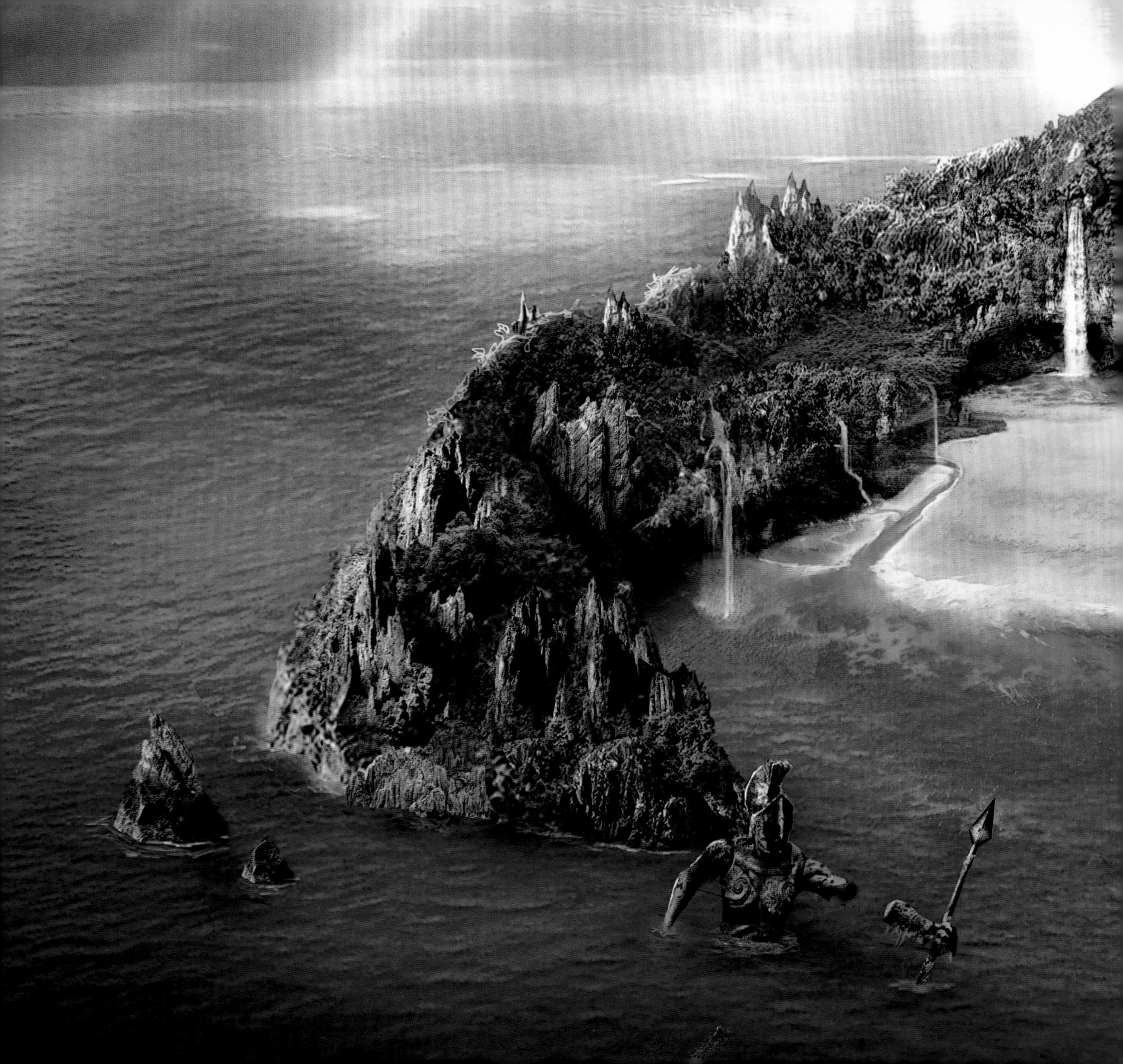

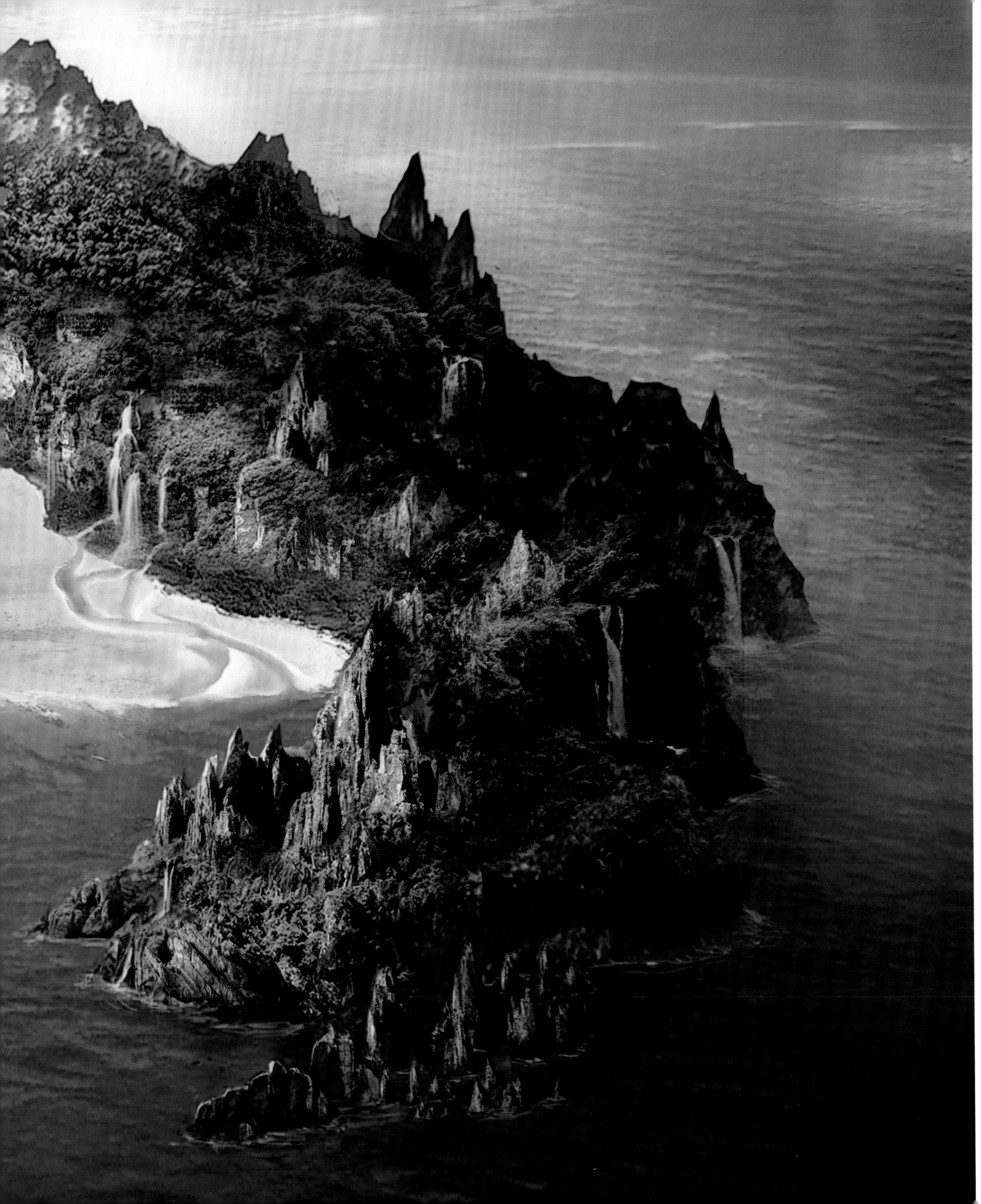

LEFT: Dead King's Island concept art by Sebastian Meyer.

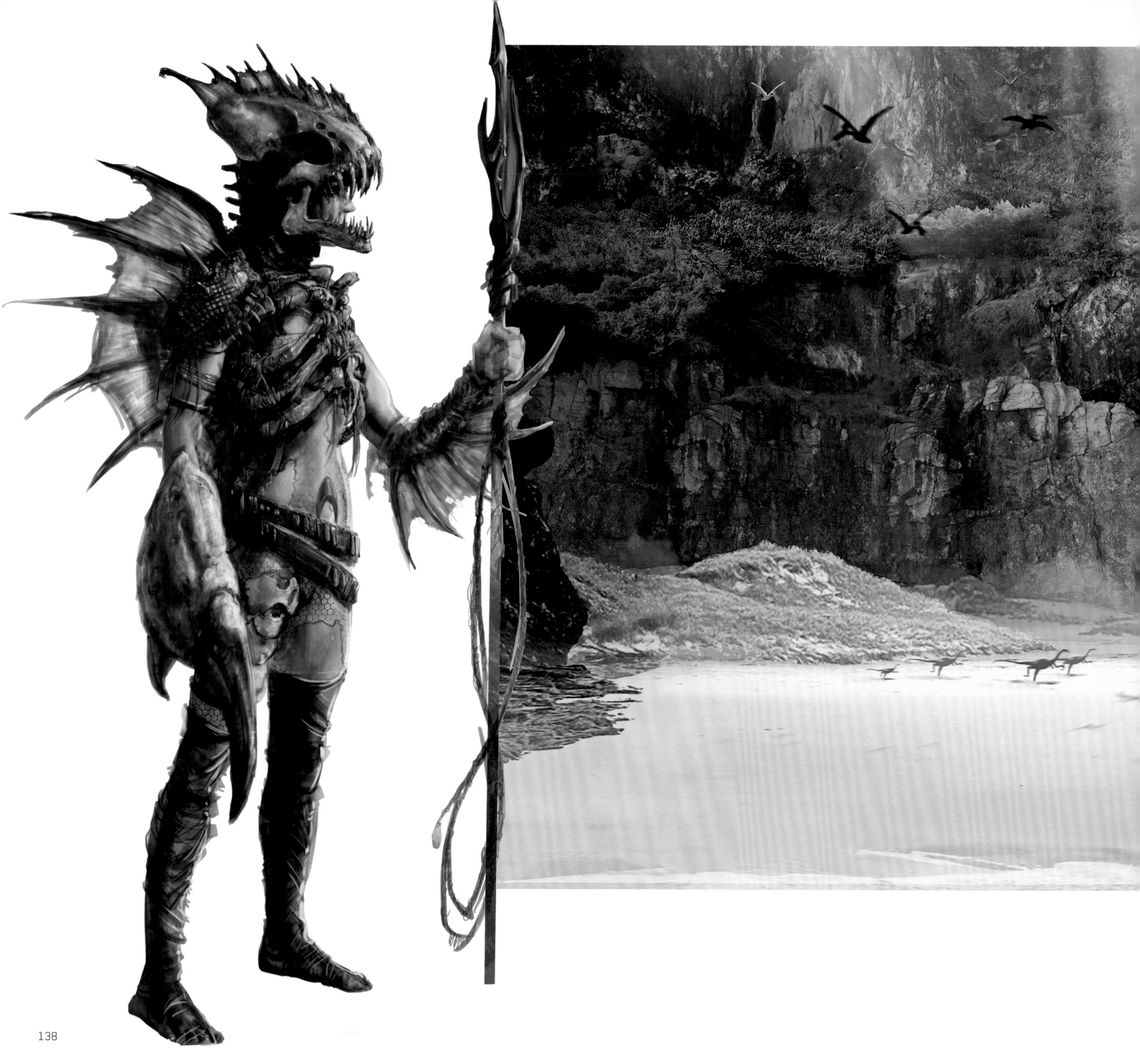

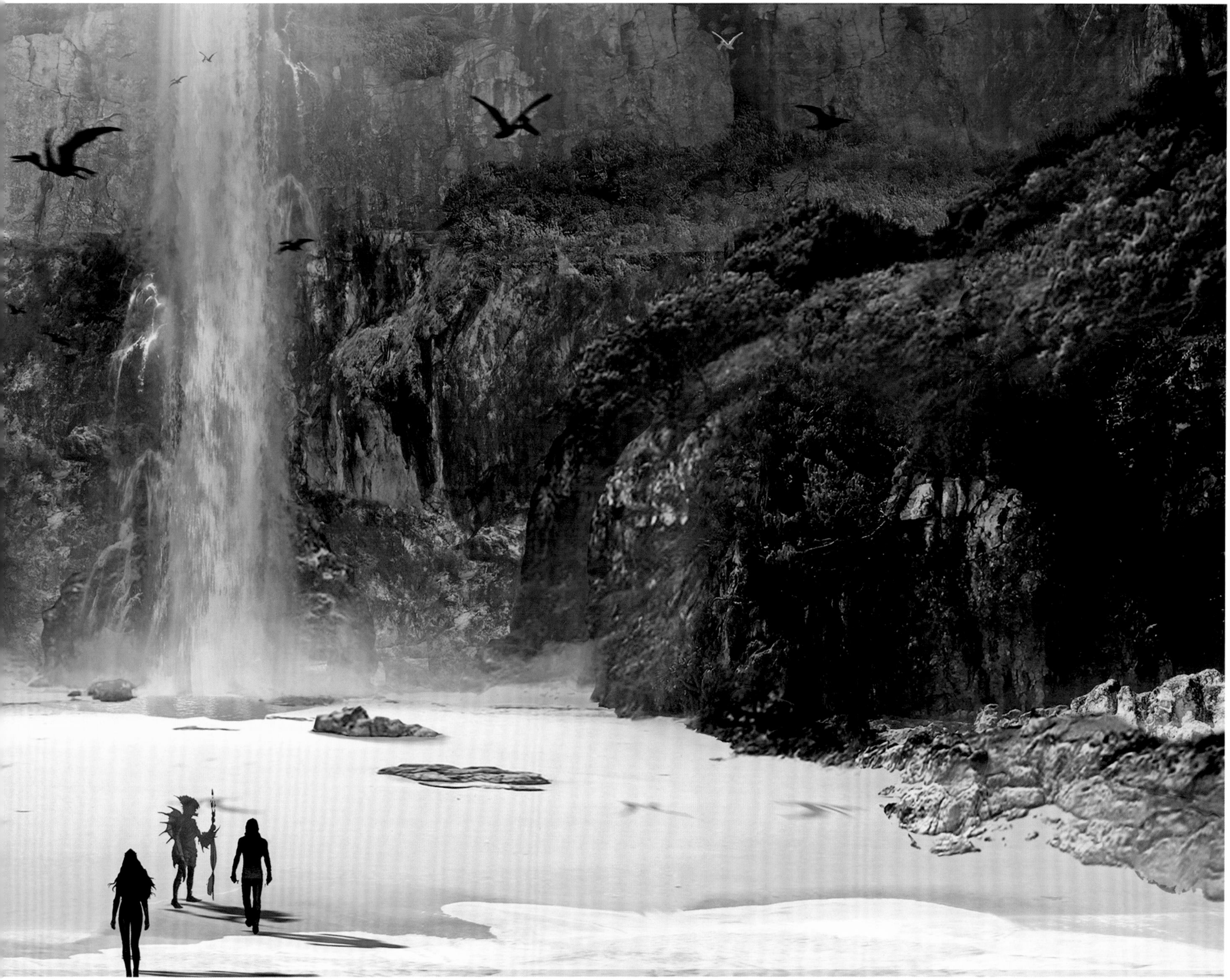

OPPOSITE LEFT: Beach survival costume concept art by Oksana Nedavniaya.
ABOVE: Dead King's Island beach concept art by Brad Nielsen.

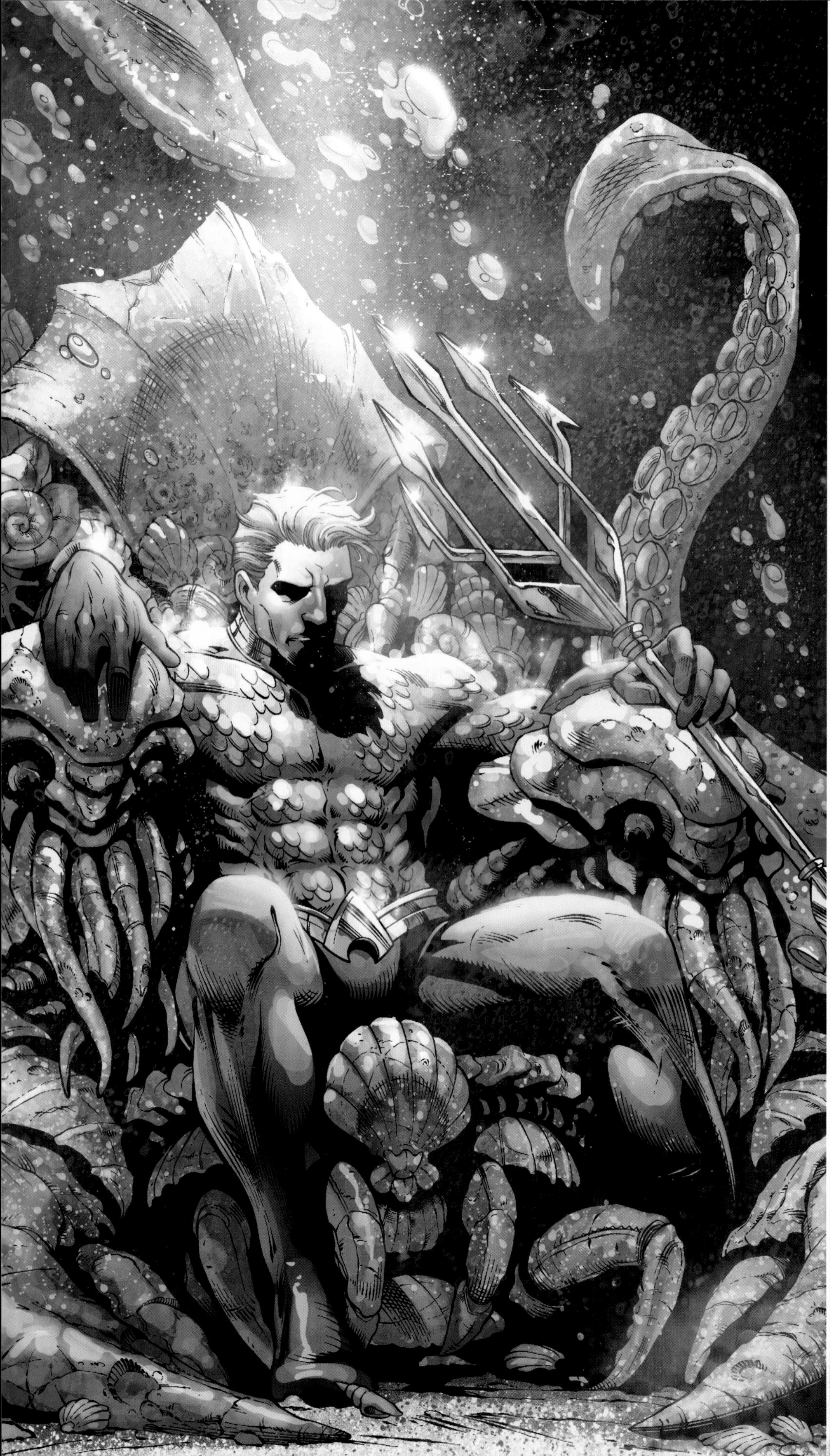
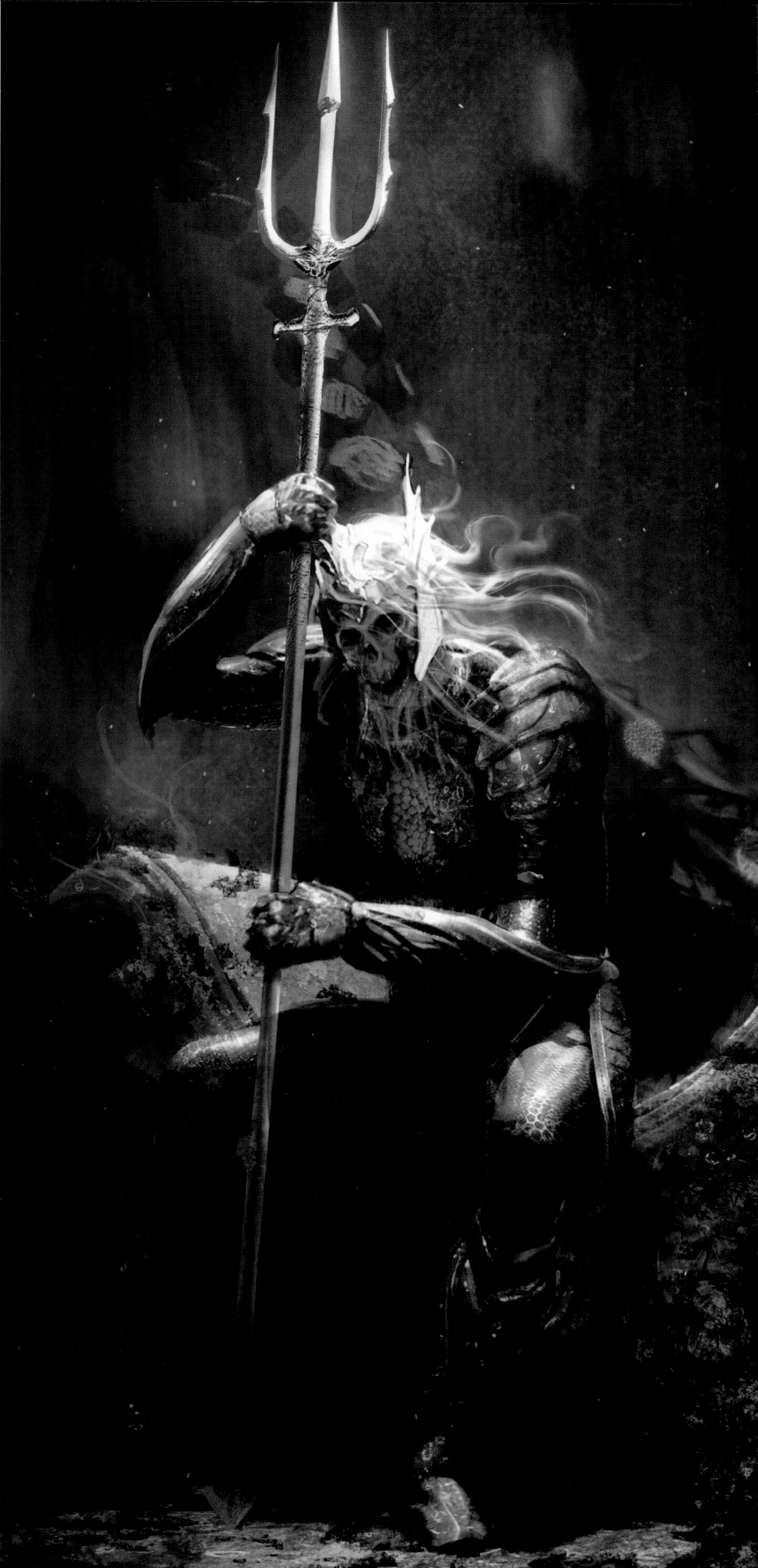

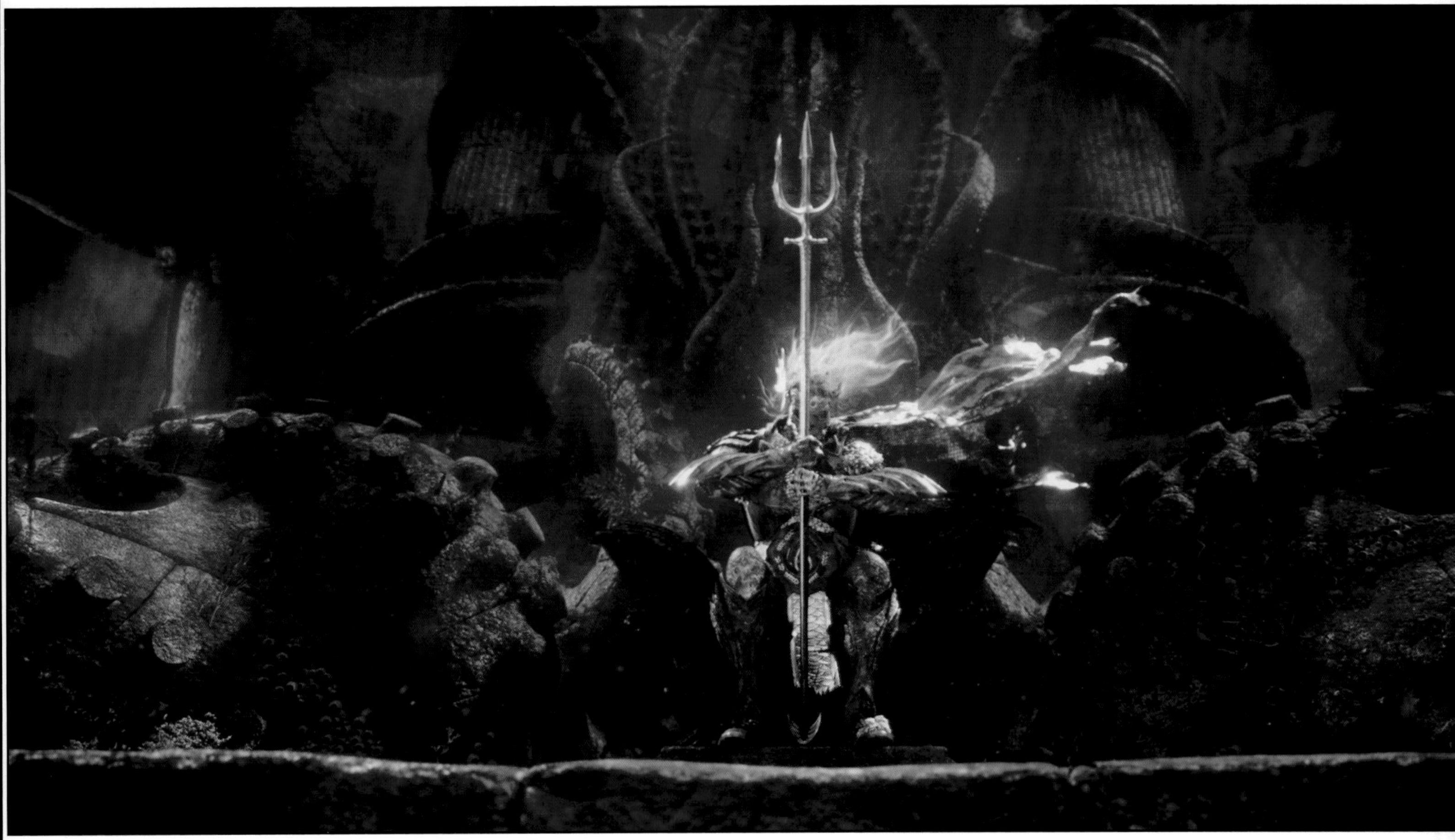

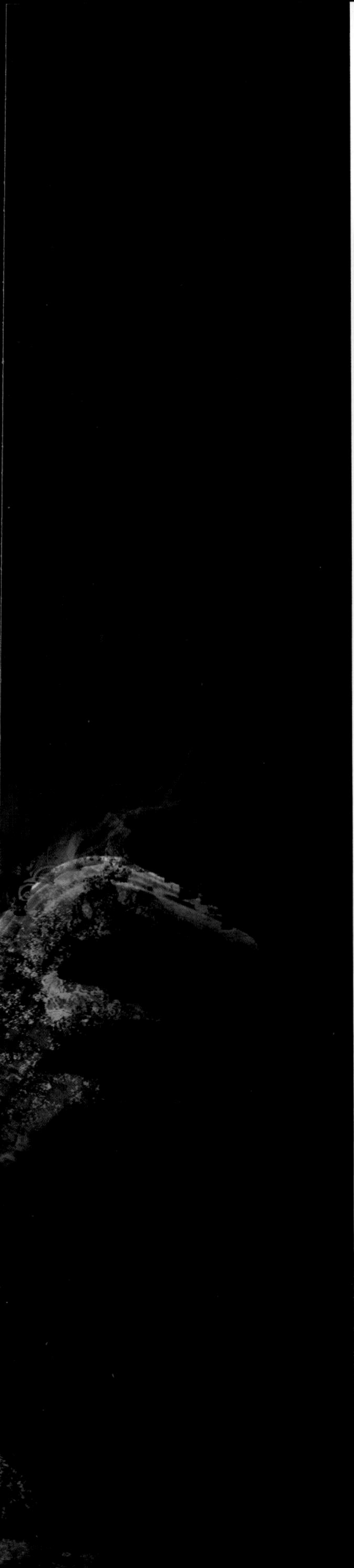

"Our evolution of Arthur's costume actually begins with King Atlan, who ruled Atlantis when it was still above the sea. His royal attire is an earthbound version of the Aquaman suit, and when we see his remains during a crucial part of the film, he's still wearing it. His cape has rotted away over time, but the chainmail and armor is still there. When Arthur reclaims the trident, he also takes the Ancient Atlantean chainmail and puts it on."

—Kym Barrett, Costume Designer

OPPOSITE LEFT: *Aquaman*, Vol. 7 #18 (May 2013) cover art by Paul Pelletier, Sean Parsons, and Rod Reis.
OPPOSITE RIGHT: Dead King concept art by Brad Nielsen.
ABOVE: The sacred trident rests with the body of King Atlan.

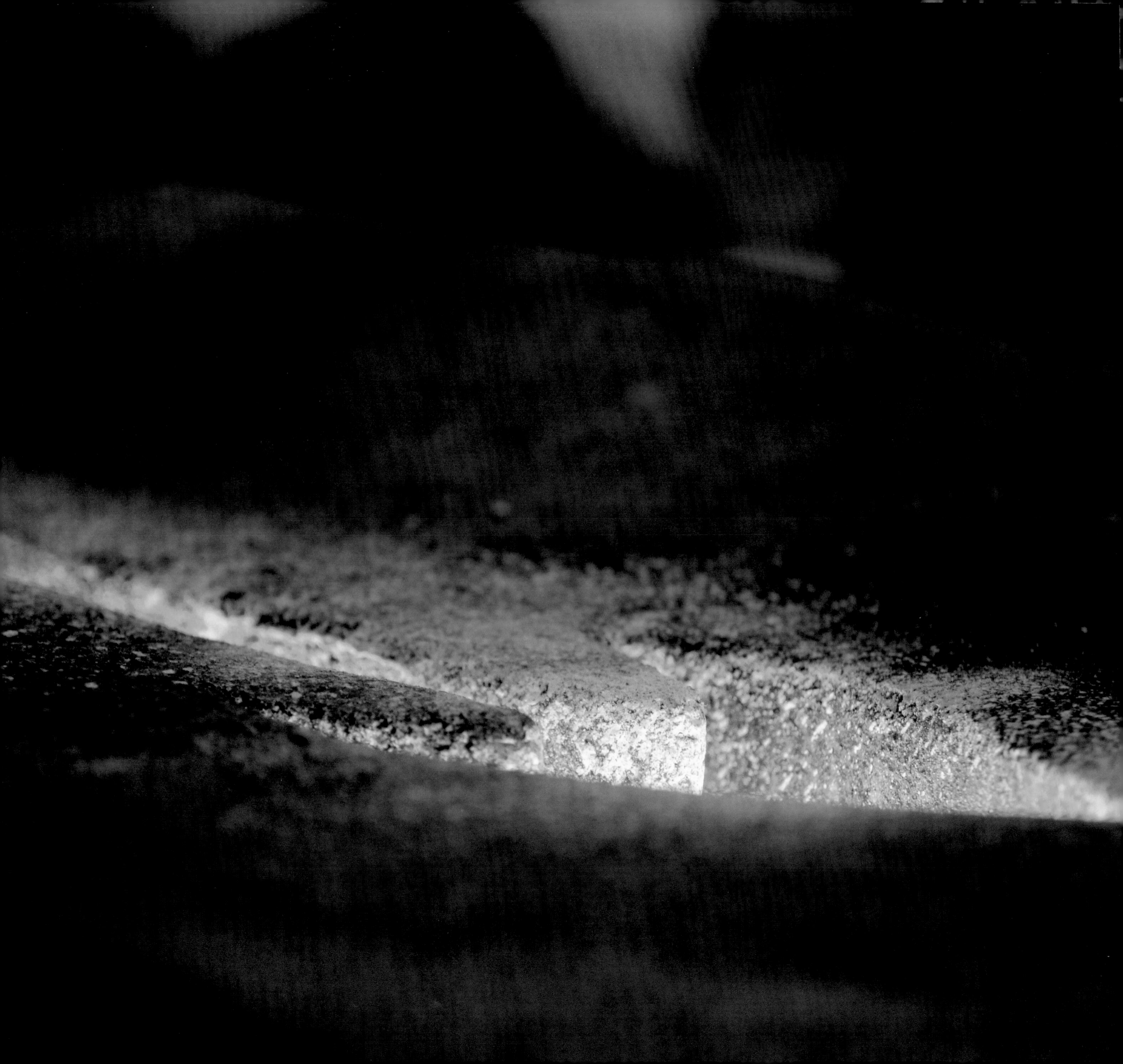

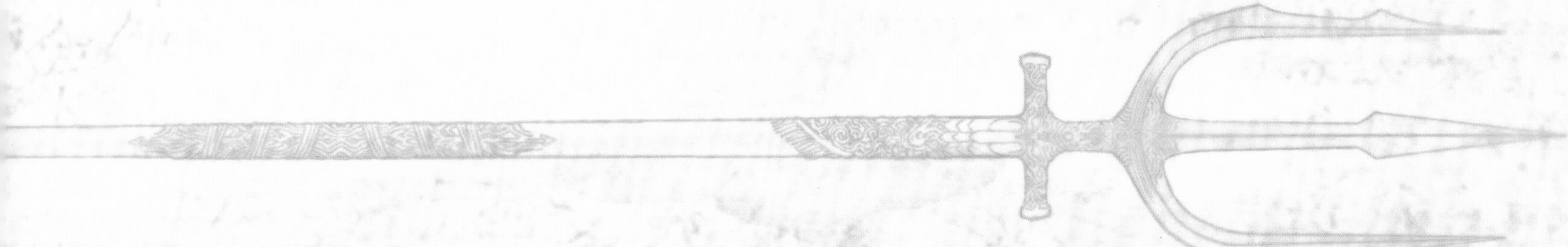

THE SACRED TRIDENT

There is a bedtime story buried deep in Arthur Curry's subconscious. It is one his mother used to tell him at an age so young, it almost seems like he dreamed it. The story is about a magical weapon, a trident that could only be wielded by the strongest person within the mightiest culture in all of civilization: Atlantis. That trident gave King Atlan control over the seven seas. But as the timeless tale goes, the ocean itself was envious of Atlan's power and created an earthquake to sink Atlantis in retribution. The trident was lost forever, and the kingdom was irrevocably fractured. Legend says a new leader will one day rediscover the trident and use it to bring Atlantis together again.

The lost trident of King Atlan is the thrust of *Aquaman*–the prize that Arthur and Mera seek to try to prevent Orm's war with the surface world. The sacred trident is the most important artifact in Atlantean civilization. It's a mighty weapon as well as a symbol of the greatness of Atlantis. Whoever wields it will be considered the rightful ruler of Atlantis. When Vulko tells Arthur about the history of Atlantis, a flashback sequence shows how the trident was assembled from Poseidon steel in the Hall of Armory. The royal advisor then gives Arthur and Mera the sharkskin map with clues that could lead them to the lost trident.

The hunt for mythical treasure recalls classic adventure movies. And that is exactly the flavor James Wan was going for when he agreed to direct *Aquaman*. "James really wanted this to be a fun, globetrotting quest movie," explains screenwriter David Leslie Johnson-McGoldrick, who worked with Wan on *The Conjuring 2*. "The object the movie revolves around is the trident, and it's up to Arthur to go and retrieve it, take the throne, and stop Orm's war."

"THE COSTUME DEPARTMENT WAS VERY influential to the trident design process. But our first references, of course, come from the DC Comics. This was an invaluable resource of inspiration. Also we wanted to honor the DC legacy and represent the characters as the fans identify them so the tridents were important to not stray too far from the comic art but to refine them to blend into our world."

–Richie Dehne, Prop Master

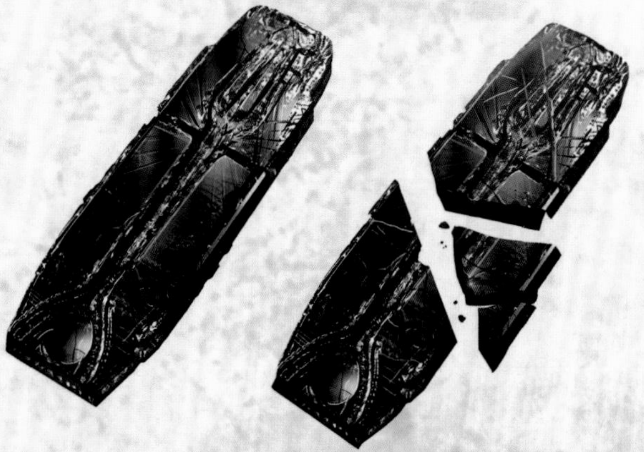

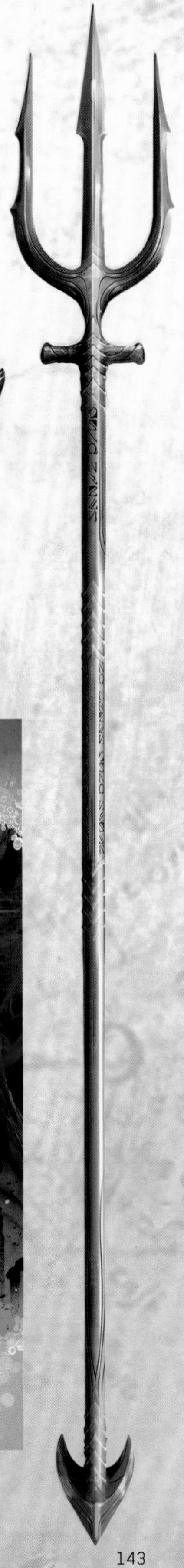

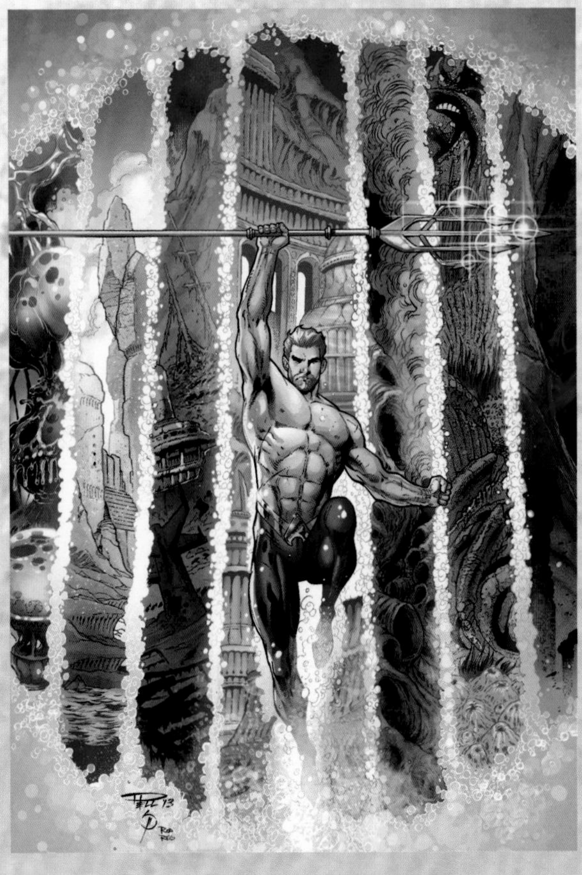

OPPOSITE: The forge of the trident from the Deserters Kingdom flashback.

TOP AND RIGHT: Trident mold design by Christian Scheurer and prop photo of the trident.

BOTTOM: *Aquaman*, Vol. 7 #24 (December 2013) cover art by Paul Pelletier, Sean Parsons, and Rod Reis.

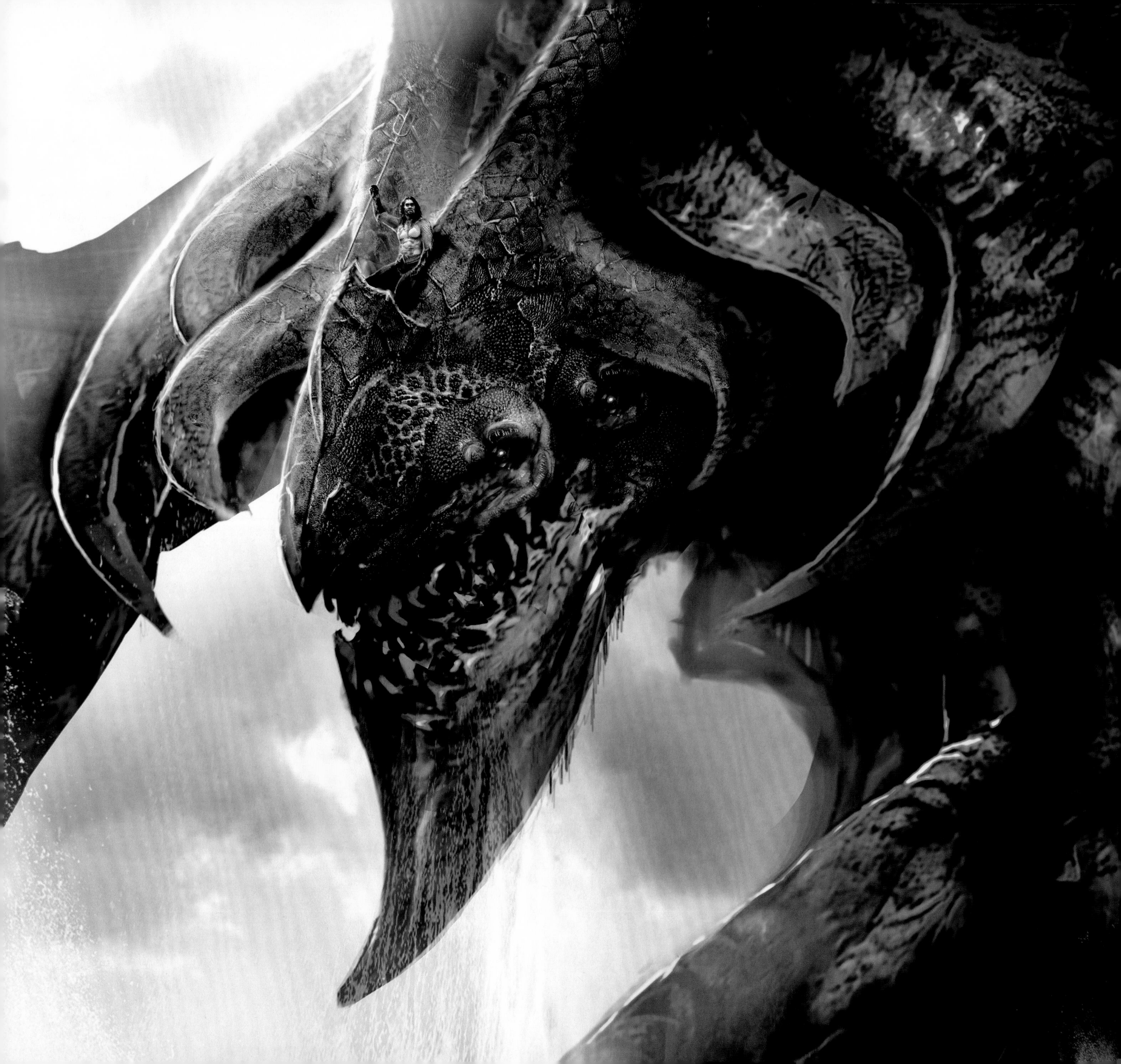

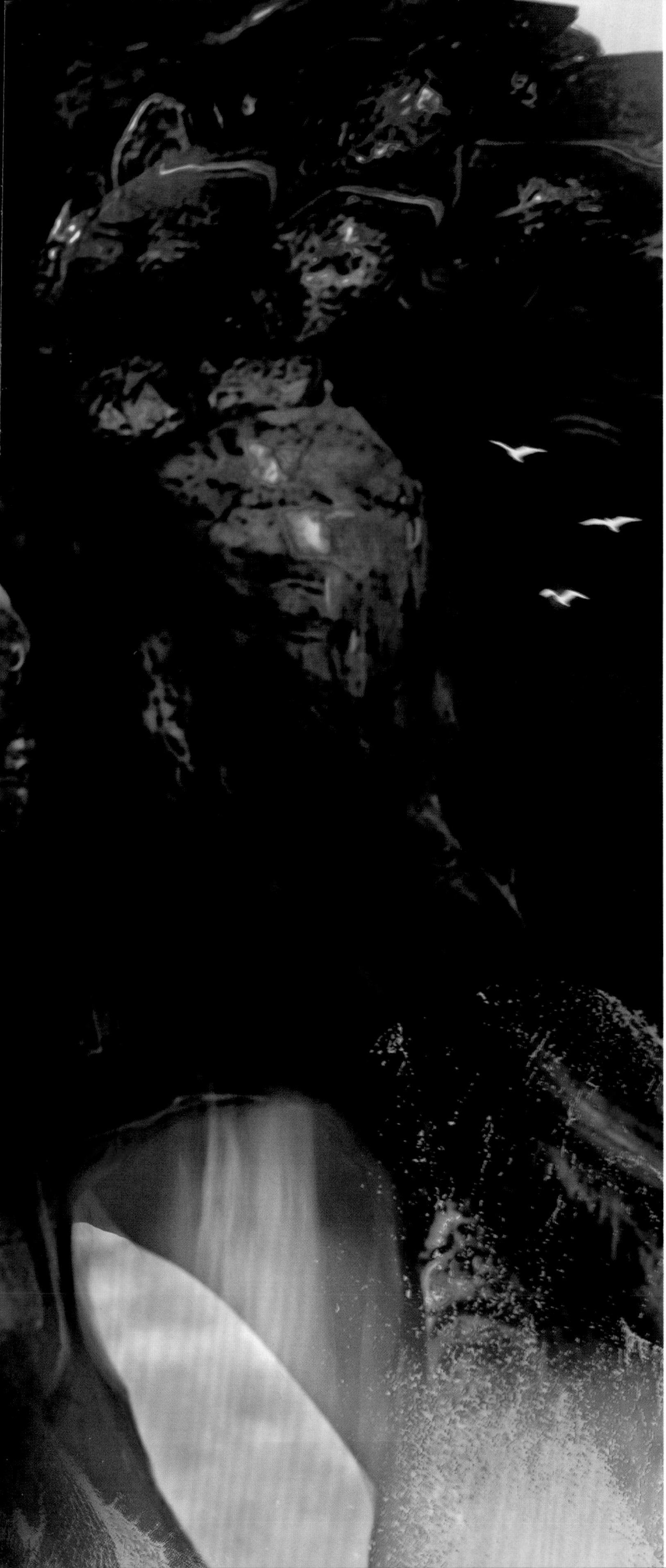

KARATHEN

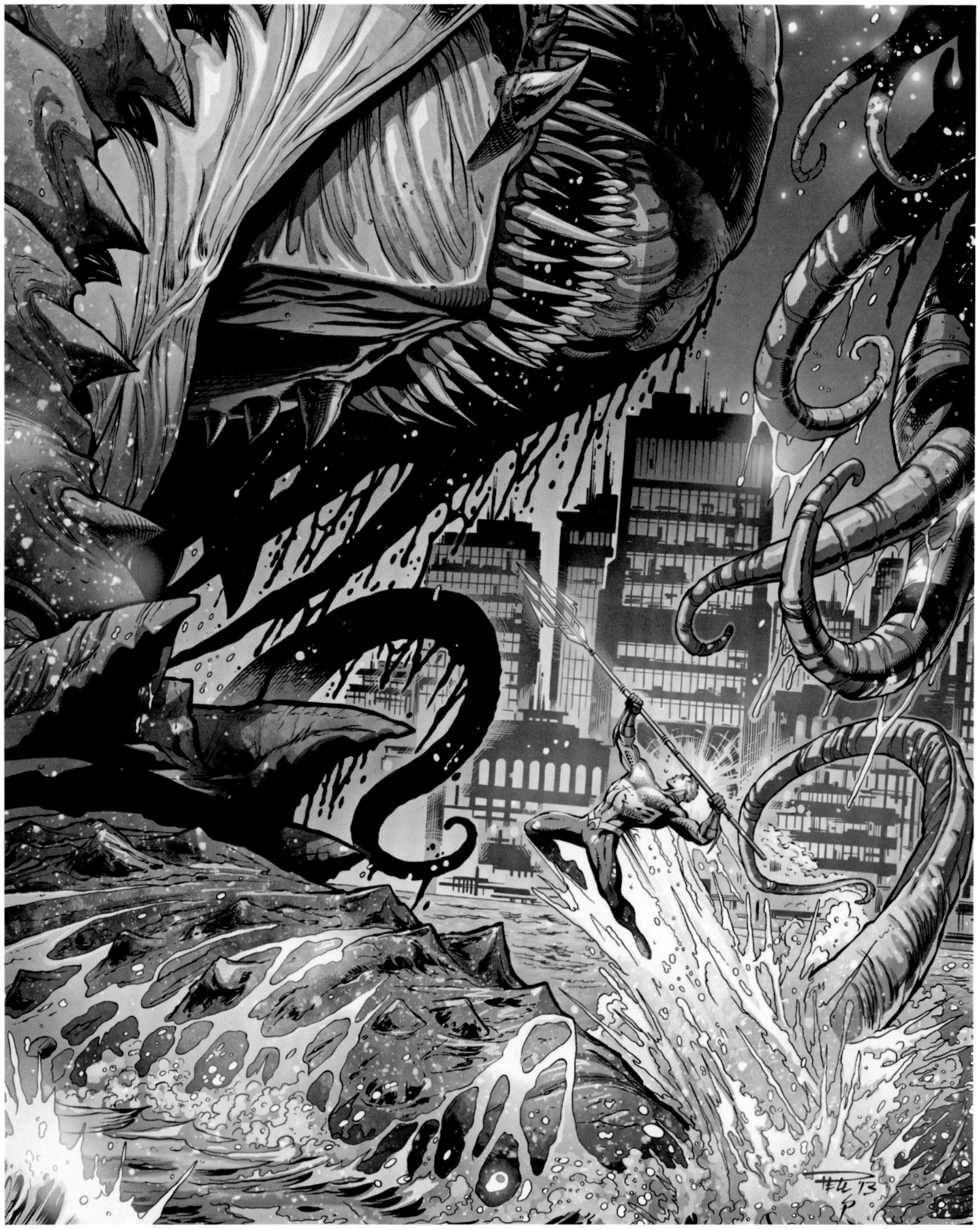

LEFT: Karathen concept art by Sebastian Meyer.

ABOVE: *Aquaman*, Vol. 7 #27 (March 2014) cover art by Paul Pelletier, Sean Parsons, and Wil Quintana.

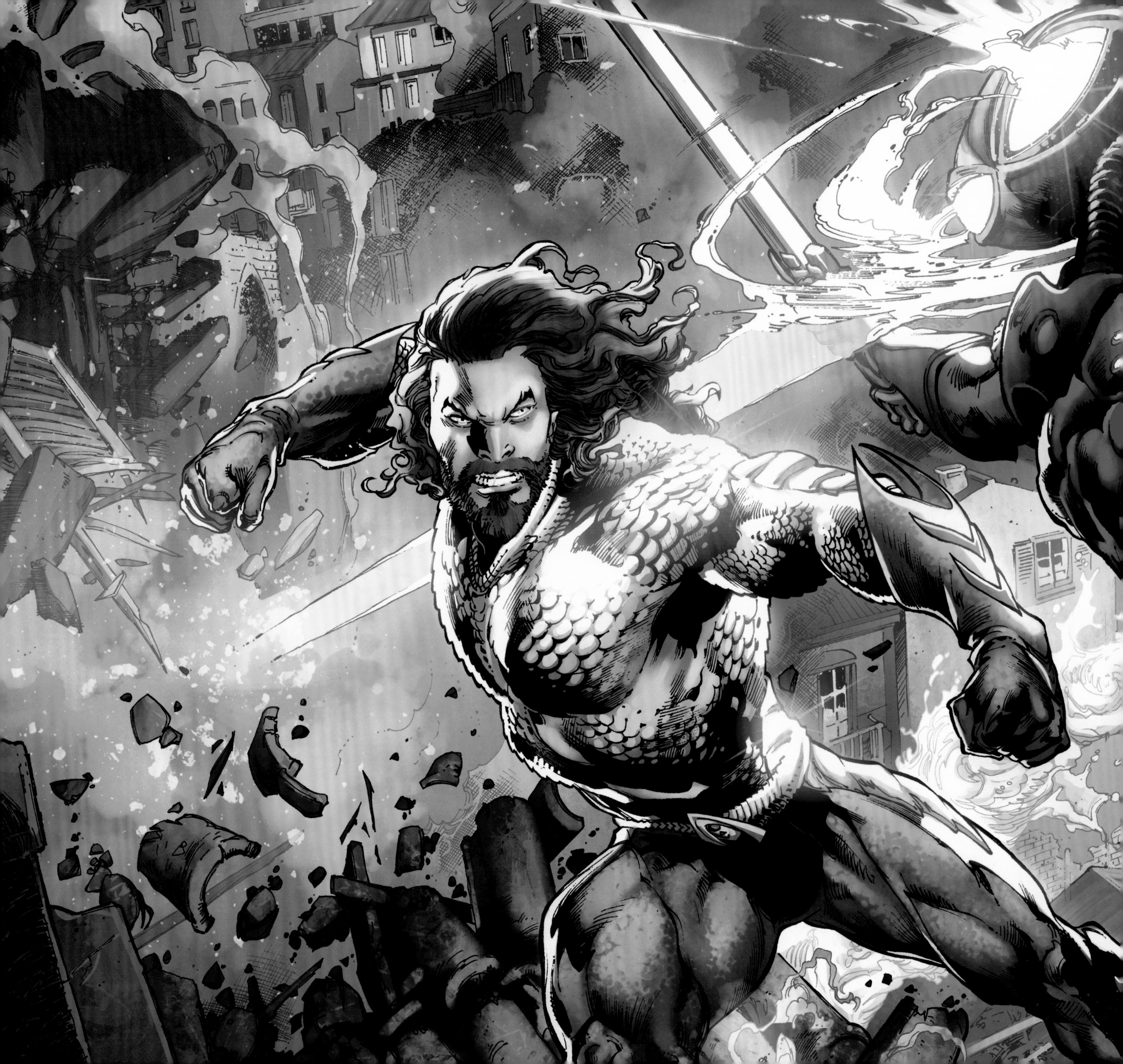

THE RISE OF AQUAMAN

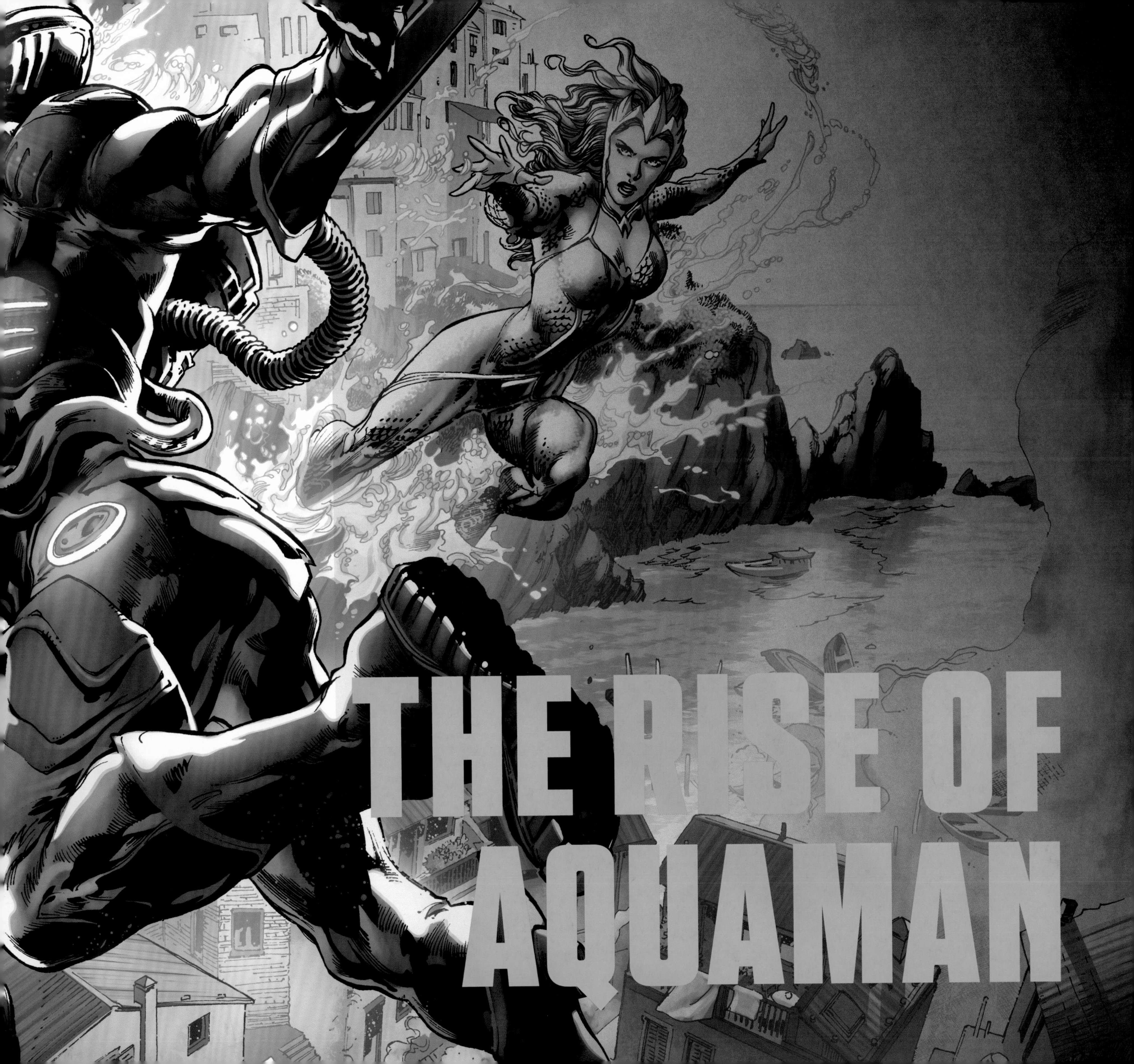

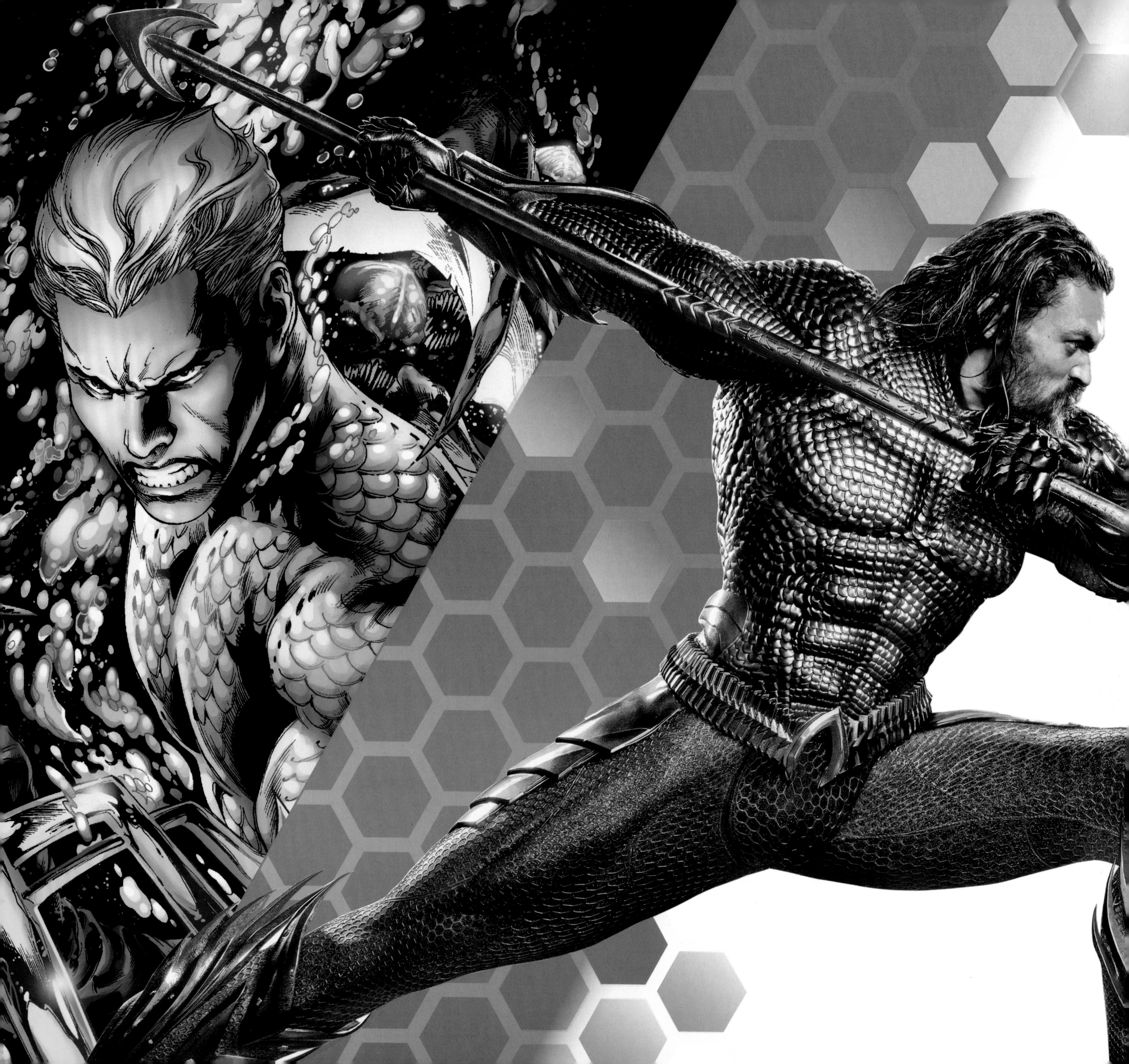

AQUAMAN

RULER OF THE SEVEN SEAS

A hero's journey doesn't always begin with one single event. The people of the surface world were referring to Arthur Curry as the Aquaman long before he sets foot in Atlantis for the first time. He's already saved the world once prior to the opening scenes of *Aquaman*. When we meet him, he is already a hero in many ways, but it is through his journey to accept his heritage and claim his identity that he becomes the *Super* Hero known as Aquaman.

Arthur's call to action is a simple request for help, to save the people of both worlds to which he belongs. The journey that follows takes him around the globe visiting the fallen kingdoms of Atlantis while his brother, Orm, collects the surviving kingdoms into his army. With Mera at his side, Arthur fights against the most powerful forces in the seas, but he also solves the mysteries of the fallen kingdoms of Atlantis and finds the lost trident of King Atlan. In learning about his past, Arthur takes control of his future and earns one more title: King of the Seven Seas.

PAGES 146–147: Aquaman and Mera vs. Black Manta art by Ivan Reis, Joe Prado, and Marcelo Maiolo.
OPPOSITE LEFT: *Aquaman*, Vol. 7 #1 (November 2011) cover art by Ivan Reis and Rod Reis.
LEFT: Jason Momoa dons the armor of King Atlan, taking on the role of King of the Seven Seas.

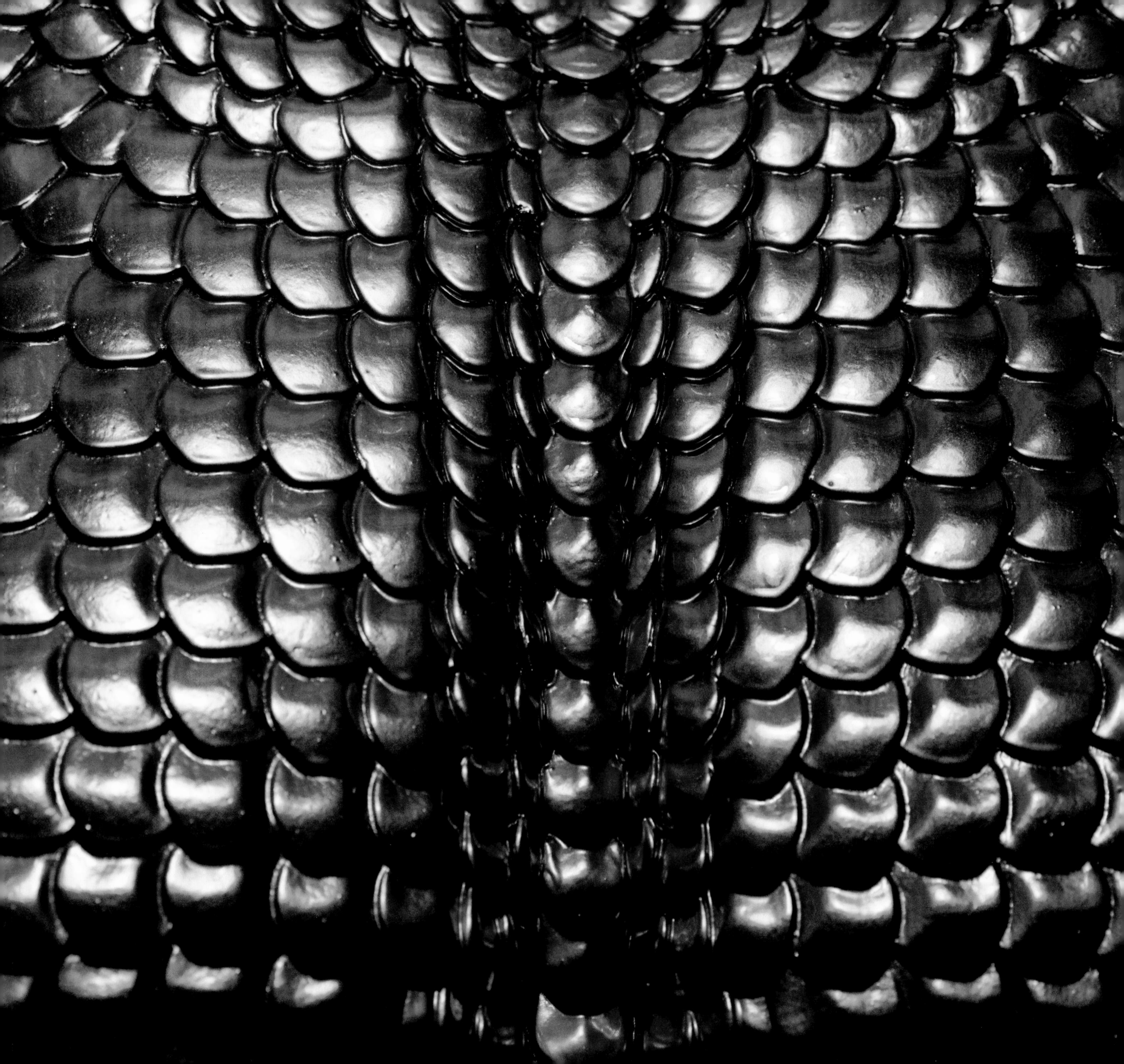

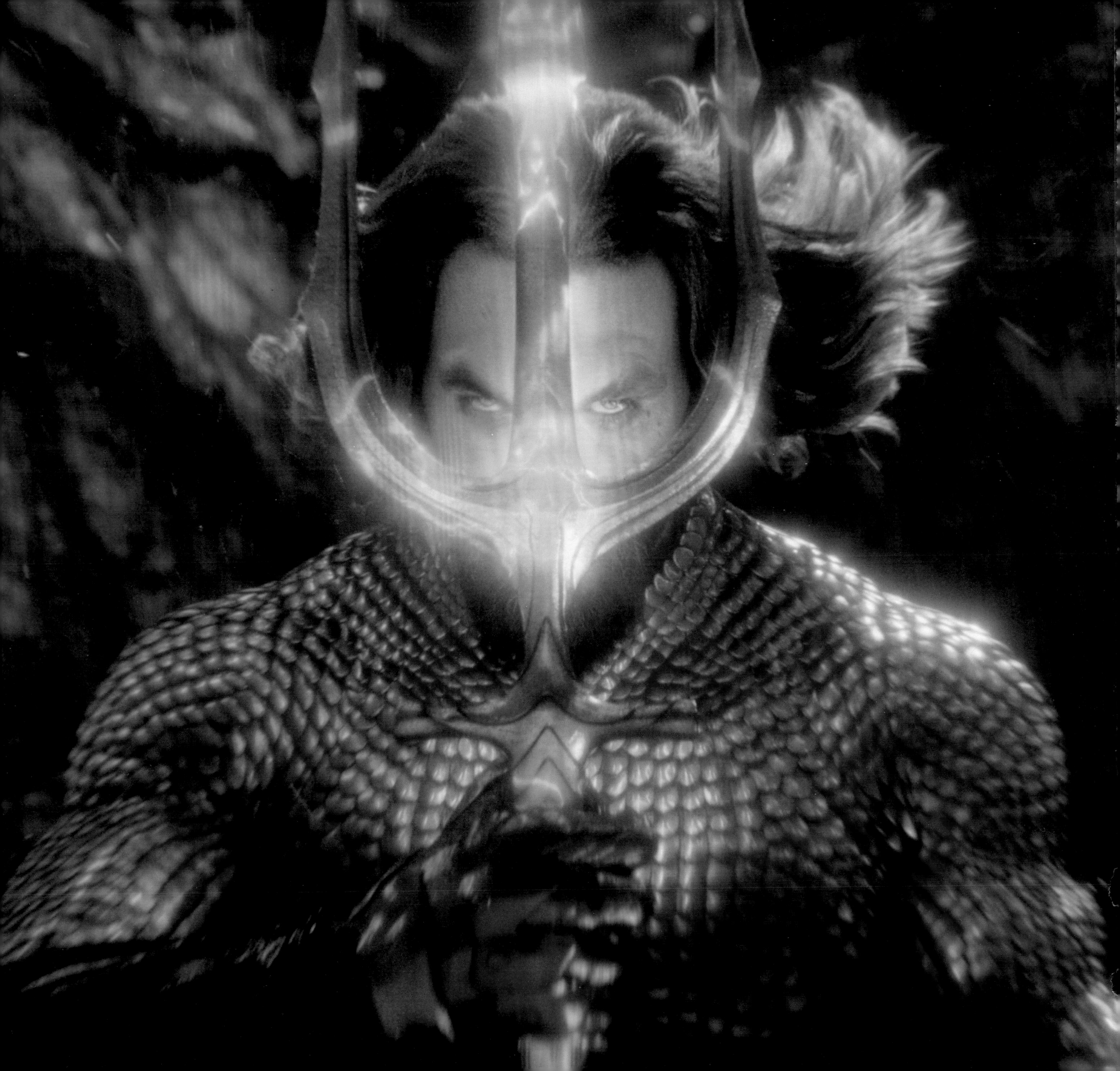

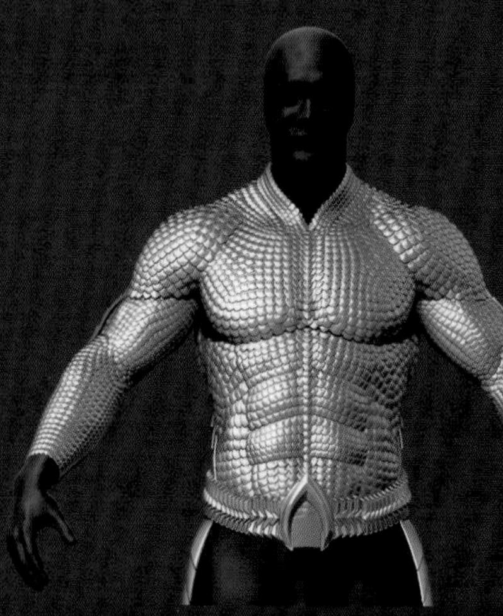

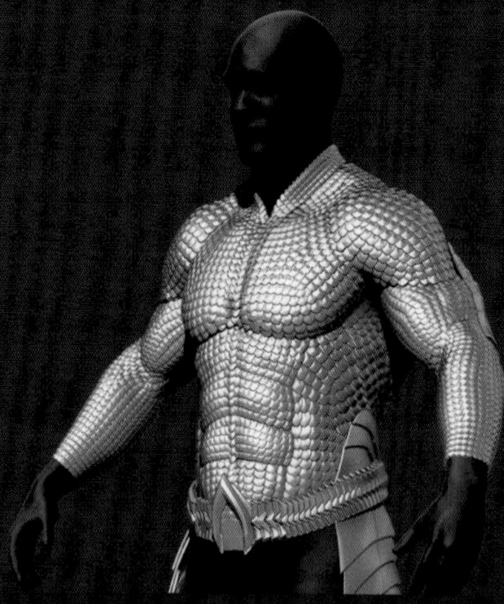

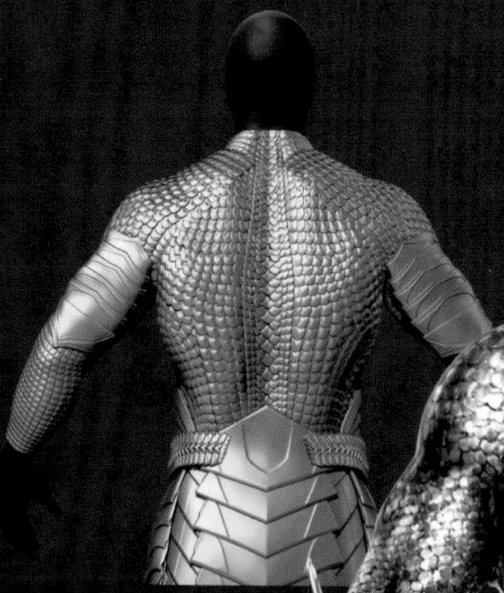

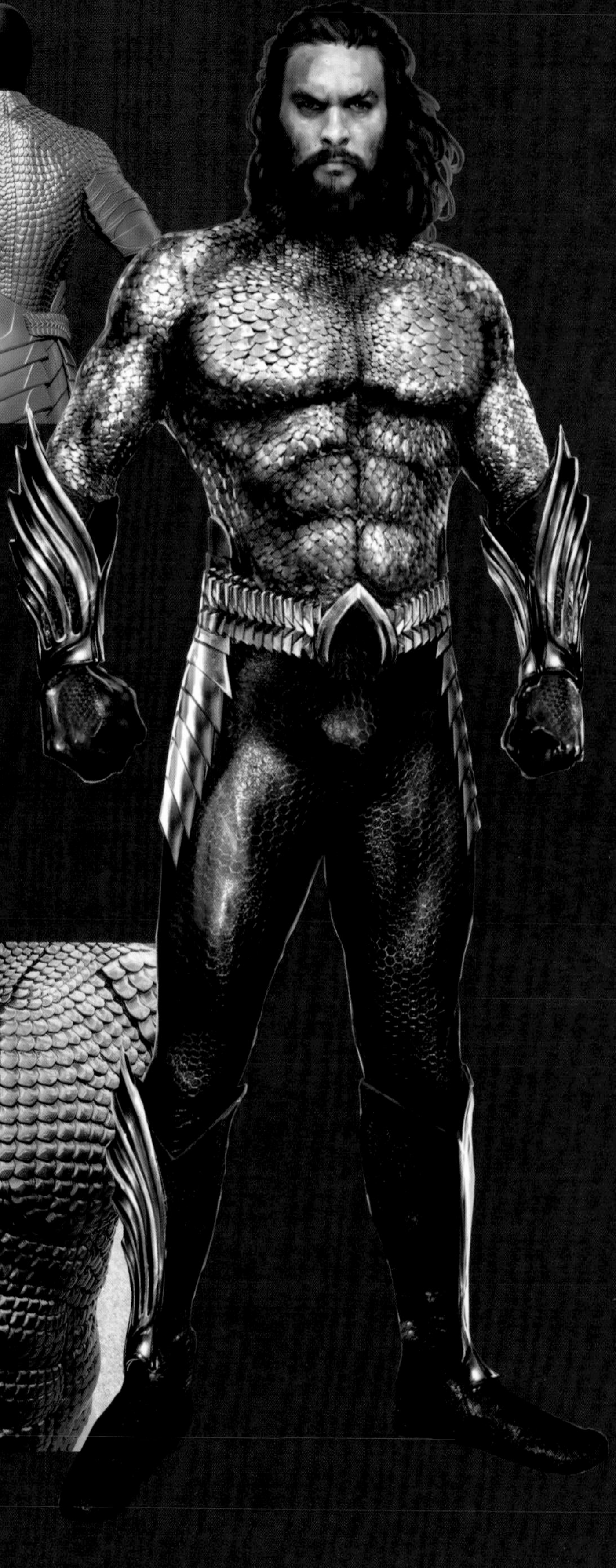

"I knew that sketches weren't going to really tell us a lot, so when we presented to the studio, we made a 3D rendering of the suit sketch and then we made an actual maquette that we painted. The finished costume is very similar to the maquette that we made to the show the studio, but we did make modifications along the way. That was mainly due to Jason and his physique. He's six-foot three and you really have to work on proportions when you're costuming an actor of that size. Also, you have a bright gold, and green-black color, so proportion is key. I didn't want to put out too many sketches because it was important we see how the costume design looked on Jason."

—Kym Barrett

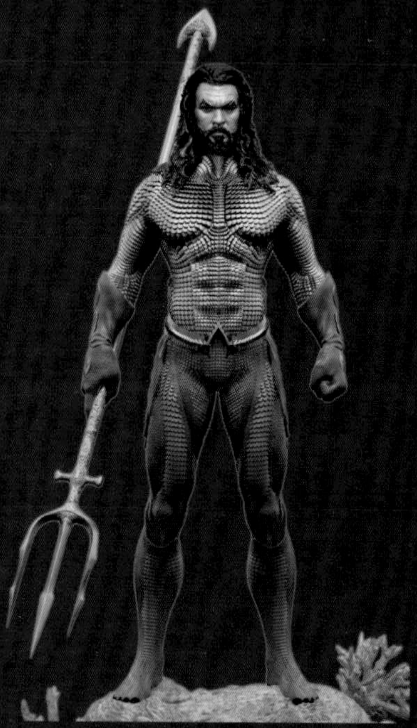

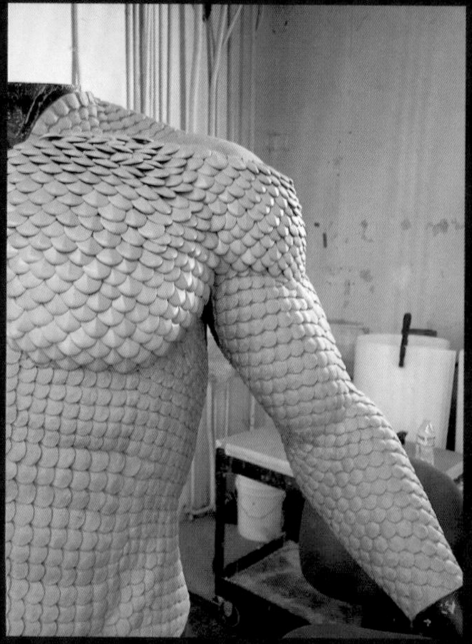

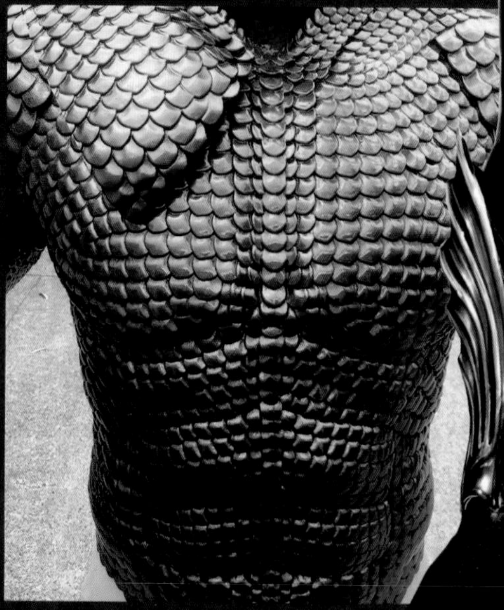

A HERO'S ARMOR

"As Aquaman's costume is a gold-coin type of chainmail that resembles scales, but not quite, we created a gold chainmail that had a slight scale shape to it, but not that overtly. King Atlan wears the gold chainmail, along with a dark green chainmail armor; it's almost black, that's how dark we made it. But it looks very much like the modern Aquaman suit in the comics."

—Kym Barrett, Costume Designer

GATEFOLD: The design process for creating the Aquaman hero costume included sketches, a model, and digital turnaround renders before construction began on what would be the most recognizable costume in the film.

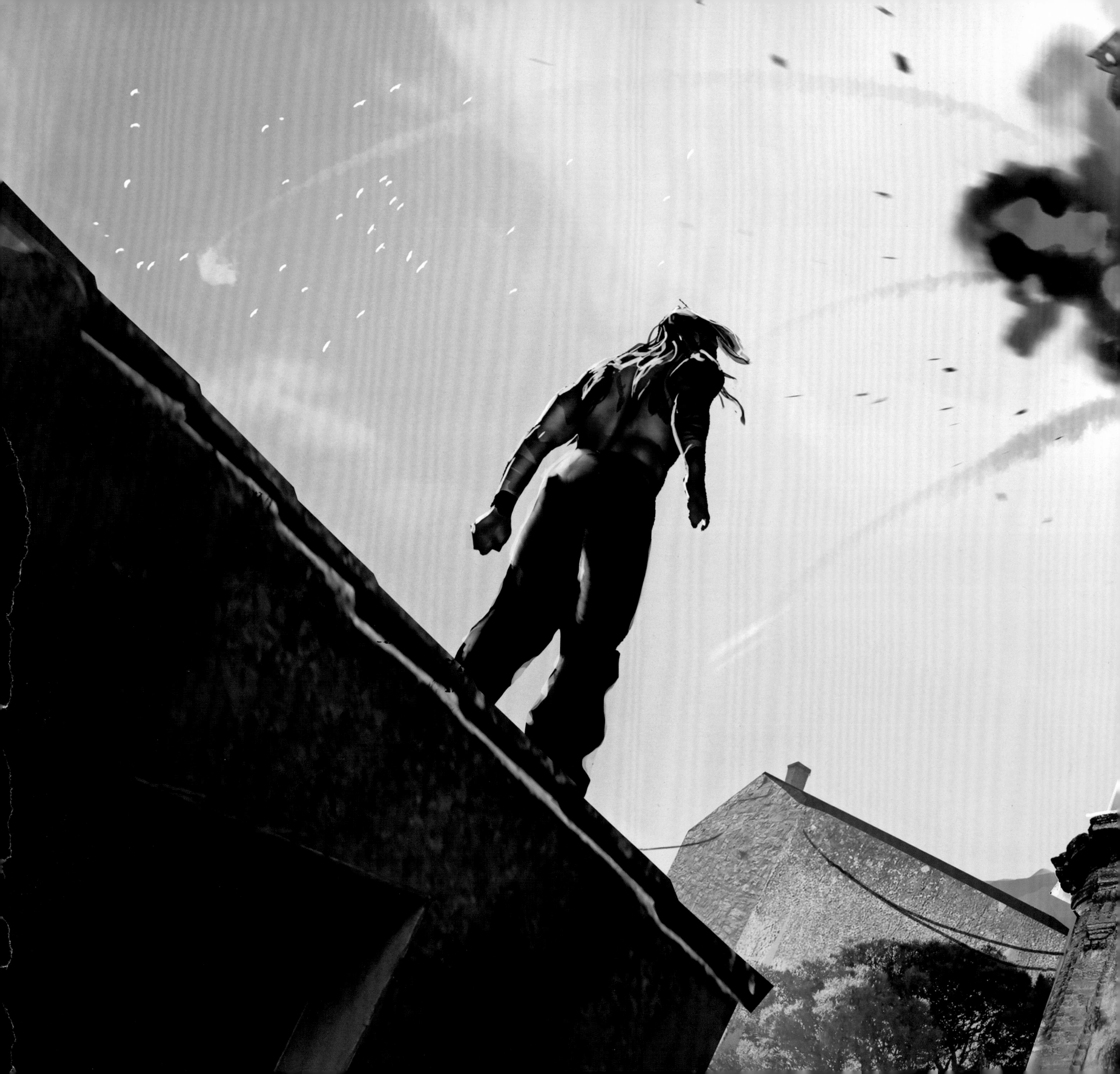

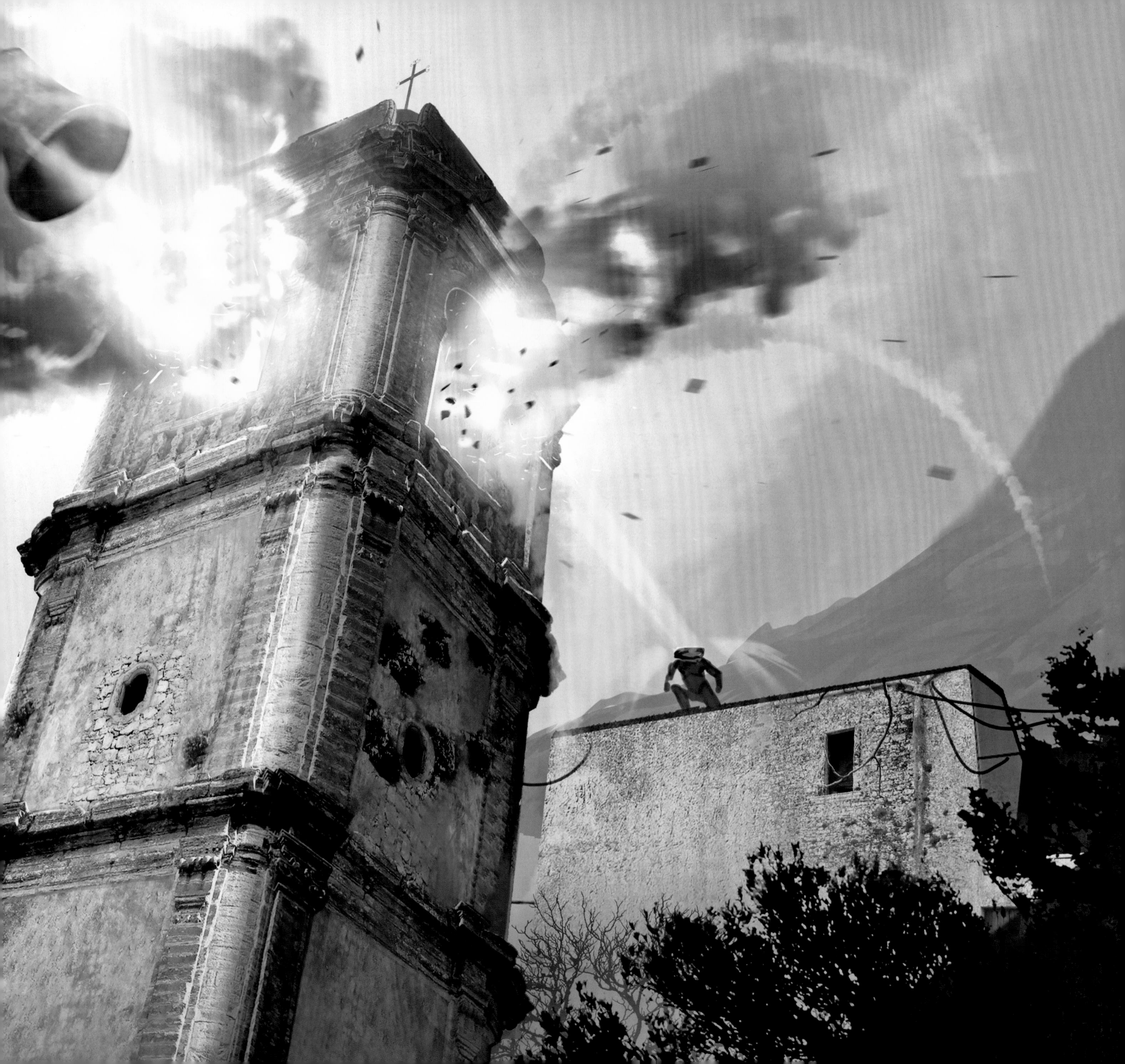

BLACK MANTA

SON OF VENGEANCE

Portraying one of the most recognizable villains in the DC Comics canon is a task no savvy actor would take lightly. Yahya Abdul-Mateen II was fully aware that fan expectations would be high for his performance of longtime Aquaman nemesis Black Manta. "I definitely want to do the character justice," the actor says, "because the fans know and they'll be able to point and they'll say, 'Nope.'"

David Kane, also known as Black Manta, is a mercenary and a dangerous adversary—and Aquaman is, in a way, responsible. Kane and his father are pirates hired by Orm to execute a submarine attack at the Council of the Kings. Orm planned it to look like an attack by humans, in an effort to convince the Xebellian king to join Orm's crusade against surface world. When Arthur Curry shows up, Kane's father is injured in the ensuing battle. Arthur ignores Kane's plea to help save his father, and as a result, the elder Kane dies. It upends Kane's life. Aquaman's inaction is the motivating factor behind Manta's quest for vengeance. Instead of being a ruthless gun for hire, Manta becomes consumed with making Aquaman pay for letting his father die. To Abdul-Mateen, Black Manta believes what he is seeking is justice, not revenge. "From his perspective, he's right, you know? Aquaman killed his father."

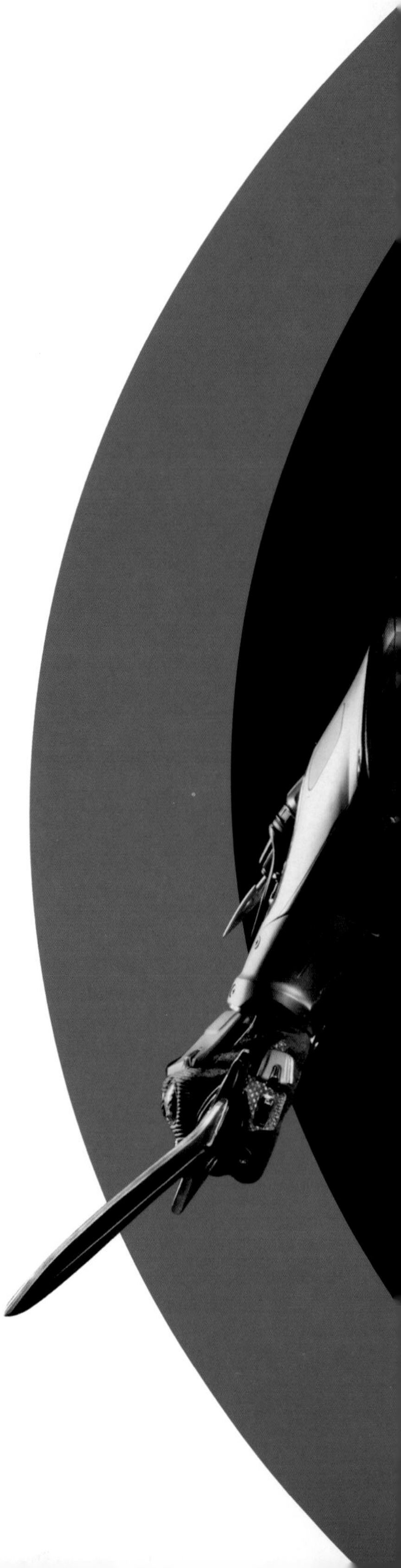

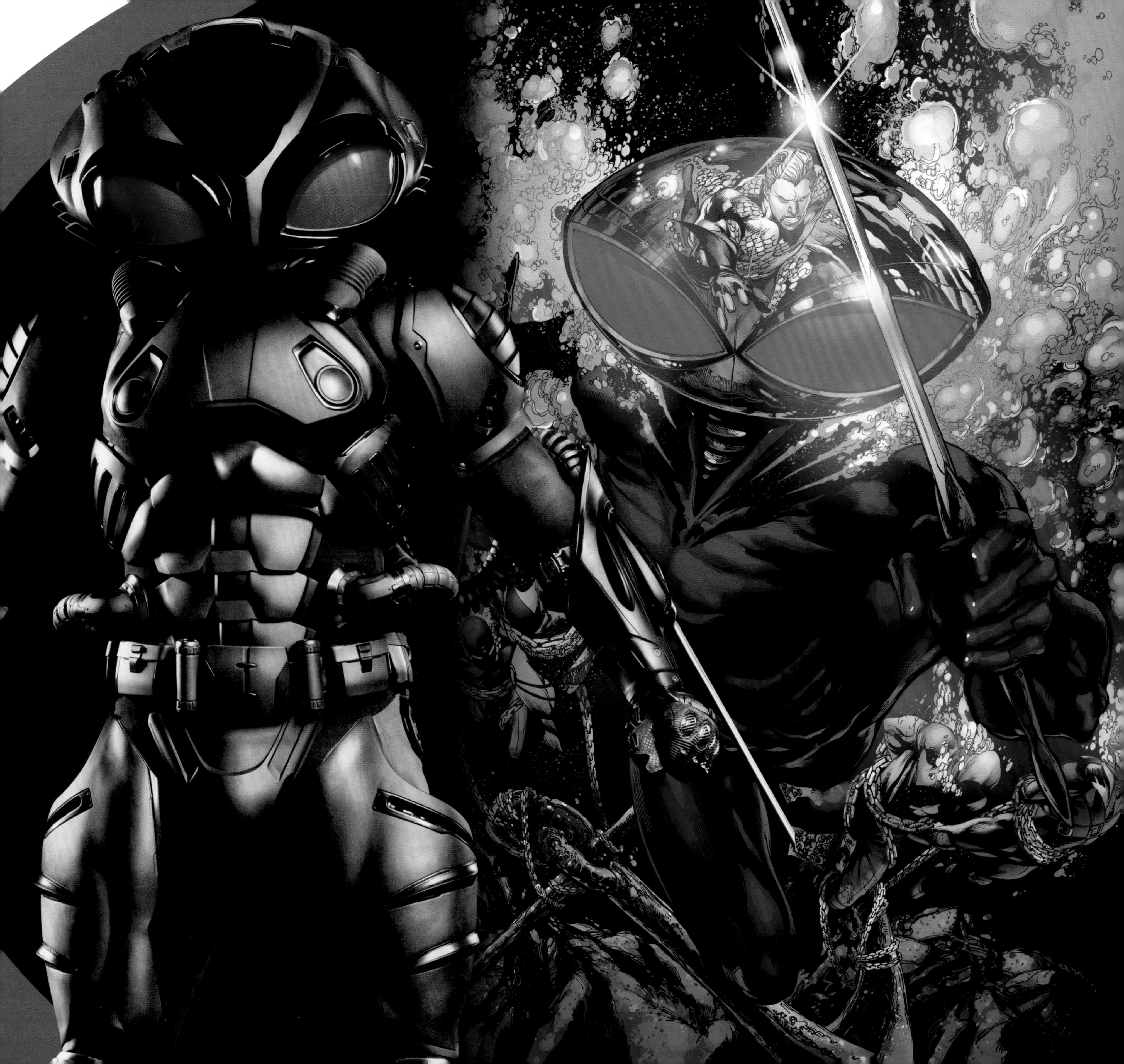

Abdul-Mateen's goal was to portray Black Manta such that the audience understands his intentions and motivations. "I want to steal as many fans as possible from Jason and I want them to say, 'No, I want Black Manta to win. He's right,'" he says. Unlike Cadillac, the charismatic and impulsive gangster he played on the Netflix series *The Get Down*, Black Manta is much more cunning and calculated, and infinitely scarier as a result, says Abdul-Mateen.

According to producer Peter Safran, Abdul-Mateen was the only person seriously considered for the role. "We just met with him and we're like, this is the guy. It was really important for Manta to be a guy that both has a humor to him but also a true intensity so that he can be a scary, scary adversary," Safran explains. "Yahya just embodied that." While Aquaman's half brother Orm is the principal villain in movie, the filmmakers quickly realized as they were developing the script that that they could not miss the chance to integrate Black Manta and show the genesis of the character. Unlike the character in the comic book origin story, the Black Manta in *Aquaman* the movie is a product of anger, loss, and Atlantean technology.

Because of their shared desire to see Arthur Curry dead, Orm and Black Manta are inextricably linked. Their relationship is based on necessity. They need each other to achieve their common goal. It is Orm who supplies Kane with the Atlantean weapons and armor that he will eventually fashion into the iconic Black Manta suit. He gives Kane a hydrostatic suit made of the next-generation material that Atlantis's soldiers wear, which also provides the wearer with enhanced strength. Orm also arms Manta with an experimental rifle that converts water into plasma beams. With the advanced suit and weapons, Manta is now able to hold his own against his nemesis. When he and Aquaman face off in the Sicilian village during one of the film's biggest action moments, he catches Arthur off guard with his newfound abilities.

A Yale drama school graduate, Abdul-Mateen admits that until he auditioned for the role, he knew very little about comic books and the mythologies they chronicled. "Then a friend of mine, and fellow actor, Mamoudou Athie, told me about comic books, so I said I would start buying them online," he recalls. "My friend told me, 'No. You have to go to the store. You have

to buy and read it that way.' So I gave in and I went to the comic book shop. And then I was like, 'Oh, yeah. This is some pretty cool stuff. So I'm into it now, man."

One of the key weapons in Black Manta's vendetta against Aquaman is his undersea vessel. The Manta Submersible is remarkably faithful to the ship the super-villain used in the comics. Mimicking the look of an actual manta ray, the Manta Sub's sleek design belies an array of technological advancements within that make Black Manta a legitimate threat to Aquaman.

PAGES 154–155: Attack concept art by Brad Nielsen.

PAGES 156–157: Black Manta costume and *Aquaman*, Vol. 7 #12 (October 2012) cover by Ivan Reis, Joe Prado, and Rod Reis (*right*).

BELOW: *Aquaman*, Vol. 8 #15 (March 2017) variant cover art by Brad Walker, Andrew Hennessy, and Gabe Eltaeb.

OPPOSITE: Manta Sub concept art by Ed Natividad.

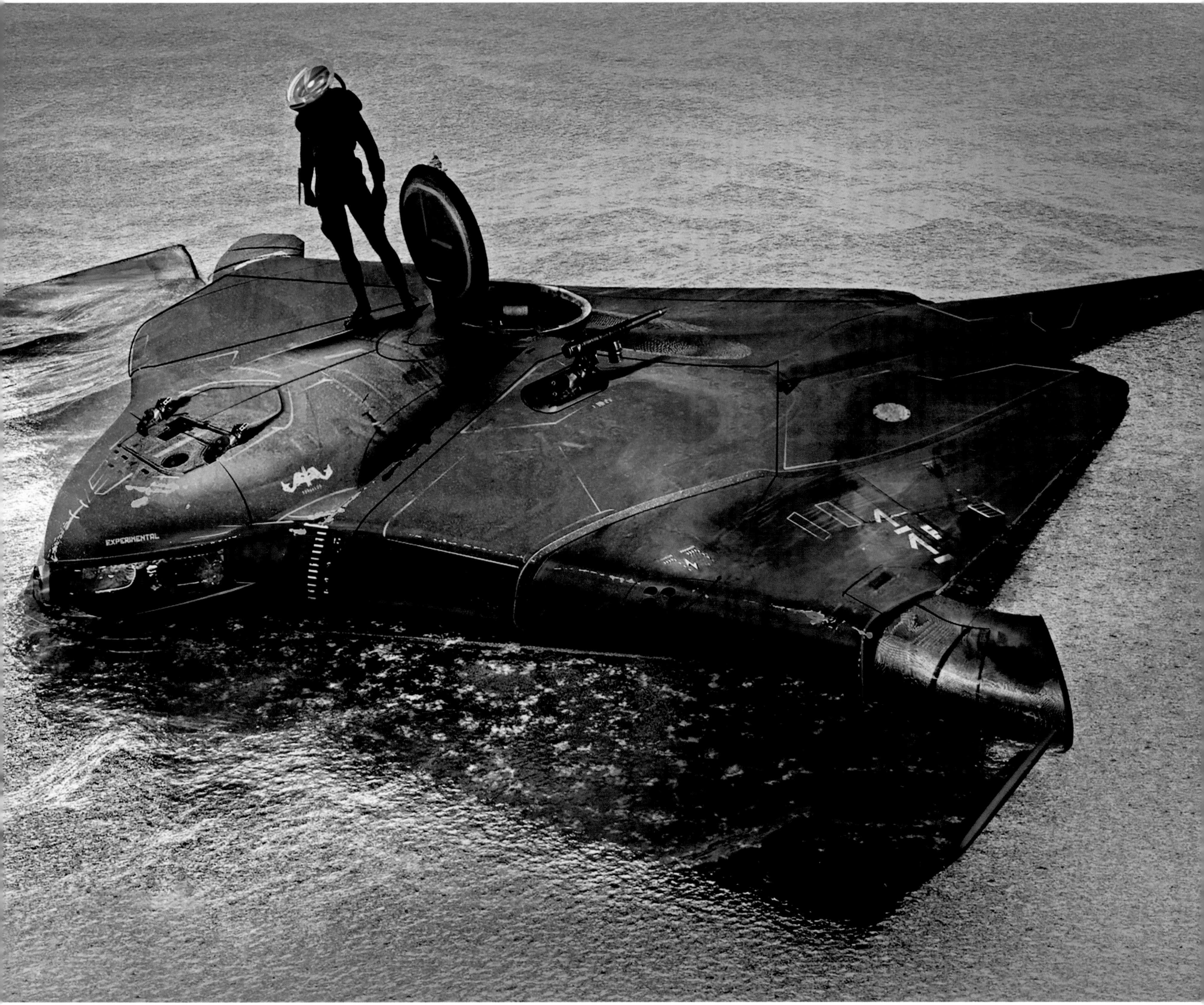
EXPERIMENTAL

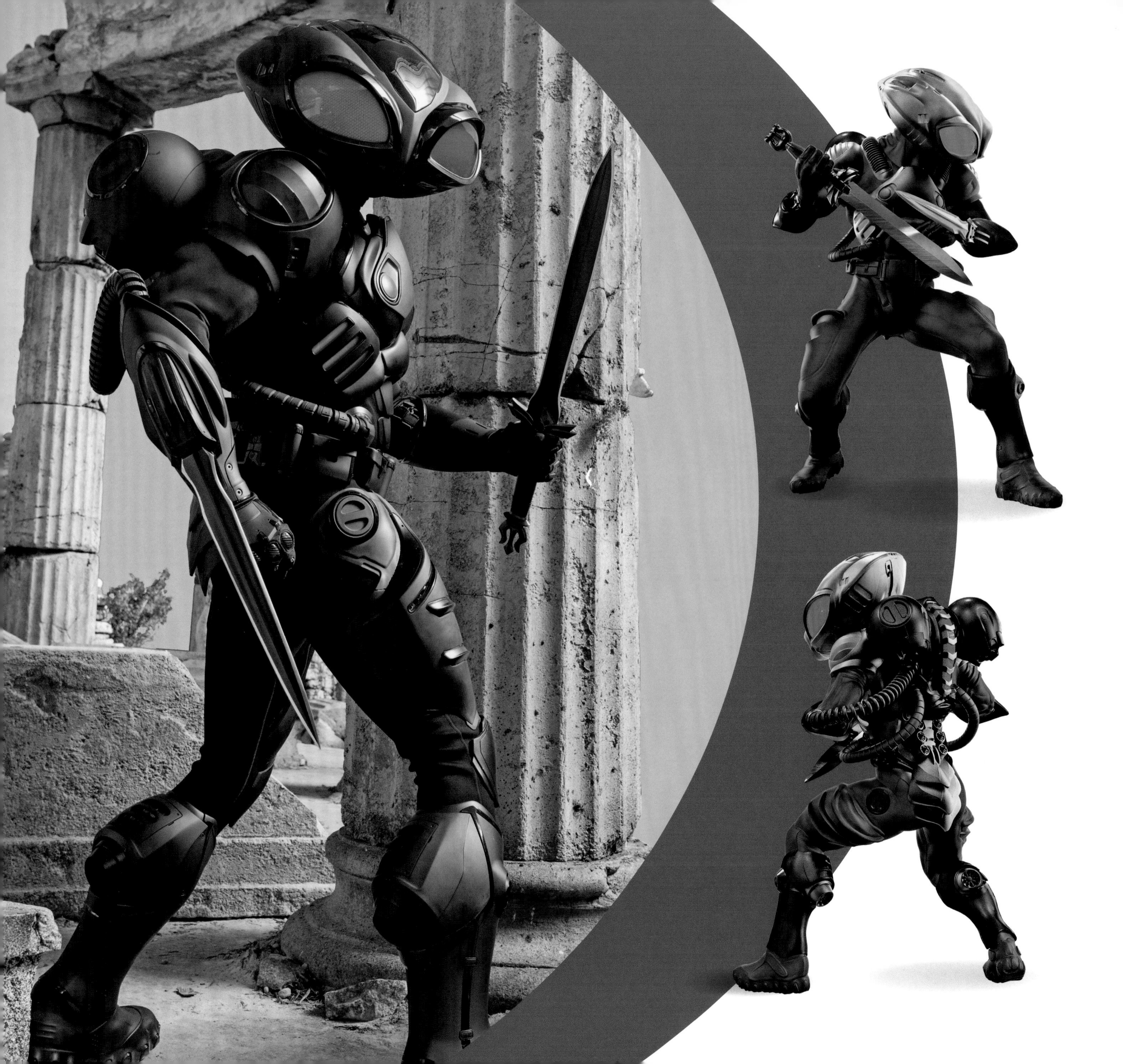

While the character's arsenal of weapons and his armored suit are Atlantean creations, the Manta Sub is actually a stolen Navy prototype undersea vessel. Set decorator Beverley Dunn crafted the interior design of the Manta Sub with stainless steel sheaves and piping to capture a sleeker look. Bulky pipes are outfitted in repetitive fashion, to create a more high-tech appearance. One other element on display inside the Manta Sub is the villain's obsession with Arthur Curry, as evidenced by a wall with a *Time* magazine cover featuring Aquaman and other newspaper clippings about the hero. Manta has been tracking Arthur's movements and related sightings in hopes of finding him.

The Manta Submersible has another material benefit: high probability of merchandising success. Director James Wan is a collector himself and had always wanted to make a movie that lent itself to merchandising spinoffs, such as a Manta Sub toy ship. "I finally get the chance to make a movie where I can actually create fun, interesting toys as well," he says. "It's the bonus part of making a film like this. We can cultivate all the different visuals, all the different characters, different vehicles and weapons. It's just such an incredible playground to literally assemble all your different toys and figurines."

OPPOSITE LEFT: Black Manta strikes a threatening pose.
OPPOSITE RIGHT: Digital turnaround designs for the Black Manta costume.
BELOW: Yahya Abdul-Mateen II as David Kane, aka Black Manta.

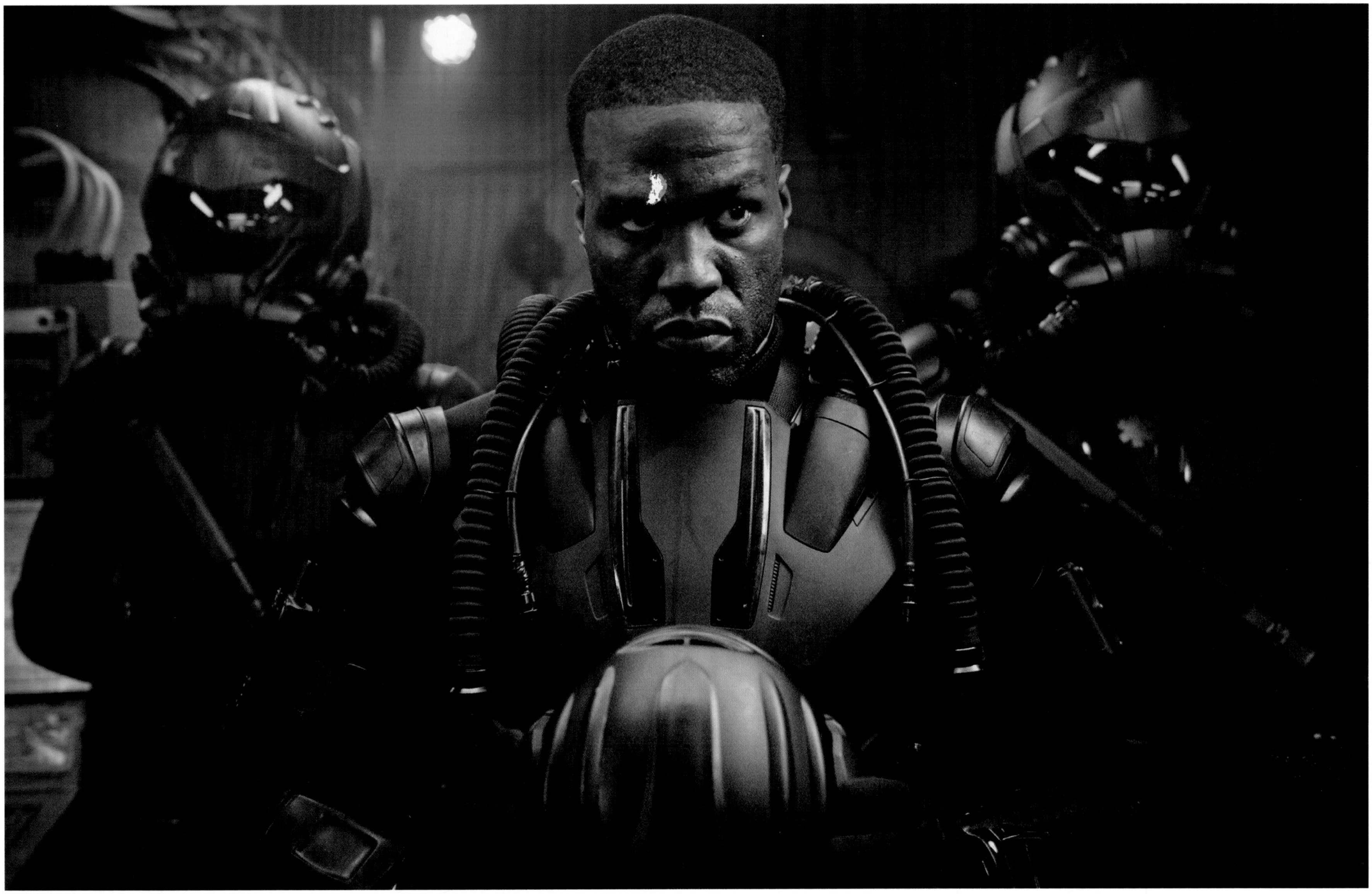

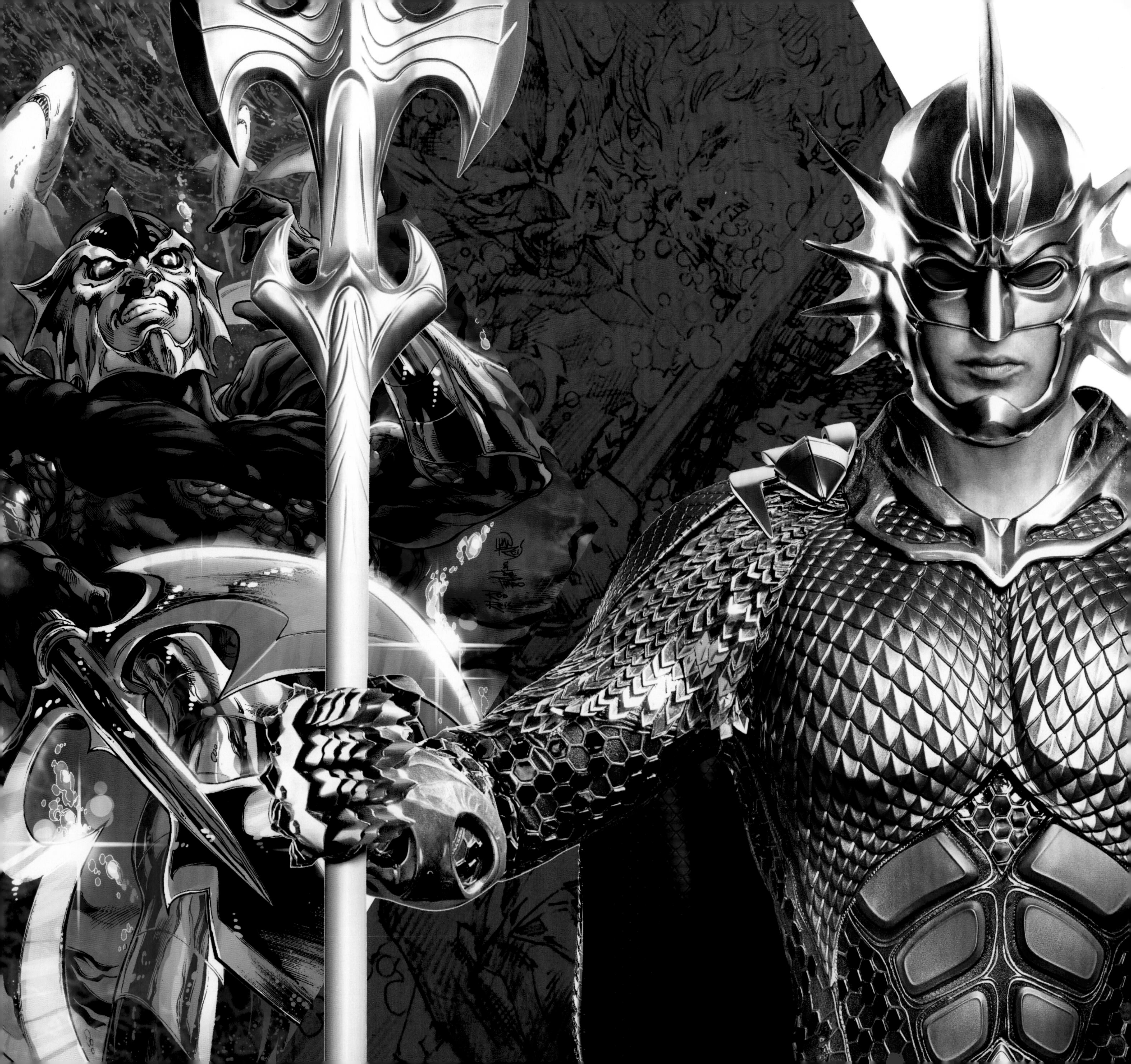

OCEAN MASTER

CONQUEROR OF KINGDOMS

Orm's path to power is more direct than his brother's. By conquering the remaining kingdoms of Atlantis, Orm earns the title of Ocean Master and believes himself to be the true ruler of the seas. His goal to protect his people from the devastating effects of surface dwellers' actions on the oceans over the centuries may be noble, but his methods for achieving that goal are twisted into something dark and evil. As he prepares to unleash his most devastating attack on the surface, only one person can stop him. The brothers' paths converge when the Ocean Master's army makes its move, leading to an epic battle that ultimately turns one brother into a villain and the other into a true hero.

OPPOSITE LEFT: *Aquaman*, Vol. 7 #14 (January 2013) cover art by Ivan Reis, Joe Prado, and Rod Reis.
OPPOSITE RIGHT: Ocean Master vs. Aquaman sketch from the graphic novel *Aquaman: Throne of Atlantis*.
LEFT: Patrick Wilson accepts the mantle of Ocean Master.
PAGES 164–165: Orm's battle cruiser bridge concept art by Jeremy Love.

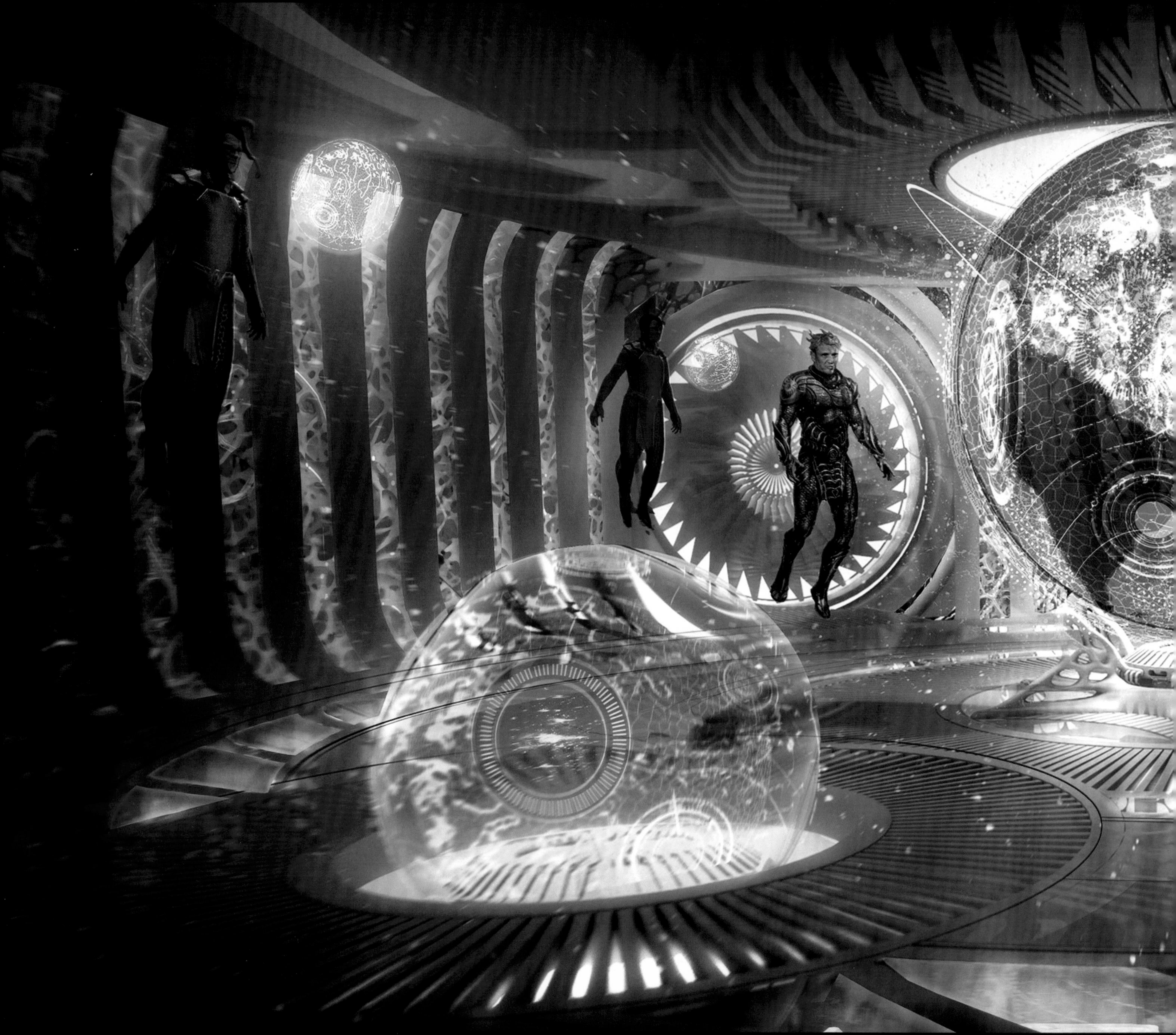

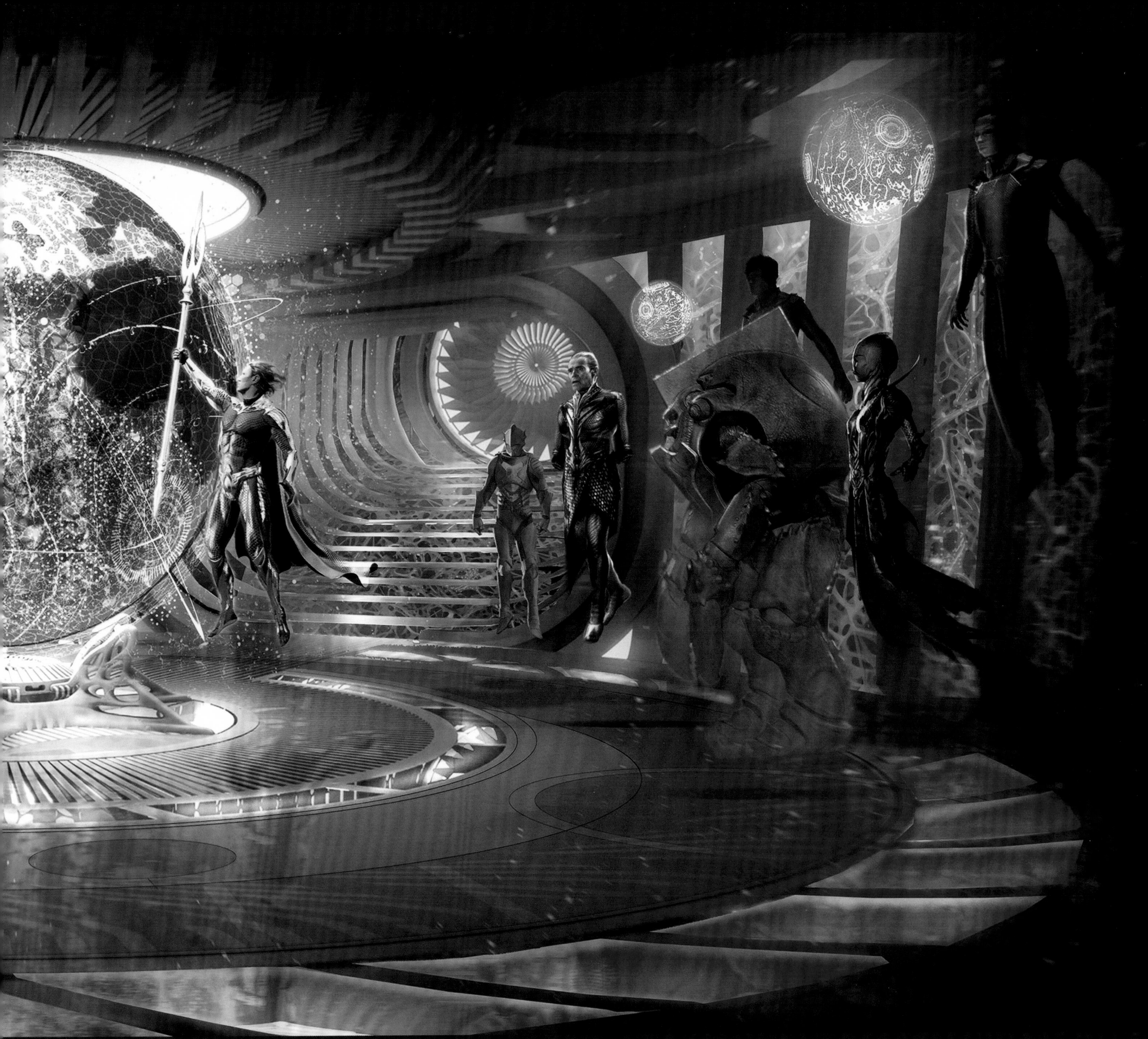

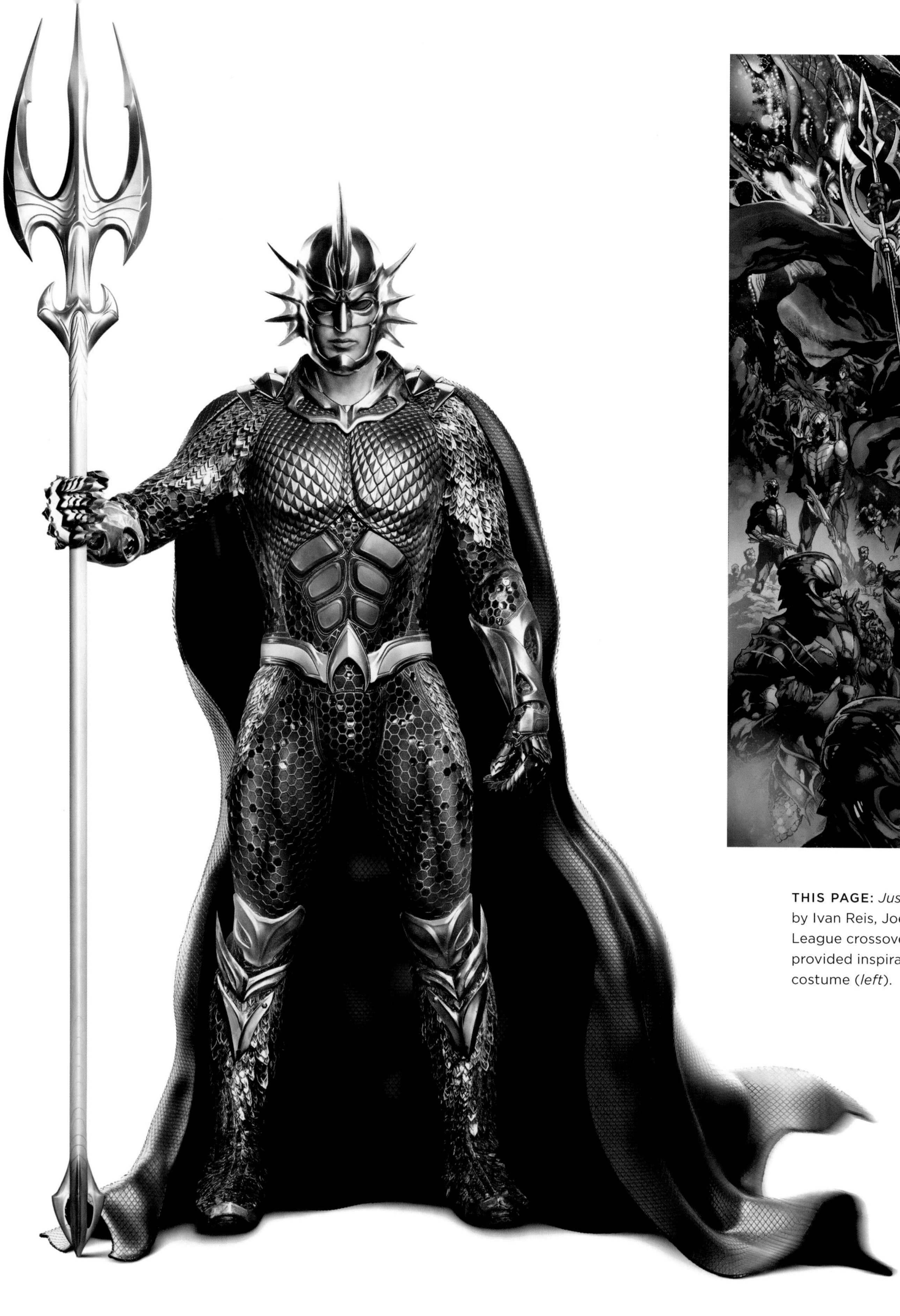

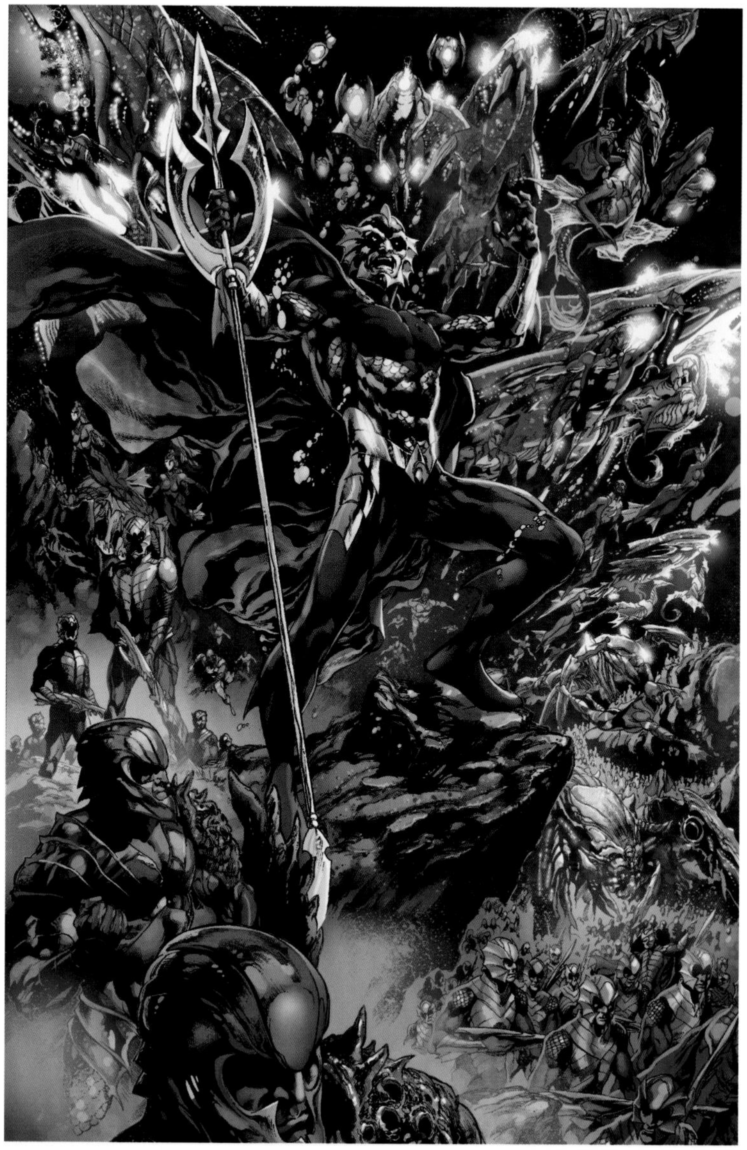

THIS PAGE: *Justice League*, Vol. 2 #15 (February 2013) art by Ivan Reis, Joe Prado, and Rod Reis. The Aquaman/Justice League crossover event Throne of Atlantis from the New 52 provided inspiration for the film as well as Ocean Master's costume (*left*).

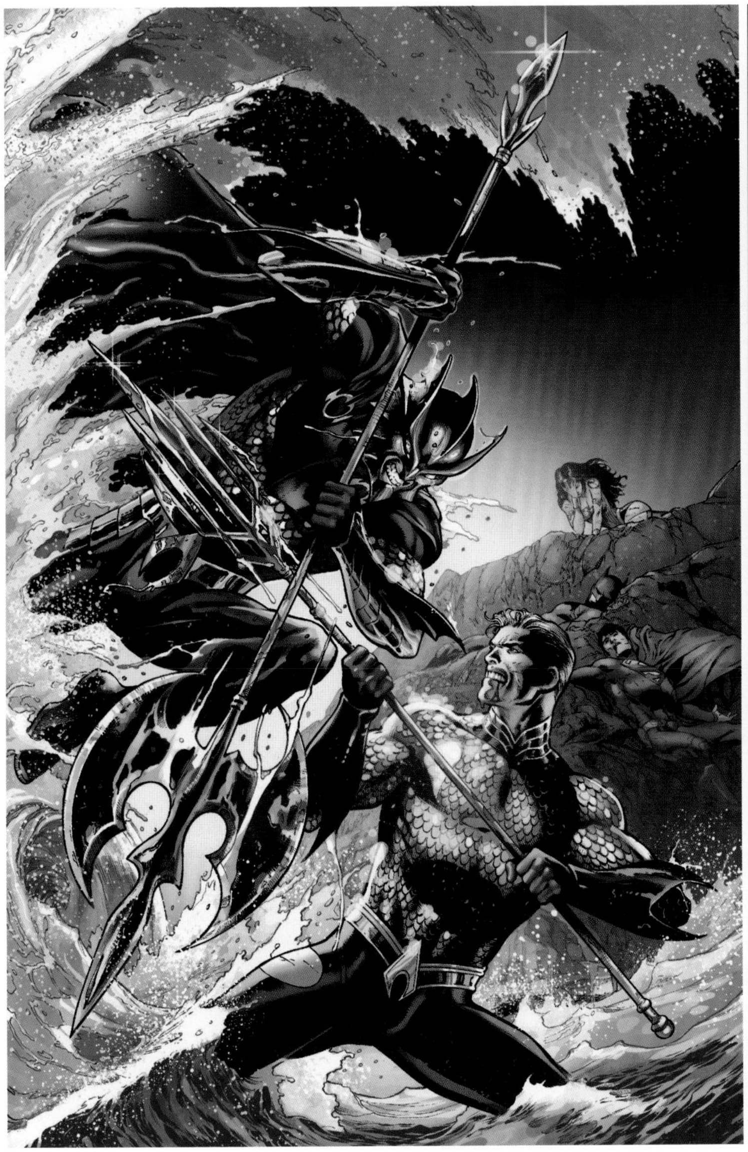

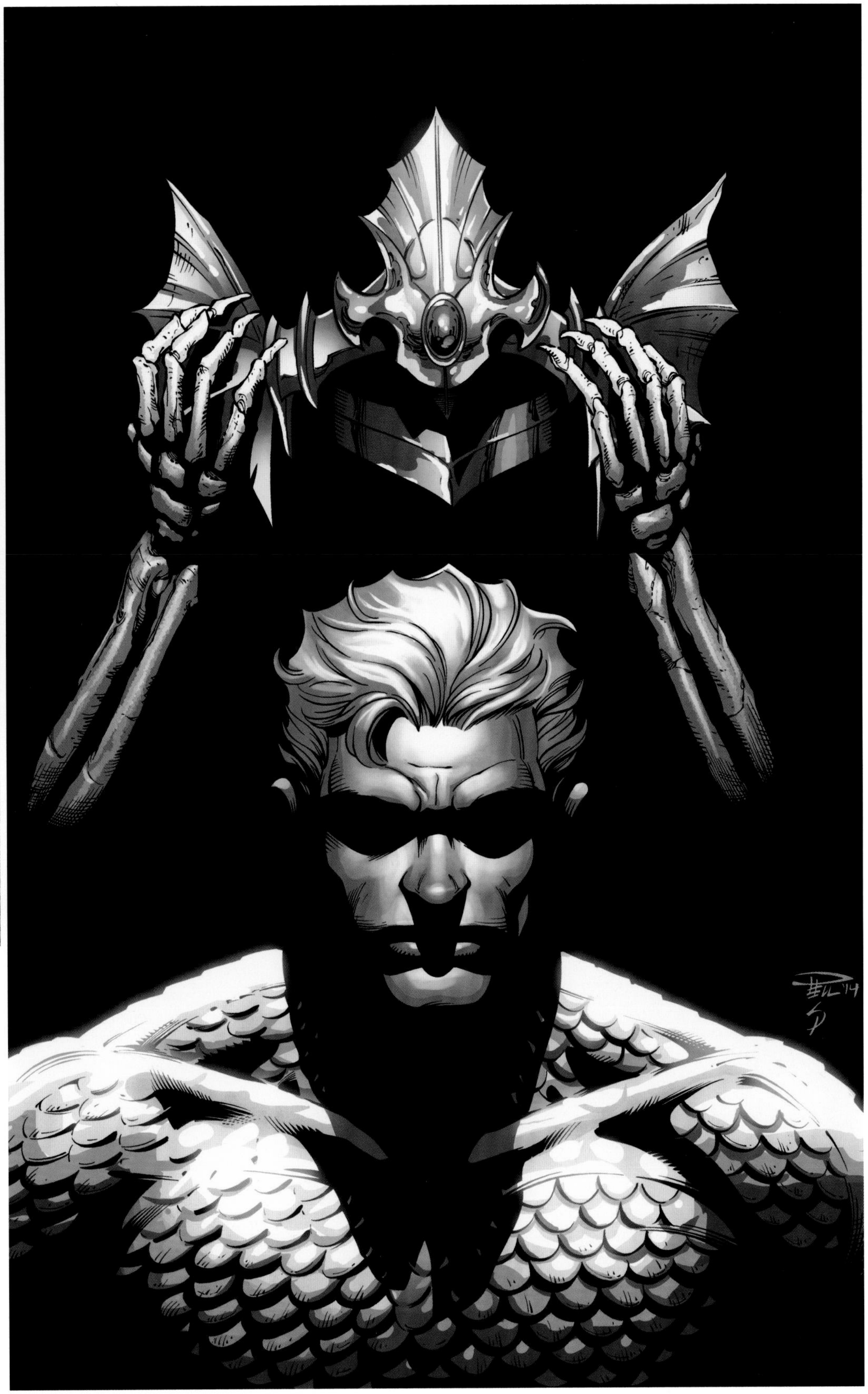

ABOVE: *Aquaman* Vol. 7 #15 (February 2013) cover art by Eddy Barrows, Eber Ferreira, and Rod Reis.

RIGHT: *Aquaman* Vol. 7 #35 (December 2014) cover art by Paul Pelletier and Sean Parsons.

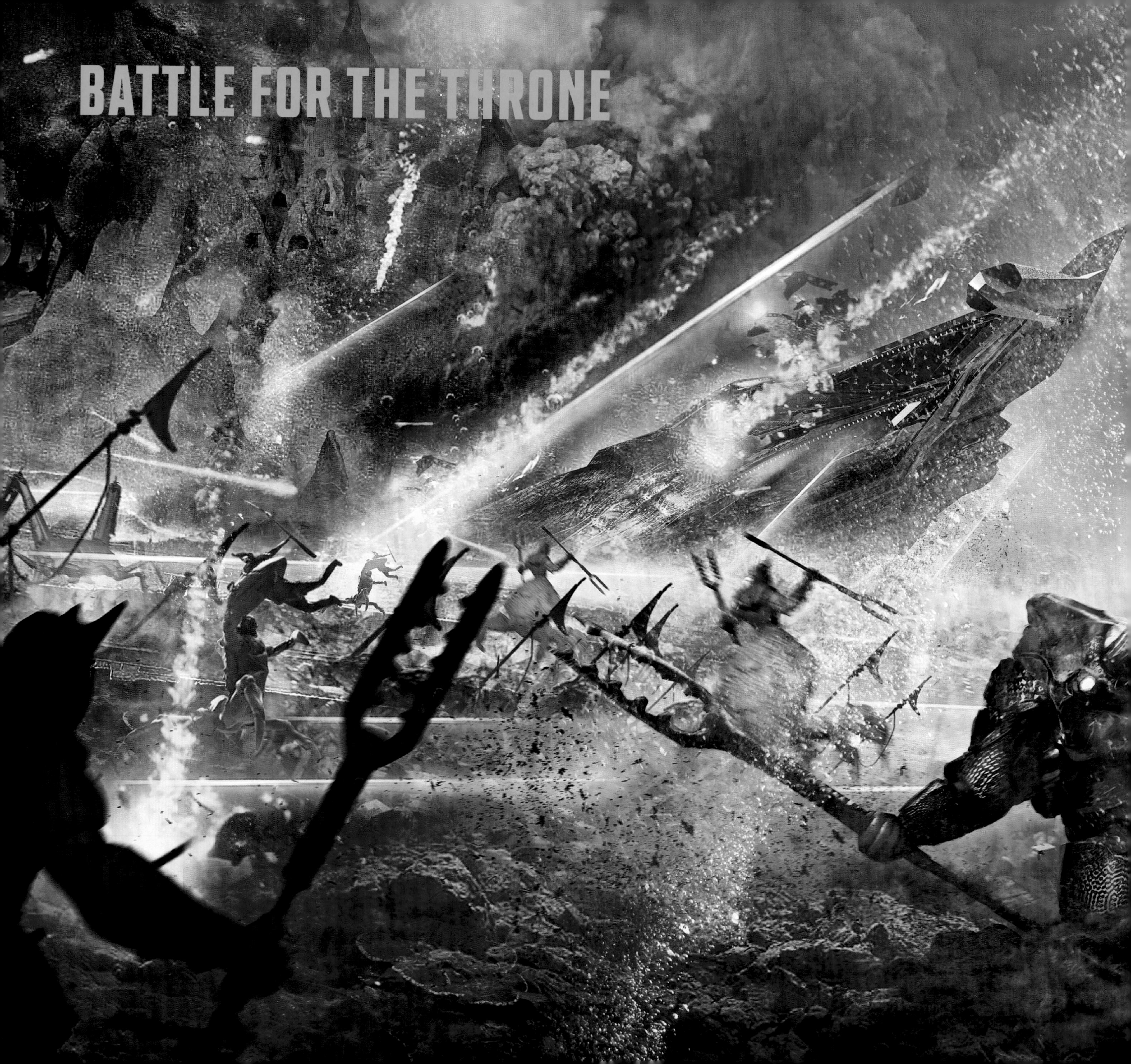
BATTLE FOR THE THRONE

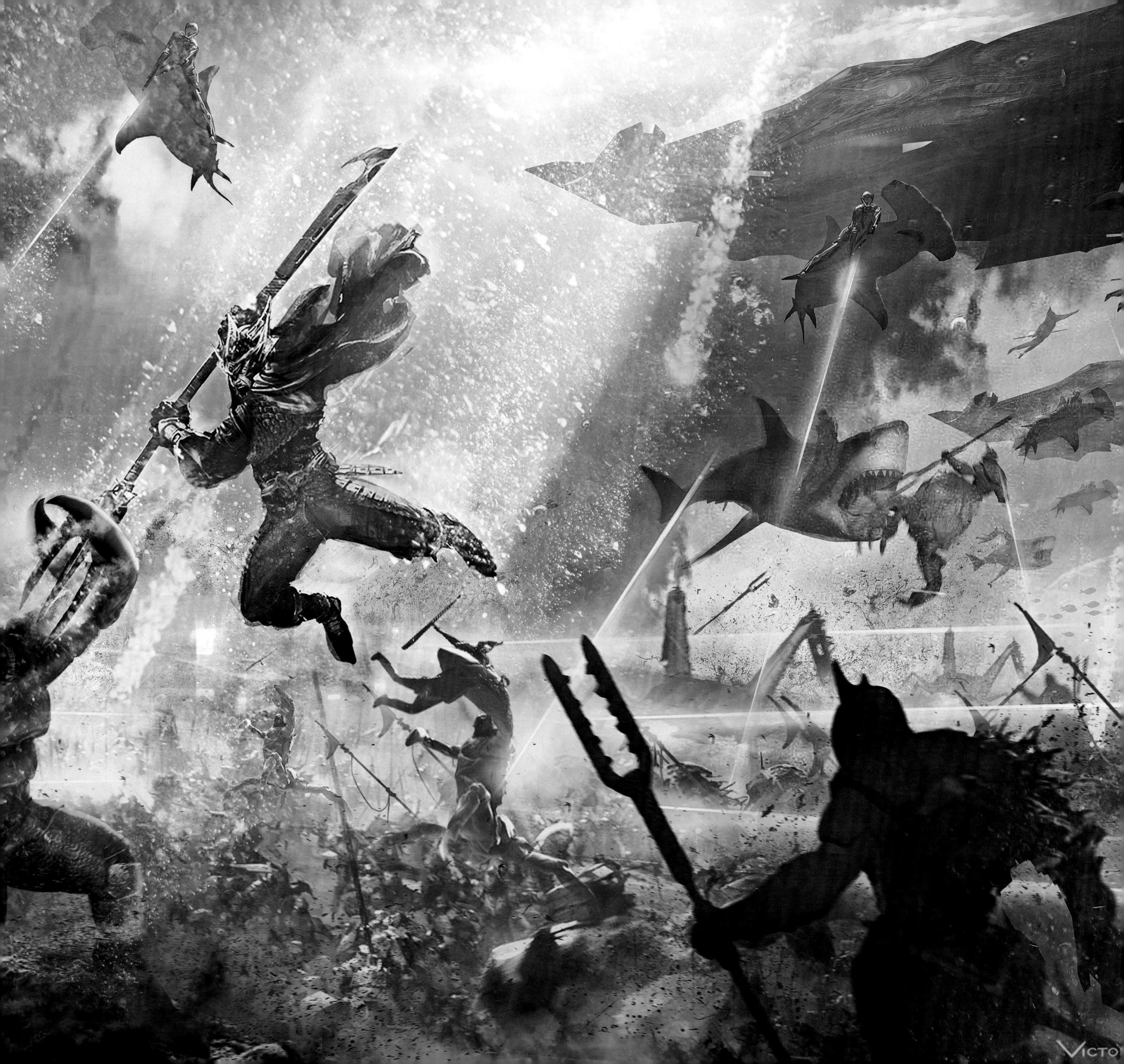

The climactic battle at the end of *Aquaman* begins with Orm's attack on the Brine Kingdom and then escalates to include Arthur and the unlikely army that he now commands. The epic combat might be a typical scene in a science fiction space adventure, except that most of the ships are submersibles while others are massive sea creatures. This final confrontation in *Aquaman* is a unique entry in the superhero subgenre: The action takes place on and under the water, with intricate visual effects sequences never before seen on film. But no matter how large the confrontation becomes, at its core it is about two brothers who barely know one another but hold the fates of two worlds in their hands. This final fight between Orm and Arthur becomes the first true confrontation between Ocean Master and Aquaman.

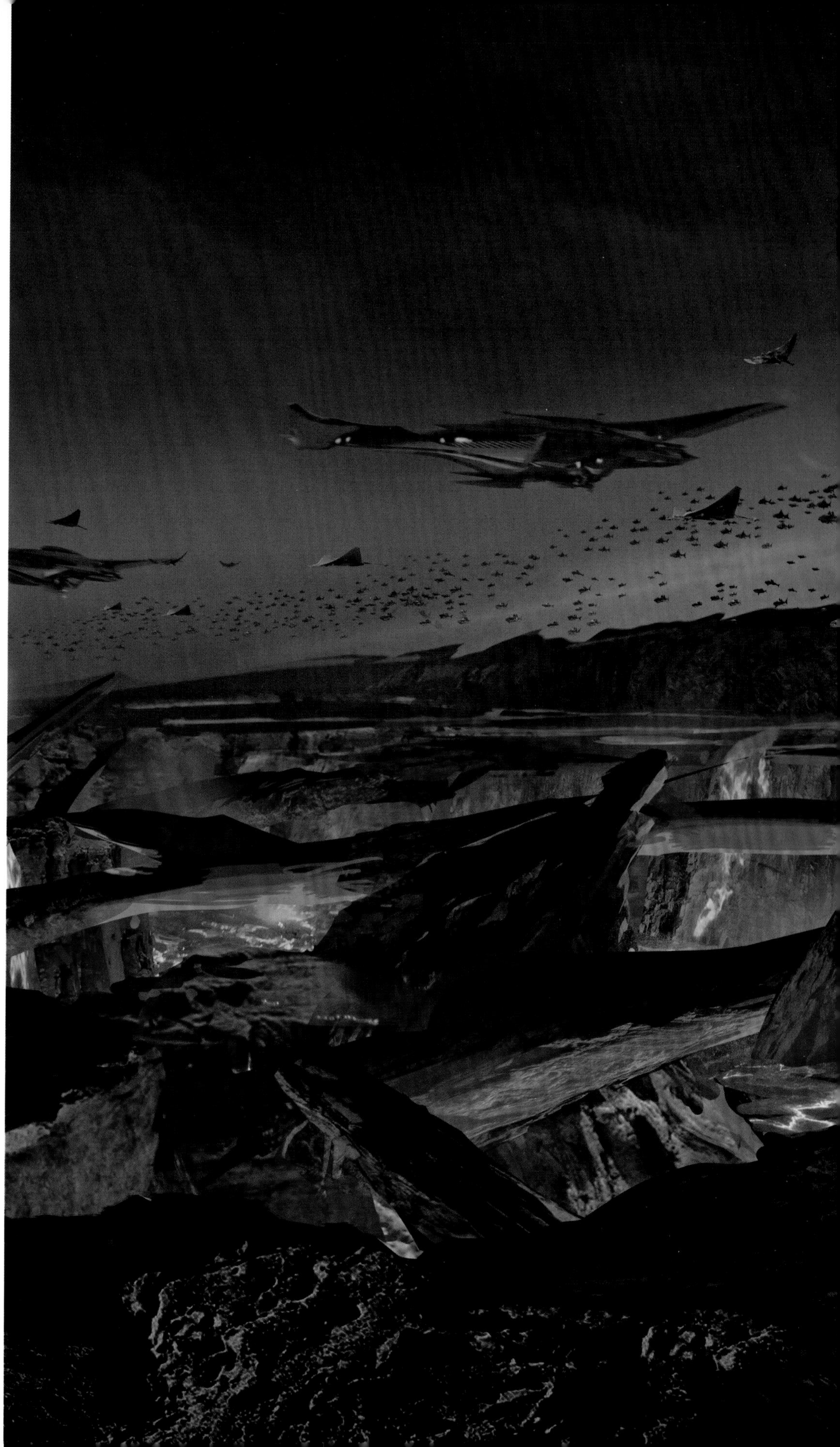

PAGES 168–169: Brine battle concept art by Victor Martinez.
RIGHT: Atlantean forces invade the Brine Kingdom in concept art.
PAGES 172-173: Overturned warship battle art by Brad Nielsen (*main image*) and Ed Natividad (*inset*).
PAGES 174-175: Final battle concept art by Ed Natividad.
PAGES 176-177: Lighthouse sunset concept art by Scott Lukowski.

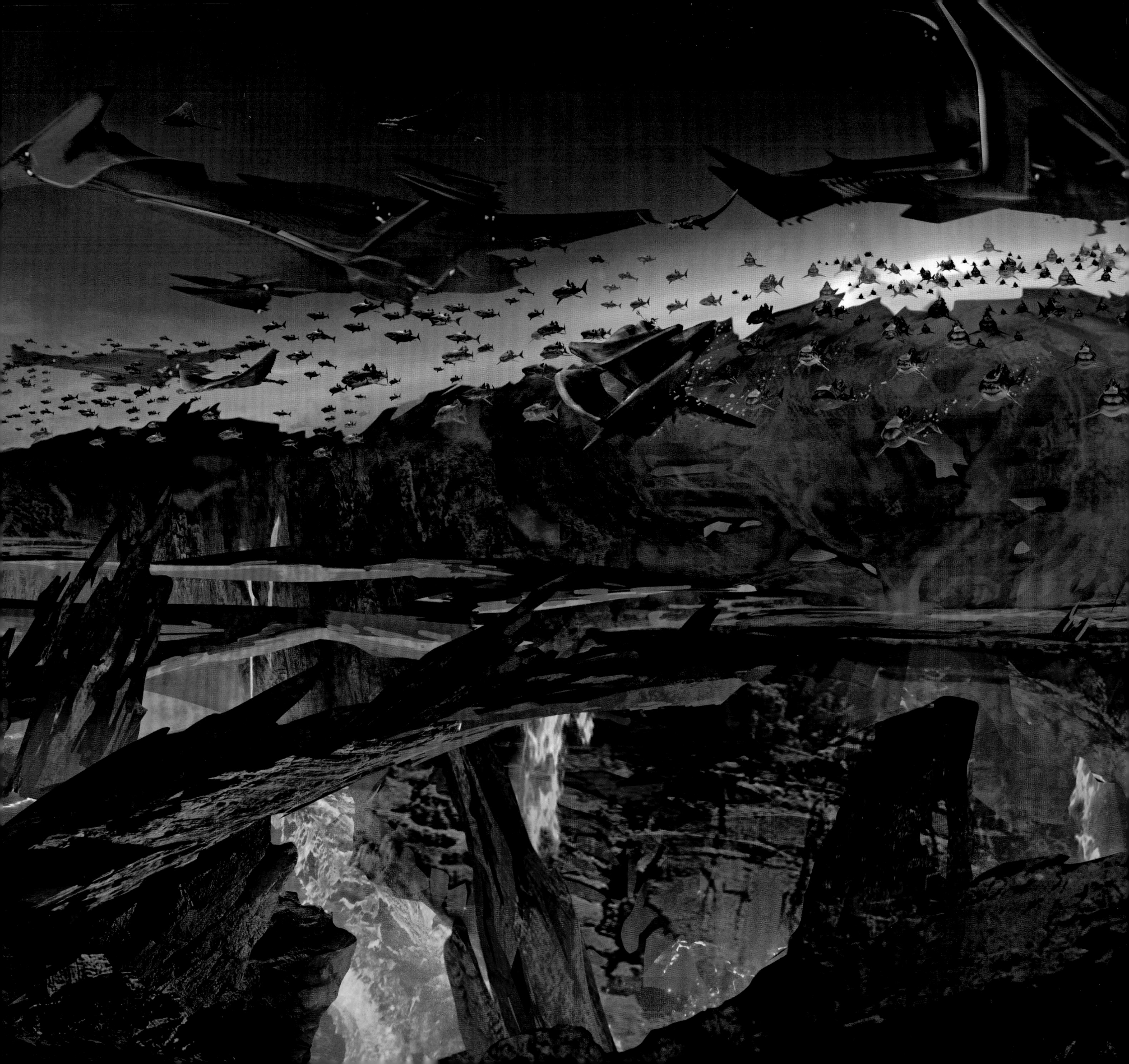

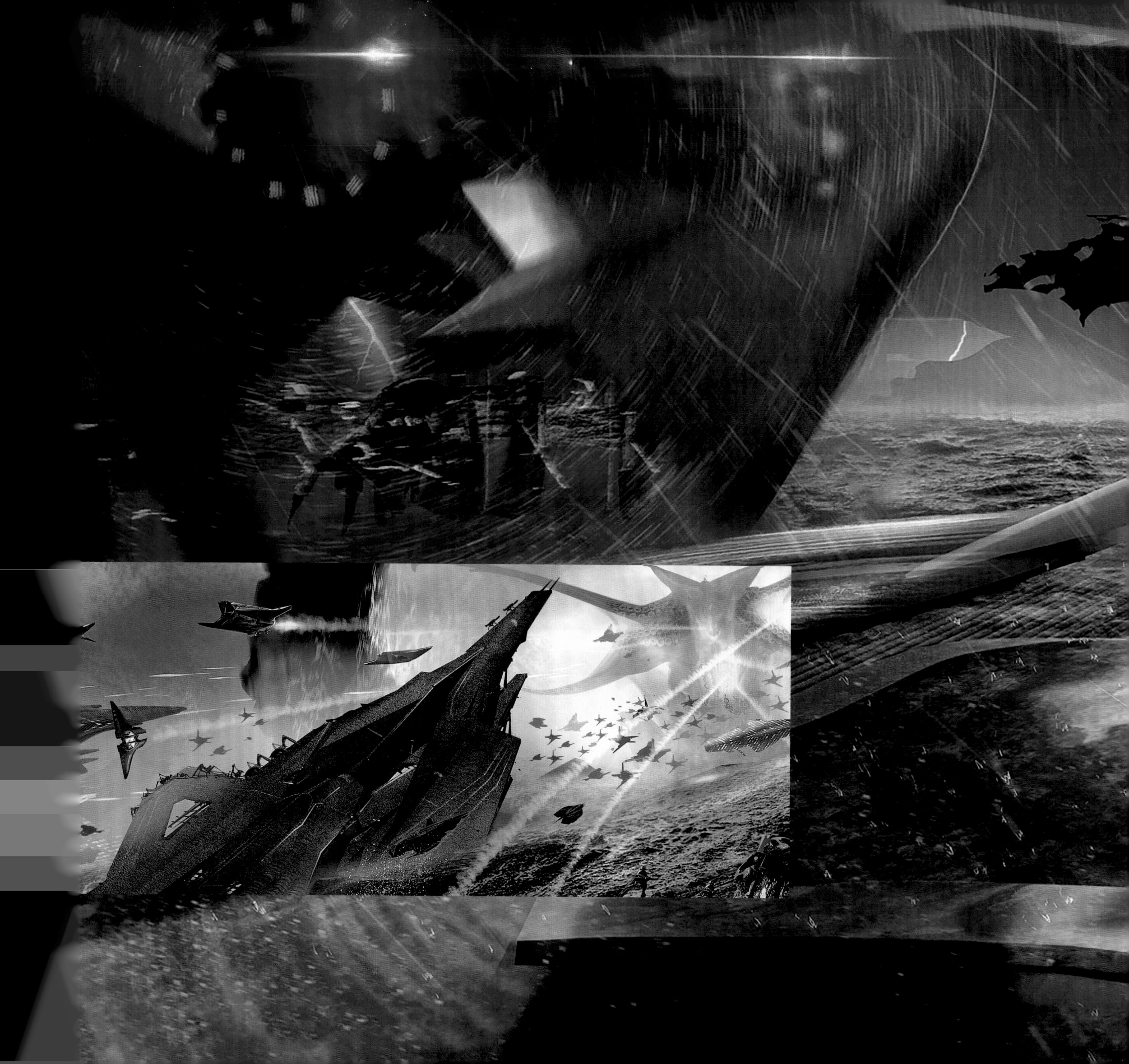

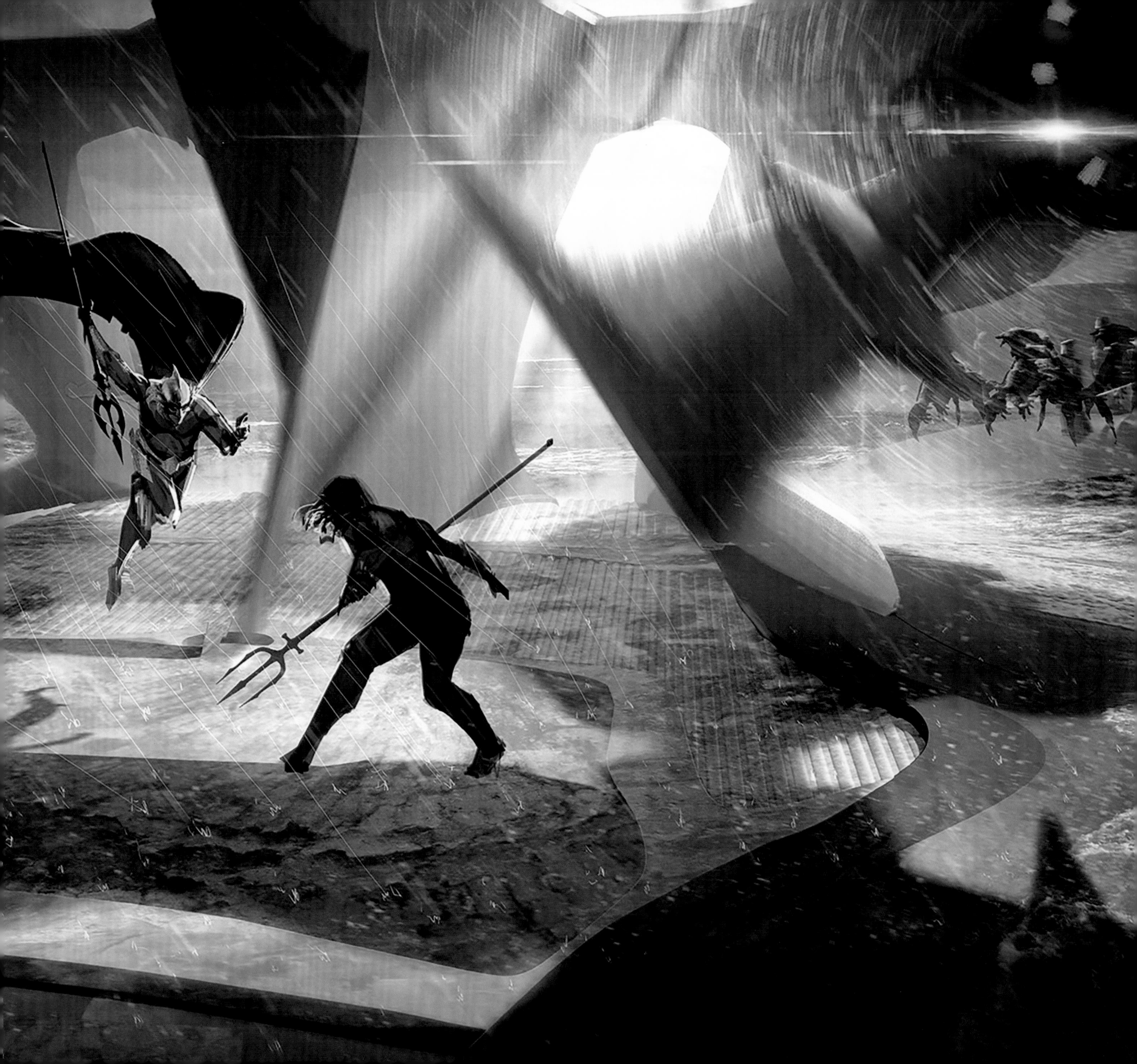

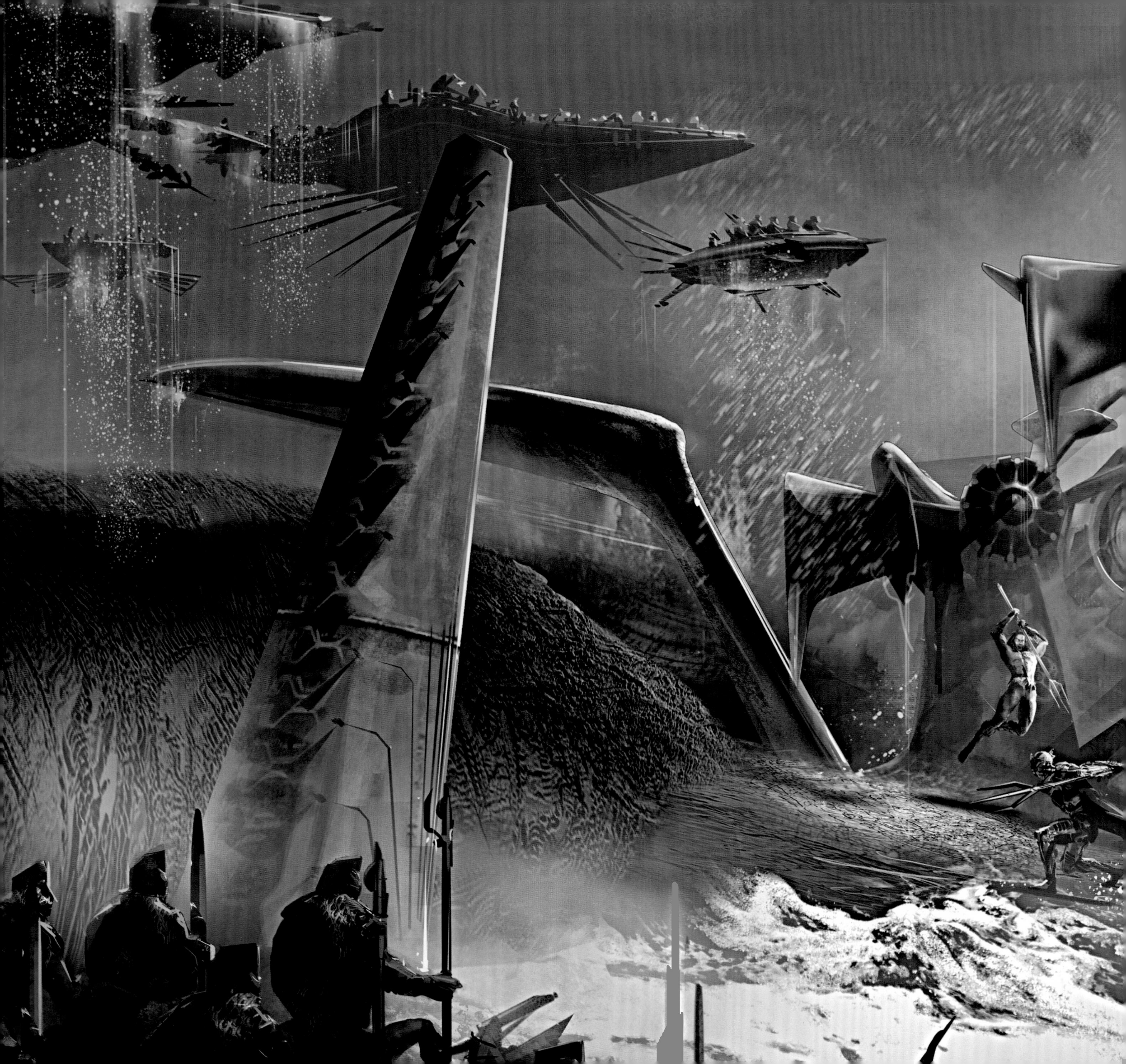

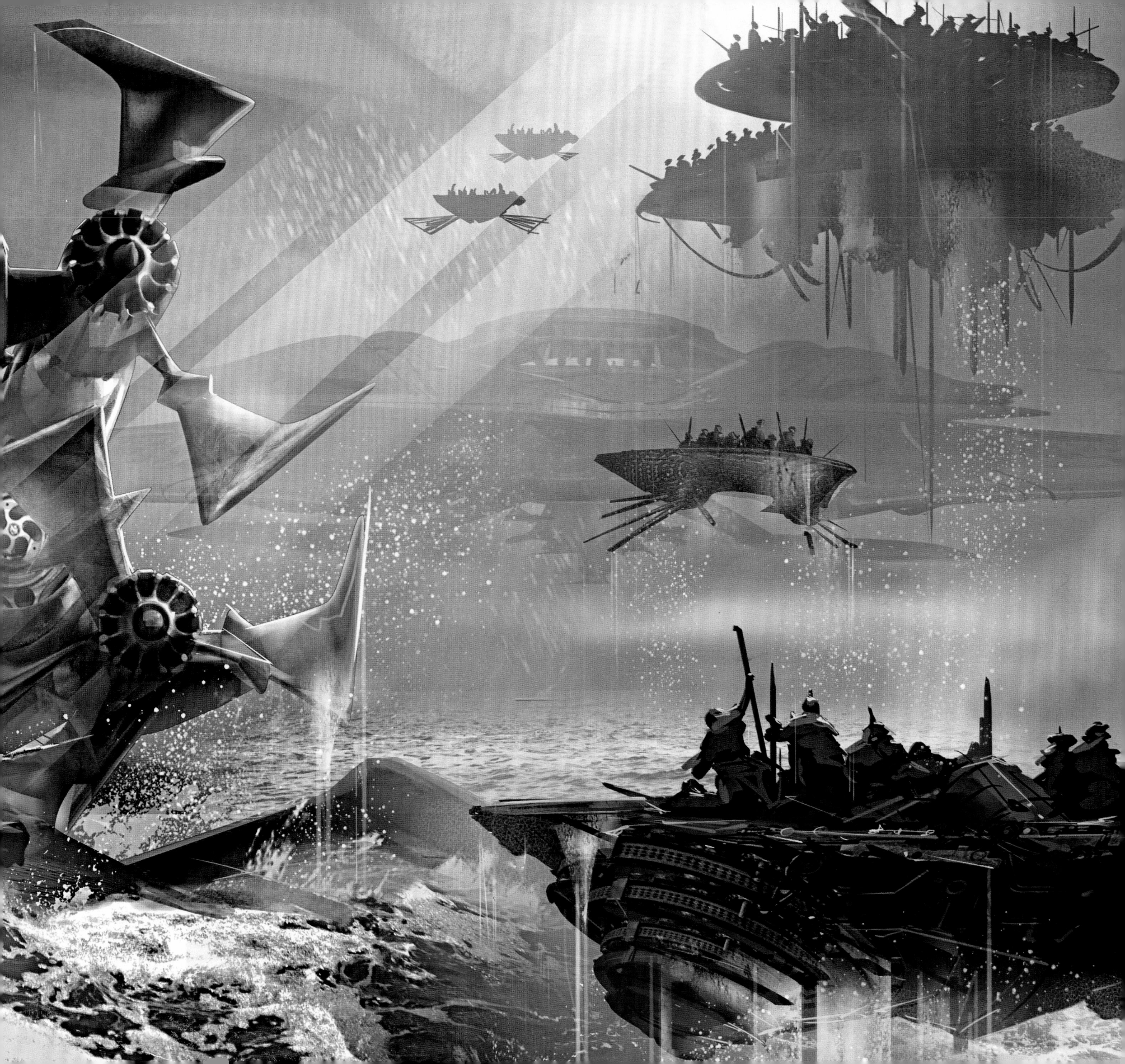

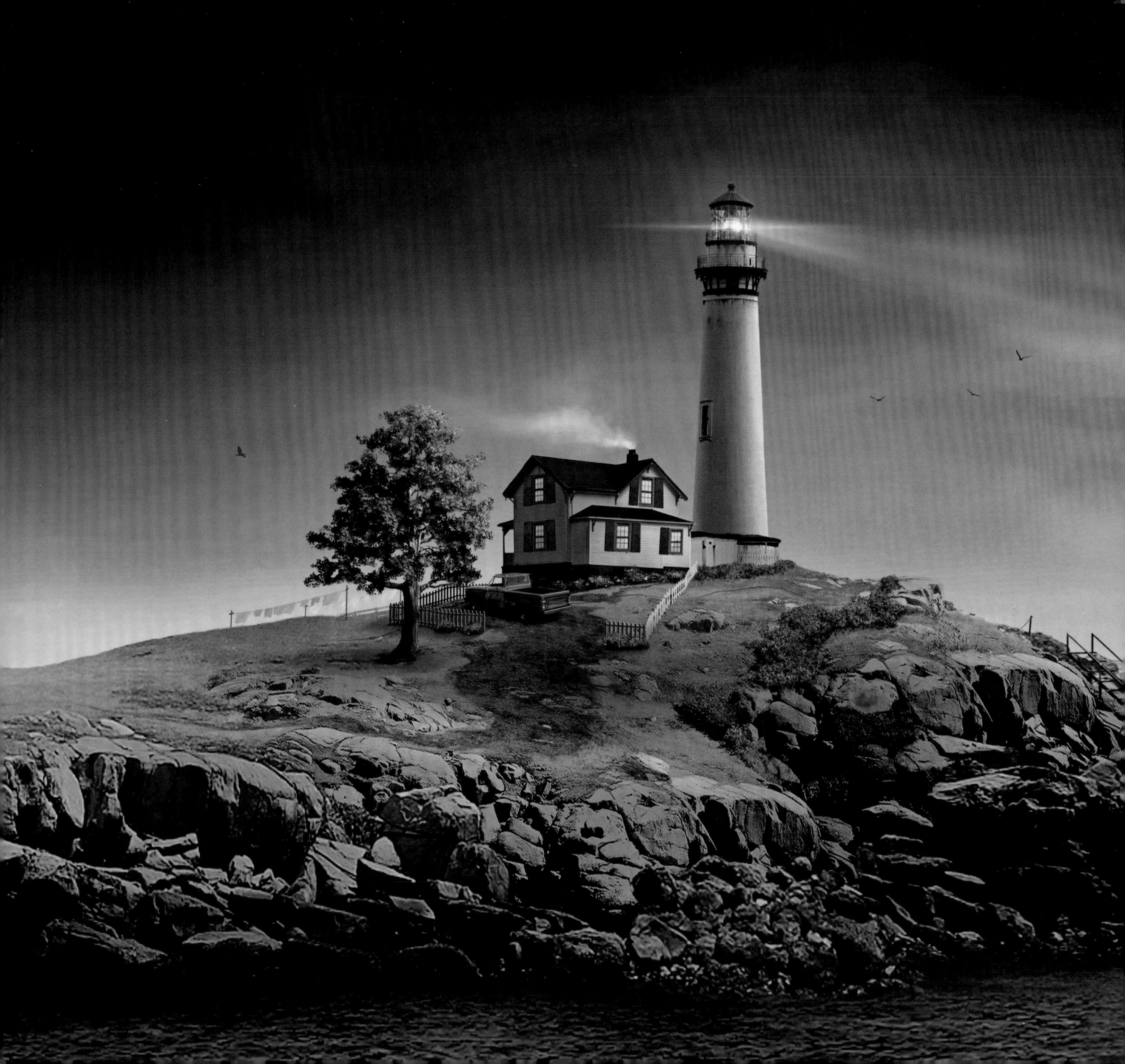

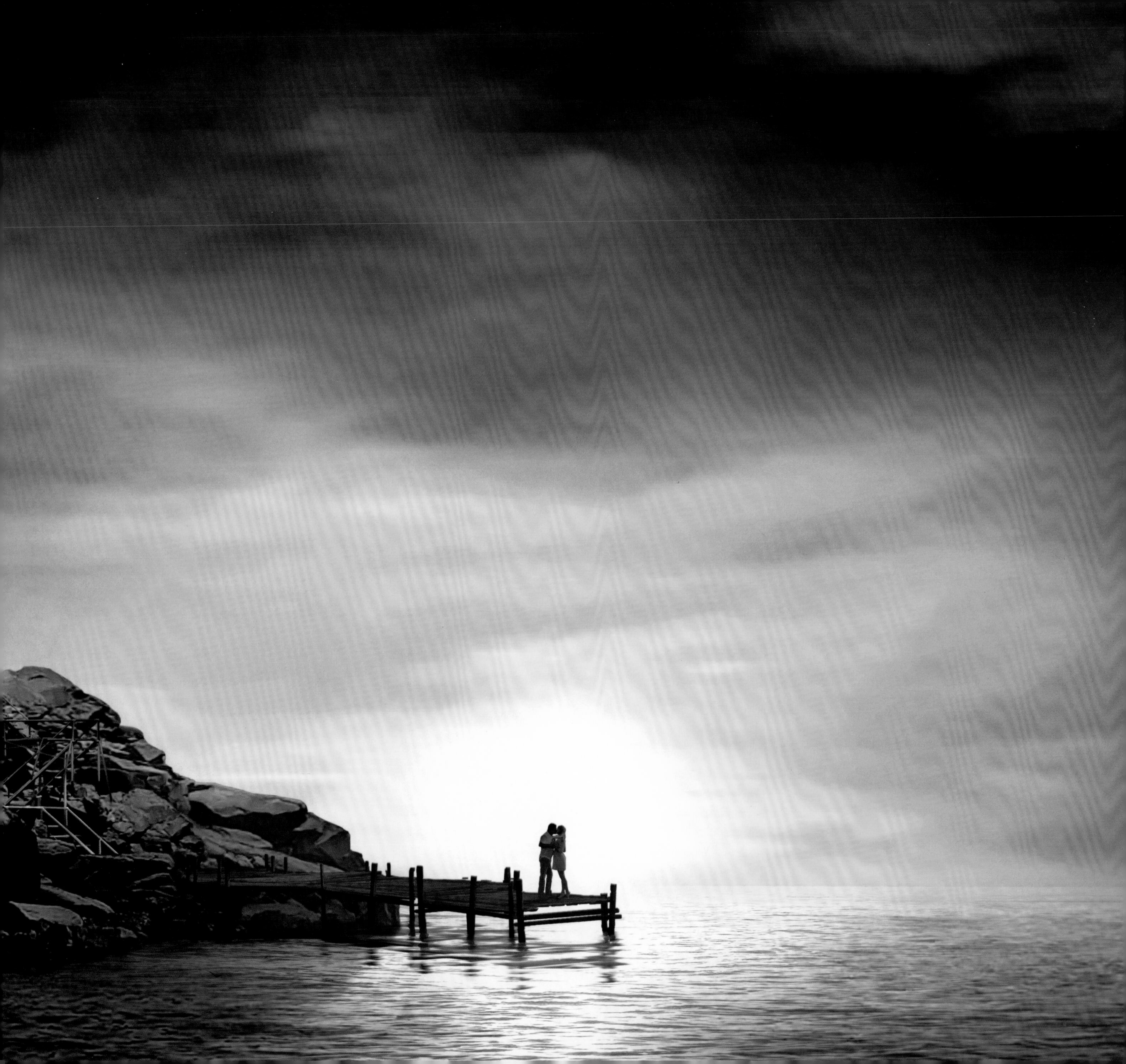

INSIGHT EDITIONS

PO Box 3088
San Rafael, CA 94912
www.insighteditions.com

Find us on Facebook: www.facebook.com/InsightEditions
Follow us on Twitter: @insighteditions

INED41487

ISBN: 978-1-68383-503-5

Publisher: Raoul Goff
Associate Publisher: Vanessa Lopez
Creative Director: Chrissy Kwasnik
Designer: Ashley Quackenbush
Senior Editor: Paul Ruditis
Editorial Assistant: Kaia Waller
Production Editor: Lauren LePera
Senior Production Editor: Rachel Anderson
Production Director/Subsidiary Rights: Lina s Palma
Senior Production Manager: Greg Steffen
Production Associate: Eden Orlesky

ACKNOWLEDGMENTS

The author would like to take a moment to note the contributions of certain people without whom this project would have sunk like a stone to the bottom of the Mariana Trench. These generous souls shared their time and insight to make sure we chronicled the creation of this project with the detail it deserved. They include: Josh Anderson, Gary Barbosa, Kym Barrett, Bill Brzeski, Mitchell Davis, Richie Dehne, Spencer Douglas, Kelvin McIlwain, Jason Momoa, Massey Rafani, Peter Safran, Shane Thompson, James Wan, and Amy Weingartner.

On a personal note, I would also like to thank my colleagues Tara Bennett and Paul Terry for their guidance and their generosity. Finally, I would like to dedicate this book to my wife Cindi and our two girls, Alexia and Talia, who are now bigger Aquaman fans than they ever thought they would be.

ROOTS of PEACE   REPLANTED PAPER

Insight Editions, in association with Roots of Peace, will plant two trees for each tree used in the manufacturing of this book. Roots of Peace is an internationally renowned humanitarian organization dedicated to eradicating land mines worldwide and converting war-torn lands into productive farms and wildlife habitats. Roots of Peace will plant two million fruit and nut trees in Afghanistan and provide farmers there with the skills and support necessary for sustainable land use.

Manufactured in China by Insight Editions

10 9 8 7 6 5 4 3 2 1

ABOVE: Artwork by Ivan Reis, Joe Prado, and Marcelo Maiolo.